The Next Great Globalization

The Next Great Globalization

How Disadvantaged Nations Can Harness Their Financial Systems to Get Rich

Frederic S. Mishkin

Princeton University Press
Princeton and Oxford

Published by Princeton University Press, 41 William Street, Princeton, New Jersey 08540
In the United Kingdom: Princeton University Press, 3 Market Place, Woodstock, Oxfordshire OX20 1SY

Second printing, and first paperback printing, 2008
Paperback ISBN: 978-0-691-13641-7

The Library of Congress has cataloged the cloth edition of this book as follows

Mishkin, Frederic S.
The next great globalization : how disadvantaged nations can harness their financial systems to get rich / by Frederic S. Mishkin.
p.   cm.
Includes bibliographical references and index.
ISBN-13: 978-0-691-12154-3 (cloth : alk. paper)
ISBN-10: 0-691-12154-0 (cloth : alk. paper)
1. Finance—Developing countries.   2. Monetary policy—Developing countries.   3. Globalization.   I. Title.
HG195.M57   2006
332.09172'4—dc22

                                                        2006010252

British Library Cataloging-in-Publication Data is available

This book has been composed in Adobe Palatino and Berkeley Old Style Book and Black by Princeton Editorial Associates, Inc., Scottsdale, Arizona

Printed on acid-free paper. ∞

press.princeton.edu

Printed in the United States of America

10   9   8   7   6   5   4   3

To Peter and Jane,
Two extraordinary editors who love their work—and it shows

Contents

Preface

Many prominent economists, financiers, politicians, and other apparent authorities regard globalization and, in particular, the international financial system as a potential danger to the world's poor. Even some of globalization's exponents speak of it warily. Partisans at both ends of the political spectrum have jumped on the anti-globalization bandwagon.

Instead of a danger, globalization is an opportunity. The globalization of trade and information of the past century has lifted vast numbers of the world's people out of extreme poverty. The *next great globalization*, that of the financial systems of emerging economies, can help transform the labors of disadvantaged people into greater wealth for them and create greater prosperity and stability for the world at large.

This book explains how the next great globalization can work. It differs from other books on globalization because it focuses on *financial* globalization, the opening up of a country's financial system to capital flows and financial firms from other countries. For emerging countries to reach the next stage of development and get rich, financial globalization must go much further than it already has. In particular, the financial systems in emerging economies must be more tightly integrated with those in the developed countries in order to partake in the benefits of financial investment, the lifeblood of the industrialized world.

Without successful financial globalization, poor countries will not be able to realize their potential, and their continued poverty will engender further instability and breakdowns in political relations with other nations. But while financial globalization is vital in promoting economic growth and reducing poverty, it is not a panacea. It can lead to economic crises that are destructive to a country and its citizens. Recent crises in emerging countries illustrate the costs and benefits of financial globalization and present some cautionary lessons for countries hoping to globalize successfully. Only by taking financial globalization seriously can we learn to reduce its destructive downside while promoting its remarkably productive upside.

Globalization is not the cause of the economic problems in disadvantaged countries. On the contrary, it is the beginning of the solution to these problems. To think otherwise is wrongheaded and dangerous. The next great globalization needs to be financial and it needs to happen soon. This book demonstrates how it can, and should, be done.

One

The Next Great Globalization: A Force for Good?

In 1960 South Korea was one of the poorest countries in the world, with an average income per person less than that in many countries in sub-Saharan Africa. It was only minimally engaged in trading goods and services with the rest of the world,[1] and the flow of capital from abroad into South Korea was minuscule, amounting to less than $400 million per year. Today South Korea is a member of the rich-countries club, the Organisation for Economic Co-operation and Development (OECD), and the booming metropolis of Seoul looks like any prosperous, world-class city. International trade is a key feature of the Korean economy, with over a third of the economy engaged in exporting, and the annual net flow of foreign capital into South Korea has increased over twentyfold to more than $10 billion.[2]

What has happened to South Korea to allow it to grow like this? *Globalization*, the increasing involvement of its economy in world markets.[3]

What Is Globalization?

Globalization is a term that is often used imprecisely and can mean many things. This book focuses on *economic globalization*, the opening up of economies to flows of goods, services, capital, and businesses from other nations that integrate their markets with those abroad.

Economic globalization takes many forms. When a New Yorker orders a Mercedes that is made in Germany, rather than a Cadillac built in America, she is taking advantage of the globalization process. When MGM sells a DVD of one

1

of its hit movies to a teenager in Singapore, this also is a result of globalization. When a company based in London makes use of an Indian computer programmer in Bangalore, globalization is again at work. All of these examples of globalization involve international trade, the flow of goods (Mercedes cars and DVDs) and services (computer programming). Globalization of trade in goods and services has expanded at an extremely rapid pace in the past forty to fifty years, growing from a little over $1 trillion (at current prices) in 1960 to over $15 trillion today.[4]

Economic globalization can take another form: the movement of capital and financial firms across borders, a process called *financial globalization*. When a Japanese investor buys a U.S. Treasury bill or a share of IBM stock, capital has moved from Japan to the United States, and the purchase is an example of financial globalization. Citibank's loan to a Malaysian shoe manufacturer is also financial globalization. The opening of a Spanish bank office in Santiago, Chile, is a further move toward financial globalization. Financial globalization has also expanded dramatically. Since 1975, when the data were first collected, international capital flows have increased more than eightfold to over $1.4 trillion per year today.[5]

The globalization process has given a new name to a class of countries that have only recently opened up their markets to the flows of goods, services, and capital from other nations: *emerging market economies.* The advent of emerging market economies and the huge increases in international trade and international capital flows suggest that we have entered a new Age of Globalization.

The First Age of Globalization, 1870–1914

The current Age of Globalization is the second great wave of globalization of international trade and capital flows. The first occurred from 1870 to 1914,[6] when international trade grew at 4% annually, rising from 10% of global output (measured as *gross domestic product* or GDP) in 1870 to over 20% in 1914, while international flows of capital grew annually at 4.8% and increased from 7% of GDP in 1870 to close to 20% in 1914.[7] John Maynard Keynes captured the feel of this era with the following famous passage from his *The Economic Consequences of the Peace,* which was published in 1919:

> What an extraordinary episode in the economic progress of man that age was which came to an end in August 1914! The inhabitant of London could order by telephone, sipping his morning tea in bed, the various products of the whole earth, in such quantity as he might see fit, and reasonably expect their delivery upon his doorstep; he could at the same moment and by the same means adventure his wealth in the natural resources and new enterprises of any quarter of the world, and share, without exertion or even trouble, in their prospective fruits and advantages; or he could decide to couple the security of his fortunes with the good

faith of the townspeople of any substantial municipality in any continent that fancy or information might recommend.[8]

This first wave of globalization was accompanied by unprecedented prosperity. Economic growth was high: from 1870 to 1914, world GDP per person grew at an annual rate of 1.3%, while from 1820 to 1870 it grew at the much smaller rate of 0.53%.[9]

But did this greater economic growth translate into a better deal for the poor of the world? If economic growth during this Age of Globalization had been associated with growing income inequality, then the poor might not have benefited. However, this is not what happened for countries involved in the globalization process. The income gap narrowed between wealthy and poor nations that actively participated in global markets (although there was little effect on income distribution within these countries).[10] Japan provides an extraordinary example. Starting in the seventeenth century, Japan completely cut itself off from the rest of the world, allowing only one Dutch ship per year to land in Nagasaki to engage in a small amount of trading. When Commodore Matthew Perry and his black ships arrived on Japanese shores in 1853 to force Japan to trade with the United States, Japan began to open up to the rest of the world. The resulting shake-up of Japanese society eventually led to the Meiji restoration in 1868, as a result of which Japan became fully engaged in the global economic system. In 1870, at the start of this period, Japan was a backward country with an average income per person that was less than a quarter of that in the United Kingdom. From 1870 to 1913, its income was able to grow at 1.5% in comparison to a growth rate of 1.0% for the United Kingdom, thereby narrowing the gap. Argentina's growth experience during this period was even more extraordinary. From 1870, when its income per person was a little over 40% of that in the United Kingdom, its income grew at 2.5% through 1913, raising its income per person to over 75% of that in the United Kingdom. The Japanese and Argentine examples illustrate how poverty was reduced in the countries that were active in the globalization process.

However, not all countries engaged in that process. Globalizers did well, but, as critics of globalization point out, some countries were unable to take advantage of globalization. For example, countries like India and China actually deindustrialized during this period,[11] with China's income per person falling from 24% of the United Kingdom's in 1870 to 13% in 1914.[12] However, this increase in income inequality between globalizers and non-globalizers occurred because non-globalizers did so badly relative to globalizers. For countries that were able to take advantage of the globalization process, income inequality actually fell because globalizers that were initially so poor did so well relative to globalizers that started out rich. Increasing income inequality between countries during the period was clearly not the fault of globalization. It was rather a consequence of the inability or unwillingness of some countries to enter the global economic system.

The End of the First Age of Globalization: The Great Reversal, 1914–1939

The first Age of Globalization came to an end with the advent of World War I. The war caused a disruption of capital flows and trade between nations that continued even after the conflict ended. From 1914 to 1929, the average level of international trade fell from 22% of world GDP to 16%, and capital flows dried up, falling from close to 20% to 8% of world GDP.[13] And worse was yet to come. In 1929 the Great Depression started in the United States, and it quickly spread to the rest of the world. The economic devastation was immense. Unemployment reached a peak of 25% in the United States, and the income of the average person had fallen by 30% by 1933 and was only slightly above 1929 levels by 1939. However, the consequences of the Depression were far worse elsewhere. The economic collapse in Germany and Italy helped bring the fascists and Nazis into power. The world then entered the worst nightmare imaginable: a second world war. From 1939 to 1945, over fifty million people died, over half of whom were innocent civilians. The inhumanity of the Holocaust resulted in the slaughter of six million Jews and five million people of other religious and ethnic backgrounds in concentration camps.[14]

The collapse of this first Age of Globalization, which has been given the name the "Great Reversal" by Raghuram Rajan and Luigi Zingales,[15] provides two important lessons: (1) Globalization is not an immutable economic force; it can be reversed. (2) The economic and political nightmares of the interwar period should warn us that a backlash against globalization can be disastrous.

The Second Age of Globalization, 1960 to the Present

The aftermath of World War II has been an extraordinary period. Even before the war ended, the soon-to-be victorious allies realized that the mistakes of the interwar period should not be repeated. They met in Bretton Woods, New Hampshire, in 1944 to develop a new international system to promote world trade and prosperity after the war. They created two new international financial institutions (IFIs) both of which were headquartered in Washington, D.C., just across the street from each other: the International Monetary Fund (IMF), whose job was to oversee the international financial system and ensure that it would facilitate trade between countries, and the International Bank for Reconstruction and Development, which became known as the World Bank, whose job was to provide long-term loans to war-torn Europe and to developing countries to aid in their economic development. An additional organization arising out of the Bretton Woods meeting, but not established until 1947, was the General Agreement on Tariffs and Trade (GATT), headquartered in Geneva. Created to regulate the conduct of trade between countries, this organization evolved into the World Trade Organization (WTO).

These new institutions were created to promote globalization, and in this they were extremely successful. Once the world economy had returned to normal by the end of the 1950s, globalization advanced at a rapid pace. From 1973 until today, world trade grew at 11% annually, rising from just over 22% of world GDP to 42%.[16] Since 1973 the flows of capital between countries have also exploded, rising from 5% to 21% of world GDP.[17] We are clearly in the second wave of globalization.

Have the participants in this new Age of Globalization experienced the good economic outcomes and the reduction of poverty associated with the previous Age of Globalization? Data suggest that they have. World economic growth from 1960 to today has been at the highest pace in the history of the world: world income per person has been rising at a 2% annual rate.[18] Critics of globalization point out that income inequality across countries has grown and argue that for this reason globalization has not been good for the poor. But they have not looked carefully enough at the data. Income inequality across countries has risen only because, as in the period before World War I, those countries that have been active in global markets have grown very rapidly. Meanwhile those who have not (such as most countries in sub-Saharan Africa) have not only seen their position relative to globalizers fall but also experienced absolute drops in income per person. As before, the globalizers have won and the non-globalizers have lost. In 1960 the income of the average person in Somalia was 10% higher than that of his South Korean counterpart. Over the next forty-five years, Somalians experienced a drop in their income, so that Somalia's income per person is now less than one-tenth that of South Korea's: Somalia's income per person decreased by 33% while South Korea's increased by more than 1000%.[19]

What we have seen in this new Age of Globalization is a convergence of income per person among countries that have been able to take advantage of globalization by becoming export oriented. For this set of countries, income inequality has decreased; for the non-globalizers, it hasn't.[20] Furthermore, there is little evidence that globalization has increased income inequality within developing countries.[21] (There has, however, been an increase in income inequality within rich countries in recent years that might be related to globalization.)[22] Thus we are led to the same conclusion that we reached for the pre–World War I era: this new Age of Globalization has seen a reduction of poverty in developing countries that have been willing and able to globalize.

Another way of looking at the data also suggests that globalization has been associated with reductions in poverty. If, instead of looking at inequality across countries, where all *countries* are weighted equally, we instead look at inequality across the world population, where each *person* is weighted equally, we get a very different picture. The great success stories in recent years have been in Asia, which has two of the most populous countries in the world, India and China. Both countries came to globalization late and have sometimes used unorthodox methods to develop their economies, but their embrace of globalization has had high payoffs. Rapid growth in India and China has removed over a billion people from extreme poverty. When we realize that these billion make up a sixth of the world's population, it becomes obvious why research that weights every human being equally in computing inequality finds that income inequality has actually fallen, not risen, in recent years.[23] The great success stories of India and China in reducing poverty are reflected not just in economic data but also in life expectancy. In 1955 life expectancies in India and China were thirty-nine and forty-one years, respectively; today they have risen to sixty-two years in India and seventy years in China.[24]

These success stories are not meant to minimize the terrible plight of certain parts of the world, such as sub-Saharan Africa, where poverty has increased and life expectancy has actually fallen to disastrously low levels in recent years because of the AIDS epidemic. (Those in poverty, defined as having income of less than $2 per day, rose from 73% of the population to over 76% today, while life expectancy has dropped from fifty years in 1990 to less than forty-six years currently.)[25] The plight of these countries, however, is due not to globalization but rather to the failure to globalize. This observation has been cogently expressed by economists Peter Lindert and Jeffrey Williamson: "As far as we can tell, there are no anti-global victories to report for the postwar Third World."[26]

A word of caution: The association of the reduction in poverty with countries that have globalized could be the result of reverse causality. That is, countries that had the capability to grow fast were also the ones that could take advantage of globalization. Evidence and analysis presented later in this book, however, suggest that causality *is* likely to run from globalization to high economic growth and reductions in poverty.

Financial Globalization in Emerging Market Economies: The Next Great Globalization?

Although economic globalization has come a long way, in one particular dimension it is far from complete. As is documented in Maurice Obstfeld and Alan Taylor's book, *Global Capital Markets*, financial globalization is primarily confined to rich countries.[27] Despite the huge increase in international capital flows in recent years, they primarily flow from North to North, that is, from rich countries to other rich countries that are mostly in the Northern Hemisphere, rather than from North to South, from rich to poor countries.[28] Most international capital flows are exchanges of assets between rich countries and are undertaken primarily for diversification. These flows enable people in rich countries to put their eggs into different baskets by holding assets from other rich countries. International capital does not generally flow to poor countries to enhance their development.

As Nobel laureate Robert Lucas has pointed out, this feature of international capital flows is a paradox: Why doesn't capital flow from rich to poor countries?[29] We know that labor is incredibly cheap in poor countries, and so we might think that capital would be especially productive there. Just think of how hugely profitable a factory might be in a poor country where wages are one-tenth of what they are in the United States. We should expect massive flows of capital from rich countries (where the returns on capital should be far lower) to poor countries (where they should be higher). While there has been a big increase in the amount of capital moving to emerging market countries in recent years, capital still flows primarily from one rich country to another, where the returns on capital are similar.[30]

The amount of private capital flowing to emerging market countries increased dramatically in the 1990s, and its annual rate is now over $300 billion. That may sound like a lot, but it is only one-fifth of total international capital flows from private sources.[31] When governments are added into the picture, recent developments are even more surprising. Emerging market countries have actually been sending capital *back* to rich countries. The United States is currently running enormous trade and current account deficits of over $600 billion because Americans are buying more goods and services from other countries than they are selling to other countries. These deficits are being financed by loans from foreigners, with emerging market countries providing the United States with about $200 billion per year. The Chinese government, for example, has accumulated almost $800 billion of foreign assets, and it is now one of the largest holders of U.S. Treasury securities in the world.

Also remarkable is the finding that capital flows from North to South relative to total capital flows are far smaller than they were in the first Age of Globalization in the late nineteenth and early twentieth centuries. By 1914 around half of the capital in Argentina was supplied by rich foreign countries, particularly Great Britain.[32] Today less than one-tenth of Argentine capital is being supplied by foreigners.[33] This change in the pattern of capital flows has not been confined to Argentina. In 1913 over 25% of the world stock of foreign capital went to countries with income per person less than one-fifth that of the United States; by 1997 this figure had fallen to around 5%.[34]

As these numbers show, financial globalization is far from complete. Will financial systems in emerging market economies become more integrated with those in the rest of the world? Will the next great globalization be financial? If it is, will further financial globalization benefit poorer countries?

Is Financial Globalization Always Beneficial?

The benefits of globalization of trade in goods and services are not a controversial subject among economists. Polls of economists indicate that one of the few things they agree on is that the globalization of international trade, in which markets are opened to flows of foreign goods and services, is desirable.[35] (Globalization of trade is, however, controversial among the general public and more will be said about it in Chapters 8 and 12.) *Financial* globalization, opening markets to flows of foreign capital, is, however, highly controversial even among economists.

The important role of its financial system in a nation's economy is not well understood by the average person. Even many economists are shocked by the high salaries paid to investment bankers and other financial professionals.[36] After all, what do these financial professionals produce? Nothing concrete comes from their highly paid work.

Even high-level government officials underestimate the importance of the financial system. George Bush's first treasury secretary, Paul O'Neill, whose job involved designing policies to deal with financial markets, displayed this ignorance in an interview shortly after he took office. He belittled the value of participants in currency markets: "The people who benefit from roiling the world currency markets are speculators, and as far as I'm concerned, they provide not much useful value."[37] O'Neill couldn't have been more wrong.

Getting the financial system to work well is critical to the success of an economy. To understand why, we need to recognize that the financial system is like the brain of the economy: it is a coordinating mechanism that allocates capital to building factories, houses, and roads. If capital goes to the wrong uses or does not flow at all, the economy will operate inefficiently and economic growth will be low. Even the strongest work ethic cannot compensate for a misallocation of capital. Working hard will not by itself make a country rich, because hard-working workers will not be productive unless they work with the right amount and kinds of capital. Brain is more important than brawn, and similarly an efficient financial system is more important than hard work to an economy's success.

Financial globalization has several important benefits in emerging market economies. First, by bringing in new capital, it lowers the cost of capital, thereby encouraging investment; this in turn promotes growth. Second, when foreign capital and financial institutions are allowed to enter a country, they improve the allocation of capital. Third, globalization of the financial system helps promote the development of better property rights and institutions, both of which make the domestic financial sector work better in putting capital to productive uses. To reap these benefits, financial globalization must be extensive enough that the entry of foreign capital and foreign institutions increases competition in domestic financial markets. (More about this in Chapters 2 and 3.)

Even with all these powerful benefits, financial globalization is not necessarily always a force for good: it can go very wrong.[38] As we will see in Chapters 4–7, opening up the financial system to foreign capital flows can lead, and has led, to disastrous financial crises, which have resulted in great pain, suffering, and even violence. (There was widespread ethnic violence in Indonesia after its crisis in 1997, and in the wake of Albania's financial crisis in 1996–97 there were some 2500 casualties.)[39] This is why financial globalization is so controversial. Joseph Stiglitz, a Nobel Prize–winning economist, is critical of globalization in his book *Globalization and Its Discontents;* he believes that the opening of financial markets in emerging market economies to foreign capital leads to economic collapse.[40] Even Jagdish Bhagwati, one of the most prominent economists defending globalization (his book is titled *In Defense of Globalization*)[41] is highly skeptical of *financial* globalization: "the claims of enormous benefits from free capital mobility are not persuasive."[42] George Soros, one of the world's most prominent financiers, opens his book *On Globalization* with an introductory chapter entitled "The Deficiencies of Global Capitalism."[43]

The case studies of financial crises in Latin America and East Asia presented in Part Two show that financial globalization is likely to produce financial crises in emerging market countries when bad policies in those countries encourage excessive risk taking by financial institutions. Unfortunately such policies are often promoted by political and business elites in these countries for their own aggrandizement. Thus the issue is not whether financial globalization is inherently good or bad; I argue that, when it is done right, financial globalization has substantial benefits. But when financial globalization is perverted by policies that lead to an explosion of the financial system, it can go very badly.

Another Great Reversal?

As we have seen, the second Age of Globalization, in which we currently find ourselves, has many similarities with the first age, which occurred in the late nineteenth and early twentieth centuries. Could there be another Great Reversal, in which globalization again retreats and the world suffers great political, social, and economic upheaval and destruction? Could we experience déja vu all over again?[44]

Unfortunately the answer is yes. The backlash against globalization in Latin America is currently very strong. Much of the public in Latin America has turned against globalization because they have been disappointed in the amount of economic growth since 1990, when they opened up their economies, particularly to foreign capital flows. Some countries (such as Mexico, Ecuador, and Argentina) have also experienced disastrous crises that have led to depressions. In the immediate aftermath of its economic crisis in 2001–02, for example, Argentina experienced an unemployment rate of nearly 20% and an income per person that was 18% below the level it had reached in 1998.[45]

Given its depression, Argentina has been pursuing policies that make it harder for it to participate in the global system. This is exactly what happened in the aftermath of the Great Depression of the 1930s. Before this period Argentina was a full-fledged participant in globalization and was one of the richest countries in the world, with income per person that was actually higher than the average for countries in Europe.[46] Indeed, Argentina was one of the most desirable destinations for immigrants. At the turn of the century, when poor Italians were choosing whether to get on a boat for Buenos Aires or New York, it was a coin toss as to which destination was better. The success of Argentina before the Great Depression is reflected in the fact that, of twenty-seven countries for which data are available, it had the highest growth rate from 1870 to 1930.[47] In the aftermath of the Depression and World War II, however, the country turned its back on globalization and closed off its economy to the rest of the world. Over the next fifty years, Argentina had low economic growth, and it has since fallen into genteel poverty, with its income per person falling to only one-half that of the average for European countries. The same study of twenty-seven countries that found that Argentina had the highest growth rate from 1870 to 1930 ranked it last in terms of growth for the period 1930–92.

Argentina seems to be going down the same path again. The 2001–02 crisis discredited the policy in the 1990s of opening up the Argentinean economy. Given the backlash against globalization, it is not surprising that the Peronist government of Nestor Kirschner, harking back to the disastrous policies after World War II of the founder of its political party, Juan Perón, has been pursuing anti–free market policies that increase the likelihood that Argentina will turn its back on the global economic system. One of the most egregious examples is a measure implemented by the Argentine government in March 2006 to restrict exports of beef for six months in order to increase the domestic supply and lower the price, thereby halting most beef shipments abroad for the world's fifth largest beef producer.[48] The country is poised to lose another fifty years of economic growth.

The backlash against globalization has also manifested itself in countries such as Bolivia and Venezuela. Demonstrations against further opening up of the economy led to the ouster of the Bolivian president in 2003 and again in 2005, while Venezuela's president, Hugo Chavez, has advocated policies that turn it away from global markets (as well as democracy).

Only one Latin American country, Chile, has completely embraced globalization. Since 1990 Chile has opened up its economy completely, to both international trade and capital flows, and it has experienced rapid growth. From 1990 to 2003 it has had an average growth rate of 5.6% per year, by far the highest in Latin America. Indeed, Chile has been given the nickname the "Latin Tiger" to compare it to successful Asian countries dubbed the "Asian Tigers."

However, Chile is a small country, with a population of only 16 million, less than one-thirtieth the total population of over 500 million in Latin America.

Which way will the remaining countries of Latin America go? Will they follow Venezuela and Argentina and retreat from globalization, or will they emulate the successes of Chile and embrace it? Recent elections in Latin America have seen a further shift to the left with the success of candidates espousing anti-globalization rhetoric. Evo Morales, a former coca grower and opponent of globalization, was elected president of Bolivia in December 2005, while Ollanta Humala, a left-wing candidate for Peru's presidency who opposes free trade, won the first round of the presidential election in April 2006.

Similarly, the public in many of the *transition countries*, former communist countries that are a subcategory of emerging market economies, also has doubts about the benefits of globalization. This is less of a problem for the transition countries in Eastern Europe that are entering or are likely to enter the European Union soon; by doing so they will automatically become a part of a globalized economy. However, there is a danger that Russia and many of the other countries that were part of the former Soviet Union may turn inward and reject globalization and economic freedom in general.

The Asian public seems to be far more supportive of globalization because they have experienced rapid growth, but the backlash against globalization might reach them too. It would be premature to assume that they will continue down the globalization path.

The backlash against globalization manifests itself in rich countries as well as poor. Protectionist measures to restrict the flow of goods from developing countries, especially China, have been proposed regularly in the U.S. Congress. Protectionist sympathies are also strong in Europe. One French protester described his fears of globalization by saying that he was worried that French workers would get "eaten with a Chinese sauce."[49] Most extraordinary have been recent government efforts in France, Italy, and Spain to block corporate takeovers when the acquiring firm is foreign, even if the acquiring country is a member of the European Union. (Protectionist concerns might also have been behind congressional pressure that blocked the takeover of six U.S. ports by Dubai Ports World in March 2006.)[50]

The possibility of another Great Reversal is very real. This book argues that turning their backs on globalization would be disastrous for both emerging market *and* rich countries. Developing countries, in particular, must embrace globalization so that they can reach their full potential and get rich.

How Can Poor Countries Get Rich?

Most people think that the way for poor countries to get rich is to make sure their citizens get a good education and are healthy, and it is not surprising that so much charitable aid goes into improving health care and education. Public health and education *are* important to economic growth, but increasing pub-

lic spending in these areas does not always produce higher growth.[51] Throughout this book, I argue that the only way for poor countries to get rich is for them
to provide incentives for capital (including capital devoted to health care and
education) to be supplied to its most productive uses.

If allocating capital to productive uses is necessary to promote economic
growth and development, how do you get it to happen? The short answer is,
"Develop good institutions that allocate capital efficiently."[52] But what are these
institutions?

The most basic set of growth-promoting institutions are those that promote
property rights (such as the rule of law, constraints on government expropriation, and the absence of corruption, all of which are discussed in the next chapter). If you live in a country where it is easy for others to take your property
away, either at gunpoint or through a corrupt government, you would be crazy
to make investments there. Without these investments, workers in your
country will be unable to earn high wages because there won't be sufficient
capital to provide the machines, buildings, and computers to make them
highly productive. Poverty will be severe.

Even if investments are made, if they go to the wrong place they will be use-
less. Thus the second, related set of institutions are ones that make sure that
those offering the best investment opportunities can actually get external
funds to make investments. This is the crucial role of the financial system. These
institutions promote an efficient financial system through financial regulation
and strong enforcement of financial contracts.

The problem for many poor countries is not that they can't get money
for investment but that the investment is counterproductive. In the 1970s,
for example, the World Bank provided lending to finance a huge shoe factory
in Tanzania that was to produce four million pairs of shoes a year, three-
quarters of which were to be exported to Europe. However, the factory, with
its aluminum walls and no ventilation system, was ill suited for Tanzania's climate, with the result that it never produced more than 4% of its installed capac-
ity and never exported a single shoe.[53]

Nations are poor because they are disadvantaged in many important areas:
their institutions are weak; they are "institutionally challenged." We can
classify poor countries into two types. The poorest group includes countries
that do not even have basic property rights, either because they are subject
to civil strife or because they are run by rapacious governments. Many
countries in sub-Saharan Africa, where average income per person is less than
one-twentieth of what the average American earns, are in this group.[54] The second group of poor countries has basic property rights and they are far better
off and far less poor than countries in the first group. These emerging market
countries are opening up their markets to the flows of goods, services, and capital from other nations, but they do not yet have institutions that support a well-
functioning financial system.

The terms "less-developed," "developing," "poor," and "emerging market" are often used interchangeably to describe disadvantaged nations, but there are subtle differences. Because this book outlines how disadvantaged nations can improve their financial system, it applies more to emerging market countries. They are the ones at a stage of development where it becomes possible to create a well-functioning financial system. Many of the policy prescriptions offered here, however, also apply to a wider group of countries that includes not only the emerging market countries but also those at the lowest level of development who do not have even basic property rights. When I refer to "less-developed," "developing," or "poor" countries, I am referring to the entire set of disadvantaged countries, including the poorest. When I use the term "emerging market," I am referring to those countries that are ready to develop financial systems that can move them up to rich-country status.

Institutional development (more precisely defined here as measures that promote effective property rights and an efficient financial system) is the key to economic development.[55] Since good institutions exist in rich countries, you might think that these institutions could just be exported to disadvantaged nations to enable them to get rich. Good institutions, however, need to be home grown; institutional frameworks that have been developed in the rich countries frequently do not translate well to poorer countries. This is a lesson that many in the advanced countries of the world have yet to learn. The development of good institutions in the advanced countries took hundreds of years as they grew and adapted to local conditions. Poor countries must ultimately develop their own institutions, and the citizens of these nations must feel they have ownership of those institutions or else the institutions will be ineffective and short-lived.

It is also important to recognize that the impediments to developing good institutions reside in the less-developed countries themselves. Developing good institutions is hard: it takes time and effort for a country to plan, establish, experiment with, evolve, and adapt its institutions to its historical, cultural, and political circumstances. It takes a long time for any nation to achieve strong property rights and an effective financial system.

It is even harder to develop good institutions in less-developed countries because of the political environment. Rich elites and special interests often have considerable political clout; they have much to lose from institutional development that encourages an efficient financial system and promotes competition. Globalization, however, can be an important force in promoting the development of better institutions: it weakens the profits and power of the rich elites and special interests who oppose institutional development, and it can even encourage them to support institutional reforms to restore their profits. Globalization can therefore help generate the political will for institutional reform. We have seen this happen in emerging market economies like Chile, China, India, Singapore, South Korea, and Taiwan that have experienced rapid growth.

Yet globalization, particularly of the financial kind, does not always produce good outcomes. Just as rich elites block needed institutional development to increase their profits, they often pervert the financial globalization process for the same reason, which is why financial globalization often does not work. There are those (including prominent economists Joseph Stiglitz and Jagdish Bhagwati) who put the primary blame for the failures of financial globalization in emerging market countries on outsiders, specifically on the IMF or the Wall Street–Treasury Department complex.[56] The evidence discussed throughout this book has brought me to the conclusion that they are just plain wrong. To be sure, institutions like the IMF or the U.S. Treasury Department are not blameless; public and private financial institutions active in the international capital markets have often aided and abetted poorly designed financial globalization, although this was not necessarily their intention. (More on this in Chapters 5–7 and 11.)

What Can the Rich Countries Do?

How can rich countries help? The key is to provide the right incentives. Currently the IMF and the World Bank often find it hard to deny loans to governments in the less-developed world that misallocate the funds or refuse to develop the institutions that are needed to make a nation's economy successful. The inability to "just say no" creates the wrong incentives for ill-run nations. Money should be used as a carrot to encourage poorer countries to develop good institutions. If a government in one of these countries is unwilling to do this, the IMF and the World Bank must use the stick and cut off the flow of money. This approach sounds harsh, but it is better to engage in tough love than to allow countries to continue down the wrong path.

International financial institutions such as the IMF and World Bank and other governmental organizations in the rich countries (like the Group of Seven or G7) have also had a tendency to impose on less-developed countries institutions patterned too directly after those that have worked well in advanced countries. They have often also pushed standard "one size fits all" prescriptions for less-developed countries, such as flexible over fixed exchange-rate regimes or complete and precipitous abolition of capital controls. The arrogance of these institutions and governments is greatly resented in the less-developed world. The standard prescriptions often don't work, and they also have a strong element of hypocrisy because many of the conditions imposed on the less-developed countries are not met by the rich countries themselves.

The international financial institutions and advanced countries can help in several ways. Although less-developed countries need to develop their own institutional frameworks to make globalization work, there is considerable expertise in institutions like the IMF and the World Bank on which these countries could draw. Technical assistance from these organizations can be of great value, and indeed it has been in South Korea and Turkey, both of which asked for help after their financial crises. The right incentives from the international financial institutions can also help encourage economic and political elements in the less-developed countries to overcome blocking of institutional development by rich elites.

What about direct financial aid? Wouldn't more aid from rich countries help poor countries to develop? Many people lament the paltry amount of foreign aid that rich countries provide to poor countries: U.S. foreign aid as a percentage of its gross national income is only a meager 0.04%.[57] Although aid in the form of technical assistance has often had important successes, as William Easterly has pointed out in his book *The Elusive Quest for Growth*,[58] aid has generally not worked well in promoting development because it has typically not provided the right incentives.[59] Indeed, Easterly cites the extraordinary example of Zambia: if the $2 billion of aid Zambia has received from the advanced countries and international aid organizations since its independence had gone into productive investments, the nation would now have an income of over $20,000 per person, putting it in the rich-nations club. Instead Zambia has an income of $600 per person, one-third lower than its income at independence.

Just as throwing money at poor countries does not seem to work, simply boosting investment and the amount of capital in a country is also not the key to economic growth, because putting capital in the wrong place does not produce a healthier economy. Only when capital is allocated to its most productive uses does the economy benefit: this is why development of an efficient financial sector is key to economic growth.

What we know does work to promote development is encouraging poorer countries to pursue an external orientation and develop a successful export sector. This approach not only forces the economy to become more efficient, it also creates a demand to improve institutions that encourage financial development. Along with technical assistance and incentives for institutional development, advanced countries can also help to alleviate poverty in the rest of the world by opening up their markets to exports from poorer countries, which they often have not done, particularly in agricultural products. Trade, not aid, will make the world a better, safer, and more economically and politically stable place to be.

Why the Anti-Globalizers Are Wrong

Anti-globalizers have it completely backwards: globalization is not the enemy. Particularly disturbing to me are elements of the left that are against globalization. They say they care about poor people, and I believe they do. They are correct in saying that the globalization process has often been perverted by rich elites and that simplistic solutions like privatization and the establishment of free markets often do not work. They are also right that globalization will not cure all the ills of poor nations. By itself globalization, in both finance and trade, is not enough to ensure economic development. But to be against globalization is most assuredly to be against poor people in the rest of the world, and this is a morally indefensible position. Less-developed countries cannot get rich unless they globalize, and, in particular, they must globalize their financial sectors. Financial globalization is not a choice: it needs to be the focus of the next great globalization.

Those in rich countries who protest against free trade in the name of helping poor people also misunderstand what it takes to promote economic development. As I have already argued and will argue later in the book, opening up rich-country markets to goods and services from less-developed countries is far more important than financial aid in alleviating world poverty, and such openness also promotes financial stability in emerging market countries. Those who are against opening up our markets—although they often don't realize it—are also against reducing poverty abroad and even at home. True, closing off our markets in rich countries may help *some* workers in the short run (although in the long run it will make the *average* worker worse off because it will lower productivity growth). But this help comes at the expense of the far poorer worker in the less-developed world. Protesting in advanced countries against free trade is the result of ignorance or narrowly defined self-interest.

This book is meant to challenge those who oppose globalization to rethink their objections. As Kofi Annan, the secretary-general of the United Nations, has put it, "The main losers in today's very unequal world are not those who are too much exposed to globalization. They are those who have been left out."[60] Rather than opposing or limiting globalization, we in the rich countries and those in the less-developed countries must, as a moral imperative, work together to make globalization work for the general good of people all over the world.

Part One

Is Financial Globalization Beneficial?

Two

How Poor Countries Can Get Rich: Strengthening Property Rights and the Financial System

In America and many other cultures, we are taught that the key to success is hard work. Yet, when we look at many less-developed countries, we see people who work extremely hard for long hours. Their wages are low and so they remain poor, and their countries as a whole remain poor. If hard work does not make a country rich, what does?

The right institutions make a country rich. Nobel laureate Douglass North defines institutions as the "rules of the game in a society, or, more formally, humanly devised constraints that shape human intervention."[1] The institutions that are most crucial to economic growth enable a country to allocate capital to its most productive uses. These institutions establish and perpetuate strong property rights, an effective legal system, a stable financial system, and sound government regulation of the financial sector.[2]

Strong Property Rights and an Effective Legal System

A country can have a successful economy only if it has strong property rights, that is, if it protects a person's property from expropriation by the government or other parties. Property rights are the most fundamental institution required for economic growth. Without them, people will have little incentive to make investments because the fruits of their investments (the returns) can be easily taken away. Weak property rights thus lead to low investment, and without investment an economy cannot grow.

Residents of advanced nations like the United States often take property rights for granted. The founding fathers of America and their British forebears understood the importance of property rights to the success of the economy, and there is a vast body of U.S. law that protects private property. The government cannot just take your property when it wants to; people who steal property are jailed; and people who make use of our property (either physical or intellectual) without our permission can be sued in courts of law.

The Role of the Legal System: Why We Shouldn't Kill All the Lawyers

Everyone loves to bad-mouth lawyers. Jokes galore make fun of ambulance chasers and shifty filers of frivolous lawsuits. Hostility to lawyers is not just a recent phenomenon: in Shakespeare's *Henry VI*, written in the late sixteenth century, Dick the Butcher recommends, "The first thing we do, let's kill all the lawyers." Is Dick right?

Most legal work is actually not about ambulance chasing, frivolous lawsuits, and criminal law. Instead it involves the writing and enforcement of contracts, which is how property rights are established. When you start thinking about the role that lawyers play in establishing and protecting property rights, you almost start to feel warm and fuzzy about them.

A good system of laws, by itself, does not provide incentives to invest, because property rights without enforcement are meaningless. This is where lawyers come in. When someone encroaches on your land or makes use of your property without your permission, you turn to a lawyer to stop them. Without lawyers, you would not be able to protect your investments and you would be unwilling to invest. With no or limited investment, there would be little of the economic growth that is the road to riches.

The Anglo-Saxon legal system, based on common law, requires more legal services than other systems. The United States is alleged to have more lawyers per person than any other country in the world. It is also among the richest countries in the world, with a financial system that is superb at putting capital to new and productive uses, such as in the technology sector. Is this just a coincidence? Or could the U.S. legal system actually be beneficial to its economy?

As we will see in the next chapter, recent research suggests that the Anglo-Saxon legal system is a big plus for the United States.[3] Once we understand the important role of property rights in producing wealth, we begin to see that a sound legal system, which requires many lawyers, is actually critical to eradicating poverty and thus highly beneficial to society. So we shouldn't kill all the lawyers.

Why Laws and Lawyers Are Not Enough
to Protect Property Rights

Having laws on the books and plenty of lawyers to protect property rights and enforce contracts is still not enough to encourage the allocation of capital to its most productive uses, which is key to economic growth. The legal system also needs to be honest and efficient, that is, it must operate quickly and at low cost.[4] Douglass North has emphasized the importance of the legal system to economic growth: "The inability of societies to develop effective, low-cost enforcement of contracts is the most important source of both historical stagnation and contemporary underdevelopment in the Third World."[5]

The inadequacy, by themselves, of a good set of laws and plenty of lawyers in promoting growth is illustrated by the poor economic performance of the Philippines, once a U.S. territory. The Philippines has a legal system based on U.S. law, yet its judiciary is known to be one of the most inefficient in the world. In the World Bank publication *Doing Business in 2005*, the Philippines is ranked as having one of the highest costs of recovering a debt, exceeding 50% of the debt's face value. (In the United States the average cost of recovering a debt is 7.5% of face value.)[6] Given its high cost of contract enforcement, the Philippines has not surprisingly enjoyed much lower growth rates than the rest of Asia. India has a legal system based on the British model, but lawsuits of all kinds, including property rights suits, can take years to settle there because its overburdened judicial system has over three million backlogged cases in higher courts, over 300,000 of which are ten years old or older.[7] The German airline Lufthansa is still in court in Brazil after almost a quarter of a century over a wrongful-termination lawsuit.[8]

Corruption, which is endemic in many less-developed countries, is another obstacle to a well-functioning property rights system. If judges can be bribed, then property rights can be expropriated by the highest bidder for the judge's "services." An entrepreneur with a good idea or investment cannot protect it from the rich and powerful elites who can use the courts as a weapon to take it away and reap any rewards for themselves. If a government official has to be bribed to allow you to conduct your business, he has in effect appropriated part of the value of your property.[9] Corruption is like a cancer in the body of an economy: it weakens and sickens the economy by reducing the incentives for entrepreneurs to make investments and work hard to make profits. Corruption is particularly pernicious because it creates so much uncertainty for entrepreneurs: they can never be sure when the bribe is enough or whether the corrupt official will keep coming back to them over and over again to demand more money. Research finds that both lower investment relative to GDP and lower economic growth are associated with increases in corruption.[10]

The high cost of setting up a legal business or legally purchasing land is another barrier to establishing clear property rights in many developing countries. In countries like the United States, opening a legal business is a simple procedure that requires filling out a form and paying a nominal licensing fee. But, as economist Hernando De Soto has documented in his fascinating book *The Mystery of Capital,* setting up a business in a less-developed country can be a nightmare. De Soto's researchers found that to legally register a small garment workshop with one worker in Peru required 289 days, working six hours a day, at a total cost of $1231—a figure thirty-one times the monthly minimum wage.[11] In contrast, to set up a similar business in the United States takes only 5 days at a cost of $210.[12] Peru may be an extreme example, but this problem is endemic in less-developed countries. Recent research on a group of developing countries found that, on average, ten bureaucratic procedures and sixty-three days, at a cost of one-third of average annual income per person, were required to open a typical business.[13] The result of these barriers to legally registering businesses is that only the rich can operate legal businesses that have access to the legal system.[14] The resulting lack of property rights for others in these countries is a serious impediment to development.

Even having property laws on the books does not guarantee them. Many governments or their officials in less-developed countries simply expropriate an idea, a business, or an investment because they want to. Robert Mugabe, the president of Zimbabwe, has impoverished his country by expropriating land and giving it to his cronies. When land can be taken away from a landowner without adequate compensation, landowners will stop investing in their land and farm production will fall. Zimbabwe, which was once a highly successful producer of farm products and exported over 700,000 tons of corn in 1990, now exports less than one-twentieth of this amount.[15] Andrei Schleifer and Robert Vishny have coined the term "the grabbing hand" to describe the often rapacious behavior of such governments, which have been given the name *kleptocracies* because they steal from their citizens in a variety of ways.[16]

Kleptocracies have been particularly common in Africa since its colonies became independent in the 1960s. This characteristic of many African economies explains, in large part, why Africa not only has failed to keep up with other regions in its economic growth but has even seen a decline of income per person and an increase in poverty in many countries. Haiti, the poorest country in the Americas, has suffered a similar fate. The Duvaliers, Papa Doc and Baby Doc, dictators from 1957 to 1986, were notorious for stealing on a grand scale. Jean-Bertrand Aristide, a democratically elected president of Haiti and a former priest, has been viewed by many as not much better. His close ties to street gangs such as the Cannibal Army and accusations of corruption and election manipulation eventually led to his overthrow by a rebel group in 2004. The history of Haiti does not inspire confidence that a new government will enforce property rights and help the country develop.

Property rights will also not exist if the rule of the gun supersedes the rule of law. Continual wars and rebellions diminish rights to property because the threat of force allows aggressors to take property. We usually think of the cost of war in terms of the number of dead and wounded, but the economic cost is horrendous as well. Because the threat of war or rebellion makes it hard to retain the profits from productive investment, investment will not occur. A continual state of warfare, in addition to years of kleptocratic rule, goes a long way toward explaining the awful growth experience of many of the countries of sub-Saharan Africa since they gained independence in the 1960s.

How Property Rights Evolve

Developing a strong property rights system is a complicated endeavor. The Magna Carta, the thirteenth-century document that protected the rights of nobles under King John, was an early step in this development for Anglo-Saxon countries, including the United States, but it did not protect the property rights of the average citizen. It is only through many twists and turns, over hundreds of years, that property rights have come to their present form.[17]

Property rights also need to evolve to suit local conditions. In *The Mystery of Capital,* De Soto describes how British property rights for land, which were based on a long-established title system, were not easily applied in the new lands of North America.[18] As the settlers moved west, good records of titles and accurate surveys were not to be had, so different legal procedures were developed to provide ownership to settlers who had improved the land on which they settled. Under British law, when someone squatted (lived and worked on land owned by someone else without their approval), the squatter was not entitled to any of the improvements he had made, even if he had squatted on the land by mistake. If this legal framework had been retained in the colonies and later in the United States, there would have been little incentive to invest in improving the land by clearing fields of trees, putting up fences, building barns, and so on. To encourage land improvements, many of the colonies adopted a new legal framework, called preemption, under which a squatter was allowed to buy the land he had settled on at a price set by a local jury if the rightful owner was unwilling to compensate the squatter for the improvements made on the land. De Soto's example illustrates how effective protection of property rights evolves over time. Indeed, this evolution continues today as courts decide whether a new computer program or a new process for genetically modifying a plant is patentable. If it is, users of the idea or process must pay a licensing fee to the patent holder. This example also demonstrates that a system for defining property rights in one country may not work effectively in another. Effective protection of property rights must reflect local conditions.

China's recent approach to defining property rights illustrates that the evolution of such rights under local conditions also takes place in less-developed countries.[19] After the death of Mao Zedong, the Chinese government realized that the nation's economy would not grow without some form of property rights that would give incentives to invest. However, communist doctrine, which objects to private property, was a barrier to establishing property rights as we know them in the West. Having such rights would have been a tacit acceptance of capitalism. Instead the Chinese government decided to allocate property rights in nonstandard ways.

To stimulate agricultural output, which had plummeted under Mao's disastrous policies, the Chinese government developed the Household Responsibility System (HRS), under which local officials assigned land to individual households according to their size. Farmers could develop their land, produce food, and sell it for their own profit, thus giving them the incentive to increase production. This approach was highly successful and led to a huge increase in the output of such crops as rice and wheat.

To increase manufacturing output, the government allowed the establishment of town and village enterprises (TVEs), in which the ownership rights to businesses were given to the local government of the township or village and not to individuals. Because the TVEs could keep the profits and use them to provide goods and services to the community, they had an incentive to make good investments and to produce goods and services as efficiently as possible. This approach also worked: TVEs were a primary source of growth in China until the mid-1990s. With the increase in the scale of manufacturing activity, however, firms needed to grow beyond the scale of TVEs: these larger firms have now become the primary drivers of Chinese economic growth.

Although the HRS and TVEs did not confer private property rights as Westerners know them, they probably worked far better in China at its early stage of development than more standard forms of private property rights. Such standard forms would not have been enforceable because a proper legal system was not in place and corruption would have been high. Indeed, having local governments own the enterprises gave the governments an incentive to make sure that the profits could not be appropriated by the central government or its officials.

The experience in China raises an important theme that we will encounter throughout this book. Institutions that function well in advanced countries may not always work in developing countries; they may have to be adapted to the local environment in order to promote investment and growth.[20] This was true when America was a developing country in the eighteenth and nineteenth centuries and the British system of property rights for land had to be modified to suit local conditions. Even in China, what has worked in the past is less likely to work in the future. Their system of property rights will have to change because entities like the TVEs are often too small to be long-term engines of economic growth. As we will see in later chapters, the Chinese government has recognized the need for changes, although it is not yet clear whether it will be successful in developing a system of property rights that can take China to the next stage of its economic development. The examples presented here provide a warning that, as part of the globalization process, simply taking institutions from advanced countries and imposing them on developing countries may not work.

A Sound Financial System

Property rights by themselves do not ensure that capital will flow to its most productive uses. Secure property rights provide individuals with the incentives to invest if they already have the money to do so and are thus a first step in achieving productive investment. However, people who have saved and have money to invest in new businesses, products, and ideas are often not the same people who have productive investment opportunities. Merely being rich does not mean you have good ideas.

Unless those with surplus funds can channel their money to those who have good investment opportunities and need funds, a substantial amount of productive investment will never take place. If surplus funds go to the wrong place and fund unproductive investments, the funds will be squandered. It is the financial system, the brain of the economy, that performs the essential coordinating function of channeling funds from households and firms that have surplus funds to those individuals and firms that have a shortage of funds *and* can make productive investments. Developing a well-functioning financial system that directs funds where they can do the most good is thus a second, crucial step on a nation's path toward producing wealth.

Getting the financial system to channel funds efficiently is not an easy task. To understand the function of the financial system, look at the schematic diagram in Figure 2.1. Those who have saved and are lending funds are at the left, and those who must finance their spending by borrowing are at the right. Most people think that funds move directly from savers to borrowers via financial markets: this is the *direct finance* route shown at the bottom of the figure. With direct finance, borrowers borrow funds directly from savers by selling them *securities* (also called *financial instruments*), which are claims on the borrowers' future income or assets. For example, if a textile company in Malaysia needs to borrow funds to pay for a new factory to produce shirts, it might borrow the funds from savers in the United States by selling them equities, like common stock, or bonds.

What is less well known is that most funds get to borrowers through the much more circuitous *indirect finance* route shown at the top of the figure. With indirect finance, a financial intermediary (a bank, insurance company, finance company, mutual fund, or pension fund) obtains funds from savers and then uses them to make loans to borrowers. Such *financial intermediation* is the primary route for moving funds from lenders to borrowers. This is especially true

Figure 2.1. Flows of Funds through the Financial System

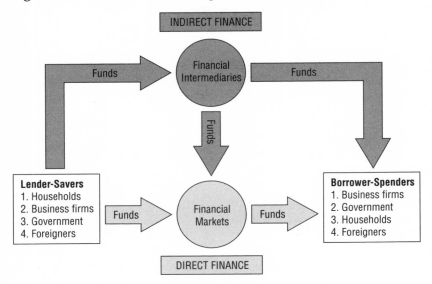

in developing countries, where almost all lending is done by financial inter-mediaries because securities markets are often tiny or nonexistent. (In devel-oping countries financial intermediation often occurs in informal credit markets through rural moneylenders, pooling of funds in rotating savings and credit associations, lending within family groups, or microcredit schemes.) Most borrowers in advanced countries also obtain credit through financial inter-mediation, even in the United States, which has the most active securities mar-kets in the world. Although the U.S. media focus their attention on securities markets, particularly the stock market, most Americans would be surprised to learn that financial intermediaries are a far more important source of financ-ing for businesses than securities markets. They supply close to 60% of the funds flowing to nonfinancial businesses.[21] This figure even understates the impor-tance of financial intermediaries, because around half of all stocks and much more than half of all bonds are purchased by financial intermediaries in finan-cial markets (the downward arrow in the figure).

Why can't the financial system get funds directly to those who need them? Why do we need financial intermediaries at all? Why isn't it simpler to get funds directly to those who need them the most?

Why Is It So Hard to Get a Financial System to Work Well?

What impedes the direct movement of funds to those with the best investment opportunities is a problem known as *asymmetric information*, a situation in which one party to a transaction has much less accurate information than the other. For example, managers of a Russian company know whether they are honest and have better information about how well their business is doing than the stockholders who own the company or the bondholders who have lent it money. This imbalance is particularly strong if the stockholders and bondholders are foreigners and do not know the ins and outs of doing business in Russia. Similarly, a person seeking a loan to buy a car knows her ability to make monthly payments, but a potential lender like a bank may not. And your son may be using his allowance to buy lunch—but he could be buying drugs instead.

In a financial system, asymmetric information creates two types of problems that make it hard to get capital to where it belongs: adverse selection and moral hazard.

Adverse selection occurs before a transaction is completed. The party who is most eager to engage in a transaction is the one most likely to produce an undesirable (adverse) outcome for you. Someone who knows that she is not going to pay you back will be the most eager to get a loan from you. If you have no way of knowing that this person is a poor credit risk (if information in this transaction is asymmetric), then you might make the loan and be very sorry afterwards. Because adverse selection makes it more likely that loans will be made to bad credit risks (whether someone seeking money to buy a car or a foreign company planning to build a new factory), lenders may decide not to make any loans at all, even though there are good credit risks in the marketplace.

Moral hazard is the second problem created by asymmetric information, and it arises after a transaction occurs. Once you have agreed to give something to someone else, there is the risk (*hazard*) that the other party will engage in activities that are undesirable (*immoral*) from your point of view. For example, if you give someone a loan, even if she was initially a good credit risk, once she has your money in hand she may go to Las Vegas and gamble, a highly risky endeavor that makes it unlikely you will be repaid.

Similarly, suppose you, the manager of a bank, decide to make a loan to a software company that you know is developing a sure-thing product: an accounting program for businesses. The software company might decide instead to forgo the safe investment and pursue the development of something far more risky, but with a high payoff in the unlikely event it succeeds, say, a new operating system to replace Microsoft Windows. If the riskier project succeeds, the owners of the software company will get incredibly rich. If the investment in developing the operating system doesn't work out, as is much more likely, you won't get repaid, yet all the company will have lost is its reputation. Clearly the software company has an incentive to take the big risk of developing the operating system—at your expense.

If you knew what the software company was doing, you might be able to stop it from engaging in moral hazard and investing your money in the riskier project. Instead you would make sure that it put the money into the more conservative accounting software project. However, because it is hard to keep track of what the company is doing with your money—that is, because information is asymmetric—there is a good chance that the company will invest in the get-rich-quick scheme and you will not get paid back. Therefore, even if you were sure that you would be repaid if the company put the money into the conservative investment, the risk of moral hazard might keep you from making the loan in the first place.

Solving Asymmetric Information Problems: Why Financial Intermediaries, Especially Banks, Are So Important

How do individuals and businesses avoid being burned by the adverse selection and moral hazard problems that result from asymmetric information? The answer is obvious—you need to collect information to eliminate the information asymmetry—but its implementation is not. An important impediment to information collection is the *free-rider problem:* private investors who do not spend their resources on collecting information can take advantage of (get a *free ride* on) the information that other investors collect.

To understand the free-rider problem, just imagine that you are Warren Buffett and have spent a lot of time and money on gathering information that tells you which firms are good investments and which are bad. You believe that the resources you have spent are worthwhile because you can make up the cost of acquiring this information, and then some, by purchasing the securities of good firms that are undervalued.

Once you have started buying, however, other savvy free-riding investors, knowing that you have produced good information—after all, you are Warren Buffett—will buy right along with you, even though they have not paid for any of the information you have gathered. The increased demand for the undervalued good securities will cause their low prices to be bid up immediately to reflect their true value, before you have been able to buy all you might want.

Because of all these free riders, you will not be able to capture most of the profits from your information production, and so you will cut back on the amount of resources you spend on producing it. Other investors who might think about spending resources on gathering information will come to the same realization, and they will also cut back on information collection. The inability to fully profit from information collection means that not enough information will be available in the marketplace, and so asymmetric information problems will remain severe.

Well-functioning financial intermediaries play a key role in solving asymmetric information problems. Financial intermediaries make it their business

to collect information to overcome adverse selection and moral hazard problems, and they can avoid the free-rider problem by primarily making private
loans. Because private loans are not traded, it is hard for anyone else to ride
free on the financial intermediary's information collection activities.[22] The
intermediary making private loans thus receives the benefits of its information collection and will therefore find it profitable to continue the activity. The
ability to profit from information collection explains why indirect finance, which
involves financial intermediaries, is the most prevalent source of funds for households and businesses.

Of all the types of financial intermediaries, banks are the most important.
Their basic business is taking in deposits and using these funds to make
loans. In the United States, banking institutions (which include commercial
banks, savings and loan associations, mutual savings banks, and credit unions)
are the most significant category of financial intermediaries, with over $11 tril-
lion in assets at the end of 2005 as compared to the next largest category,
mutual funds, with $6 trillion.[23] The dominance of banks is even more strik-
ing in other countries. While banks supply only 18% of total credit to nonfinancial businesses in the United States, they supply 56% in Canada, 76% in
Germany, and 78% in Japan.[24] In developing countries, banks are even more
important than in advanced economies.[25]

Banks are particularly critical in the financial system because they have unique
advantages over other financial intermediaries in using several practices to solve
asymmetric information problems.

Screening. Collecting information before a transactions occurs, to avoid
adverse selection problems, is called *screening.* Lenders check out potential borrowers carefully and ask a lot of personal questions. When a bank is thinking
about giving you a mortgage loan, it asks you about your income, your
employment record, your bank accounts, the value of the house, and so on.[26]
Banks are particularly good at screening because they develop long-term
relationships with potential borrowers.[27] This enables them to know their
customers well, making it cheaper for them to screen out bad borrowers.

Monitoring. Collecting information after a transaction occurs, to prevent moral
hazard, is called *monitoring.* After a financial institution makes a loan, the loan
officer checks on how the borrower is using the funds lent to him and will call
him if she sees risky behavior. Banks have a natural advantage in monitoring
a borrowing firm's behavior because they observe a firm's checking account,
which yields a great deal of information about the borrower's financial condition. For example, a sustained drop in the borrower's checking account
balance may signal that the borrower is having financial trouble. Unusual
account activity may suggest that the borrower is engaging in risky activities.
A change in suppliers, as indicated by the payees on the firms' checks, may

suggest that the borrower is pursuing a new line of business.[28] Banks' long-term relationships with their customers also give them an advantage in monitoring borrowers. If the borrower has borrowed from the bank before, the bank has already established procedures for monitoring that customer, making it cheaper to monitor the new loan.

Banks also try to prevent moral hazard by writing provisions into debt contracts, called *restrictive covenants,* that restrict borrowers' activities. For example, banks often write provisions into their loan contracts that forbid borrowers from going into risky businesses. Such a covenant would prevent undesirable behavior that would make it less likely they will be repaid. They also write covenants that promote desirable behavior. For example, a loan contract might require the firm to keep a certain percentage of its assets in cash so that it is more likely to be able to pay off the loan. Another type of covenant requires the firm to provide information periodically about its activities in the form of quarterly accounting and income reports, thereby making it easier for banks to monitor the firm.

But what if a lender does not think through every contingency when it writes the restrictive covenants into the loan contract? There will always be risky borrower activities that have not been explicitly ruled out. Banks have an advantage in avoiding this problem because they can use the threat of cutting off lending in the future to improve a borrower's behavior.[29] If a bank doesn't like what a borrower is doing even when the borrower isn't actually violating any restrictive covenants, the bank can threaten not to give the borrower any new loans in the future. Banks thus have an ability to deal with unanticipated moral hazard contingencies that is often unavailable to other participants in the financial markets.

Collateral. Another tool used by financial institutions to solve adverse selection and moral hazard problems is *collateral,* property promised in the loan contract to the lender if the borrower defaults on its debt. Most household debt is collateralized: a house is collateral for a mortgage and an automobile is collateral for an auto loan. (The only form of noncollateralized loan that households tend to have is credit card debt.) In the United States, commercial and farm mortgages, for which property is pledged as collateral, make up around one-quarter of borrowing by nonfinancial businesses; corporate bonds and other bank loans also often involve pledges of collateral.

Collateral is so prevalent in loan contracts because it ameliorates both adverse selection and moral hazard problems. Adverse selection interferes with the functioning of financial markets only if a lender suffers a loss when a borrower defaults on its loan payments. Collateral reduces the consequences of adverse selection because, if a borrower defaults on a loan, the lender can sell the collateral and use the proceeds to make up for its losses on the loan. For example, if you fail to make your mortgage payments, the lender can take title to your house, auction it off, and use the receipts to pay off the loan. Lenders are thus more willing to make loans secured by collateral, and borrowers are willing to supply collateral because the reduced risk for the lender makes it more likely they will get the loan, and perhaps at a better interest rate.

Collateral also reduces moral hazard by decreasing the incentives for borrowers to take on too much risk. When borrowers pledge collateral on their loans, they have more to lose if they can't pay them back, and so they are naturally more reluctant to engage in risky activities that make it more likely they will default and lose their collateral. If you have a house that you love and the bank will take it from you if you default on your mortgage, you will surely be less of a risk taker and will thus be less of a credit risk.

Why (Again) We Shouldn't Kill All the Lawyers

Once we understand how financial intermediaries solve adverse selection and moral hazard problems, we again come to a more favorable view of lawyers and the legal system. As we have seen, restrictive covenants are a key tool to reduce moral hazard, and they cannot be written effectively without lawyers. Restrictive covenants also have to be enforced to reduce moral hazard, and here again smart lawyering comes into play. Collateral only works to mitigate the adverse selection problem if the lender can take possession of the collateral—and again, good lawyers are needed to do this. Having a large legal community is therefore critical to the ability of the financial system to solve adverse selection and moral hazard problems; without them the financial system would be unable to allocate capital to its most productive uses. Lawyers and the legal system are what make the financial system work.

Why Well-Functioning Banks Are Even More Critical to Growth in Developing Countries

We have seen that information collection in securities markets is hindered by the free-rider problem. If the quality of information is poor or if not enough information is gathered, asymmetric information problems are severe, and it will be harder for firms to issue securities. This is exactly the situation in developing countries. Information about private firms is so hard to get because these countries' accounting standards and information technology are generally weak. For these reasons, securities markets in developing countries are typically underdeveloped and banks therefore play an even more dominant role in the financial system.

If banks do not have the right incentives to solve adverse selection and moral hazard problems in these countries, then the financial system will be unable to channel capital to its most productive uses, and economic growth will suffer. Furthermore, as we will see in later chapters, with the wrong incentives, banks can distort the financial globalization process so that it does more harm than good. Making sure that banks have the right incentives is crucial to development of a sound financial system in developing countries, and this is why we focus so much attention on the issue of incentives for banks throughout the book.

As financial systems develop, information about firms becomes easier to acquire, and so asymmetric information problems will be less severe and it will be easier for firms to issue securities. The importance of banks in the financial system will then diminish. This is exactly what we have seen in the United States in the past twenty years, during which there have been incredible improvements in information technology and banks' share of total lending has fallen.[30] The advances in information technology have led to *securitization*, the process of transforming what were once illiquid, nontraded financial assets (such as residential mortgages, automobile loans, small business loans, and credit card receivables), once the bread and butter of banking institutions, into marketable securities. As Alan Greenspan has put it, a vibrant securities market is a big plus for an economy because it can act as a "spare tire" for the economy: if there is a "flat" because banks get into trouble, securities markets can allow the economy to keep rolling.[31] Unfortunately, financial information in developing countries is so poor that this spare tire is not available.

Sound Government Regulation and Supervision of the Financial Sector: Why Laissez-Faire Is Not the Answer

Many conservatives lament government interference in the economy and believe that, if the government would just let markets do their work, we would all be far better off. But the presence of asymmetric information, which impedes the functioning of the financial system, indicates that, although this might be true for some sectors of the economy, it is not true for the financial sector.

We have seen that the more information that is collected, the less information asymmetry there will be, and the better the financial system will work. However, we have also seen that the free-rider problem creates a serious impediment to information production. Can government intervention in the financial system help?

The government could, for instance, produce information to help investors distinguish good firms from bad ones and provide it to the public free of charge. This solution, the socialization of information production, has its drawbacks.[32] First, without a profit motive, the government may not have the incentives to produce good information. Second, information produced by the government is likely to become politicized and thus unreliable. A government might find it politically difficult to release negative information about certain firms, or it could be influenced by powerful business interests to paint a positive picture when it is unjustified. Third, government agencies are unlikely to be able to pay market wages to attract the best people and so would be unable to produce high-quality information. Given these shortcomings, are there other approaches that the government can use to improve the quality of information in financial markets?

Government Regulation to Promote Transparency

A more sensible approach to decreasing information asymmetry is for the government to directly promote transparency. The government can regulate financial markets in a way that encourages firms to reveal honest information about themselves so that investors can more easily determine the true performance of these firms. In the United States, the Securities and Exchange Commission (SEC) requires firms selling their securities in public markets to disclose information about their sales, assets, and earnings. Governments also have laws to force firms to adhere to standard accounting principles that make profit verification easier and to impose stiff criminal and civil penalties on individuals who commit fraud by hiding and stealing profits.

Although government regulation to increase transparency is crucial to reducing adverse selection and moral hazard problems, bad firms have strong incentives to make themselves look like good firms, because they are then able to fetch a higher price for their securities. Executives have incentives to make their firms look better than they are because, when the firm appears to be doing well, they receive higher compensation. Not surprisingly, government regulation does not always solve the problem, as illustrated by the recent collapse of Enron and accounting scandals at other corporations like WorldCom in the United States and Parmalat and Royal Dutch Shell in Europe.

Prudential Regulation and Supervision

We have already seen that banks are particularly well suited to solve adverse selection and moral hazard problems because they make private loans that help avoid the free-rider problem. However, this solution gives rise to two additional problems in the banking system. First, depositors might be reluctant to put their money into a bank if they cannot easily tell whether bank managers are engaging in moral hazard and taking on too much risk or are outright crooks. Second, depositors' lack of information about the quality of a bank's assets can lead to bank panic, the wholesale collapse of many banks at the same time, which can have harmful consequences for the economy.

To see how asymmetric information can lead to bank panics, consider the following situation. Suppose that an adverse shock hits the economy, such as a default on the government debt that banks are holding, and as a result 5% of the banks have such large losses on their loans that they become insolvent.

Because of asymmetric information, depositors cannot tell whether their bank is solid or insolvent. Depositors at bad *and* good banks recognize that they may not get back one hundred cents on the dollar for their deposits and will want to withdraw their deposits. Indeed, because banks operate on a first-come, first-served basis, depositors have a very strong incentive to show up at the bank first (leading to a *run on the bank*) because, if they are last in line, the bank may have already given out all its cash and closed its doors. Uncertainty about the health of the banking system in general can therefore lead to a run on one bank, which then can further increase uncertainty about the health of the banking system and hasten the fall of other banks. If nothing is done to restore the public's confidence, a snowball effect (also known as a *contagion*) will set in, and multiple banks can fail over a brief period of time. With banks no longer around to solve adverse selection and moral hazard problems, lending and investment will decline, and the economy will experience a sharp economic downturn, such as occurred in the United States during the Great Depression in the 1930s and in Indonesia and Argentina more recently.

The government can intervene in the financial system to short-circuit bank runs by creating a safety net for depositors. It may either provide deposit insurance (such as that from the Federal Deposit Insurance Corporation in the United States) or else make funds available directly to troubled financial institutions. This safety net can accomplish two goals. If depositors are protected and are sure they won't suffer any losses when a bank fails, they will no longer be reluctant to provide the bank with funds at the first sign of trouble, even if they are unsure of its ultimate financial health. Depositor protection also means that depositors no longer have reasons to run on the bank because they know they will get their money back no matter what. Contagion from one bank failure, potentially leading to others, will no longer be a possibility, and bank panics will no longer occur.

Although a government safety net provided by deposit insurance is usually successful in protecting depositors and preventing bank panics, it can have negative consequences, particularly in developing countries. It increases the moral hazard problem for banks because, with a safety net, depositors have less incentive to withdraw their funds if they suspect that the bank is taking on too much risk. The discipline of the marketplace is weakened because the bank will still be able to acquire funds even if it pursues actions that will make it more likely to fail. Consequently, the presence of a government safety net increases the incentive for banks to take on greater risk than they otherwise would, with taxpayers paying the bill if the bank subsequently fails.

Given the moral hazard incentives created by a government safety net, there is a need for *prudential regulation,* rules set by the government to prevent banks from taking on too much risk. The government can limit banks' risk level by adopting regulations to promote disclosure of their activities. With this information, the market is more likely to pull funds out of a bank if it is engaging in risky activities. The government can also establish regulations to restrict those activities and asset categories that it considers too risky for banks, encourage banks to diversify, promote accurate disclosure to the markets of banks' financial condition, and require that banks hold minimum levels of capital as a cushion against bad loans. To make sure that these regulations are enforced, the government must also engage in *prudential supervision*, in which it monitors banks by examining them on a regular basis.

Effective prudential regulation and supervision are needed to make the financial system work well. But what if, as is often the case in developing countries, government officials cannot be trusted and use their regulatory and supervisory powers to line their own pockets? When government regulation and supervision are inadequate, the financial system will be unable to channel funds to those with productive investment opportunities, and colossal blowups of the financial system can occur (such as those discussed in Chapters 4–7).

We can see that a large amount of institutional development is needed to make a financial system work well. Developing all the fundamental institutions to support strong property rights and a sound financial system is a daunting task. Is it worth all the effort? How can the goal be accomplished? This is the subject to which we now turn.

Three

Financial Development, Economic Growth, and Poverty

As we have seen, developing the institutions that allow a financial system to overcome the problems created by asymmetric information is challenging. Indeed, recent research finds that an important reason why many developing countries and transition (i.e., ex-communist) countries like Russia experience low rates of growth is that their financial systems are underdeveloped, a situation referred to as *financial repression*.[1] We can understand why this is so by returning to the metaphor of the financial system as the brain of an economy: just as repressing the activity of the human brain (say, by the use of drugs or alcohol) seriously impairs a person's ability to carry out even simple tasks, financial repression is a severe impediment to economic growth and the reduction of poverty.

Are Financial Development and Economic Growth Linked? The Evidence

The evidence that financial development, often called *financial deepening,* and economic growth are linked is quite strong. (I am using the term *deepening* to refer to financial development that includes not only expansion in the financial sector but also improvement in institutions, so that the financial system can allocate capital to its most productive uses more efficiently.)[2] A pioneering study by Robert King and Ross Levine using a sample of eighty countries found that those with larger financial sectors back in 1960 experienced greater economic growth over the subsequent thirty years.[3] Later studies using more sophisticated techniques have confirmed this finding; they indicate that a doubling of the size of private credit in an average less-developed country is associated with a two-percentage-point annual increase in economic growth.[4] Through the magic of compound interest, a two-percentage-point annual increase results in a doubling of national income in thirty-five years. Industries and firms that are more dependent on external sources of funds will benefit more from financial deepening and will grow faster in countries that are better developed financially.[5] Similarly, more new firms are created in countries with better-developed financial systems.[6] The evidence also suggests that financial development stimulates growth more through its improvements in the allocation of capital (which raises overall productivity) than through its encouragement of higher levels of investment.[7] These findings have led World Bank researcher Patrick Honohan to state that "The causal link between finance and growth is one of the most striking empirical macroeconomic relationships uncovered in the last decade."[8]

Although financial deepening improves an economy's rate of economic growth, it is at least theoretically possible that the degree of poverty could remain the same or even increase because the resulting growth could lead to greater income inequality. However, research finds no evidence of this effect. In countries with better financial development, the income of the poorest fifth of the population actually grows faster than average GDP per person,[9] indicating clearly that financial development is associated with reductions in poverty and even with reductions in the use of child labor.[10] This finding is in concert with the predictions of economic theory: financial development increases the access of the poor to credit, which previously was accessible largely to the rich.[11]

What Impedes Financial Development?

Despite its benefits, financial development often doesn't happen in poor countries because their financial systems face severe impediments to solving asymmetric information problems.

The Tyranny of Collateral

As we have seen, the use of collateral is a crucial tool to help the financial system in general, and financial intermediaries like banks in particular, minimize the adverse selection problem. However, to use property, such as land or capital, as collateral, a person must legally own it. Unfortunately, as Hernando De Soto has documented in his fascinating book *The Mystery of Capital*,[12] it is extremely expensive and time consuming for the poor in less-developed countries to make their ownership of property legal. Obtaining legal title to a dwelling on urban land in the Philippines, for example, involved 168 bureaucratic steps and 53 public and private agencies, and the process took thirteen to twenty-five years. For desert land in Egypt, obtaining legal title took 77 steps, 31 public and private agencies, and five to fourteen years. To legally buy government land in Haiti, an ordinary citizen had to go though 176 steps over nineteen years.[13] These barriers do not mean that the poor do not invest. They still build houses and buy equipment even if they don't have legal title to these assets. Indeed, the amount of this investment is huge: by De Soto's calculations, the "total value of the real estate held but not legally owned by the poor of the Third World and former communist nations is at least $9.3 trillion."[14]

Without legal title, however, none of this property can be used to borrow funds. Because lenders usually have little information about the spending and savings habits of the poor, the only way they are willing to lend to them is if the borrowers have good collateral. But because most of what poor people have is not legally theirs, legal contracts cannot be written to permit lenders to take over this capital if borrowers default on their loans.

Even when people have legal title to their property, the legal system in most less-developed countries is so inefficient that collateral does not mean much. Typically creditors must first sue the defaulting debtor for payment, which takes several years, and then, once a favorable judgment has been obtained, the creditor has to sue again to obtain title to the collateral. This process often takes in excess of five years, and by the time the lender acquires the collateral it is likely to have been neglected or stolen and thus has little value. In addition, governments often block lenders from foreclosing on borrowers in politically powerful sectors of a society, such as agriculture.

When the financial system is unable to use collateral effectively, the adverse selection problem will be worse, because the lender will need even more information about the quality of the borrower to distinguish a good loan from a bad one. The result is that little lending will take place, especially in transactions that involve collateral, such as mortgages. In Peru, for example, the value of mortgage loans relative to the size of the economy is less than one-twentieth of that in the United States.[15]

The poor have an even harder time obtaining loans because it is too costly for them to get title to their property and they therefore have no collateral to offer, resulting in what Raghuram Rajan and Luigi Zingales refer to as the "tyranny of collateral."[16] Even when poor people have a good idea for a business and are willing to work hard, they cannot get the funds to finance it, making it difficult for them to escape poverty. The tyranny of collateral for the poor is one reason why the rags-to-riches story that we talk about so often in Western countries is much rarer in developing countries.

The Inability of the Legal System to Enforce Restrictive Covenants

A poorly designed legal system intensifies asymmetric information problems by making it more difficult for lenders to enforce restrictive covenants, which can reduce moral hazard incentives for borrowers to take on excessive risk. Furthermore, if the judiciary is in the pockets of the rich and politically powerful, judges may be unwilling to enforce restrictive covenants for those who are less powerful. As a result, creditors may have a severely limited ability to reduce borrowers' risk taking and so will be less willing to lend. In countries where bankruptcy proceedings are not well developed and where creditors' rights are weak, there is strong evidence that less lending to firms takes place.[17] Again, the outcome of not being able to enforce restrictive covenants will be less-productive investment and a lower growth rate for the economy.

The basic design of the legal system also matters to economic growth. The common law system, in which the law is continually reinterpreted by judges, seems to protect property rights better than other systems and makes it easier to enforce restrictive covenants. For example, the rights of shareholders (who actually own corporations) and of creditors are much stronger in the Anglo-Saxon legal system than under the Napoleonic code, first developed in France and currently used in many other countries. Countries with legal systems derived from British common law are found to outperform those with systems based on the Napoleonic code in both financial development and economic growth (the performance of countries using the German or Swedish legal systems lies somewhere in between).[18]

Even more important to how well a given type of legal system works is the way it was imposed on a country to begin with. Some colonies, for example in the Caribbean, in Africa, and on the Indian subcontinent, could not be settled by large numbers of Europeans because the death rates from native diseases were so high. In these colonies, legal systems were modified to benefit the small number of Europeans that ran the countries and to enable them to exploit the countries' resources and local populations.[19] As a result, legal systems in these countries were not as effective at protecting the property rights of the average person, and as colonies became independent this was a serious handicap to their growth. On the other hand, if larger numbers of Europeans were able to settle in a colony, as in North America, they were better able to resist exploitation by the home country. (The American Revolution was a dramatic manifestation of this.) After independence, the legal systems in these countries more effectively protected property rights and promoted high rates of economic growth.[20] Indeed, differences in the quality of legal systems resulting from different patterns of European settlement can explain three-quarters of the differences in income per person between former colonies.[21]

The variations in how colonies were settled explain why even countries whose legal systems were originally based on the British system, with its emphasis on protection of property rights, have shown such different economic performance. The United States, Canada, Australia, and New Zealand, with predominantly European populations that could resist exploitation, ended up with highly effective legal systems and became rich. On the other hand, former British colonies such as Jamaica, India, Pakistan, and Nigeria, where Europeans made up only a small fraction of the population, ended up with much less effective legal systems and have remained poor.

Government-Directed Credit

Leaders of governments in developing and transition countries often have programs to direct credit to themselves, to their cronies, or to favored sectors of the economy. Governments can direct the flow of funds by creating so-called development financial institutions to make specific types of loans at artificially low rates, or by directing existing institutions to lend to certain entities or sectors of the economy. Private institutions have incentives to solve adverse selection and moral hazard problems and to lend to those borrowers with the most productive investment opportunities: if they do not make wise loans, they will not earn any profits. Governments have fewer incentives to make sure their loans are going to sound and honest companies because they are driven not by the profit motive but by political considerations. Government-directed programs are unlikely to channel funds to sectors that will produce high growth for the economy; instead they typically result in less efficient investment and slower growth.[22]

Governments can also effectively direct credit by owning banks, and state-owned banks are very common in many developing and transition countries. Again, because of the absence of the profit motive, these state-owned banks have little incentive to allocate their capital to the most productive uses.[23] Indeed, the primary loan customer of these state-owned banks is often the government, which frequently does not use the funds wisely. Greater state ownership of banks is associated with less financial development and lower growth rates, and this effect is found to be larger for poorer countries.[24] State ownership also tends to be anticompetitive, resulting in a larger share of credit going to the biggest firms, and it is also associated with a higher likelihood of financial instability and banking crises.[25] The negative features of state-owned banks have led a major World Bank study to conclude that "whatever its original objectives, state ownership of banks tends to stunt financial sector development, thereby contributing to slower growth."[26]

Underdeveloped Regulatory Systems to Promote Transparency

Government regulation can promote transparency by increasing the amount of information available in financial markets. Many developing and transition countries have an underdeveloped regulatory apparatus, which limits the provision of adequate information to the marketplace. For example, these countries often have weak accounting standards and disclosure requirements, making it hard to ascertain the strength of a borrower's financial position. As a result, asymmetric information problems are more severe, and the financial system is hampered in channeling funds to the most productive uses.

Institutional environments characterized by a lack of collateral, inefficient legal systems, weak property rights, government intervention through directed credit programs and state ownership of banks, and weak government regulation to promote transparency all help explain why many countries stay poor while others grow richer.

Is China a Counterexample?

There is one possible counterexample to the importance of institutional development: China. Despite great strides in improving property rights using the Household Responsibility System (HRS) and town and village enterprises (TVEs) after the death of Mao Zedong in 1976, China's property rights, legal system, and transparency standards remain weak by the standards of more advanced countries. Yet the nation has had one of the highest growth rates in the world over the past twenty years. How has China been so successful given its weak institutions and a banking sector that is primarily state owned?

It is important to remember that China is still at an early stage of development, with an income per person around one-eighth of that in the United States.[27] But with an extremely high savings rate, averaging 39% over the past two decades,[28] the country has been able to rapidly build up its capital stock and shift a massive pool of underutilized labor from the subsistence-agriculture sector into higher-productivity activities that require capital. Even though available savings have not been allocated to their most productive uses, the huge increase in capital, combined with the gains in productivity from moving labor out of low-productivity, subsistence agriculture, has been enough to produce high growth.[29]

As China gets richer, however, this strategy is unlikely to continue to work.[30] The former Soviet Union provides a graphic example of why this is so. In the 1950s and 1960s, the Soviet Union shared many characteristics with modern-day China: a weak legal system and an inefficient financial system dominated by state-owned banks. It had high growth fueled by a high savings rate, a massive buildup of capital, and shifts of a large pool of underutilized labor from subsistence agriculture to manufacturing.[31] During this high-growth phase, however, the Soviet Union was unable to develop the institutions needed to allocate capital efficiently. Once the pool of subsistence laborers was used up, the Soviet Union's growth slowed dramatically, and it was unable to keep up with the Western economies. Today no one considers the Soviet Union to have been an economic success story, and its inability to develop the institutions necessary to sustain growth was an important reason for its demise.

Although there are parallels between the former Soviet Union and China, we should be careful not to take them too far. In contrast to the Soviet Union, China has a vibrant manufacturing export industry and innovative approaches to property rights such as the HRS and TVEs. It is far from clear that China will face the same problems that the Soviet Union did. The Soviet Union's experience, however, does suggest that China's economic destiny is by no means assured and that some of the enthusiasm for its prospects should be tempered.

The Chinese example suggests that, in the early stages of development, economic growth can be rapid even in the face of weak institutional development. To reach the next stage of development and eventually get rich, countries like China will need to allocate their capital more efficiently. To do this, these countries have to improve their institutional infrastructure and develop financial systems that direct capital to its most productive uses. The Chinese leadership is well aware of this challenge, as we will see later, but whether they will succeed remains an open question.

Who Causes Financial Repression?

We have now seen that a severe impediment to economic growth and the reduction of poverty in poorer countries is the repression of financial systems. Why does this occur? After all, if there are such tremendous benefits to financial development, why doesn't every country put its financial house in order and head down the path to growth and prosperity?

One answer, as we have seen, is that it is difficult to build the legal and regulatory institutions that facilitate the flow of information that in turn allows financial markets to function smoothly. The development of these institutions took hundreds of years in the advanced countries of the West.[32]

Although this answer explains part of the story, it is not completely satisfactory. Since successful legal and regulatory institutions have already been developed in the advanced countries, why can't a developing country just imitate them? Indeed, this was what the Japanese did after the Meiji restoration in the late nineteenth century, and it has also been a feature of the development path taken by economies in East Asia, such as Taiwan, Singapore, and Hong Kong. Technical assistance in establishing these institutions is available from the developed countries and from institutions like the World Bank and the IMF.

A further explanation is that the benefits of financial development are enjoyed by numerous sectors of the population, while the costs are borne by narrower groups (*special interests*) who are also able to impede the development process. The benefits of an efficient financial system are spread widely: to the young couple who can now buy a house with the help of a mortgage, to the new car owner who is able to finance its purchase with an auto loan, to the entrepreneur who can get capital to start her new business, and to the corporation that can finance its investment in a new manufacturing plant. On the other side, there are relatively fewer, powerful, concentrated groups who lose from financial development and so try to slow its progress.

One such group is the government, often the primary source of financial repression. Although strong property rights are a crucial element in financial development, they severely constrain a government's ability to expropriate property and ideas whenever it wants to profit from them. Rapacious governments whose rulers treat their countries as personal fiefdoms are not uncommon—from Saddam Hussein's Iraq to Robert Mugabe's Zimbabwe to Suharto's Indonesia. Government officials, even in more democratic governments, often use the power of the state to get rich. Not surprisingly then, many governments pay lip service to property rights but do not encourage a rule of law to protect them.

Governments have strong incentives to establish and support state-owned banks because it is through them that politicians and government officials can channel funds to themselves, their families, their cronies, and businesses that support their political campaigns. Politicians often explain their support for state-owned banks by saying that these institutions will direct funds where they can do the most public good. But the reality is that the politicians know that state-owned financial institutions primarily enhance their wealth and their power.

The Principal-Agent Problem: A Special Type of Moral Hazard

To understand why politicians and governments are less likely to act in the public interest in poorer countries, we can again use the concept of moral hazard. In this situation, the moral hazard problem takes a particular form, called the *principal-agent problem*. In theory, politicians and government officials (the *agents*) are supposed to work on behalf of the public (the *principals*). However, politicians have incentives to act in their own interests, which often differ from, and are sometimes in direct opposition to, the public's. The government and politicians can get away with this behavior as long as the public cannot tell whether the politicians are acting in their own self-interest or in the public interest, that is, as long as there is asymmetric information. In addition, even if the public can monitor politicians, so that there is little information asymmetry, they may not have the ability to get the politicians to act in their interest if the state is too powerful.

The existence of the principal-agent problem in the political sphere helps explain why governments in poorer countries are less likely to act in the public interest and more likely to support financial repression. Many of these countries have uneducated populations and no tradition of institutions to promote the transparent, free flow of information. The free press that the United States has enjoyed ever since its inception may cover a few too many stories on celebrity lives and scandals, but it also serves an essential role in keeping people informed.[33] It was the free press that uncovered the Watergate cover-up, which resulted in Richard Nixon's resignation from the presidency, and that has helped to constrain the executive branch of the U.S. government from overreaching its power and spying inappropriately on its citizens. The free press brought to light the inadequacy of armor plating for Humvees used by U.S. troops in Iraq and thus stimulated the Pentagon to speed up production and installation of improved armor. The free press exposed the corrupt practices of lobbyists such as Jack Abramoff, leading to calls for restrictions on their ability to influence members of Congress.

In countries without a free press—and many emerging, transition, and impoverished countries unfortunately fall into this category—the public has a hard time monitoring what politicians are up to and thus is less able to constrain them from acting in their own interest rather than the public's. The result is that politicians are more likely to use a state-owned banking system to enhance their own wealth and power and less likely to be strong supporters of property rights.

The principal-agent analysis also explains why corruption is endemic in poorer countries. An active free press helps keep corruption in check. As Justice Louis Brandeis said, "Sunlight is the best disinfectant." Here in America, the press is always looking for the slightest hint of corruption, because uncovering it sells newspapers and wins reporters Pulitzer Prizes. Americans love to read about the latest scandal and take great pleasure when politicians are forced to step down when they are caught with their hands in the cookie jar. In poorer countries, the press is more likely to be influenced or even controlled by the government and so has little incentive for investigative reporting. Since the population is often less literate, fewer newspapers can be sold, reducing the potential revenue from exposing corruption. This makes it easier for those who are enriching themselves through corruption to buy off the press and keep their dishonesty hidden.[34]

Repressive Incumbents

As Raghuram Rajan and Luigi Zingales emphasize in their thought-provoking book *Saving Capitalism from the Capitalists*,[35] the second special interest group that often supports financial repression is the "incumbents," entrenched, rich elites who own businesses that are threatened by competitive, free markets.[36] Large, established business firms often finance new investment projects out of their previous earnings and so do not need funds from external sources in the financial markets. Incumbent financial institutions also have incentives to repress the financial system.[37] Such firms, financial and nonfinancial alike, have less to gain from development, and frequently have much to lose. They will oppose the following policies, which weaken their power but promote a more efficient financial system.

Increased transparency. Financial development requires increased transparency through better accounting standards and disclosure requirements. However, increased transparency may make it harder for rich elites to exploit their connections and conduct business as usual, and so they will often oppose it. Through their connections to established businesses, incumbent financial institutions may have the ability to collect information, not available to the public, that enables them to distinguish good credit risks from bad. Increasing transparency may not be in their interest because their best customers may then be able to bypass their services and go to other financial intermediaries or instead resort to direct finance by issuing their own securities.

Improved legal systems. Rich elites are also likely to oppose improvements in the legal system when these improvements would weaken their ability to sway the system to their own interests. If judges can be easily influenced, the incumbent elites will be able to get favorable rulings that will increase their power and wealth. Financial development would also allow capital to flow to entrepreneurs who might now be able to compete with the incumbents. Rich elites thus are often perfectly happy to see the financial system remain repressed because this subjects them to less competition. Incumbent financial institutions also discourage development of the legal system that is intended to enforce financial contracts fairly. They already have their own methods of enforcement through influence over corrupt judges or outright physical threats. Improving the legal system would not help them very much, but it would enable competitors to enter the financial sector and take away their customers.

Fewer barriers to entry. Incumbent rich elites are also likely to encourage barriers to setting up legal businesses. These barriers can be prohibitive for all but the very wealthy in less-developed countries and can discourage or even prevent new businesses from becoming established or growing. After all, new or large-scale businesses would eat into the incumbents' monopoly profits. The so-called "license raj" in India, which existed until the reforms of Rajiv Gandhi started to dismantle such regulations in the 1980s, is one notorious example.[38] Under the license raj, new businesses had to obtain hard-to-get licenses before opening their doors, and incumbents frequently spent more time lobbying government officials to prevent entrepreneurs from setting up competing businesses than on making their own businesses more productive.

More effective prudential regulation and supervision. Incumbent financial institutions often discourage effective prudential regulation and supervision over their activities. A government safety net, which insulates these firms from market discipline, enables them to take on risk, with most of the cost borne by taxpayers if their loans go sour. If financial institutions are poorly supervised, they can exploit the financial safety net to pursue risky strategies such as rapidly expanding high-risk lending—on which they make a lot of money if they bet right and lose only a small amount if they bet wrong. Because rigorous prudential regulation and supervision would stop incumbent financial institutions from doing this, they naturally oppose it. Indeed, such opposition by financial institutions occurs in rich as well as poor countries. But because poor countries have less transparency, this opposition is far more successful there, with the result that the quality of prudential regulation and supervision is typically low.

Can Globalization Help Encourage Financial Development?

How can the obstacles to financial development posed by politicians and rich elites be overcome? How can the political will to implement reforms that encourage financial deepening be created? One solution, advocated by Rajan and Zingales and a World Bank Policy Research Report, *Finance for Growth*, is globalization, the opening up of domestic markets to foreign goods and direct investment, as well as to foreign capital and foreign financial institutions.[39] Globalization can encourage financial development indirectly, by changing the distribution of economic power and increasing incentives for financial development. We will consider the indirect benefits first, but, as we will see, globalization has direct benefits, too.

Indirect Benefits

Allowing entry of foreign goods and investment produces a more competitive environment that will drive down the revenue of incumbent firms and reduce their cash flow (revenue minus outlays) so that they will have to seek out external sources of finance. Because these sources of finance will be available only if the financial system has the wherewithal to solve asymmetric information problems, incumbent firms and their rich elite owners will now have incentives to support the necessary institutional reforms to make the financial system work better. In turn, the resulting reforms will increase the size of the financial sector and will foster economic growth.[40] Greater openness to trade is indeed found to be linked to a larger financial sector,[41] and the increased competition from foreigners stimulates domestic firms to become more productive in order to survive.

Opening up to foreign capital and foreign financial institutions is another strong force for institutional reforms that promote financial development.[42] When domestic businesses can borrow from abroad or from foreign financial institutions that establish affiliates in the less-developed country, domestic financial institutions will start to lose many of their old customers. To stay in business, they will have to seek out new customers and lend to them profitably. To accomplish this, they will need the information to screen out good credit risks from bad and to monitor borrowers to make sure they do not take on excessive risk. Domestic financial institutions will thus have incentives to encourage politicians to adopt institutional reforms, such as better accounting standards and disclosure requirements, that will make it easier for them to acquire the information that they need to make profitable loans. The institutions will also see the need to improve the legal system so they can enforce restrictive covenants or be able to take title to collateral if a borrower defaults. With globalization, domestic financial institutions will support legal reform because it will not only help them make profits but also strengthen the property rights that directly encourage investment.

Yet financial globalization will only help promote institutional development if opening a country to foreign capital and foreign financial institutions actually generates more competition. If foreign financial institutions are allowed to enter with special privileges, or in such limited numbers that they are able to exploit monopolies in the same way that domestic financial firms have, financial globalization will not generate positive results. Without increased competition, foreigners will operate just like rich domestic elites, and there will be no constituency for institutional reform.

Direct Benefits

Entry of foreign financial institutions into domestic markets also plays a direct role in promoting financial development. When foreign financial institutions enter a country, domestic financial institutions have to become more efficient in order to survive, and this is exactly what happens.[43] Foreign financial institutions bring to domestic financial markets *best practices*, that is, expertise that has been gained from their past experience, and they are also likely to promote technology transfer to domestic financial institutions.[44] Entry of foreign financial institutions helps improve domestic prudential regulation and supervision because supervisors are now able to see the risk management practices that have been successfully used in foreign institutions and to insist that they be adopted by domestic institutions.[45] Foreign financial institutions also act as a constituency for institutional reform aimed at improving the quality of information in financial markets because, as outsiders, they do not have access to the same inside information as domestic institutions.

Financial globalization has additional direct benefits for domestic financial markets. Allowing foreign capital to freely enter domestic financial markets (a process called *capital account liberalization*) increases the availability of funds, which in turn increases liquidity and lowers the cost of capital, which stimulates investment and economic growth.[46] This is what has happened as countries have opened up their stock markets to foreign capital: on average dividend yields fall by 2.4 percentage points, the growth rate of investment increases by 1.1 percentage points, and the growth rate of output per worker increases by 2.3 percentage points.[47] These results have prompted Stanford University economist Peter Blair Henry to state that "the increasingly popular view that capital account liberalization brings no real benefits seems untenable."[48]

Opening up domestic capital markets to foreigners, however, does not seem to stimulate financial development when countries are extremely poor and have weak property rights.[49] The benefits of financial globalization are more apparent for emerging market countries, which have attained sufficient institutional development to take advantage of the process.[50]

Will Financial Globalization Always Work?

Given the benefits of financial globalization discussed so far, it seems as though opening up domestic financial markets to international capital should have an unambiguously positive impact on economic growth and the reduction of poverty. However, evidence from aggregate data on the benefits of financial globalization is mixed: there is no clear-cut relationship between international financial openness and economic growth.[51]

Why doesn't opening up financial markets always work? Opening up an economy to international capital flows, particularly if the transition is not managed to prevent excessive risk taking, can lead to financial blowups that are disastrous to the economy.[52] Although financial globalization can be a strong force for good, it can also go very wrong if a country doesn't manage the process properly.[53] The next chapter outlines how financial globalization can lead to financial crises that can devastate an economy. The chapters that follow present three case studies of financial crises in emerging market countries. From these chapters, we learn what can go wrong with globalization, and we can derive some lessons in how to do it right.

Four

When Globalization Goes Wrong: The Dynamics of Financial Crises

When emerging market countries open up their markets in an effort to globalize, they have high hopes that globalization will stimulate economic growth and eventually make them rich. Instead of leading to high economic growth and reduced poverty, however, globalization has often led to great depressions, with sharp increases in poverty and social unrest.[1] What has gone wrong?

In this chapter we see how financial globalization, if improperly managed, can lead to the collapse of a nation's financial system and economy. These crises are particularly disastrous for the poor in emerging market countries because the safety nets that provide assistance to those who lose their jobs (such as unemployment insurance) are much weaker.[2] In addition, these crises increase income inequality, because the rich are far better able than the poor to take advantage of the financial opportunities that arise during the crisis.[3]

To help us understand how financial globalization gone wrong can lead to such devastation, we discuss a framework that can be used to analyze and understand the dynamics of financial crises, which have become more common in recent years.[4] In Part Two, we use this framework to analyze crises that have occurred in Mexico, South Korea, and Argentina. In Part Three, we use the framework to analyze how globalization can bring prosperity, stability, and wealth to emerging market countries that understand it and that put in place the necessary institutional reforms when liberalizing their financial systems, so that they can manage globalization successfully.

What Is a Financial Crisis?

When a financial system is unable to cope with the problems raised by asymmetric information, it is unable to fulfill its crucial function of allocating capital efficiently from savers to those with productive investment opportunities. As the system breaks down, asymmetric information problems intensify and multiply until there is a full-blown financial crisis in which the financial system becomes inoperable and economic activity collapses.

The dynamics of such financial crises are outlined in Figure 4.1.

All financial crises originate in the good times that precede the collapse. During the early phases of the globalization process, the economic performance of emerging market countries is good: economic growth is high and inflation has come down to low levels, particularly by the standards of these countries'

Figure 4.1. The Dynamics of Financial Crises

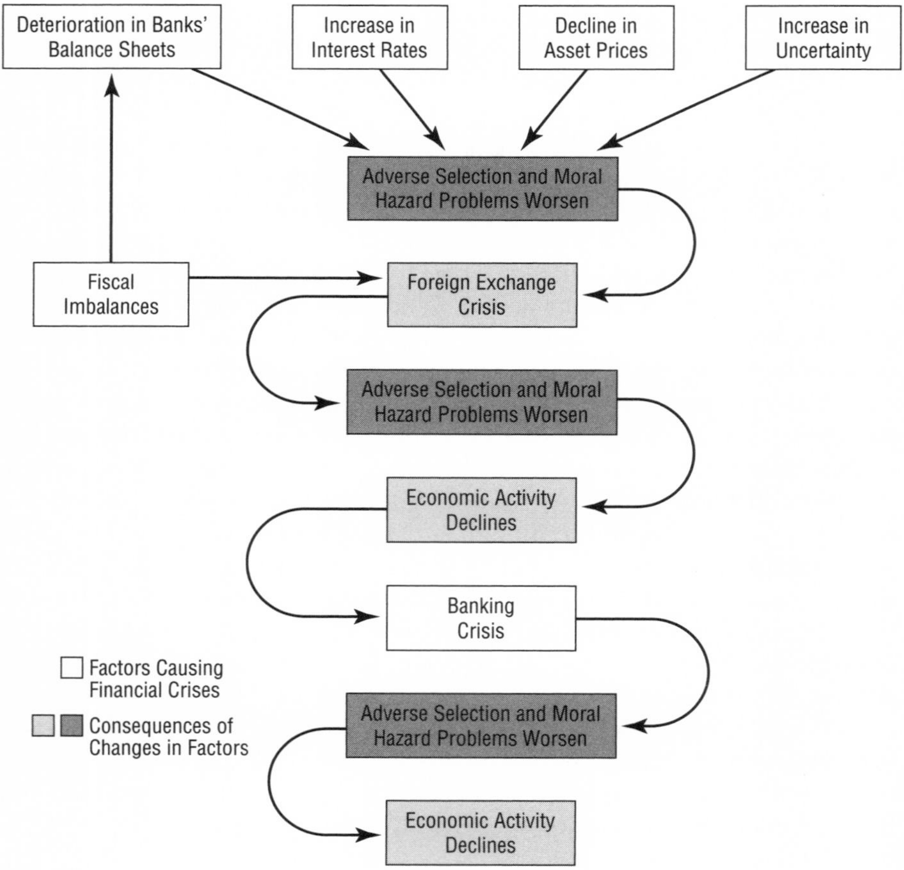

pasts. But the good times often have a dark side. There are two basic routes through which emerging market countries can find themselves in a crisis: a financial liberalization/globalization process gone wrong or a severe fiscal imbalance. We initially focus on the first of these because it is the most common culprit; it is, for example, what precipitated the crises in Mexico in 1994 and many East Asian countries in 1997.[5]

Stage One: Mismanagement of Financial Liberalization/Globalization

The seeds of a "globalization-gone-wrong" financial crisis are sown when countries liberalize their financial systems, usually several years before the crisis hits. Financial liberalization can be separated into two components. *Internal financial liberalization* involves lifting regulations that restrict domestic financial institutions from lending their funds at market rates or that set quantitative limits on the amount of credit they can allocate to particular uses. *External financial liberalization*, more commonly referred to as *capital account liberalization* or *financial globalization*, occurs when domestic financial markets are opened to flows of foreign capital and to foreign financial institutions. Internal and external financial liberalization usually go together, but they don't have to. A country could free up its domestic financial markets but still keep them closed off from the outside world. When I want to make it clear that financial liberalization includes an external component, I will use the term "financial liberalization/globalization."

Eighteen of twenty-six financial crises in the past twenty years occurred after the financial sector had been liberalized, both internally and externally, within the preceding five years.[6] Countries hit with this type of crisis often start out with solid fiscal policy: in the years before their crises hit, the countries in East Asia were running budget surpluses, and Mexico was running a budget deficit of only 0.7% of GDP, a number that most advanced countries would be thrilled to have today.[7] (By comparison, in 2004, the U.S. budget deficit was 4.5% of GDP and even Germany, once fiscally conservative, had a deficit of 3.9% of GDP.)

Lending Boom and Bust: The Deterioration of Bank Balance Sheets

Although the process of financial liberalization has the potential to be highly beneficial, it often leads banks to take on excessive risk. With internal restrictions lifted, banks go on a lending spree and expand their lending by 15 to 30% per year, which is more than double the typical lending growth rate.[8] Not only do banks increase their lending, they give out more loans to firms in industries about which they have little knowledge. Because the managers of the bank-

ing institutions in emerging market countries typically do not have the expertise to manage risk appropriately in these new lines of business and are unable
to cope with the rapid growth of lending that typically follows a financial liberalization, problems are bound to arise. Even if the required managerial
expertise is available initially, the rapid lending growth will likely outstrip the
information resources available to banking institutions. Increased lending to
industries about which banks know little results in excessive risk taking by the
banks.

Because of this lack of expertise in screening and monitoring borrowers, losses
on the loans begin to mount. These losses mean that banks' balance sheets deteriorate because the drop in the value of their loans (on the asset side of the balance sheet) falls relative to their liabilities, thereby driving down the banks'
net worth (capital). With less capital, banks become riskier, and so depositors
and other potential lenders to the banks are less willing to supply them with
funds. Fewer funds mean fewer loans and less lending. The lending boom will
turn into a lending crash.

Banks play a crucial role in financial markets because they are well suited
to collect information about businesses and industries. This ability in turn enables
banks to distinguish good loan prospects from bad ones. When banks cut back
on their lending, no one else can step in to collect this information and make
these loans, so the ability of the financial system to cope with the asymmetric
information problems of moral hazard and adverse selection is severely hampered (Figure 4.1, leftmost factor in top row). As loans become scarcer, firms
are no longer able to fund their attractive investment opportunities; they
decrease their spending and economic activity contracts.

If the deterioration in bank balance sheets is severe enough, a bank panic
may ensue, in which there are simultaneous failures of banking institutions.
In the absence of a government safety net, one bank failure can cause another,
and so on. Such a contagion can cause even healthy banks to fail. The failure
and subsequent closing of a large number of banks in a short period of time
means that there is a further reduction in information collection in the financial markets and a direct loss of financial intermediation by the banking sector. The ultimate outcome of the bank panic is an even greater worsening of
asymmetric information problems, a sharper decline in lending to facilitate productive investments, and a resulting sharp contraction in economic activity.[9]

The Government Safety Net to the Rescue?

Most governments try to prevent bank panics and encourage banks to keep
on lending during bad times by providing a safety net. If depositors and
other providers of funds to banks are protected from losses, they will keep on
supplying banks with funds so banks can continue to lend and will not fail.

However, as we saw in Chapter 2, there is a catch. The government safety net weakens market discipline for the bank because, with a safety net, depositors know that they will not lose anything if a bank fails. Thus the bank can still acquire funds even if it takes on excessive risk. The government safety net increases the moral hazard incentive for banks to take on greater risk than they otherwise would, because, if their risky but high-interest loans pay off, the banks make a lot of money. If they don't and the banks fail, taxpayers foot most of the bill for the safety net that protects depositors. Banks can play the game of "heads, I win; tails, the taxpayer loses."

The moral hazard incentives to take on excessive risk arising from the government safety net are more likely to be the source of bad loans than lack of expertise among bank managers. Even in countries with well-developed banking sectors, financial liberalization has often led to lending booms and banking crises, as the experience in the 1980s and 1990s in Japan and the United States suggests. A government safety net has the unintended consequence of making it more likely that a lending boom will occur, followed by an economic bust.[10]

The Crucial Role of Prudential Regulation and Supervision

A solution to preventing a lending boom and bust is prudential regulation and supervision of the banking system to prevent banks from taking on excessive risk. However, financial liberalization is often undertaken with completely inadequate regulation and supervision. (In contrast to the East Asian countries that suffered crises, for example, Singapore, Hong Kong, and Taiwan all had strong prudential regulatory and supervisory systems and did not suffer crises from financial globalization.)

Not only do the new lines of business and rapid credit growth stretch the managerial resources of banks, they also stretch the resources of the government's bank supervisors. After a financial liberalization, bank supervisors frequently find themselves without the expertise or the additional resources needed to appropriately monitor the banks' new lending activities. Without this monitoring, excessive risk taking by banks cannot be prevented.

The deterioration in banks' balance sheets and net worth can get even worse if regulators and supervisors practice *regulatory forbearance,* that is, knowingly allow financial institutions that are broke to continue to operate. Regulatory forbearance is common in advanced and emerging market economies; it dramatically increases moral hazard problems because it creates incentives for banks to take on even more risk because they have almost nothing to lose.[11] If they get lucky and their risky loans pay off, they become solvent again. If, as is likely, the risky loans don't pay off, the banks' losses mount, further weakening the financial system.

Adding Fuel to the Fire: Opening Up to Foreign Capital

The financial globalization process that allows domestic banks to borrow abroad, an important element of financial liberalization, adds fuel to the fire. The banks pay high interest rates to attract foreign capital and so can rapidly increase their lending. The ability of domestic banks to attract foreign capital is enhanced by the belief of foreign creditors that they are likely to be protected by a government safety net (either from the government of the emerging market country or from international agencies such as the IMF).[12] The capital inflow is further stimulated by government policies that keep exchange rates pegged to the dollar, which give foreign investors a sense of lower risk.

Capital inflows were high in Mexico and east Asia, averaging from 5 to 14% of GDP in the three years leading up to the crisis, and were an important factor in the expansion of bank lending, especially in the Asian-Pacific region.[13] The capital inflows fueled the lending boom, which led to excessive risk taking on the part of banks, which in turn led to huge loan losses and a subsequent deterioration of the balance sheets of banks and other financial institutions.

Perversion of the Financial Liberalization/Globalization Process

The story that we have told so far suggests that a lending boom and crash are inevitable outcomes of financial liberalization and globalization, but this is not the case. They occur only when there is an institutional weakness that prevents the nation from successfully handling the liberalization/globalization process. More specifically, if prudential regulation and supervision to limit excessive risk taking were strong, the lending boom and bust would not happen. Why is financial liberalization in some emerging market countries undertaken with prudential regulatory and supervisory structures that are completely inadequate? Why are more resources not devoted to prudential supervision when it is clear that the rapid growth in bank lending requires it?

The answer is that the principal-agent problem encourages powerful domestic business interests to pervert the financial liberalization process. Politicians and prudential supervisors are ultimately agents for voters-taxpayers (principals): the goal of politicians and prudential supervisors is, or should be, to protect the taxpayers' interest, because taxpayers bear the cost of bailing out the banking sector if losses occur. To act in the taxpayer's interest, prudential regulators and supervisors have several tasks: they must restrict banks from holding assets that are too risky, impose capital requirements high enough to ensure that banks have enough capital to withstand negative shocks, and close down insolvent institutions rather than engage in regulatory forbearance.

Once financial markets have been liberalized, powerful business interests that own banks will want to prevent the supervisors from doing their job properly. Because these interests contribute heavily to politicians' campaigns, they are often able to persuade politicians to weaken regulations that restrict their banks from engaging in high-risk/high-payoff strategies. After all, if bank owners can pursue growth and rapidly expand bank lending, they stand to make a fortune. But if the bank gets into trouble, the government is likely to bail it out, and the taxpayer foots the bill. In addition, these business interests can make sure that the supervisory agencies are starved for resources, so that, even in the presence of tough regulations, they do not have the capability to effectively monitor banking institutions or to close them down.

It Can Happen Here: The Lincoln
Savings and Loan Scandal, 1984–1989

The problem of powerful business interests perverting the financial liberalization process does not exist only in emerging market countries. In the United States in the 1980s, owners of savings and loans (S&Ls), a type of banking institution, lobbied Congress and President Ronald Reagan to pass banking legislation that allowed the S&Ls to engage in risky activities, such as making commercial real estate loans, purchasing junk bonds, and making direct commercial investments in real estate, common stocks, and service corporations. They were able to get their safety net extended in 1980 by persuading Congress to increase the amount of bank and S&L deposits covered by federal deposit insurance from $40,000 to $100,000. Knowing that the government would cover deposits in the event of a failure, depositors were less concerned with keeping the S&Ls in line.

When the resulting lending boom turned sour in subsequent years, the S&L industry lobbied to restrict the resources available to its supervisory agency, the Federal Home Loan Bank Board, so that it became short-staffed and was unable to carry out frequent examinations of the S&Ls it was supposed to monitor.[14] The S&Ls even worked to keep the Federal Savings and Loan Insurance Corporation, the federal deposit insurance agency for S&Ls, from having sufficient funds to close down insolvent banks. As a result, many insolvent S&Ls (which Edward Kane, a banking expert, dubbed "zombies")[15] now had huge incentives to "bet the bank": they had everything to gain and little to lose from pursuing high-risk strategies.

The most egregious example of the principal-agent problem in action was the Lincoln Savings and Loan scandal. Edwin Gray, a former chairman of the Federal Home Loan Bank Board, described it as "a story of incredible corruption. I can't call it anything else."[16] Charles Keating Jr. was able to acquire Lincoln Savings and Loan of Irvine, California, in early 1984, even though he had been accused of securities fraud by the SEC less than five years earlier. Keating had Lincoln plunge into high-risk investments, such as currency futures, junk bonds, common stocks, hotels, and vast tracts of desert land in Arizona. When the Federal Home Loan Bank Board of San Francisco recommended federal seizure of the bank and all its assets because it was violating regulations, Keating fought the board with every tool at his disposal. He engaged hordes of lawyers—eventually numbering seventy-seven law firms—and accused bank examiners of bias. He even hired Alan Greenspan, not yet chairman of the Federal Reserve, to render a favorable opinion on some of his firm's activities.

Lawyers were not Keating's only tactic for keeping regulators off his back. After receiving $1.3 million of campaign contributions from Keating, five senators—Dennis De Concini and John McCain of Arizona, Alan Cranston of California, John Glenn of Ohio, and Don Riegle of Michigan, subsequently named the "Keating Five")—met with Gray and later with four top regulators from San Francisco in April 1987. (Remarkably, two of these senators, John Glenn and John McCain, have a strong reputation for integrity.) The Keating Five complained that the regulators were being too tough on Lincoln and urged them to quit dragging out the investigation. After Gray was replaced by M. Danny Wall, Wall took the unprecedented step of removing the San Francisco examiners from the case in September 1987 and transferred the investigation to the board's headquarters in Washington. No examiners called on Lincoln for the next ten months, and, as one of the San Francisco examiners described it, Lincoln dropped into a "regulatory black hole."[17]

Lincoln Savings and Loan finally failed in April 1989, and its failure eventually cost U.S. taxpayers over $2 billion. Keating was convicted for abuses (such as having Lincoln pay him and his family $34 million), but after he had served only four and a half years in jail, his conviction was overturned in 1996. Wall was forced to resign as the head of the Office of Thrift Supervision because of his involvement in the Keating scandal. As a result of their activities on behalf of Keating, the Keating Five were made the object of a congressional ethics investigation, but they were only given a slap on the wrist in the form of minor sanctions.

The bailout of depositors at Keating's Lincoln Savings and Loan and close to a thousand other S&Ls ended up costing U.S. taxpayers $150 billion—not a small chunk of change, but still only 3% of GDP. The S&L debacle did not develop into a full-blown crisis in the United States because S&Ls were not major players in the banking system. Furthermore, the capacity of the U.S. government to raise the funds needed to bail out insolvent S&Ls allowed it to contain the crisis before it spun out of control.[18]

Why Perversion Is Worse in Emerging Market Countries

As bad as the Lincoln Savings and Loan scandal was, far worse happens on a regular basis in emerging market countries, as we will see in the case studies in the next three chapters. In these economies, business interests are far more powerful than in advanced economies, where a better-educated public and a free press monitor (and punish) politicians and bureaucrats who are not acting in the public interest. Not surprisingly, the cost to society of the principal-agent problem we have been describing here is much higher in emerging market economies. The cost to the taxpayer of the S&L bailout in the United States amounted to 3% of GDP, but the cost of banking bailouts in emerging market countries is typically up to ten times higher and sometimes in excess of 50% of GDP, as it was in Indonesia after that country's 1997 financial crisis.[19]

The principal-agent problem can also exist for regulators, even if they are not under pressure from business interests. Supervisors, who act as agents to prevent risk taking at the taxpayer/principal's expense, have an incentive to sweep problems under the rug to escape blame for a bank's poor performance. For example, supervisors need to immediately close down an insolvent bank so that it does not take on huge risks to get itself out of the hole. By weakening capital requirements or by not requiring banks to write off losses on their loans, supervisors can hide the problem of an insolvent bank and hope that the situation will improve, a maneuver called *bureaucratic gambling*.[20] If the supervisor plans to leave the job soon, a bureaucratic gamble will almost certainly pay off, since the bank failure will not occur on his or her watch.

In emerging market countries, powerful bankers make it even more likely that supervisors will sweep things under the rug, because they have made sure that supervisors are less protected from personal lawsuits. In many emerging market countries, a bank can sue a supervisor personally for actions she has taken in carrying out her job. In contrast, in countries like the United States, the law allows only the government agency to be sued, not the individual supervisor. Given the enormous resources of bankers in poorer countries to bring suits against supervisors, a supervisor will not want to risk a lawsuit that can bankrupt him. Thus, even though an emerging market country's supervisory system looks good on paper, it may not work well in practice.

Stage One: Severe Fiscal Imbalances

The second route through which emerging market countries end up experiencing a financial crisis is through government fiscal imbalances caused by substantial budget deficits that must be financed. The 2001–02 financial crisis in Argentina was of this type, but other recent crises—for example those in Russia in 1998, Ecuador in 1999, and Turkey in 2001—have some of the same elements.[21]

In contrast to Mexico and the East Asian countries, Argentina had a well-supervised banking system, and a lending boom did not occur before the crisis. The banks were in surprisingly good shape before the crisis, even though a severe recession had begun in 1998. This recession led to declining tax revenue and a widening gap between expenditures and taxes. The subsequent severe fiscal imbalances (budget deficits) were so large that the government had trouble getting both domestic residents and foreigners to buy enough of its bonds. It then had to look to other sources to finance its deficits.

When Willie Sutton, the notorious bank robber, was asked why he robbed banks, he answered, "Because that's where the money is." Governments in emerging market countries have the same attitude. When they face large fiscal imbalances and can't finance their debt, they often cajole or force banks to purchase government debt. This is exactly what the Argentine government did in the run-up to its financial crisis in 2001. When investors lose confidence in the ability of the government to repay its debt, they unload the bonds, and this causes their prices to plummet. Now the banks that are holding this debt have a big hole on the asset side of their balance sheets, with a huge decline in their net worth. The deterioration in bank balance sheets causes a decline in bank lending and can even lead to a bank panic, and this is what happened in Argentina. Severe fiscal imbalances spill over into and weaken the banking system. Adverse selection and moral hazard problems worsen, and these cause an economic contraction, as is shown in Figure 4.1.

Stage Two: Run-up to the Currency Crisis

The deterioration in bank balance sheets resulting from mishandled financial liberalization that occurs with globalization or from large fiscal imbalances sets the stage for a full-scale financial crisis. The balance sheet deterioration increases the incidence of adverse selection and moral hazard in financial markets well before the crisis starts, but other factors (shown at the top of Figure 4.1) also come into play shortly before the crisis hits.

Higher interest rates and their effects on cash flow. Another precipitating factor in some crises (e.g., the Mexican crisis but not the East Asian crises) is a rise in interest rates that comes not from domestic sources but from events abroad, such as a tightening of U.S. monetary policy. When interest rates rise, firms that are good credit risks (because they are likely to be making more conservative investments) cannot make enough to cover the high interest payments.

While good risks may stop seeking out loans, the poorer risks are all too eager to ask for money. For example, firms with speculative investments, such as those building mammoth skyscrapers, are more than happy to continue to take out loans, because, if they get lucky, they will have more than enough to pay the high interest rate and still earn a big profit.[22] Banks and other lenders, on the other hand, will now be leery of making loans because more of the firms seeking loans are likely to be bad credit risks. Therefore, when there is an increase in interest rates, there is now more adverse selection in financial markets, and lenders will want to make fewer loans. A sharp upward spike in interest rates can then lead to a steep decline in the supply of loans, which in turn will lead to a substantial decline in investment and aggregate economic activity.[23]

If a firm is borrowing, a rise in interest rates also leads to higher interest payments and a decline in the firm's cash flow, the difference between its cash receipts and the cash it must pay out to cover its costs, including its borrowing. If it has sufficient cash flow, a firm can finance its projects internally, and there is no asymmetric information because it knows how good its own projects are. With less cash flow, the firm has fewer internal funds and must raise funds from an external source, say a bank, which does not know the firm as well as its owners or managers know it. The bank cannot be sure if the firm will invest in safe projects or instead take on big risks and then be unlikely to pay back the loan. Thus lower cash flow for healthy, low-risk firms increases adverse selection (only firms with poor risks will be actively seeking loans) and moral hazard (once even a healthy firm gets a loan, it is more likely to take on higher-risk, higher-return projects because it will not bear the full costs if the projects turn out badly). Because of this increased adverse selection and moral hazard, the bank may choose not to lend even firms with good risks the money to undertake investments, even though they would have been profitable for the firms and the bank. We thus see that, when cash flow drops as a result of an increase in interest rates, adverse selection and moral hazard problems become more severe, again curtailing lending and investment.[24]

Increases in uncertainty and the decline in lending. When a prominent firm fails, the economy is in a recession, or the political system is in disarray, people become uncertain about the returns on investment projects. Uncertainty increased in Thailand and South Korea when major financial and nonfinancial firms failed just before those countries' crises. It also increased in Mexico in 1994 when Luis Donaldo Colosio, the ruling party's presidential candidate, was assassinated and there was an uprising in the southern state of Chiapas. When uncertainty increases, it becomes harder for lenders to screen out good credit risks from bad and to monitor the activities of firms to which they've loaned money. They become less willing to lend, and as lending declines, investment, and then aggregate economic activity, declines as well.

Declining asset prices and the decline in net worth. A decline in the prices of assets, whether stocks, real estate, or other types, will cause firms' net worth to decline. When the stock market crashes, for example, firms' share prices decrease. Share prices reflect the valuation of a corporation, so a market crash means that the net worth of most corporations has fallen. Net worth plays a role similar to collateral because it can be taken by the lender when a firm defaults on its loans. Lower net worth indicates to lenders that they will get less if the firm's investments go sour. When lenders are less well protected against the consequences of adverse selection, they decrease their lending not only to risky firms but also to healthy, conservative firms whose net worth has declined. As a result, investment, and in turn aggregate output, declines.[25]

In addition, because corporate net worth has decreased, firms have less to lose and thus may make riskier investments. The resulting increase in moral hazard gives lenders another reason not to lend. This is another path by which a collapse in asset prices leads to decreased lending and reduced economic activity.[26]

High interest rates, increases in uncertainty, and stock market crashes occurred shortly before and contributed to full-blown crises in Mexico, Thailand, South Korea, and Argentina. (The stock market crashes in Malaysia, Indonesia, and the Philippines occurred simultaneously with the onset of those crises.) All these factors increased asymmetric information problems; they made it harder for lenders to distinguish bad borrowers from good ones and increased the incentives for borrowers to make risky investments because they had less to lose if their investments were unsuccessful, given the decline in their net worth. High interest rates, increases in uncertainty, and stock market declines, along with deterioration in banks' balance sheets, worsened adverse selection and moral hazard problems and made these economies ripe for serious financial crises.

Stage Three: Currency Crisis

As the effects of any or all of the factors at the top of Figure 4.1 build on each other, participants in the foreign exchange market start to smell blood: they can make huge profits if they bet on a depreciation of the currency. Currencies that are fixed against the U.S. dollar now become subject to a speculative attack as speculators engage in massive sales of these currencies. As the currencies flood the market, supply far outstrips demand, the value of the currencies collapses, and a currency crisis ensues. Although high interest rates abroad, increases in uncertainty, and falling asset prices play a role, the deterioration in bank balance sheets and severe fiscal imbalances are two key factors that trigger the speculative attacks and plunge the economies into the full-scale downward spiral of currency crisis, financial crisis, and meltdown.

How Deterioration of Bank Balance Sheets
Triggers Currency Crises

When banks and other financial institutions are in trouble, it is not as easy for governments to defend their currencies by raising interest rates and thus encouraging capital inflows. If the government raises interest rates, banks must pay more to obtain funds. This increase in costs decreases bank profitability, which may lead banks to insolvency. When the banking system is in trouble, the government and the central bank face a dilemma: if they raise interest rates too much, they will destroy their already weakened banks; if they don't raise them, they cannot maintain the value of their currency.

Once the speculators in the foreign currency market recognize the troubles in a country's financial sector and realize that the government's ability to defend the currency is limited, they know that they are presented with an almost sure thing. The value of the currency has only one way to go: downward. Speculators engage in a feeding frenzy and sell the currency in anticipation of its decline, which will yield them huge profits. These sales rapidly use up the country's foreign currency reserves because its central bank has to sell those to buy the domestic currency and keep it from falling in value. Once the country's central bank has exhausted its holdings of foreign currency reserves, it no longer has the resources to intervene in the foreign exchange market and must let the value of the domestic currency fall. That is, the government must allow a devaluation.

Even though the Mexican central bank intervened in the foreign exchange market and raised interest rates sharply, it was unable to stem the speculators' attack and was forced to devalue the peso on December 20, 1994. In Thailand, three events culminated in a successful speculative attack that forced the Thai central bank to allow the baht to float downward in July 1997: concerns about the country's large current account deficit, concerns about weakness in its financial sector, and the failure of a major finance company, Finance One. Soon after the baht's devaluation, speculative attacks developed against the other countries in the region, leading to the collapse of the Philippine peso, the Indonesian rupiah, the Malaysian ringgit, and the South Korean won.

How Severe Fiscal Imbalances Trigger Currency Crises

We have seen that severe fiscal imbalances, as in Argentina, can lead to a deterioration of bank balance sheets and so can help produce a currency crisis along the lines just described. Fiscal imbalances can also directly trigger a currency crisis.[27] When government budget deficits spin out of control, foreign and domestic investors begin to suspect that the country may not be able to pay back its government debt and so will start pulling money out of the country and selling the domestic currency. Recognition that the fiscal situation is out of control thus results in a speculative attack against the currency, which eventually results in its collapse, as occurred in Argentina on January 6, 2002.

Currency Crises and Asset Price Fluctuations Can Have a Life of Their Own

Most currency and financial crises are initiated by poor fundamentals: weak regulation and supervision of the banking system or large fiscal imbalances.

However, asset prices, such as stock prices and exchange rates, have huge swings that are often hard to explain. Speculative attacks that set off currency crises can occur spontaneously even in the best-run economies. Speculative bubbles in the real estate and stock markets also appear frequently almost everywhere, and when they burst they too can lead to financial instability. Strong fundamentals do not completely insulate an economy from financial crises. Yet policies to improve prudential regulation and supervision and promote responsible fiscal policy can substantially reduce an economy's vulnerability to currency and financial crises. (For more on these policies, see Chapter 9.)

Final Stage: Currency Crisis Triggers Full-Fledged Financial Crisis

A key characteristic that distinguishes emerging market economies from advanced economies is the structure of their debt markets. In advanced economies, inflation has tended to be moderate and so debt contracts are typically of fairly long duration with fixed interest rates. About half of the residential mortgages in the United States, for instance, have fixed rates and come due in around thirty years, and corporate bonds with maturities of thirty years or longer are common.

In contrast, emerging market countries have experienced very high and variable inflation rates in the past, with accompanying wide swings in the values of their domestic currencies. One result of their experience is that debt contracts are of very short duration in order to minimize inflation risk. In many emerging market countries, for example, almost all bank lending is very short-term, with variable-rate contracts that are adjusted on a monthly, or sometimes even a daily, basis. In addition, because of the likelihood that their currency's value will change for the worse, many nonfinancial firms, banks, and governments in emerging market countries find it much easier to issue debt denominated in foreign currencies, often U.S. dollars.[28] That is, a shoe manufacturer in Mexico might need to borrow 100 million pesos, but because the bank is unsure what the value of the peso will be next year, it prefers to lend the shoe manufacturer the same amount in dollars, say $10 million if the exchange rate is 10 pesos per dollar. This phenomenon is called *liability dollarization*.[29]

When debt contracts are denominated in foreign currency (in this example, dollars) and there is an unanticipated depreciation or devaluation of the domestic currency (pesos), the debt burden of domestic firms increases in terms of domestic currency because it takes more pesos to pay back the dollarized debt. Since the goods and services produced by most firms are priced in the domestic currency, the firms' assets do not rise in value in terms of pesos, while the debt does. The depreciation of the domestic currency increases the value of debt relative to assets, and the firms' net worth declines. The decline in net worth then increases adverse selection and moral hazard problems, which lead in turn to a decline in investment and economic activity.

Although depreciation in an emerging market country under a floating-exchange-rate regime leads to financial fragility, such a regime is less likely than a pegged-exchange-rate regime to cause a full-fledged financial crisis in which financial markets seize up and stop performing their role of moving funds to those with productive investment opportunities. Under a pegged-exchange-rate regime, when a successful speculative attack occurs, the decline in the value of the domestic currency is usually much larger, more rapid, and less anticipated than when a depreciation occurs under a floating-exchange-rate regime.[30] For example, during the Mexican crisis of 1994–95, the value of the peso fell by half within only a few months, while in the recent Southeast Asian crisis the country worst hit, Indonesia, saw its currency decline by 75% within a short period of time.

In addition, a pegged-exchange-rate regime encourages liability dollarization, which makes the financial system more vulnerable when a depreciation occurs: domestic firms are more likely to borrow in dollars because the government's commitment to preventing a decline in the value of the domestic currency reduces their risk. With a guarantee that the local currency will remain fixed in terms of dollars, the domestic firm does not have to worry that the local currency will depreciate, a situation that would require the firm to use more of its local currency to pay back dollar debt.[31]

To see how a currency crisis destroys balance sheets and provokes a financial crisis, let's look at what happened in Indonesia after its 1997 currency crisis. The rupiah's value fell by 75% and dollar-denominated debt became four times as expensive in terms of rupiahs. In this situation, almost every Indonesian firm with a substantial amount of dollar debt became insolvent. The moral hazard and adverse selection problems of lending to an insolvent firm were so severe that—even if an Indonesian firm in this situation had a good balance sheet, was run well, and presented superb investment opportunities —no one would lend to it. Investment and spending collapsed, as did the entire economy: output declined by over 10% in 1998 (larger than the decline the United States experienced in the first year of the Great Depression), and the percentage of the population living in poverty doubled.[32]

For firms that export most of their output (generally priced in foreign currency), the impact of a depreciation on the balance sheet is far less severe. The depreciation leads to a rise in the prices of the goods and services the exporter produces, thereby raising the value of its assets in terms of the domestic currency. The increase in asset values helps to offset the rise in the value of the exporter's debt. This outcome suggests that, when the export sector in an emerging market economy is large, the consequences of a currency collapse for balance sheets and the overall economy will be less severe, and this is what empirical evidence finds.[33]

We now see how the institutional structure of debt markets in emerging market countries interacts with currency devaluations to propel the economies into full-fledged financial blowups, producing what economists often call the "twin crises": concurrent currency and financial crises.[34] Because so many firms in these countries had debt denominated in foreign currency, such as the dollar and the yen, depreciation of their currencies resulted in increases in their indebtedness in terms of the domestic currency, even though the value of their assets remained unchanged. When the Mexican peso lost half its value by March 1995, and the Thai, Philippine, Malaysian, and South Korean currencies lost 30 to 50% of their value by the beginning of 1998, firms' balance sheets took a big negative hit, causing a dramatic increase in adverse selection and moral hazard problems (as shown in the fourth row of Figure 4.1). This negative shock, as we have seen, was especially severe for Indonesia, which saw its currency fall by over 75%, resulting in insolvency for almost all firms with substantial amounts of debt denominated in foreign currencies.

If an economy is almost completely dollarized, that is, if most of its debts are denominated in dollars, as was true for the Argentine economy before its crisis in 2001,[35] the destruction of balance sheets is almost total and the currency collapse is truly devastating. In the aftermath of its crisis, Argentina entered the worst depression in its history from 2001 to 2002, with the unemployment rate climbing to nearly 20%, a level comparable to what the United States experienced during the Great Depression.

The collapse of a currency can also lead to higher inflation. The central banks in most emerging market countries have little credibility as inflation fighters. Thus a sharp depreciation of the currency after a currency crisis leads to immediate upward pressure on import prices, which is likely to lead to a dramatic rise in both actual and expected inflation. This happened in Mexico and Indonesia, where the annual inflation rate surged to over 50% after the currency crisis. The rise in expected inflation after the currency crises in Mexico and Indonesia led to a sharp rise in interest rates, which now had to compensate investors for inflation risk. The resulting increase in interest payments caused reductions in firms' cash flow, which led to increased asymmetric information problems since firms were now more dependent on external funds to finance their investment. As the asymmetric information analysis suggests, the resulting increase in adverse selection and moral hazard problems made domestic and foreign lenders even less willing to lend.

As shown in Figure 4.1, further deterioration in the economy occurred because the collapse in economic activity and the deterioration of cash flow and balance sheets of firms and households meant that many of them were no longer able to pay off their debts, resulting in substantial losses for banks. Sharp rises in interest rates also had a negative effect on banks' profitability and balance sheets. Even more problematic for the banks was the sharp increase in the value of their foreign-currency-denominated liabilities after the devaluation.

Thus bank balance sheets were squeezed from both sides: the value of their assets was falling as the value of their liabilities was rising.[36] Moreover, much of the banks' foreign-currency-denominated debt was very short term; the sharp increase in the value of the debt led to immediate problems for the banks because this debt needed to be paid back quickly.

Under these circumstances, the banking system will suffer a bank panic and collapse in the absence of a government safety net (as it did in the United States during the Great Depression). In many cases, however, the IMF will help emerging market nations by providing their governments with loans whose proceeds can be used to protect depositors and avoid a bank panic. (Indonesia, on the other hand, did experience a banking panic in which numerous banks were forced out of business.) However, given the loss of bank capital and the need for the government to intervene to prop up the banks, even with the IMF's help banks' ability to lend is sharply curtailed. A banking crisis that does not develop into a panic still hinders the ability of banks to lend and worsens adverse selection and moral hazard problems in financial markets, because banks are less capable of playing their role in financial intermediation. The banking crisis and the other factors that increase adverse selection and moral hazard problems explain the collapse of lending and economic activity in the aftermath of the crisis.

Contagion

So far we have been looking at shocks to the financial system that originate with actions or events inside an individual emerging market economy. But not all financial crises are homegrown. A currency or financial crisis in one country can spread to another in a process called *contagion*. Research on contagion suggests that it is particularly virulent when there have been large capital inflows that come to a "sudden stop,"[37] when the crisis in the initiating country was a surprise, and when highly leveraged common creditors (banks, mutual funds, or hedge funds) have been lending to the countries that experience contagion.[38] The 1997 East Asian financial crisis, for example, began in Thailand, with the devaluation of the Thai baht in July. Once participants in the financial markets recognized that something was wrong in Thailand's financial sector, they realized that the rest of East Asia might be in a similarly precarious financial state. Speculative attacks began against the currencies of other countries in the region. As it became clear that South Korea, Malaysia, the Philippines, and Indonesia had also experienced lending booms that weakened their banking systems, the selling pressure became so great that their currencies collapsed as well. Although the speculative pressure on these other currencies might have been triggered by the successful speculative attack on the Thai baht, the attacks on them were successful because the countries had similar problems in their domestic financial sectors. Speculators also began to sell the currencies of Singapore, Hong Kong, and Taiwan, but these countries were able to survive the attacks because strong prudential regulation and supervision had kept their banking systems in good shape. Their governments were able to successfully defend their currencies and keep them from devaluing, and financial crises did not occur. The East Asian financial crises were thus primarily homegrown, although the exact timing was probably influenced by contagion from Thailand.

Contagion from proximity to a crisis country is particularly well illustrated by the 2002 financial crisis in Uruguay, which borders Argentina.[39] Up until early 2002, Uruguay's government debt had an investment-grade rating, indicating that the credit rating agencies assessed the probability of default on this debt as low.[40] In 2002, however, the financial crisis in Argentina triggered a crisis in Uruguay because its economy and financial system were so highly integrated with Argentina's, and also because its economy was highly dollarized.[41] The depression in Argentina, in the wake of its financial crisis in late 2001 and early 2002, caused a sharp fall in Uruguay's exports and led to downward pressure on its exchange rate. In addition, Argentineans began to pull their deposits out of Uruguay; the Uruguayan banks experienced a run and saw their deposit base drop by 40%. The speculative attack that followed forced the Uruguayan government to abandon the peg of its peso to the U.S. dollar on June 19. The ensuing collapse of the peso devastated the balance sheets of nonfinancial firms whose liabilities were principally denominated in dollars, and this led to a full-scale bank panic because these firms could not repay their loans. The damage to the banking system and to the balance sheets of nonfinancial firms fed on each other to precipitate a collapse in lending and the economy at large. The contagion was complete. When Argentina's financial crisis spilled over to Uruguay in 2002, it precipitated a great depression in Uruguay as well.

Why Are Financial Crises So Different in Advanced Countries?

Advanced countries also experience financial crises, although in recent years the effects have typically not been as devastating as those in emerging market economies. The United States experienced banking and financial crises every twenty years or so in the nineteenth and early twentieth centuries, with the last major one being the Great Depression of the 1930s.[42] In the 1980s, the S&L crisis was a limited banking crisis, but it was contained by the government and so did not lead to a full-scale financial crisis. As painful as this episode was to the U.S. taxpayer, its impact on the economy was limited. Finland, Norway, and Sweden experienced banking crises even larger, relative to GDP, than the S&L crisis in the United States. In the early 1990s, for example, Finland needed to spend over 10% of its GDP to bail out its banks, and it experienced a severe depression. Japan's banking crisis lasted from the early 1990s until recently, and it has been an important factor in the economic stagnation that has led to income per person in Japan falling farther behind that in the United States in recent years.

However, the dynamics of financial crises in advanced economies are very different from those in emerging market economies. For example, advanced economies are rarely hit with the twin crises (currency and financial) because their debt structure is diametrically opposite to that of emerging market economies.[43] It is denominated in domestic currency and is long term. When the currency of an advanced economy depreciates, the depreciation has little impact on its firms' balance sheets because their debt is denominated in domestic currency. Thus a depreciation does not trigger a financial crisis.

To see the difference between what happens in advanced versus emerging market economies when a currency crisis hits, we can look at the experience of British firms after the September 1992 currency crisis there. A speculative attack against the British pound led the British to exit the Exchange Rate Mechanism (ERM), a precursor to the European Monetary Union under which the British pound was pegged to the deutsche mark. After Britain exited the ERM, the pound was allowed to depreciate by 10%. Because a British firm would have its debt denominated in pounds, the fall in the value of the British currency had no adverse impact on the firm's balance sheet. Indeed, if the British firm was an exporter, it actually benefited from the depreciation, because its exports now became cheaper in foreign currency and thus more competitive. The speculative attack and the currency crisis increased demand for British goods, and this increase helped the British economy to outperform those of other European countries (such as France) that did not devalue against the deutsche mark.

Although speculators made enormous profits at the expense of the Bank of England, which bought pounds that later fell in value while defending its currency (George Soros, one such speculator, is reported to have made $1 billion for his hedge fund), these speculators may have done Britain a favor. Their successful attack on the British pound, which caused the pound to depreciate, helped make British goods cheaper relative to foreign goods, and this increased demand for British goods, which in turn helped the weak British economy to recover. Contrast this situation with that in Indonesia in 1997, where the successful speculative attack devastated the balance sheets of Indonesian firms and led to a financial crisis and a great depression.

My research on financial crises resulted in my proudest moment as a forecaster. In August 1997, I was presenting a paper, "The Causes and Propagation of Financial Instability: Lessons for Policymakers," at the Federal Reserve Bank of Kansas City's Jackson Hole Conference.[44] This annual conference is attended by the who's who of central bankers throughout the world. The paper outlined the analysis of financial crises (the same as that presented in this chapter) and applied it to the Mexican crisis of 1994–95. One of the conference participants wondered why the decline in the East Asian countries that had started with the devaluation of the Thai baht in early July was such a big deal. After all, depreciations of similar magnitudes in industrialized countries were common and yet had little negative impact. I replied that this was an apples-to-oranges comparison because debt structure was so different in emerging market versus advanced economies. I stated that the depreciations in East Asia, if they were large enough, would lead to financial crises and to a collapse of East Asian economies. Over the next couple of months my prediction came true. (Note that my forecasts aren't always this accurate. When Apple Computer was first touting the mouse, I told one of my classes at Columbia that it wouldn't be successful because it was too cumbersome to use.)

These different outcomes from similar events show how emerging market countries differ from advanced economies and should remind us that drawing conclusions from the experiences of advanced countries and applying them to emerging market countries can be dangerous. Understanding the differences between the two types of economies is crucial to developing helpful, growth-oriented policy prescriptions, as we will see in Part Three of this book.

Part Two

Financial Crises in Emerging Market Economies

Five

Mexico, 1994–1995

The framework described in the previous chapter presents the bare bones of the genesis, buildup, and downward spiral of a generalized financial crisis as it occurs in an emerging market economy. To really understand the specifics of why financial globalization can go so wrong and what policies are needed to make it work, we need to examine specific crises in more detail. We will look at the villains, and sometimes the heroes, in these episodes.

The case studies in this chapter and the two that follow illustrate many key themes of this book. First, financial crises are primarily homegrown and can result from inadequate prudential regulation and supervision, perversion of the financial globalization process by powerful business interests, irresponsible fiscal policy, or any combination of these factors. Second, a pegged-exchange-rate regime and liability dollarization (in which debt is denominated in foreign currency) are a deadly combination that leaves emerging market countries highly vulnerable to financial crises. Third, because strategies that work well in advanced countries often do not translate to emerging market countries, "one size fits all" policies can be dangerous. Fourth, government officials often delay the inevitable and sweep difficult problems under the rug shortly before financial crises begin, making the crises much worse. Fifth, crises become far worse if the response to them is slow and confidence is not restored quickly.

In this chapter we look at the Mexican crisis of 1994–95, which Michel Camdessus, then the managing director of the IMF, described as the "first financial crisis of the twenty-first century, meaning the first major financial crisis to

71

hit an emerging market economy in the new world of globalized financial markets."[1] (Actually, Chile had had a similar, but less well-known, crisis over ten years earlier; it had devastating effects on the country's economy, which saw a decline in GDP of 14% in 1982 and another 3% in 1983.)[2] The next chapters examine the South Korean crisis in 1997 (archetypical of the crises that struck East Asia) and the Argentine crisis of 2001–02 (illustrative of how fiscal imbalances and bad luck can lead to disaster).

Macroeconomic Fundamentals before the Crisis

In the years preceding the Mexican financial crisis of 1994–95—which has been dubbed "the Tequila Crisis" in honor of Mexico's national drink—the macroeconomic fundamentals appeared quite solid. There had been a tremendous success on the inflation front, with the annual inflation rate falling from 130% in 1987 to 7% by 1994. Right before the crisis began in 1994, the economy was growing solidly at an annual rate of 4.4%, while the government budget was just slightly in deficit, at 0.7% of GDP as compared to the over-4% numbers we have seen in the United States in recent years.[3]

The only uncomfortable number was the current account deficit, at 7.2% of GDP (as compared to 6% in the United States now). The current account is, in effect, a cash flow number for countries: a current account deficit meant, in the most general terms, that Mexico had outlays on items such as imports that were larger than its receipts from items such as exports. This negative cash flow had to be financed by inflows of foreign capital, which increased Mexico's vulnerability: if the capital flows reversed, there would be a sharp decline in the value of the currency. Although Mexico's current account deficit was large, many other countries have had numbers this large and yet have not experienced a crisis. The primary source of the Mexican financial crisis does not appear to have been macroeconomic problems. Instead, the seeds of the Tequila Crisis were planted with the financial liberalization that started in the late 1980s and the adherence to a fixed-exchange-rate regime.

Stage One: Mismanagement of Financial Liberalization/Globalization

To understand how the Tequila Crisis occurred, we have to step back a decade. In 1982 the government of Mexico (then headed by President José Lopez Portillo) defaulted on its debt. Even though it was the government's policies that had led to the default, the banks served as a useful scapegoat. Using the excuse that they were to blame, the government took over all the banks in Mexico.[4] The takeover was labeled a "nationalization," giving the impression that the banks had been foreign owned. This was not the case, however: foreign banks had been banned from engaging in retail banking in Mexico since the latter part of the eighteenth century.

When Carlos Salinas de Gortari became the president of Mexico in 1988, his administration espoused a more probusiness philosophy and immediately pursued a financial liberalization policy under which it removed credit controls and lending restrictions and allowed interest rates on loans to be set freely in the markets. As part of this process, the Salinas government decided in 1991 to privatize the banking system by selling the government-owned banks to Mexican citizens. The hope was that a private banking system would be more efficient and help stimulate economic growth, and that the sale of the banks would provide needed revenue for the government.

The U.S. government and the IMF also tried to persuade Mexico to open up its financial markets to foreign capital flows, and capital account liberalization was further encouraged by Mexico's application to enter the Organisation for Economic Co-operation and Development (OECD), which it did in May 1994, and by the North American Free Trade Agreement (NAFTA), which was signed by the Salinas and Bush administrations in 1992. With the opening of the capital account, foreign portfolio investment climbed from less than $5 billion per year in the late 1980s to over $20 billion per year in the early 1990s.

Opening the Door to Disaster

The cozy and often corrupt relationship between the Mexican government and rich, powerful elites with business interests in the financial sector has been a long-standing one.[5] To ensure that it would get a high price for its banks in the 1991 privatization, the government adopted measures to ensure that they would be profitable.[6] First, the government indicated that competition in the industry would be restricted. The largest four banks (which held a combined 70% of bank assets) were not broken up into smaller pieces for the sale, thus leaving the banking system very concentrated. (In comparison, the top four banks in the United States held less than 40% of total bank assets in 2003.)[7] The government also signaled that it would restrict entry into the banking industry by requiring that bank charters be obtained only with the permission of the secretary of the treasury. In addition, the government would not allow foreign banks to enter Mexico, another long-standing tradition.[8]

When it came time to sell the banks, the Salinas government always sold to the highest bidder, without taking into account the management capabilities of those to whom it was selling. In addition, under pressure from potential buyers, the government made it easier for them to employ leverage and buy the banks with other people's money.[9] As a result, the new owners of the banks did not always have much of their own money invested in the banks, and with so little to lose there was great incentive for them to make risky loans.

If the high-risk/high-payoff loans paid off, the banks would be hugely profitable, and, with their highly leveraged positions, the owners would make a ton of money. If the loans went sour, they would lose very little of their own money. The moral hazard incentives for risk taking were significant.

To make matters worse, a government safety net left the markets with very little incentive to monitor the banks. The government had put in place deposit insurance that not only insured small depositors, as in the United States, but also provided a blanket guarantee for *all* deposits. As a result depositors, even the most sophisticated, had no incentive to monitor the Mexican banks because they would not incur any losses if a bank failed.[10]

With market discipline so weak and with the owners of banks potentially having little to lose, Mexican bankers had tremendous incentives to engage in moral hazard and have their banks take on risk. They were not shy about doing so. Particularly egregious was the massive amount of so-called connected or insider lending: 20% of all large loans outstanding from 1995 to 1998 went to bank directors.[11] Insider lending is a form of looting, in which insiders make a sweetheart deal that makes them rich but increases risk for the institution they manage. These insider loans had interest rates 4 percentage points lower than those on other loans, a 33% higher default rate, and a 30% lower recovery rate for collateral. Although the insiders were getting a good deal, the banks were not.

No One to Shut the Door

This moral hazard problem could have been addressed by effective government regulation and supervision of the banks. Since such supervision was not in the interests of the bankers, who wanted to pursue their business without any constraints, the government put in place a weak regulatory regime. Mexican accounting rules, for example, were much less tight than those generally accepted in other countries. One of the most flagrant abuses of good accounting practice was that bankers could avoid revealing losses on their loans by "evergreening" bad loans: that is, the bank could provide the borrower with a new loan that would be used to pay off the principal and past-due interest on the loan—which in reality had gone sour. With this practice in place, bank supervisors could engage in regulatory forbearance. Banks were not forced to write off bad loans, and, even though they had inadequate, or even negative, net worth, they were allowed to stay in business. The creation of "zombie" banks with nothing to lose gave bankers huge incentives to take excessive risk, just as had been the case in the U.S. savings and loan crisis. In addition, the National Banking Commission (Comision Nacional Bancaria), the regulator and supervisor of the banks, was not given the resources to develop the necessary expertise to monitor the banks' loan portfolios and management practices. Thus the Commission could not prevent the banks from taking outrageous risks or close down banks that were insolvent.

Stage Two: Run-up to the Currency Crisis

Clearly the financial liberalization process had been so perverted that a disaster was bound to follow, and that is exactly what happened.

Deterioration in Bank Balance Sheets

The huge incentives to take on risk and the flow of foreign capital into Mexico to fund bank lending resulted in extremely rapid growth of bank credit to private nonfinancial enterprises, which grew from 10% of GDP in 1988 to over 40% of GDP in 1994.* Before the bank privatization, the government-owned banks, naturally enough, had directed about 50% of their lending business to the government. When the banks were privatized in the early 1990s, their expertise in making loans to private firms and individuals was limited because they did not have a "credit culture," that is, they had little ability to screen out good credit risks from bad or to monitor borrowers to prevent excessive risk taking. For example, Mexican banks did not have formal credit departments, nor were there credit bureaus (like TRW or Equifax in the United States) to gather information on how much households and small businesses had borrowed from other sources.[12] If they couldn't find out how many outstanding loans borrowers had, the banks could not tell whether the borrowers would be capable of paying them back. Nonetheless, the banks aggressively sought out this loan business, setting off a lending boom.

The inability of the National Banking Commission to effectively supervise the banking system became even more pronounced with the rapid growth of the banking sector. This lack of supervisors (bank examiners) was exacerbated not only by the bank lending boom but also by the tremendous expansion in lending by other financial institutions, such as credit unions, thrifts, and leasing companies. With the incentives that were in place and the inability of the Commission to restrain excessive risk taking, the banks made many bad loans. The official measure of nonperforming loans from the Bank of Mexico, expressed as a percentage of total loans, rose steadily, from below 5% at the beginning of the 1990s to above 15% after the crisis. With the lax accounting principles that the government had put in place for recognizing bad loans, however, even these numbers are gross underestimates. Later estimates of Mexican

*Figures that display the data and outline the sequence of events described in this chapter are on pages 76–77.

Figure 5.1. Sequence of Events in Mexico's Financial Crisis, 1994–1995

Bank credit to private firms rose...

A. Bank Credit to Private Enterprises, 1988–1995 (percentage of GDP)

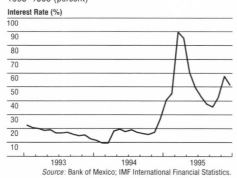

Percentage of GDP

Source: Bank of Mexico.

...and many of the loans were bad.

B. Nonperforming Loans as Share of Total Loans, 1990–1995 (percent)

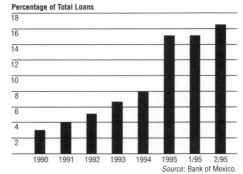

Percentage of Total Loans

Source: Bank of Mexico.

Interest rates rose.

C. Interest Rates on Interbank Loans, 1993–1995 (percent)

Interest Rate (%)

Source: Bank of Mexico; IMF International Financial Statistics.

The stock market declined as uncertainty increased.

D. Stock Market Prices on the Bolsa, 1993–1996 (index value)

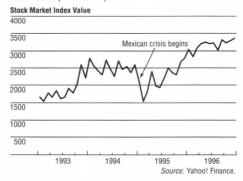

Stock Market Index Value

Mexican crisis begins

Source: Yahoo! Finance.

International reserves to support the peso shrank.

E. Mexico's International Reserves, 1994–1995 (trillions of U.S. dollars)

Trillions of U.S. Dollars

Source: Total reserves (excluding gold), including foreign exchange, reserve position with the IMF, and special drawing rights at end of period: line 1L in IMF International Financial Statistics. End of period: Bank of Mexico, IMF International Financial Statistics.

Dollar-denominated bonds outpaced peso-denominated bonds.

F. Cetes and Tesobonos Amounts Outstanding, 1993–1995 (trillions of new pesos)

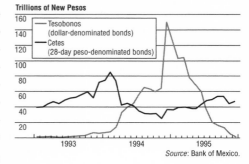

Trillions of New Pesos

— Tesobonos (dollar-denominated bonds)
— Cetes (28-day peso-denominated bonds)

Source: Bank of Mexico.

The peso was halved in value, ...

G. Peso-Dollar Exchange Rate,
1993–1995 (U.S. dollars per peso)

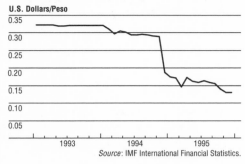

U.S. Dollars/Peso

Source: IMF International Financial Statistics.

...contributing to the deterioration of household and business balance sheets...

H. Net Creditor (+) or Debtor (−) Position with the Domestic Financial System, 1987–1995 (percentage of GDP)

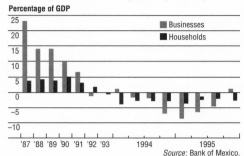

Percentage of GDP

Source: Bank of Mexico.

...and leading to a dramatic rise in inflation.

I. Consumer Price Inflation, 1993–1996 (annual percent)

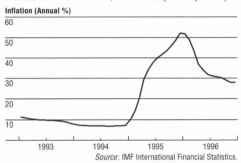

Inflation (Annual %)

Source: IMF International Financial Statistics.

Adverse selection and moral hazard problems intensified, and foreign lenders pulled out funds, ...

J. Annualized Quarterly Flows of Foreign Portfolio Investment, 1993–1995 (billions of U.S. dollars)

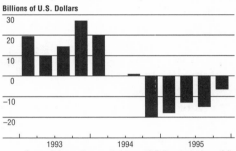

Billions of U.S. Dollars

Source: Balance of payments data; portfolio investment is portfolio equity and money market investment, Bank of Mexico.

...the economy collapsed, ...

K. Real GDP Growth, 1994–1995 (percent)

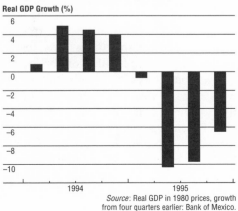

Real GDP Growth (%)

Source: Real GDP in 1980 prices, growth from four quarters earlier: Bank of Mexico.

...and unemployment rose.

L. Unemployment Rate, 1993–1995 (percent)

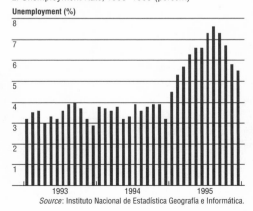

Unemployment (%)

Source: Instituto Nacional de Estadística Geografía e Informática.

nonperforming loans based on generally accepted accounting principles were about three times higher, exceeding 50% after the crisis.[13]

Given the incentives created by the perversion of the financial liberalization process and the resulting deterioration in bank balance sheets, the financial system would surely have collapsed at some point. But the exact timing of the collapse was determined by a set of specific precipitating factors.

Higher Interest Rates and Their Effects on Cash Flow

The first precipitating factor was a rise in interest rates abroad. Beginning in February 1994, the Federal Reserve began to raise the interbank federal funds rate to proactively prevent inflationary pressures from taking hold. Although this policy kept inflation in check in the United States, it put upward pressure on Mexican interest rates. Interest rates had to be raised so that investors would continue to find holding peso-denominated assets attractive at the exchange rate of 3.1 pesos per dollar, the floor set by the Mexican government.[14]

Higher interest rates increased adverse selection problems in the Mexican financial markets because, at these higher rates, only poorer credit risks who wanted to pursue high-return/high-risk investments were willing to borrow. Because most Mexican debt was very short term (much of it had interest rates reset on a daily basis), interest payments made by firms and households immediately rose and cash flows declined. In turn, reduced cash flow forced firms and households to seek funds in external financial markets where adverse selection and moral hazard problems were likely to be severe. As asymmetric information theory suggests, the rise in interest rates and the decline in cash flow made lenders reluctant to lend when the crisis hit in late 1994, and investment and spending declined.

Increases in Uncertainty and the Decline in Lending

The second precipitating factor was an increase in uncertainty in Mexico's financial markets, much of it on the political front. The first major blow occurred when Luis Donaldo Colosio, the presidential candidate of the ruling party, the Institutional Revolutionary Party (Partido Revolucionario Institucional; PRI), who was almost sure to be elected, was assassinated in March 1994. In September the secretary-general of the PRI was assassinated. In October negotiations to contain a major uprising in the southern state of Chiapas broke down, leading to increased violence there just before the new president of Mexico, Ernesto Zedillo, took office. These events increased uncertainty in financial markets and decreased the quality of information, making it harder to screen credit risks or monitor borrowers. The increase in asymmetric information eventually made lenders leery, and lending fell further.

Falling Asset Prices and the Decline in Net Worth

Partially as a result of the increased uncertainty, stock prices on the Bolsa, the Mexican stock exchange, fell nearly 20% from the peak in September 1994 to the middle of December 1994. The decline in firms' net worth, which acts like collateral, meant that lenders were less protected against the consequences of adverse selection. Firms also now had more incentives to take on risk because, with less net worth, they had less to lose, thus increasing moral hazard problems. The decline in asset prices, which increased adverse selection and moral hazard problems, added to the initial conditions that worsened asymmetric information problems and made the Mexican economy ripe for a serious financial crisis. It was then that the currency crisis struck.

Stage Three: Currency Crisis

As part of an earlier stabilization plan to lower inflation, the Mexican government had committed to a high floor for the peso (3.1 pesos per dollar) that overvalued the currency.[15] Because it was not allowed to fall below this floor, the peso was in effect pegged to the U.S. dollar.

The effective exchange rate peg had three undesirable consequences. First, it helped encourage the capital inflows that fueled the lending boom, because it gave foreign investors a false sense of security that they would be protected from currency risk. Second, it encouraged liability dollarization (the issuing of domestic debt denominated in U.S. dollars) because, with the government's commitment to keep the peso fixed in terms of dollars, a domestic borrower no longer had to worry that the peso would depreciate and that it would be forced to come up with more pesos to pay back the dollar debt. Third, it made possible a speculative attack on the currency.

With the Colosio assassination and the political uncertainty from the Chiapas uprising, currency traders suspected that a devaluation of the Mexican peso might soon occur, and this increased downward pressure on the peso. Speculators began to unload their pesos in the foreign exchange market, and the currency came under attack. To keep the peso from falling through the floor set by the government, the Banco de Mexico intervened in the foreign exchange market to purchase pesos, resulting in a substantial loss of foreign exchange reserves. To make things worse, the markets became aware that the Mexican banking system was in deep trouble and that a rise in interest rates that would increase the cost of funds would sink the banks. It then became clear that the Banco de Mexico would not be able to prop up the peso by raising interest rates enough to attract capital inflows. Selling pressure on the peso increased.

The Mexican government was unwilling to raise interest rates to defend the peso, not only because doing so would cause many banks to collapse but also because it did not want to raise interest rates right before a presidential election (an action that might cause the ruling party's candidate to lose). When presented with an almost impossible situation like this one, politicians often gamble, hoping that, if they take measures to delay the problem, it might just go away. The Salinas government did exactly this by deciding on a dangerous, and eventually very costly, gambit to prop up the currency. Instead of financing its debt with peso-denominated bonds, it dramatically increased its issuance of dollar-denominated bonds, called tesobonos. The tesobonos provided foreign exchange reserves, and the government hoped that the day of reckoning might be avoided. But this was not to be.

The government also tried to hide the fact that it was running out of foreign exchange reserves: it did not reveal that a substantial amount of its holdings had to be paid back in the near future. Once speculators perceived that the government would be unlikely to be able to defend the currency, they were given a one-way bet and began to pile on. Furthermore, the huge prospective deficits arising from the future bailout of the distressed banks raised questions about the solvency of the Mexican government, providing another reason why the speculators would sell pesos.[16] Even though the Mexican central bank raised interest rates sharply, the hemorrhaging of foreign exchange reserves forced the authorities to devalue the peso on December 20, 1994.

Final Stage: Currency Crisis Triggers
Full-Fledged Financial Crisis

The institutional structure of debt markets in Mexico now interacted with the peso devaluation to propel the economy into a full-fledged financial crisis. By March 1995 the value of the peso had fallen by 50%. Because so many firms had debts denominated in dollars, the decline in value led to an immediate sharp increase in their indebtedness in pesos, while the value of their assets remained unchanged. The depreciation of the peso led to an especially sharp negative shock to the net worth of private firms, causing a dramatic increase in adverse selection and moral hazard problems.

The collapse of the Mexican peso also led to a sharp rise in import prices, which, because the perceived ability of the Banco de Mexico to control inflation was not great, fed immediately into higher actual and expected inflation. Higher expected inflation, combined with the desire of the Banco de Mexico and the Mexican government to limit the peso's depreciation by raising interest rates, meant that interest rates on peso-denominated debt went sky high (exceeding 100% at an annual rate), and the Mexican stock market crashed, falling a further 30% in peso terms and by over 60% in dollar terms. Given the resulting huge increase in interest payments because of the short duration of the Mexican debt, households' and firms' cash flow dropped dramatically, leading to a greater need for them to obtain external loans. Moral hazard and adverse selection problems became more severe for both domestic and foreign lenders because they had difficulty obtaining information about what was going on in the Mexican economy. Foreign lenders were then even more eager to pull their funds out of Mexico, and this is exactly what they did. Annual foreign portfolio investment inflows to Mexico, which were on the order of $20 billion in 1993 and early 1994, reversed course, and the annual outflows exceeded $10 billion beginning in the fourth quarter of 1994. The sharp decline in lending helped lead to a collapse of economic activity: real GDP growth fell from an annual rate of 4 to 4.5% in the last half of 1994 to negative growth rates in the vicinity of –10% in the second and third quarters of 1995.

Further deterioration in the economy occurred because the collapse in economic activity and the deterioration in the cash flows and balance sheets of firms and households led to a worsening banking crisis. Many firms and households were no longer able to pay off their debts, and the banks suffered substantial loan losses.

In addition, the depreciation of the peso had a direct negative impact on the banks' balance sheets, because Mexican banks were highly exposed to currency risk. The balance sheets of Mexican banks had a "matched book" in which the amounts of foreign-currency-denominated liabilities and assets were almost equal: foreign-currency-denominated liabilities were 116 billion pesos at the end of 1993, while foreign-currency-denominated assets amounted to 123 billion pesos. At first glance, the banks looked as though they were protected from a collapse of the peso. When the peso fell from 3.1 to the dollar to 5.3 to the dollar immediately after the currency crisis, the value of foreign-denominated liabilities immediately jumped by 98 billion pesos, but this increase was more than offset by the increase in foreign-denominated assets of 103 billion pesos. On paper, the banks had made a profit of 5 billion pesos![17] In reality, however, Mexican banks were highly exposed to currency risk, because a large percentage of their foreign-currency loans were made to domestically oriented firms whose income was primarily tied to the peso; they were unable to pay back loans denominated in (now highly appreciated) dollars.[18]

Could the international bank regulatory standards adopted in 1988 have helped reduce Mexican banks' exposure to currency risks? These standards, together known as the Basel Accord, were created by advanced countries under the auspices of the Basel Committee on Bank Supervision, operating out of the Bank for International Settlements in Basel, Switzerland. The purpose of the accord was to standardize and improve bank capital requirements worldwide, but it had little to say about currency risk from liability dollarization. This is not surprising, because in advanced countries a currency depreciation does no damage to firms' balance sheets. Indeed, it can actually improve them: a depreciation makes domestic firms more competitive because their goods become cheaper relative to foreign goods, while the depreciation does little harm to firms' balance sheets because liability dollarization is not widespread.

Compliance with these international standards would not have helped Mexican banks weather the currency crisis, and they were inadequate to ensure the safety and soundness of banks in an emerging market country like Mexico.[19]

Even more problematic for the Mexican banks were the short terms of many of their foreign-currency-denominated liabilities; the sharp increase in the value of these liabilities led to liquidity problems for the banks because they had to be paid back quickly. The problems of the Mexican banking system would have made its collapse inevitable in the absence of a government safety net. Instead the Mexican government provided the funds to protect depositors, thereby avoiding a bank panic. However, given the banks' loss of capital and the need for the government to intervene to prop up the banks, the banks' ability and willingness to lend were sharply curtailed. As we have seen, a banking crisis that hinders the ability of banks to lend also makes adverse selection and moral hazard problems worse in financial markets, because banks are no longer as capable of playing their traditional financial intermediation role.

The issuance of the tesobono dollar-denominated debt also complicated matters for the Mexicans. The collapse of the currency meant that this debt had more than doubled in terms of pesos, creating an additional fiscal burden on the government that would have to be paid for by future taxes. The tesobono gambit was a bet that did not pay off. With the stock of outstanding tesobonos reaching 150 billion pesos before the crisis and the peso falling to about half its value after the crisis, the Mexican government had to pay on the order of 300 billion pesos, an extra 150 billion, or over 10% of GDP, to redeem this tesobono debt—a costly mistake indeed.

The impact of the Tequila Crisis on the Mexican economy was devastating. Not only did GDP fall precipitously, but unemployment rose to over 7.5% and the poverty rate rose dramatically, to over 35%.[20] The social fabric of Mexican society was also shredded. Mexico City became one of the most dangerous cities in the world as its crime rate rose by over 50% in the wake of the crisis.[21] One of my academic colleagues and his wife were kidnapped there while attending a conference, while a Mexican central banker told me a harrowing story of how home invaders threatened him with a gun and tied him up while they robbed his house. Financial crises are not only devastating from an economic point of view; they destabilize a society and deprive its citizens of a sense of security.

Recovery

Mexico had one big advantage that helped its recovery: location, location, location. Given the two countries' long common border, the U.S. government could not afford to have a Mexico that was both destabilized and economically devastated. The U.S. Treasury began discussions with the Mexican government about providing a support package of $18 billion, with the U.S. government to provide half that amount and the rest coming from international financial institutions like the IMF. The debate over the support package in the U.S. Congress, however, became heated, and the negotiations with the Mexican government dragged on.[22] The support package was delayed for close to two months, during which time the crisis had become worse. By the time the support package was finally signed into law on February 21, 1995, the amount of funds needed had more than doubled to $50 billion, with $20 billion coming from the U.S. government and the other $30 billion from the IMF and other sources.[23] These funds were to be used by the Mexican government to prop up the currency and also to help get the Mexican banking system back on its feet. In addition, the U.S. economic recovery and the adoption of NAFTA increased demand for Mexico's exports.[24]

The Mexican peso stabilized at around 6 pesos per dollar, about half of its value before the crisis. The bailout of the banking system continued from 1994 to 2001. The government—through the Fondo Bancario de Protección al Ahorro, a deposit insurance agency known by its initials as FOBAPROA—provided funds to build up bank capital to international standards and took over banks' nonperforming loans. The Mexican National Banking Commission found that fifteen banks were in such bad shape that they had to be closed by either liquidation or being sold off to other financial institutions. However, because the Mexican government dragged out the cleanup over several years, the cost of the bailout, which was ultimately borne by Mexican taxpayers, was higher than it had to be, and confidence in the Mexican financial system and economy was slow to recover.[25] The estimated cost of the bailout ended up being close to 20% of the country's GDP.[26]

The government eventually successfully recapitalized the banking system and beefed up regulation and supervision of the banks to reduce moral hazard problems. Connected (insider) lending was restricted by regulations that prevented banks from making loans to their officers or employees (except when the loans were part of an employee benefits package). Banks were also required to publish consolidated accounts (which included their subsidiaries), so connected lending would be more obvious. Capital requirements were increased to be in line with international norms, and deposit insurance was no longer unlimited. In addition, in order to obtain foreign funds to help recapitalize the banking system, the government lifted restrictions on foreign ownership of Mexican banks. Today over 80% of the banks in Mexico are foreign owned.[27] Bringing in foreign expertise, along with the beefing up of accounting standards, has returned the Mexican banking system to health: nonperforming loans have dropped steadily, falling below 5% by 2001; the ratio of capital to total bank assets now exceeds 10%; and banks have returned to profitability.[28]

Financial Reforms Are Only Halfway There

Although the measures to put the Mexican banking system on a sound footing have been successful, and indeed are ones recommended for other emerging market economies (discussed in Part Three of the book), Mexican economic growth since the crisis has been disappointing. This is even more troubling given the boost that NAFTA was supposed to provide for the Mexican economy. Why has the Mexican economy not done better?

One important factor is that the financial and banking systems in Mexico still do not work very well. Mexico continues to have an extremely inefficient legal system that makes it hard to enforce financial contracts: it does not have effective bankruptcy laws, and the adjudication process is notoriously slow.[29] As we noted in Chapter 2, this weakness in property rights make it very difficult for banks to lend to private parties. Loan rates in Mexico are high relative to the cost of funds, and the real value of commercial, housing, and consumer lending has fallen to a quarter of what it was in 1994.[30]

Thus Mexico still does not have a financial system that is capable of channeling funds to those with the most productive investment opportunities. The inefficiency of the financial system is reflected in the low rate of Mexican financial development: bank loans are around 15% of GDP, while this number averages around 100% in advanced countries.[31] Instead of relying on the financial system to get funds, most Mexican firms get their financing from their suppliers.

Although Mexico has recovered from the Tequila Crisis, reforms of its financial system have only gone halfway. The country is making progress: the Mexican congress has passed laws establishing a new bankruptcy code and strengthening the rights of creditors to collect collateral. Without more work, however, the Mexican economy will never live up to its potential, leaving the United States with a next-door neighbor burdened by poverty and instability.

Six

South Korea, 1997–1998

Prior to its crisis in 1997, South Korea was one of the great economic success stories in history. In 1960, after the Korean War, the country was extremely poor, with an annual income per person of less than $2,000 (in today's dollars).[1] During the postwar period, South Korea pursued an export-oriented strategy that helped it become one of the world's major economies. With an annual growth rate of nearly 8% from 1960 to 1997, it became one of the leaders in the "Asian miracle," as what were once desperately poor countries embarked on a period of rapid economic growth. By 1997 South Korea's income per person had risen by more than a factor of ten, qualifying it in 1996 for membership in the rich-countries club, the Organisation for Economic Co-operation and Development (OECD).

South Korea had embraced globalization, and the process was putting the country on the road to wealth. But then globalization went wrong. South Korea's story is one of tragedy and triumph. The unfolding of the Korean crisis has many features in common with the story of the Mexican crisis. As in Mexico, financial liberalization and globalization were perverted by powerful business interests. What distinguishes the Korean crisis from the Mexican one is the extremes to which these business interests perverted the process, and particularly the bizarre policies that governed how the economy was opened up to foreign capital. This perversion led in turn to a banking crisis, a currency crisis, and finally a full-fledged financial crisis.

The Korean crisis has its villains: the family-owned conglomerates called *chaebols* and their allies in the precrisis Korean government. The Korean crisis also has heroes. The government of Kim Dae-jung, with technical advice from the IMF and the World Bank, adopted financial reforms in the immediate aftermath of the crisis that quickly put South Korea back on the road to prosperity.

Macroeconomic Fundamentals before the Crisis

South Korea's macroeconomic fundamentals were strong before the crisis, even stronger than Mexico's. In 1996 inflation in South Korea was below 5%, real output growth was close to 7%, and the country was expected to grow at a rate of more than 6% in 1997. The government budget was in slight surplus, while the current account deficit had fallen from 4.4% of GDP in 1996 to less than 2% in 1997. From a macroeconomic point of view, the South Korean economy seemed well managed, so the financial crisis cannot be attributed to macroeconomic fundamentals. Instead, as in Mexico, the source of the crisis was perversion of the financial liberalization process, which had some particularly strange elements.

Stage One: Mismanagement of Financial Liberalization/Globalization

Starting in the 1960s, South Korea pursued what became known as the Korean model of economic development. This involved a partnership between the government and the business sector, represented by the chaebols.[2] The Korean government directed credit to favored industries, especially in the export sector, through state-owned banks, by issuing government guarantees of repayment for particular loans and by tightly controlling the banking system so that in effect it acted as an agent of the government. This state-directed, export-oriented strategy, with the chaebols playing a central role, was in general highly successful. Yet as the South Korean economy grew, the government-supervised allocation of capital that had worked well during the earlier stages of economic development was becoming less viable. Korea needed a well-functioning financial system.

The Korean government recognized that, in a maturing economy, it would be less able to pick winners—the right industries for productive investment. It was also aware of its past mistakes in resource allocation, such as the Heavy and Chemical Industry policy of the 1970s, under which funds were directed to the steel, petrochemical, automobile, machine tool, shipbuilding, and electronics industries. The government began to consider more market-oriented policies, including deregulation and liberalization of the financial system. The push to open up Korean financial markets to foreign capital flows and financial institutions arose in the late 1980s, not only from the desire for more market-oriented policies but also in response to pressure from the U.S. government, which wanted U.S. financial services firms to have access to Korean markets.[3] South Korea's desire to fulfill the requirements for membership in the OECD and encouragement from the IMF also played a role in stimulating the Korean government to embark on a financial liberalization and globalization process, which accelerated in the mid-1990s.

Opening the Door to Disaster

The financial liberalization process in South Korea had many features in common with the process followed in Mexico. The government made it absolutely clear that banking institutions would be bailed out in a crisis, as indeed they were. As in Mexico, supervision of the banking system was lax, making it easy for Korean banks to hide their nonperforming loans through evergreening schemes in which new loans were made to borrowers so they could pay off the old, nonperforming loans. Just as in Mexico, lax banking regulation and supervision were no accident: it was in the interest of both the banks and the firms that borrowed from them that they be allowed to do their business unfettered by bothersome regulations and inspections. The government safety net and weak banking regulation and supervision put in place the moral hazard incentives for banks to take excessive risks in their efforts to earn high returns.

Although there are similarities in the ways in which the financial liberalization process was perverted in South Korea and Mexico, Korea's situation had some extraordinary elements owing to the unique role of the chaebols. Because of their massive size (sales of the five largest chaebols accounted for nearly 50% of GDP),[4] the chaebols were politically very powerful. One result of their influence was that the government safety net was extended far beyond the financial system because the government had a long-standing policy of viewing the chaebols as "too big to fail": the chaebols would receive direct government assistance or directed credit if they got into trouble. Not surprisingly, given this guarantee, the chaebols borrowed like crazy and were highly leveraged, taking on huge amounts of debt relative to their equity capital: the debt-to-equity ratio for the top thirty chaebols was four (as compared to less than two for the manufacturing sector in the United States).[5] This high leverage meant that, if they were profitable, the chaebols' profitability per dollar of equity capital (return on equity) would be very high. On the other hand, relative to their size, they had only a small amount of equity capital to act as a cushion against negative shocks.

Because of the government safety net for the chaebols, banks had little need to develop a credit culture in which they would screen out good credit risks from bad and monitor the chaebols to which they were lending. The banks knew they would make money from these loans no matter what. Bank managers extended credit based on the size of the borrower, favoring those whose large size, it was thought, made them too big to fail. The resulting concentration of loans to the chaebols meant that Korean banks were not diversifying their lending—a situation that made them vulnerable to any unfavorable shocks that might hit the nation's economy.

By the 1990s the chaebols were in trouble: they weren't making any money. From 1993 to 1996, the return on assets for the top thirty chaebols was never much more than 3% (a comparable figure for U.S. corporations is 15 to 20%).* In 1996, right before the crisis hit, the rate of return on assets had fallen to 0.2%. Furthermore, only the top five chaebols had any profits: the sixth- through thirtieth-largest chaebols never posted a rate of return on assets much above 1%, and in many years they actually had negative rates of return. With this kind of profitability and their already high leverage, any banker in his right mind would have pulled back on lending to the conglomerates—*if* there were no government safety net. But because the banks knew the government would make good on the chaebols' loans if they were in default, the opposite occurred: the banks continued to lend to them, evergreened their loans, and, in effect, threw good money after bad, knowing that the government would in turn throw its money at the chaebols to enable them to pay off their creditors if necessary.[6]

Even though the chaebols were getting substantial financing from commercial banks, it was not enough to feed their insatiable appetite for credit. They decided that the way out of their troubles was to go for growth, and they needed massive amounts of funds to do it. Even with the vaunted Korean national savings rate of over 30%, which is several times the current U.S. rate, there were just not enough loanable funds available to finance the chaebols' planned expansion. Where could they get the cash? The answer lay in the international capital markets.

To gain access to the funds they needed to grow, the chaebols encouraged the Korean government to accelerate the process of opening up Korean financial markets to foreign capital. In 1993 the government expanded the ability of domestic banks to make loans denominated in foreign currency by expanding the types of loans for which this was possible. At the same time, the government effectively allowed unlimited short-term foreign borrowing by financial institutions, while maintaining quantity restrictions on long-term borrowing as a means of managing capital flows into the country. Opening up short-term but not long-term borrowing to foreign capital flows made no economic sense. It is *short-term* capital flows that make an emerging market economy financially fragile: short-term capital can fly out of the country at the first whiff of a crisis.

Opening up primarily to short-term capital, however, made complete political sense: it is much easier to borrow short-term funds at lower inter-

*Figures that display the data and outline the sequence of events described in this chapter are on pages 90–91.

est rates in the international market, because long-term lending is much riskier for foreign creditors. Keeping restrictions on long-term international borrowing, however, allowed the government to say that it was still restricting foreign capital inflows and to claim that it was opening up to foreign capital in a prudent manner. In the aftermath of these changes, Korean banks opened twenty-eight branches in foreign countries, thus gaining access to foreign funds.

The Basel international standards for banking regulation had the unintended consequence of encouraging short-term borrowing from abroad.[7] Under the Basel Accord, loans to non-OECD banks with maturities less than one year had one-fifth the capital requirement of loans with maturities over one year. The accord thus provided further encouragement for foreign banks to lend short-term rather than long-term to Korean banks and businesses. (This is an example of how policies developed for advanced countries may have perverse effects in emerging market countries.)

Although Korean financial institutions now had access to foreign capital, the chaebols still had a problem. They were not allowed to own commercial banks and so still might not get all the bank loans they needed. What was the answer? The chaebols needed to get their hands on financial institutions that they could own, that were allowed to borrow abroad, and that were subject to scant regulation. This way the financial institutions could engage in connected lending, borrowing foreign funds and then lending them to the conglomerates that owned the institutions.

There is a type of financial institution specific to South Korea that perfectly met the chaebols' requirements: the merchant bank. Merchant banking corporations are wholesale financial institutions that engage in securities underwriting, leasing, and short-term lending to the corporate sector. They obtain funds for these loans by issuing bonds and commercial paper and by borrowing in interbank and foreign markets.

At the time of the Korean crisis, merchant banks not only were allowed to borrow abroad, they were virtually unregulated. The chaebols saw their opportunity. They persuaded government officials, often through bribery and kickbacks, to permit many finance companies, which were not allowed to borrow abroad, to be converted into merchant banks, which could.[8] Some of these companies were already owned by the chaebols. In 1990 there were only six merchant banks and all of them were foreign affiliated. By 1997, after the chaebols had worked their political magic, there were thirty merchant banks; of these, sixteen were owned by chaebols, two were foreign owned but had chaebols as major stockholders, and twelve were Korean owned but independent of the chaebols.[9] The conglomerates were now able to exploit connected lending with a vengeance: the merchant banks channeled massive amounts of funds to their chaebol owners, who made unproductive investments in steel, automobile production, and chemicals.

Figure 6.1. Sequence of Events in South Korea's Financial Crisis, 1997–1998

The chaebols were unprofitable.

A. Return on Assets of Thirty Largest Conglomerates, 1993–1997

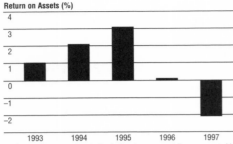

Source: Averages of each chaebol's return on asset figures reported in S. W. Joh, "The Korean Corporate Sector Crisis and Reform," Korea Development Institute mimeo, August 1999.

Credit issued by financial institutions took off, ...

B. Domestic Credit of Financial Institutions, 1986–1998

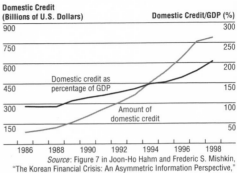

Source: Figure 7 in Joon-Ho Hahm and Frederic S. Mishkin, "The Korean Financial Crisis: An Asymmetric Information Perspective," Emerging Markets Review 1, no. 1 (2000): 21–52.

...fueled by massive borrowing from foreigners, ...

C. External Liabilities, 1992–1998

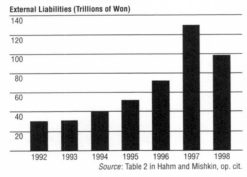

Source: Table 2 in Hahm and Mishkin, op. cit.

...which led to a deterioration in bank balance sheets.

D. Adjusted Bank Capital as Percentage of Total Bank Assets for Twenty Domestic Commercial Banks, 1992–1998

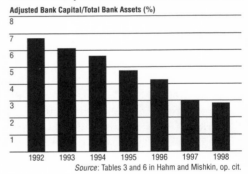

Source: Tables 3 and 6 in Hahm and Mishkin, op. cit.

The stock market declined as uncertainty increased.

E. Stock Market Index (KOSPI), 1990–1999

Source: Figure 2 in Hahm and Mishkin, op. cit.

International reserves to support the won shrank.

F. Foreign Exchange Reserves, 1996–1998 (billions of U.S. dollars)

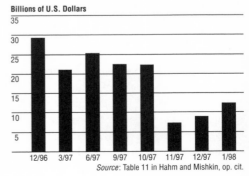

Source: Table 11 in Hahm and Mishkin, op. cit.

The won halved in value.

G. Won-Dollar Exchange Rate,
1996–1999 (U.S. dollars per won)

U.S. Dollars/Won

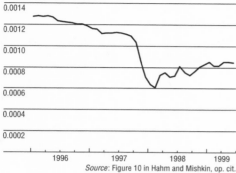

Source: Figure 10 in Hahm and Mishkin, op. cit.

Market interest rates rose...

H. Interest Rates on Benchmark Three-Year
Corporate Bonds, 1996–1999 (percent)

Interest Rate (%)

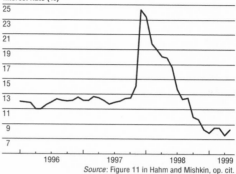

Source: Figure 11 in Hahm and Mishkin, op. cit.

...and inflation rose but came back down quickly.

I. Annualized CPI Inflation Rate (percent)

Percentage Change in CPI over Previous Year

Source: IMF International Financial Statistics.

Adverse selection and moral hazard problems intensified and foreign lenders pulled out funds, ...

J. Annual Flows of Foreign Portfolio Investment,
1993–1999 (billions of U.S. dollars)

Billions of U.S. Dollars

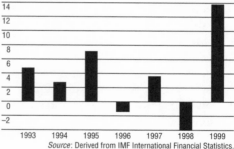

Source: Derived from IMF International Financial Statistics.

...the economy collapsed, ...

K. Real GDP Growth, 1990–2002
(year-over-year growth rate)

Real GDP Growth (%)

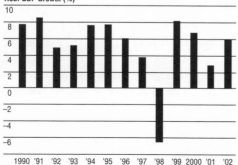

Source: World Development Indicators.

...and unemployment rose.

L. Unemployment Rate, 1990–2000 (percent)

Unemployment (%)

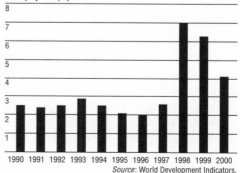

Source: World Development Indicators.

Key to the ability of Korean financial institutions to be able to borrow abroad was an implicit safety net for foreign lenders. Foreign lenders assumed—quite rightly as it turned out—that they would suffer only minor losses if Korean financial institutions got into trouble. They would be protected from losses either by the Korean government or by international institutions such as the IMF, which would provide the South Korean government with the necessary funds to bail them out. The presence of this safety net meant that foreign lenders did not have sufficient incentives to monitor the Korean financial institutions and pull their money out if they learned those institutions were taking on too much risk.

Stage Two: Run-up to the Currency Crisis

The perversion of the financial liberalization process by the chaebols created conditions that eventually led to economic disaster along the lines of the Mexican crisis. Thanks to the government safety net and the "too big to fail" policy regarding the chaebols, commercial banks had huge moral hazard incentives to increase risk taking by rapidly increasing their lending to the chaebols. The problem was even worse for the merchant banks and other non-bank financial institutions that were largely owned by conglomerates (more than 30% of total assets in the nonbank financial industry were held by chaebols). While the central bank had supervisory authority over commercial banks, the supervisory system for these other financial institutions was fragmentary and lacked accountability. The opportunities for risk taking were enormous. The percentage of merchant banks' loans going to chaebols was very high, so they were not sufficiently diversified. The merchant banks often borrowed over the short term and so could quickly suffer losses of funding. In addition they invested in relatively long-term, high-yield assets that were quite risky.

The inadequate monitoring of nonbank financial institutions by supervisors sometimes resulted in illegal off-balance-sheet transactions to move funds of affiliated financial institutions to ailing subsidiaries. For example, Daehan Life Insurance, the third-largest life insurance company in South Korea, extended more than 3 trillion won of loans to subsidiaries of its parent company, in violation of regulations against connected lending. When these loans went sour, Daehan had to be bailed out by the government. Similarly, Daehan Merchant Bank and Dongseo Securities became insolvent as a result of extending credit to ailing parent and affiliated companies.

Given these incentives, as in Mexico, credit issued by financial institutions took off, expanding at an extremely rapid annual rate of 20% from 1992 to 1997. Real domestic credit more than quadrupled from 1988 to 1997, while domestic credit as a share of GDP rose from around 100% to nearly 200% of GDP (five times higher than the comparable number for Mexico just before its crisis).[10] This lending boom was fueled by massive foreign borrowing. From 1993 to 1996, gross external liabilities climbed from $67 billion to $165 billion; relative to GDP, they rose from 19.4% to 31.6%. That over half of the foreign borrowing was short term made the financial system even more vulnerable.[11]

With the lack of a credit culture and the laxity of prudential supervision, the lending boom was surely going to lead to bad loans. Remarkably (and, as it turns out, erroneously), official estimates of the ratio of nonperforming loans to total loans actually showed a decline from 1993 to 1996, suggesting that loan quality was improving up to 1996. Official estimates of the ratio of bank capital to total assets, however, did show a decline before the crisis, but the government estimates of the ratio of capital to assets remained above 4% (a comparable figure in the United States currently is around 7%).

Yet even these estimates were too favorable. In research that I conducted with Joon-Ho Hahm, we found that more accurately valued bank capital showed a deterioration on bank balance sheets, with the ratio of bank capital to total assets falling well below 4% by 1996.[12] The rosy picture of nonperforming loans and the bank balance sheets painted by bank supervisors provides further evidence of the laxity of bank supervision in Korea. Political pressure on bank supervisors led to regulatory forbearance: the supervisors were not forcing banking institutions to reveal their bad loans and were allowing insolvent institutions to stay in business. The incentives for these institutions to take on even more risk thus increased even further. Troubles in the banking sector were also reflected in the stock market: from 1994 onward, the bank stock index began to underperform the overall market index by a significant margin.

As in Mexico, considering what was going on in the financial sector, a Korean financial crisis was inevitable. But the exact timing of the crisis was influenced by when particular shocks occurred. First, the South Korean economy was hit by bad luck in its export markets. Depreciation of competing countries' currencies, such as the Japanese yen, meant that prices of major export goods, especially semiconductor chips, steel, and chemicals, fell significantly during this period. For example, the unit price of semiconductor chips fell by more than 70%, leading in part to an overall decline of 20% in the relative price of exports.[13]

The negative shock to export prices (a so-called negative terms-of-trade shock) hurt the already-thin profit margins of the chaebols and the small and medium-size firms that were tied to them, resulting in major corporate bankruptcies in 1997. The monthly average number of firms defaulting on promissory notes rose by nearly 50% in 1997.[14]

On January 23, 1997, a second major shock occurred, creating great uncertainty for the financial system: Hanbo, the fourteenth-largest chaebol, declared bankruptcy. This event signaled that the government was no longer able to maintain its "too big to fail" policy for chaebols and that the decline in the relative price of exports might require a large-scale restructuring of the corporate sector. Indeed, the bankruptcy of Hanbo was just the beginning. Five more of the thirty largest chaebols declared bankruptcy before the year was over.[15]

As a result of the greater uncertainty created by these bankruptcies and the deteriorating condition of financial and nonfinancial balance sheets, the stock market declined sharply. From a peak value of 980.9 at the end of April 1996, the South Korean stock market index (KOSPI) fell to 677.3 by the end of March 1997, a decrease of more than 30%. After this drop, the market recovered a little bit, but with the subsequent chaebol bankruptcies throughout 1997, the KOSPI continued to decline. Just before the outbreak of the currency crisis, it had dropped to 470.8, more than 50% below its peak a year and a half earlier.

The facts of the run-up to the Korean financial crisis nicely fit the asymmetric information story outlined in Chapter 4. The increase in uncertainty, the decrease in net worth that resulted from the stock market decline, and the deterioration in corporate balance sheets increased asymmetric information problems. It became harder to screen out good borrowers from bad; the decline in net worth decreased the value of firms' collateral and increased their incentives to make risky investments, because there was less equity to lose if the investments were unsuccessful. All of these events worsened adverse selection and moral hazard problems and made the South Korean economy ripe for a serious financial crisis.

Stage Three: Currency Crisis

Although South Korea did not officially have a fixed-exchange-rate system, the country in effect pegged its exchange rate within narrow bands through the Market Average Exchange Rate System, which it had instituted in 1990. As in Mexico, the effective exchange rate peg helped stimulate capital inflows, which added fuel to the fire of the lending boom, and promoted liability dollarization, which left the Korean economy highly vulnerable to a speculative attack on its currency.

Given the weakness of balance sheets in the financial sector and the increased exposure of the economy to a sudden stop in capital flows because of the large amount of short-term, external borrowing, a speculative attack on Korea's currency was inevitable. With the collapse of the Thai baht in July 1997 and the announced closing of forty-two finance companies in Thailand in early August 1997, contagion began to spread as participants in the market wondered whether similar problems existed in other East Asian countries. Soon speculators recognized that the banking sector in South Korea was in trouble. They knew that the Korean central bank could no longer defend the currency by raising interest rates, because this would sink the already weakened banks. Just as in the Mexican crisis, speculators were presented with a one-way bet and so pulled out of the Korean won, leading to a speculative attack.

The attack differed from those in Mexico and the other East Asian countries because at that time South Korea, unlike the other countries, did have some capital controls in place in the form of tight regulation on forward contracts. Furthermore, there was no currency futures market inside South Korea. Thus direct sales of Korean won were restricted. Instead of outright sales in currency markets, the attack was driven by a run on Korean financial institutions and chaebols by foreigners who were unwilling to roll over their loans and by foreign investors who wanted to exit the Korean stock market.

Just as the Mexican government used the tesobono gambit to delay the inevitable and to make its foreign exchange reserves look better than they were, the Koreans used their foreign exchange reserves to try to prop up their domestic banks. Because the Korean banks, faced with declining credit standing, were finding it increasingly difficult to refinance their foreign debt, the Bank of Korea, the central bank, encouraged by the Ministry of Finance, decided to prop up the banks by depositing its foreign exchange reserves in their foreign branches.[16] (The Bank of Korea thus aided and abetted the regulatory forbearance committed by the prudential supervisors, by giving the banks the funds to stay in business.) Because central bank foreign exchange reserves were already pledged to help Korean banks, they could not be used to defend the currency.

The Bank of Korea did not make its actions known. The amount of foreign exchange reserves it officially reported appeared to remain high, with little downward trend before the currency crisis. However, if one subtracts the reserves that the central bank deposited at foreign branches of domestic banks from the officially reported reserves, to obtain the usable amount of foreign exchange reserves, a downward trend becomes clear. Once foreign investors got wind that the official reserves number was meaningless, devastating rumors circulated about the actual size of usable foreign exchange reserves. Investors realized that the central bank no longer had the resources to defend the won and that its devaluation was inevitable. They started selling off their supplies of won, putting even more downward pressure on the currency's value.

(The tendency to hide the bad news of a decline in foreign exchange reserves during a currency crisis is not uncommon in emerging market countries. The Thai monetary authorities also hid the fact that they were running out of foreign exchange reserves to defend the currency by engaging in forward transactions in foreign exchange, which they did not report but which committed their foreign exchange reserves to others at a future date.)

The policy mistake of obscuring the true amount of usable foreign exchange reserves was compounded by another. The merchant banks were in particular trouble when the financial crisis started to unfold, because many of them had increased their lending to other East Asian countries (particularly Thailand) during 1995 and 1996 and now had substantial losses on this lending. Instead of closing these institutions down, the government encouraged commercial banks to lend to the merchant banks, while the Bank of Korea provided commercial banks with liquidity.[17] This policy had two negative outcomes. First, it signaled to the market that the Korean government was willing to bail out financial institutions without providing a serious plan to remedy the fragility of the banking sector. Restoring confidence in the financial system is crucial to promoting recovery, yet this policy did just the opposite: it suggested that the government would try to sweep the problems of the financial sector under the rug. Second, the expansion of liquidity by the central bank indicated that the bank would be unwilling to tighten monetary policy to defend the currency. Confidence in the government's willingness to take measures to strengthen the currency was weakened, thus making a greater depreciation of the won much more likely. And this is exactly what happened: from October until the end of 1997, the won depreciated by 47%.

Final Stage: Currency Crisis Triggers Full-Fledged Financial Crisis

The sharp depreciation of the won raised import prices, which feed directly into inflation, and weakened the credibility of the Bank of Korea as an inflation fighter. As a result, expected inflation rose. Market interest rates soared to over 20% by the end of 1997 to compensate for the higher inflation risk. They also rose because the Bank of Korea pursued a tight monetary policy in line with recommendations from the IMF. High interest rates caused investment and spending to fall. In addition, they led to a drop in cash flows, which forced firms to obtain external funds and increased adverse selection and moral hazard problems in the credit markets.

Although the depreciation also caused inflation to rise, it peaked at a little under 9%, far below the peak seen in Mexico (35%). Because inflation and interest rates came back down quickly, the damaging effects of higher interest rates on cash flow were much smaller and shorter-lived than in Mexico. These more transient effects are an important reason why South Korea's economic downturn was less severe.

Because both nonfinancial and financial firms had so much foreign-currency debt, the nearly 50% depreciation of the won led to a severe erosion of net worth. According to estimates from the Korea Stock Exchange, in the last two months of 1997 the loss as a result of the exchange rate devaluation amounted to 17.5 trillion won, nearly 20% of the entire equity capital for listed nonfinancial corporations in South Korea. This loss of net worth led to a severe increase in adverse selection and moral hazard problems in Korean financial markets, not only for domestic lenders but for foreigners as well. Domestic lending dried up while annual foreign portfolio investment inflows into South Korea, which had been on the order of $10 billion in 1996 before the crisis, now reversed; the annual outflows exceeded $2 billion in 1998.[18] The steep decline in domestic and foreign lending led to a sharp economic contraction: real annual GDP growth fell from 5.7% in the first half of 1997 to −5.4% in the second half of 1997.

As in Mexico, the deterioration in the cash flow and balance sheets of firms led to a worsening banking crisis. Bank balance sheets were devastated because the banks had to pay off their foreign-currency borrowing with more won and yet could not collect on the dollar-denominated loans they had made to domestic firms. In addition, the fact that financial institutions had been encouraged to make their foreign borrowing short term increased their liquidity problems, because they had to pay these loans back so quickly. The government stepped in to guarantee all bank deposits and prevent a bank panic, but the loss of capital meant that banks had to curtail their lending. The banking crisis sent the economy into a deeper, steeper tailspin.

The financial crisis hit the South Korean economy hard, and it experienced a negative growth rate of –5.8% in 1998. But there was a high human cost too. The ranks of the poor swelled from 6 million to over 10 million,[19] suicides and divorces jumped by nearly 50%, drug addiction climbed by 35%, and the crime rate rose by over 15%.[20]

Recovery

The downturn in South Korea was actually short-lived, and its recovery, which began by the end of 1998, was the strongest among all the emerging market countries that have experienced financial crises in recent years. What did South Korea do to reverse the situation so quickly?

South Korea clearly had some advantages going into its crisis, which helped the recovery. First, the South Korean economy was very open, with a large export sector. Many of the firms that had debts denominated in foreign currency also had the prices of their goods denominated in foreign currency. Thus firms whose won indebtedness increased because of the currency depreciation were mostly compensated by receiving higher prices in won for their goods. Second, South Korea's performance on inflation before the crisis had been quite good: inflation had remained below 5% and the country did not have a recent history of very high inflation, as did Mexico. As a result, the collapse of the won in late 1997 did not lead to a large surge in inflation, and so interest rates did not climb nearly as high as they did in Mexico. This meant that the negative effects on cash flow were much less than in countries like Mexico.

While initial conditions helped speed its recovery, the reaction of its government to the crisis was the key to South Korea's success after the crisis. Like Mexico, South Korea was the beneficiary of a large support package, on the order of $60 billion, arranged in December 1997 by the IMF, the World Bank and other development banks, and foreign governments. Given South Korea's strategic location and the presence of American troops there, a large U.S. support package for South Korea is no surprise. Finally, an eleventh-hour deal between South Korea and its major bank creditors was brokered, and this kept Korea's credit lines open and rescheduled its short-term debt, giving it more time to pay it back.[21] With this assistance, in early 1998 the Korean government was able to negotiate a rollover of $25 billion in short-term debt held by foreign banks, thus giving it breathing space to deal with the crisis.

The Korean government then put forth a remarkable effort to institute, extremely rapidly, a widespread set of financial reforms to deal with the crisis. These reforms promoted solid fundamentals that directly helped promote recovery. They also restored confidence and reduced uncertainty, thereby encouraging lending and spending. Higher lending and spending enabled the economy to begin growing again. How did this rapid reform take place?

Political Changes

The crisis in South Korea discredited powerful business interests and emboldened entrepreneurial reformers.[22] For example, nongovernmental organizations (NGOs) such as the People's Solidarity for Participatory Democracy, which had advocated reforms to improve corporate governance and had monitored progress in financial and corporate restructuring, came to the fore. By fortunate timing, national elections took place in December 1997, and South Koreans voted for change, throwing out the ruling Grand National Party and electing a new government headed by President Kim Dae-jung.

The Kim government embarked on a set of widespread reforms, which had the additional political benefit of reducing the power of the chaebols, who had been strong supporters of the former ruling party. The government was in the enviable position of doing good while doing well: its reforms would both strengthen the financial system and weaken the political opposition.

Although the new government coalition of the National Congress for New Politics and the United Liberal Democrats did not have a parliamentary majority, the Grand National Party was blamed for the financial crisis and so was unable to block the new government's reform initiatives. At the end of December, thirteen financial reform bills were pushed through the National Assembly, including an act establishing a new financial supervisory authority, the Financial Supervisory Commission (FSC). Existing supervisory agencies were consolidated into the Financial Supervisory Service (FSS), administered by the FSC. The FSC and FSS were given statutory authority to restructure financial institutions through write-offs of loans, mergers, suspensions, and closures of troubled financial institutions. In addition the Korea Asset Management Corporation (KAMCO) was provided with a fund to resolve nonperforming loans by purchasing them from financial institutions. The Bank of Korea was also given more independence from the government, thus enabling it to take stronger measures to control inflation.

President Kim then used the bully pulpit to get the Korean public to support financial reform. In January 1998 he conducted a highly publicized meeting with business leaders to argue for corporate restructuring emphasizing transparency, accountability, and financial soundness. The government also campaigned to get ordinary Koreans to contribute their personal holdings of gold to help cope with the crisis. President Kim conducted televised town hall meetings, in which he urged Koreans to work together to overcome the national crisis. And, strikingly, he never played the "blame the foreigner" card during the crisis. He made it clear that the source of the crisis was not evil foreigners but the bad policies of the Korean government and Korean businesses. His approach thus contrasted sharply with, for example, that of Dr. Mohamad Mahathir, the prime minister of Malaysia, who blamed his country's crisis on foreign speculators. Where Mahathir's pronouncements weakened confidence that the government would take the proper steps to reform the economy, Kim Dae-jung's strengthened it.

The resulting rapid restoration of confidence had immediate effects on the economy. In early 1998 the won stabilized and began to recover, regaining half the value it had lost by the end of that year. At the same time, interest rates began to decline, and, by the end of 1998, they were actually lower than they had been prior to the crisis. The rebound of the won helped repair some of the damage done to balance sheets by the prior devaluation, thus reducing asymmetric information problems in the credit markets. In addition, lower interest rates directly stimulated spending and helped improve firms' cash flows, which diminished adverse selection and moral hazard problems. These stimulative forces led to a recovery in the economy later in the year, and economic growth resumed.

Financial Reform: Restructuring and Recapitalizing

With the political structure to sustain reforms in place, the government got to work on restructuring and recapitalizing the financial system. First it assessed the problem in the financial sector. Before the crisis, government supervisors had been lax in classifying loans as nonperforming, identifying them as such only after payments were over six months past due. In March 1998 the government began to follow internationally accepted standards, classifying as nonperforming those loans whose payments were three months overdue; this doubled the estimate of nonperforming loans to a face value of 118 trillion won, around 28% of GDP.[23] In June 1998 the government closed five insolvent banks; seven others were required to submit plans for restructuring by the end of July 1998 (five of these eventually merged into other banks). Between 1997 and 2001, KAMCO purchased 101 trillion won of nonperforming loans for 39 trillion won. Eventually the government injected close to 160 trillion won ($130 billion, about 30% of GDP)[24] into the financial system and closed or merged out of existence 617 financial institutions.[25]

The resulting consolidation of the financial system was enormous. Most striking is that the infamous merchant banks, which had played so prominent a role in the crisis, were almost entirely eliminated. Of the thirty merchant banks that had existed before the crisis, twenty-two were closed outright and six were merged into other institutions. By June 2002, only three merchant banks were left, two survivors and one new entry.

The commercial banking industry also underwent substantial consolidation. The number of commercial banks shrank from twenty-six in 1997 to fifteen in 2001, a decrease of over 40%. The number of employees also shrank by 40%, from 114,000 to 68,000. However, this reduction in the number of banks and employees was not the result of a contraction in the banking sector. Bank assets in 2001, at 641 trillion won, were 6% higher than before the crisis.[26] This slight increase in the size of the banking sector, with a 40% reduction in the number of workers, signaled a huge increase in bank efficiency and productivity.

The banking system returned to health. By the end of 2001, nonperforming loans had fallen to 3.3% of assets, from a peak of 13.6%.[27] Capital in Korean banks now exceeds the international standards mandated by the Bank for International Settlements by over 2 percentage points, and the banks once again became profitable in 2001, with an average return on assets nearing 1% and a return on equity of 16%. These numbers not only exceeded those before the crisis, they are comparable to returns we see today in the United States.

The recapitalization of the financial sector was rapid indeed. Compare how quickly the South Koreans restructured and recapitalized their banking system to what the Japanese have done (or not done) in recent years. For over ten years after the bursting of the Japanese economic bubble in 1990 (which led to a huge number of nonperforming loans), the Japanese government was unwilling to pursue policies to restore the banking system to health. It is only in the past year or so that the system has begun to recover and has begun lending again. Even the United States didn't come to grips with problems in its banking sector for a long time. The need for restructuring and recapitalization of the U.S. banking sector, especially the savings and loans, was clear by the mid-1980s, and yet the process did not start in earnest until 1989 and then took several more years to complete.[28]

Other Financial Reforms

The Korean government did not stop with restructuring and recapitalizing the banking system. It also instituted reforms to cope with moral hazard in the financial and nonfinancial sectors. The government recognized that, to reduce incentives for banks to engage in risky lending, it had to introduce a more forward-looking approach to classifying loans, one which took into account the potential future performance of borrowers. In December 1999 bank regulators made banks adopt forward-looking criteria for assessing risk, including managerial competence, future cash flow, and the financial condition of the borrower. Loans had to be classified as substandard when the ability of the borrower to make debt payments was deemed considerably weakened. In March

2000 the forward-looking criteria were further enhanced so that loans could be classified as nonperforming when future risks were high, even if no interest payments were overdue.

Before the crisis, the government had signaled that it would protect all depositors from any losses, and this is exactly what it did after the crisis. As we have seen, this policy created incentives for banks to take on excessive risk by reducing the incentives for depositors to monitor banks. To reduce these incentives, as part of the reform package the government also overhauled the deposit insurance system. All deposit insurance was consolidated under the Korea Deposit Insurance Corporation (KDIC) in 1998, and, starting in January 2001, the amount of deposits that would be insured by the KDIC was limited to 50 million won (around $40,000), substantially less than the $100,000 limit in the United States.

The government also made clear that it would no longer guarantee that large corporations would not be allowed to fail. By the end of 1999, of the thirty largest chaebols that had existed before the crisis, fourteen were allowed to go bankrupt or had to be restructured. Through corporate reorganizations (both court-ordered and those handled out of court), the managements of many chaebols were thrown out, and controlling shareholders saw their equity stakes written down or wiped out altogether.

The government's handling of Daewoo, one of the five largest chaebols, made it clear that the business environment had changed. At the onset of the crisis, the government indicated that the top five chaebols would be shielded from out-of-court restructurings, thereby offering these firms an implicit guarantee against bankruptcy. Given this guarantee, Daewoo which was in deep trouble after the crisis, was still able to issue 17 trillion won of new corporate bonds and commercial paper up until September 1998. To constrain Daewoo's expansion of debt, in October of that year the government imposed caps on the amount of corporate bonds from any single chaebol that could be held by financial institutions: 10% of capital for banks and 15% for investment trust companies. Finally, in August 1999, the "too big to fail" doctrine for chaebols was laid to rest when the government allowed Daewoo to go broke. The government did step in to bail out small investors, giving them 95% of the face value of Daewoo's bonds. But the fact that those investors still sustained a loss of 5% marked an important departure from the past. The failure of Daewoo ended up threatening the health of investment trust companies, which held a large number of Daewoo's bonds, and the government did bail them out. Thus the government did not eliminate *all* guarantees against losses from holding debt issued by large corporations, but it did limit the guarantees.

The demise of the "too big to fail" doctrine has caused a sea change in the way investors view Korean corporations. Knowing that they can be subjected to losses has increased their incentives to monitor corporations and pull their money out if a corporation is taking on too much risk. In addition, in July 2000 the government required all investment funds to mark the value of their assets to market prices, so that they would have to reveal losses at an earlier stage. All of these steps have reduced moral hazard incentives in South Korean financial markets and are helping to promote a credit culture in which individuals and financial institutions have the incentives to screen out good credit risks from bad and to monitor firms to ensure that they do not take on excessive risk once they have received funds. Not surprisingly, financial institutions have been more cautious in lending to large corporations. However, overall bank lending has not been scaled back. It has recovered to precrisis levels, but it has shifted to include consumer and housing loans, promoting financial deepening in those markets. By the end of 2001, the share of corporate lending in the stock of won-denominated bank loans had fallen below 50%, from a high of 75% at the end of 1996.

Corporate Reforms

The Korean government has also taken measures to strengthen corporate governance. These include the compulsory appointment of outside directors, regulations on external audits, compliance with international standards of accounting, requirements for audit committees and upgrading of internal accounting and compliance systems, reform of accounting standards, and strengthening of minority shareholders' rights.[29]

Increased Globalization

The government has continued down the path of financial globalization. It has liberalized foreign exchange transactions to more fully open its capital markets and has adopted a floating-exchange-rate regime in which the won is allowed to go to its market clearing level. (However, the government still intervenes by buying and selling won in the foreign exchange market.) Restrictions on mergers and acquisitions of Korean firms by foreigners have been abolished, and foreigners are now allowed to invest in the Korean bond and stock markets. As a result the share of market capitalization in the Korean stock market owned by foreign investors doubled from 1997 to 2001, reaching 37%. Restrictions on foreign direct investment have been reduced in both the financial and nonfinancial sectors. For example, Newbridge Capital, an American investment fund, was allowed to purchase Korea First Bank, and the new management made radical changes in the operations of the bank, even going so far as to refuse to support government initiatives to continue extending credit to troubled firms.

Opening up the South Korean financial markets to foreigners has helped bring best practices to the financial sector and has stimulated a convergence of accounting and governance standards with those of advanced countries. The result has been a substantial expansion of Korean capital markets since the crisis. The market capitalization of the Korean stock market more than doubled from 146 trillion won at the end of 1998 to 308 trillion won at the end of 2001; over the same period the Korean bond market increased from 336 trillion won to 483 trillion won.[30]

All of these measures have produced a Korean capital market in which there is an improved assessment of risk and capital is flowing to more productive uses. The Korean financial system is becoming more like its counterpart in the United States, in which markets play a more prominent role. Not only has this helped restore confidence in the Korean financial system, which has stimulated lending and spending, it is leading to a more efficient Korean economy. Both of these effects are a key reason why South Korea had the strongest recovery among all countries that have experienced financial crises in recent years.

The Need for Further Reform

By 2001, with the economy recovered, the South Korean reform process began to slow markedly, and there has even been some backsliding, with barriers raised to foreign investors and financial institutions. Reform fatigue has set in. South Korea cannot afford to be complacent, however, because it still has a long way to go to develop financial markets on a par with those in advanced countries. It has made substantial progress in improving regulation and supervision of the banking sector, but banks still do not have strong enough risk management capabilities, and this is especially important given their shift into new businesses. The reform process has been less successful in the nonbank financial sector. Insurance companies continue to be weak and undercapitalized, as are securities firms and nonbank deposit-taking institutions such as credit unions. Insulation of supervisors from political pressure and from threats of lawsuits by financial institutions—both of which may induce them not to do their jobs properly —is still weak.[31]

Although corporate governance has improved dramatically in South Korea, it is still far behind what it needs to be. This is manifest in the so-called Korea discount, the low valuations of Korean stocks relative to what the valuations would be if management were more focused on maximizing shareholder value.[32] Auditing and accounting practices are also not sufficiently developed, and corporate disclosure is not strong.

To reach the next stage of development and achieve its dream of becoming one of the richest countries in the world, South Korea has to complete its reform process. If it does so and develops a financial system that is up to the standard of those found in Europe and North America, and in Asian economies like Hong Kong, Singapore, Taiwan, and Australia, there will be no stopping South Korea. The drive and high educational attainment of its population will then have enormous payoffs, and South Korea may even give the United States a run for its money.

The Role of the IMF and the World Bank

The international financial institutions (IFIs) in Washington, D.C., the IMF and the World Bank, are often seen as villains who have created great hardship in emerging market countries, but in the Korean case they were the unsung heroes. Although the Korean government had the will to clean up the country's financial system, it did not know how to do it. The IMF and the World Bank provided extensive technical assistance. Experts from these organizations supplied the South Korean authorities with basic frameworks within which the restructuring and recapitalization of the financial sector could be carried out effectively. They also recognized that the Korean authorities could benefit from the experience of other countries that had been through major financial crises, and they chose three of them: Sweden, Chile, and Mexico. They brought in consultants from these countries to outline what worked and what didn't in their bank restructuring. They asked experts in corporate restructuring from Mexico to help the Koreans fix on a strategy for restructuring the failed chaebols. They also used the carrot of technical assistance and the stick of threatening to hold back funds to provide incentives for the Korean government to make the hard decisions that politicians sometimes find so difficult.

What is also clear from my discussions with staff at the IFIs is that they established a partnership with the Korean authorities. They recognized that they needed to work together not only at the technical level but also at the political level. They understood the need to listen to the political authorities; even though they sometimes felt that a given strategy would produce better outcomes, that strategy might not have been politically feasible. If the right thing to do is politically infeasible, it is not likely to work in practice.

Despite a common criticism that the IMF and the World Bank have been misguided and incompetent in helping countries emerge from crisis, I formed a totally different impression when I visited South Korea in September 2000 as a member of an international advisory board to the FSS. I was struck by how appreciative Korean officials were of the help they received from the IFIs. Clearly the money had helped, but they indicated that without the technical support they would have been far less successful in restructuring and recapitalizing the financial sector. They also told me that they often were able to overcome political resistance against doing the right thing only because of the stick that the IFIs carried. This does not mean that there were no criticisms of IMF policies. The tight monetary and fiscal policies recommended by the IMF were, and still are, controversial, as we will see in later chapters. The success of South Korea was primarily due to the willingness of government officials to reform the financial system, but without the assistance of the IMF and the World Bank the reform process would have been far less successful.

Lessons from the Korean Crisis

The story of the Korean crisis drives home many of the themes we encountered in the Mexican crisis, which will motivate policy prescriptions in later chapters. First, the financial liberalization process led to a blowup of the South Korean economy because there was inadequate prudential regulation and supervision to limit risk taking, a perverse approach to opening up to foreign capital flows, an effective pegged-exchange-rate regime that encouraged a speculative attack, and extensive liability dollarization, which meant that balance sheets would be devastated by a currency crisis. Second, international standards for banking regulation designed for advanced countries did not work well in the Korean context. Third, a rapid response to the crisis, including reforms, had high payoffs because it restored confidence quickly, helping explain why South Korea's recovery was so much stronger than those of other countries that have experienced similar crises. Finally, successful recovery from a financial crisis in an emerging market country can be facilitated by a successful collaboration of the country's government with the IMF and the World Bank.

Seven

Argentina, 2001–2002

The story of Argentina is the most depressing of all the case studies in this book.
Argentina did many things right in developing a financial system that would
promote economic growth. Unfortunately these efforts were not enough to
ensure success for this emerging market economy. Structural problems in the
Argentine economy, a failure to deal with fiscal problems, and some bad luck,
which weakened macroeconomic fundamentals, led to a financial crisis that
was far more devastating in a more long-lasting way than the crises in Mexico and South Korea.

Macroeconomic Fundamentals before the Crisis

Argentina's sad story begins with the high hopes engendered by a major
shift in economic policy under the presidential administration of Carlos
Menem: the adoption of the Convertibility Plan in April 1991.[1]

The Convertibility Plan

After a bout of hyperinflation in which inflation rose above 2000% in 1990,
Argentina, under its minister of the economy, Domingo Cavallo, embarked on
a bold plan of reform with the enactment of the Convertibility Law in April
1991. This law put in place a strong commitment to fixing the exchange rate
of the Argentine peso, called a currency board. A currency board fixes the

exchange rate (at one peso to one U.S. dollar in the case of Argentina) and requires that the central bank stand ready to exchange the domestic currency for the foreign currency (or vice versa) at this rate whenever the public requests it.[2] Convertibility was intended to stop inflation in its tracks, and Cavallo, the plan's designer, hoped it would also produce institutional reform in fiscal policy, labor markets, and bank regulation to improve the Argentine economy.

A key feature of the currency board was that discretionary monetary policy was no longer possible. The monetary authorities could not expand or contract the money supply through their own policy decisions because they were bound by the Convertibility Law to exchange pesos for dollars at the one-to-one rate. Because the monetary authorities were no longer able to conduct an independent monetary policy, the labor markets and product markets would need to become more flexible in order to deal with shocks to the economy that would otherwise be addressed by monetary policy. For example, if aggregate demand fell, an expansionary monetary policy was no longer an option, so wages and prices would need to be adjusted downward to restore the economy to full employment. Thus labor market reform became necessary, to increase the flexibility of the economy so it could respond appropriately to negative shocks. This provided an impetus for change in the well-known rigidity of Argentine labor and product markets.

Convertibility also meant that the monetary authorities no longer had the option to expand the money supply (a practice often referred to as "printing money") to buy government bonds to finance deficits, thus limiting the ability of the government to pursue irresponsible fiscal policies. If the government could no longer finance its spending by having the central bank print money, there would be a greater need for the government to get its fiscal house in order. The hope was that convertibility would force reforms that would put the government on the path to fiscal responsibility.

Since the monetary authorities could no longer print money, convertibility also meant that they would lose the ability to act as the "lender of last resort," that is, they could no longer provide liquidity to the banking system to prop it up if it got into trouble. Without the backstop of a lender of last resort, there would be a greater need to put the financial system on a sounder footing. The impetus for banking sector reforms would be strengthened, making banks sounder and more efficient, and thus promoting financial deepening.

Convertibility was a gamble to promote institutional reform that would kill four birds with one stone: it would (1) keep inflation under control, (2) promote banking reform to strengthen the financial system, (3) make labor and product markets more flexible, and (4) promote fiscal responsibility. Convertibility did, for a time, help kill the first two birds, but it did not even wing the last two. Inflexibility and irresponsibility, along with vulnerabilities that the Convertibility Plan itself created, led to the downfall of the Argentine economy.

The Initial Success of the Convertibility Plan: Inflation Control

In its initial phase, the Convertibility Plan delivered everything that had been hoped for on the inflation front. With the peso tied to the U.S. dollar, inflation in Argentina rapidly decreased toward U.S. levels. From a high of 2300% in 1990 it fell to below 5% by 1994.* Economic growth was also rapid: for the four years from 1991 to 1994, real output grew at an average of 7.6% per year, although some of the growth reflected the economy's rebound from its sorry state prior to the introduction of convertibility.[3] This rate was well above that in the rest of Latin America (which averaged 4.3% over the same period) and was comparable to the growth rates in Asia. On the macroeconomic front, convertibility was a spectacular success.

The Tequila Crisis

When the Mexican financial crisis, the so-called Tequila Crisis, started with the collapse of the peso in December 1994, there was fear that Argentina's peso might also collapse. As the public rushed to exchange Argentine pesos for U.S. dollars, Argentina suffered a run on its currency. The central bank had to buy pesos to prop up the value so that the currency board would survive, and the resulting decline in the quantity of pesos held by the public led to a sharp drop in the money supply. With less liquidity in the economy, interest rates rose. At first depositors in Argentine banks just switched their peso deposits into dollar deposits. But when they became concerned about the liquidity of the banking system, they began to pull their money out of the banks whether the deposits were denominated in dollars or in pesos, and a run on the banks began. Within a couple of weeks, bank deposits fell by 18%, and both the banking system and the currency board looked like they might collapse. At this point the IMF came to the rescue with a package of $1.5 billion to help support both the peso and the banking system, and both the currency board and the banking system survived.

The Argentine economy did not emerge unscathed, however. The rise in interest rates made financing more expensive, so spending fell. Because firms had to pay more to finance their debt, the interest rate increase also reduced firms' internal cash flows, forcing more firms to seek funds in external financial markets. Adverse selection and moral hazard problems were likely to be severe in these external markets because potential lenders did not know the firms well. Furthermore, the decline in bank deposits meant that banks had fewer resources to lend and so were less able to use their expertise to cope with adverse selection and moral hazard problems in the credit markets. The com-

---

*Figures that display the data on macroeconomic fundamentals and outline the sequence of events before the crisis are on pages 110–11.

bination of these forces led to a decline in lending and spending, which sent the Argentine economy into a recession. From its 1991–94 average of 7.6%, Argentina's annual growth fell to –2.8% in 1995.[4]

Financial Reform in the Aftermath of the Tequila Crisis

The close call from the Tequila Crisis made clear to Argentineans that the central bank could not shore up the banking system by acting as a lender of last resort. Argentinean officials recognized the need to strengthen their financial system to make it less vulnerable to contagion. A talented group of technocrats at the central bank, led by its president Roque Fernández, began to develop new regulatory frameworks to overhaul the banking system.

They created one of the most innovative bank regulation and supervisory regimes in the world. They called it BASIC: *bonos* (bonds), *auditoria* (auditing), *supervisión consolidada* (consolidated supervision), *información* (information), and *calificadoras de riesgo* (risk rating).[5] The BASIC system went further than supervisory systems in advanced countries by taking an explicit multifaceted approach to bank supervision with its five elements: (1) the requirement that banks issue subordinated debt, which is paid off after all other debt and so provides more sensitive price signals about the amount of risk the bank is taking; (2) a program to ensure adequate internal and external audits of banks; (3) consolidated supervision of financial conglomerates; (4) a program to increase the quality and dissemination of information; and (5) the requirement that every bank have an annual rating of its credit risk by a rating agency registered with the central bank. In addition to the BASIC system, the Argentine bank regulatory system instituted capital requirements that were even more stringent than the international standards in the Basel Accord. The regulatory system also had strict liquidity requirements, which by 1998 required the banks to hold 20% of short-term deposits (those with maturities under ninety days) in safe and liquid international assets or as interest-bearing deposits at the central bank.

In the aftermath of the Tequila Crisis, Argentina also passed a banking law that improved the system for closing down banks.[6] As a result, between 1995 and 2000, Argentine regulators were able to close down twenty troubled banks, some of them quite large, and the Argentine banking system underwent substantial consolidation, going from 166 banks in 1994 to 89 in 2000.[7] The government arranged the privatization of sixteen provincial state-owned banks, leading to a 50% reduction in the number of state-owned banks. To further strengthen the banking system, the Argentine authorities encouraged the entry of foreign banks (mostly Spanish), a step that increased their share of total bank assets from 15% in 1994 to over 70% in 2000.[8] Argentina also enacted a new bankruptcy law that provided a better basis for rehabilitation or liquidation of corporations, and it instituted reforms to improve the enforcement of creditor rights.

Figure 7.1. Macroeconomic Fundamentals in Argentina before the Crisis, 1990–1998

After enactment of the Convertibility Law in April 1991, inflation fell precipitously...

A. Inflation, 1990–1998 (percent)

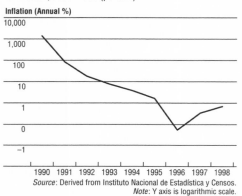

Source: Derived from Instituto Nacional de Estadística y Censos.
Note: Y axis is logarithmic scale.

...and economic growth was rapid.

B. Real GDP Growth, 1990–1998 (percent)

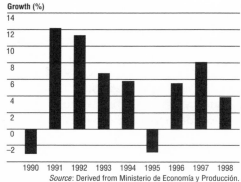

Source: Derived from Ministerio de Economía y Producción.

The Mexican Crisis led to a run on the Argentine peso, which led to a rise in interest rates, ...

C. Interest Rates, 1993–1998 (percent)

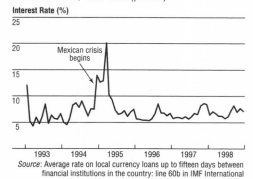

Source: Average rate on local currency loans up to fifteen days between financial institutions in the country: line 60b in IMF International Financial Statistics.

...and concerns about the health of the banking system led to a sharp decline in bank deposits.

D. Bank Deposits, 1991–1998 (billions of pesos)

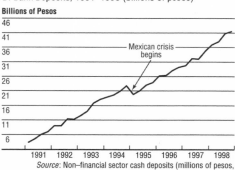

Source: Non–financial sector cash deposits (millions of pesos, not seasonally adjusted): Banco Central de la República Argentina Boletín Estadístico.

After the Mexican Crisis, the government improved banking supervision, and financial deepening occurred.

E. Private Credit as Percentage of GDP, 1990–1998

Private Credit as Percentage of GDP

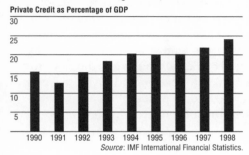

Source: IMF International Financial Statistics.

Instead of falling, the degree of liability dollarization increased.

F. Percentage of Credit Denominated in U.S. Dollars, 1990–1998

Percentage of Credit Denominated in U.S. Dollars

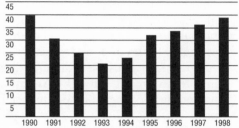

Source: Total external debt less total international reserves as percentage of nominal gross domestic product: line 99b in IMF International Financial Statistics.

During good times, the Argentine government did not exercise tight fiscal management, and the ratio of debt to GDP rose.

G. Public Debt as Percentage of GDP, 1992–1998

Public Debt as Percentage of GDP

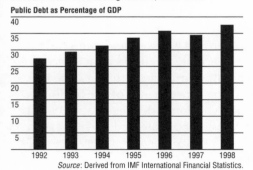

Source: Derived from IMF International Financial Statistics.

As a result of these reforms, by 1998 the World Bank ranked Argentina second among emerging market economies for the quality of its regulatory environment (behind Singapore, tied with Hong Kong, and ahead of Chile).[9] In addition, the Bank assessed Argentina's compliance with insolvency and creditor rights to be consistent with its principles.[10]

Given these financial reforms it is not surprising that financial deepening occurred. The ratio of credit to GDP rose from less than 15% in 1991 to over 30% by 1999.[11] The banking system became far sounder and more resilient. The BASIC system of prudential supervision made excessive risk taking by banks far less likely. It is striking that, even after two years of recession and increased loan losses, the balance sheets of Argentine banks were still quite healthy in 2000. The amount of bank capital relative to assets, even after loan write-offs, remained in excess of 10% (high by international standards), and bank capital relative to risk-weighted assets was well in excess of requirements under the Basel Accord. Banks also bought insurance against deposit outflows by arranging for credit lines from international banks (although this did not protect them later, because the international banks stopped providing these credit lines when times got tough). Argentineans could be proud of the strengthening and development of their financial system. But convertibility had imposed hidden vulnerabilities.

The Seeds of Destruction Sown during Good Times: Dollarization, Imprudent Fiscal Policy, and Labor and Product Market Inflexibility

In 1996 the Argentine economy began to recover, with output growing at an annual rate of more than 5% and inflation continuing to fall. Yet, despite the extraordinary strides on the inflation and financial development fronts, all was not well.

Dollarization. In the discussion of the Mexican and Korean crises, we saw that a pegged exchange rate made their economies more fragile because it encouraged liability dollarization, the use of a foreign currency (in this case the U.S. dollar) to denominate debt transactions. One consequence of convertibility, which provides a strong ("hard") peg for the domestic currency, is that it encouraged liability dollarization: the percentage of private credit denominated in dollars rose from below 50% in the early 1990s to over 60%; for credit to the public sector this percentage rose to over 90%.

This increase in financial dollarization left the Argentine economy far more vulnerable to an exchange rate shock. Argentina was (and still is) a fairly closed economy, with a small export sector that prices its goods in foreign currency. With most debt denominated in dollars, a devaluation of the peso would lead to the insolvency of many firms: their debt would increase in terms of pesos, but the value of their assets (their products) would not, because they were priced in pesos. Particularly problematic was the banks' tendency to lend in dollars to firms in the nontradable sector—over 75% of the debt for non-tradable firms was denominated in dollars.[12] If the peso fell in value, nontradable firms would be unable to pay the banks back, and there would be a sharp decline in bank capital.

Although the Argentine regulators had gone beyond the international regulatory capital standards called for in the Basel Accord, they did not force banks to take into account the fact that, if convertibility were abandoned, they would be highly exposed to currency risk even if they had matched books with equal amounts of dollar-denominated assets and liabilities. As in Mexico and South Korea, a depreciation of the domestic currency would devastate bank balance sheets, because the banks would now have to pay back their dollar liabilities with more pesos and yet could not be repaid on the dollar-denominated loans they had made to domestic firms.

Argentine regulators were not as likely to attempt to limit currency risk arising from liability dollarization because they were following international standards that did not focus on currency risk. The Basel standards had been developed primarily for banks in advanced countries. These countries do not suffer from currency risk arising from liability dollarization because loans there are generally denominated in domestic currency.

Another reason why the regulatory authorities may not have put in place prudential regulations to discourage the use of dollarized debt was to avoid suggesting that they lacked confidence in the currency board arrangement. After all, if they forced banks to hedge against losses that might occur from a collapse of the peso's value, wouldn't this mean that the government doubted its ability to stick to convertibility? The government may have issued mostly dollar-denominated debt to demonstrate its commitment to the one-for-one peg, since abandoning the peg would have left the government with a higher debt burden.

International capital standards as represented by the Basel Accord also did not take account of the riskiness of government bonds. The accord had a weighting scheme for measuring bank risk according to which government bonds were classified as being the least risky of all assets that a bank could hold. This classification makes sense for the virtually default-free government bonds of advanced countries, but it is inappropriate for emerging market countries, whose government debt can be highly risky—as the banks in Argentina later found out. Following international capital standards thus did not provide sufficient controls for keeping risk low at Argentine banks. Argentina's predicament again illustrates one of the main lessons in looking at emerging market countries: what works in advanced economies may not work in emerging market economies. The differences between the economies of advanced and emerging market countries must always be kept in mind in designing policies in the latter.

Imprudent Fiscal Policy. The second vulnerability of the Argentine economy was on the fiscal front. In contrast to advanced countries, emerging market countries have often defaulted on their sovereign debt (government debt sold in international markets). As a result, investors are much less forgiving of fiscal imbalances: they will pull their money out of sovereign debt issued by emerging market countries when the ratio of debt to GDP is far lower than in advanced countries. This feature of markets for the debt of these countries is sometimes referred to as "debt intolerance."[13] Debt intolerance often leads to a default because the emerging country's debt, which is generally very short-term and so comes due frequently, cannot be rolled over. Thus emerging market countries have to be particularly vigilant in controlling their government budget deficits so they can avoid investor flight from their sovereign debt. During bad times, when GDP falls and tax revenue declines, deficits naturally rise, and the ratio of debt to GDP rises. To provide a cushion against bad times, emerging market countries must keep a tight lid on fiscal policy during good times and reduce or keep their debt-to-GDP ratios under 35%, well below levels often reached in advanced countries. Only if the debt-to-GDP ratio is kept low during good times will its rise during bad times leave it at a sustainable level. If this ratio is kept at a reasonable level, investors won't pull out and a default will not occur.

As forcefully argued by Michael Mussa, the former chief economist of the IMF, who was in the trenches there from 1991 to 2001, this is not what the Argentine authorities did.[14] From 1993 to 1998, while the Argentine economy had a robust average annual growth rate of 4.4%, the ratio of government debt to GDP rose from 29.2% to 41.4%. (Also contributing to the growth of government debt was a pension reform adopted in 1993–94 that increased fiscal deficits in the short run, even though it would put finances on a sounder footing over the long term.)[15] This government debt increase was even more dangerous because most of the debt was denominated in dollars, and it and the debt-to-GDP ratio would jump dramatically in value if the peso depreciated significantly (as it eventually did).

There are two reasons why Argentine fiscal policy was profligate. First, federal government spending increased under President Menem, who wanted to continue to be reelected despite constitutional barriers and was successful in this endeavor in 1995. (His attempt to run for reelection to a third term in 1999, however, was unsuccessful when it was declared unconstitutional, and corruption accusations against him forced him to leave the country.)

Second, Argentina has always had difficulty keeping its budgets under control because of the fiscal relationship between its provinces (similar to states in the United States) and the federal government.[16] In Argentina the provinces have control of a large percentage of public spending, but the responsibility for raising the revenue is left primarily to the federal government. With this system, the provinces have incentives to spend beyond their means and the federal government is called on periodically to assume responsibility for provincial debt. As a result, Argentina is perennially in deficit. Contrast this with the system in the United States, in which state and local governments are responsible for raising the revenue to pay for their spending, and there is a federal government policy of not bailing them out. As a result, state and local governments typically balance their budgets.

It was hoped that the Convertibility Plan would encourage fiscal responsibility in Argentina, but this did not happen. Instead the plan made the fiscal situation worse because it made it easier for the government to borrow foreign funds.[17] External government debt rose from $52 billion in 1993 to $77 billion in 1998, an increase of 48%, while nominal GDP during this same period increased by only 26%.

Even during the good times up until 1998, Argentina's government was increasing its debt burden, signaling that the country was incapable of fiscal discipline. If bad times came, the markets would surely get nervous about the ability of Argentina to repay its debt, and a debt crisis would ensue.

Labor and Product Market Inflexibility. The third vulnerability of the Argentine economy was the continuing rigidity of its labor and product markets, given the fixed exchange rate under the Convertibility Plan. Labor market rules in Argentina, similar to those in Europe, make it hard to fire workers or lower their pay if the firm faces reduced demand for its products or encounters financial difficulties. Despite the hope that convertibility would lead to labor market reforms that would make wages and employment policies more flexible, such reforms did not occur. Similarly, reforms to promote competition in Argentine product markets were not forthcoming, and these markets also remained rigid. With the peso fixed to the dollar one for one, if the dollar appreciated relative to the currencies of Argentina's trade partners, the peso would appreciate as well, making Argentine industry less competitive. Given the rigid labor and product markets, wages and prices in Argentina would not be able to adjust downward, leading to declining demand and rising unemployment. Alternatively, if Argentina experienced a negative shock to its terms of trade (a decline in the demand for Argentina's exports relative to imports), demand for Argentine production would fall. Again, rigid wages and product prices would lead to a decline in output and higher unemployment.

Stage One: Severe Fiscal Imbalances

Toward the end of 1997, bad luck hit Argentina, exposing the vulnerabilities of the convertibility system. The economy was hit by four negative shocks. In mid-1997, the U.S. dollar began to appreciate, and by early 1999 it had appreciated by 15%.[18] With the Argentine peso fixed one for one with the dollar, it also had to appreciate, making Argentine goods more expensive relative to those of its trading partners.[19] The second shock was a decline in the terms of trade, as demand fell for such Argentine exports as edible oils, wheat, corn, and aluminum.[20] The third negative shock hit in the fall of 1998, when the Russian financial crisis led to a decline in capital inflows. The fourth shock hit in early 1999, when Argentina's most important trade partner, Brazil, experienced a foreign exchange crisis. By the end of January, the value of the Brazilian real had fallen by over a third.[21] The collapse of the real, which lowered the price of Brazilian goods relative to those from Argentina, made Argentine industry even less competitive. The situation only worsened when the U.S. dollar appreciated by another 10% in 2000 and 2001, taking the peso with it. By 2000 the peso was estimated to be overvalued (above its long-run equilibrium value) by as much as 50%.[22] The Argentine export sector was having trouble selling its goods, while the lower price of imports further decreased demand for Argentine products.

When capital suddenly stopped flowing into Argentina after the Russian crisis and the collapse of the Brazilian real, the resulting shortage of loanable funds drove interest rates sky high: the rates on Argentine sovereign bonds rose from below 500 basis points (5 percentage points) above U.S. Treasuries to well over 1000 basis points above them. Although this interest rate spread later decreased, it still remained above 500 basis points in 1999 and 2000.* The high interest rates arising from the sudden stop of capital inflows and the uncompetitive tradable goods prices due to the peso's appreciation put the economy into a prolonged recession. Output fell by 3.4% in 1999 and declined by about 2% per year in 2000 and 2001. Unemployment rose from near 13% in 1998 to over 15% in 2000.

By 2000 the weak economy had made the fiscal situation in Argentina unsustainable. The new administration of president Fernando de la Rúa tried to restore growth and get budget deficits under control, but it was unsuccessful. The recession meant that tax revenue was falling, and so budget deficits increased. In addition, the decline in GDP meant that the ratio of debt to GDP was rising. The Argentine economy had now entered a "growth-debt trap" in which low economic growth dramatically reduced the likelihood of the government being able to pay back its debt.

Given the higher probability of default, investors naturally required a higher interest rate on Argentine debt to compensate them for their increased risk. The resulting higher interest payments added to government expenditures, and deficits rose even higher, as did the ratio of debt to GDP. The higher debt-to-GDP ratio caused interest rates to rise further, and so on and so on. The growth-debt trap meant that the spread between the interest rate on Argentine sovereign debt and U.S. Treasury debt would spiral upward, leading to an eventual default.

*Figures that display the data and outline the sequence of events during the Argentine financial crisis are on pages 118–19.

In December 2000 the IMF stepped in with a bailout package of around $12 billion in new funds for Argentina (although the announced package was for a possible disbursement of up to $40 billion). There was a brief drop in the spread between Argentine sovereign debt and U.S. Treasury debt, but the Argentine government was still not able to get its fiscal house in order. In March 2001, the minister of the economy, Ricardo López Murphy, resigned after only two weeks in office because of strong opposition to his fiscal austerity plan. The interest rate spread resumed its relentless climb.

Stage Two: Run-up to the Currency Crisis

At this point, President de la Rúa appointed Domingo Cavallo, the highly respected architect of the Convertibility Plan, to take over as his economy minister on March 19, 2001. Most notably, Cavallo was given special powers to enact economic measures by presidential decree. Cavallo, who had strong political ambitions, decided that he would gamble on radical measures to rescue Argentina's economy. In doing so, he trod the well-worn route of so many government officials in emerging market countries, by pursuing policies that tried to delay the inevitable. As we will see, his gamble made the crisis far worse. In the minds of many Argentineans, Cavallo is the arch-villain of the story. He became so disliked that, after the Argentine economy blew up, he left the country for the United States.

Upon taking office, Cavallo immediately pursued a number of measures to get the economy growing again and to deal with the fiscal crisis. Hoping to engineer a devaluation for trade transactions and stimulate demand for Argentine products, he imposed a tax on imports and subsidized exports. To allow for a change in the peg so that it would stay in line more with the euro (the currency used by most of Argentina's trading partners) than with the dollar, Cavallo proposed an amendment to the Convertibility Law. The amendment would drop the one-peso-to-one-dollar peg and replace it with a peg to a basket consisting of euros and dollars with equal weight, once the dollar-euro exchange rate hit one dollar per euro.

These measures did not help get the economy growing again but instead only made things worse. They fostered doubts about the government's support for convertibility, one of the few economic institutions in which Argentineans believed.

The public also interpreted Cavallo's measures as a weaker commitment by the government to maintain the value of the peso. Investors began to think that a collapse of the currency board and a sharp decline in the peso were likely. This expectation was reflected in the behavior of interest rates on bank deposits denominated in pesos, which rose sharply relative to interest rates on deposits denominated in dollars. This "currency premium," which reflected the risk of a devaluation of the peso, jumped from around 10 basis

Figure 7.2. Sequence of Events in Argentina's Financial Crisis, 2001–2002

The Argentine peso became overvalued, while the sudden stop of capital inflows led to a jump in interest rates, ...

A. Interest Rate Spreads on Argentine Sovereign Bonds, 1998–2001 (basis points)

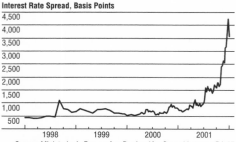

Source: Ministerio de Economía y Producción. Spread between RA 17 global government bond and similar maturity U.S. Treasury notes.

...pushing the Argentine economy into recession...

B. Real GDP Growth, 1998–2004 (percent)

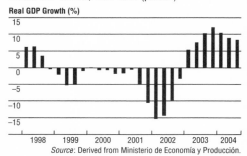

Source: Derived from Ministerio de Economía y Producción.

...as unemployment rose.

C. Unemployment Rate, 1998–2002 (percent)

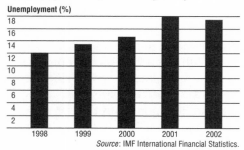

Source: IMF International Financial Statistics.

The weaker commitment of the government to maintain the value of the peso led to a rise in the currency premium.

D. Currency Premium, 1998–2001: Spread between Interest Rates on Peso-Denominated versus Dollar-Denominated Bank Deposits (basis points)

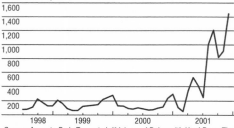

Source: Augusto De la Torre et al. "Living and Dying with Hard Pegs: The Rise and Fall of Argentina's Currency Board," Figure 8, panel c, page 65.

Doubts about the soundness of banks led to a decline in bank deposits.

E. Bank Deposits, 1998–2004 (billions of pesos)

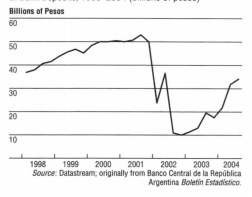

Source: Datastream; originally from Banco Central de la República Argentina *Boletín Estadístico*.

With a banking panic and government bond default imminent, investors sold pesos and international reserves fell, ...

F. International Reserves, 1998–2004
(billions of U.S. dollars)

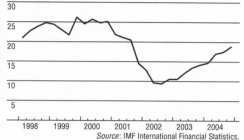

Source: IMF International Financial Statistics.

...leading to the collapse of the currency board and the Argentine peso.

G. Dollar Value of the Argentine Peso, 1998–2004

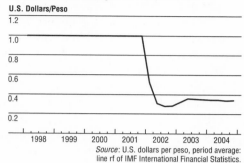

Source: U.S. dollars per peso, period average: line rf of IMF International Financial Statistics.

Inflation surged...

H. CPI Inflation, 1998–2004 (percent per year)

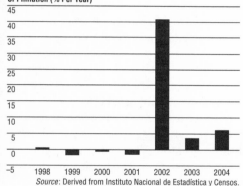

Source: Derived from Instituto Nacional de Estadística y Censos.

...and interest rates rose.

I. Interest Rates, 1998–2003 (percent)

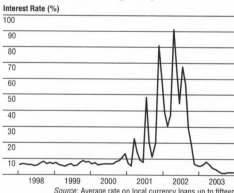

Source: Average rate on local currency loans up to fifteen days between financial institutions in the country: line 60b in IMF International Financial Statistics.

The economy collapsed...

J. Real GDP Growth, 1998–2004 (percent)

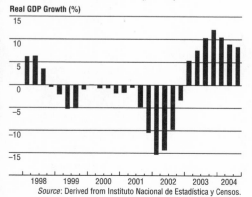

Source: Derived from Instituto Nacional de Estadística y Censos.

...and unemployment climbed above 20%.

K. Unemployment Rate, 1998–2003 (percent)

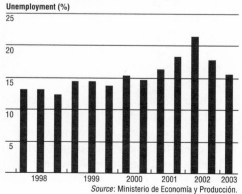

Source: Ministerio de Economía y Producción.

points just before Cavallo took office to 600 basis points in late April. A devaluation of the peso meant that the value of the government's dollar-denominated debt, which accounted for the bulk of its debt, would necessarily increase in terms of pesos. The debt-to-GDP ratio would increase, making it even more likely that the government would be forced to default on its debt. Concerns about a possible devaluation thus made the growth-debt trap even worse, and the interest rate spread between Argentine sovereign debt and U.S. Treasury debt continued to rise.

Cavallo then raised the stakes in his bid to be the Great Rescuer. With the growth-debt trap spiraling out of control, he needed to take desperate measures. Although much of the government's debt had been sold to the recently created private pension system, government debt was becoming harder to sell, as reflected in its higher interest rates. Cavallo needed to find new buyers. He realized that he needed to tap the money in Argentine banks, particularly the foreign-owned banks that dominated the banking system. Argentine banks were already big holders of government bonds before Cavallo came into office, with 15% of their assets in these bonds, but Cavallo needed them to buy more. How could he achieve this? In the words of Mario Blejer, a former president of the Argentine central bank, "What started as a seduction ended up as a rape."[23]

The answer to getting banks to buy more government bonds was to change the banking regulations so they could hold more government bonds. This change meant weakening the strong prudential regulatory and supervisory regime administered by the central bank. Inconveniently for Cavallo, the bank's president, Pedro Pou, a highly regarded official who was seen as a guardian of a strong banking system, was unwilling to go along. To clear the way for his plan, Cavallo engineered a campaign to get rid of Pou. The bank president was accused of failing to prevent money laundering by some Argentine branches of foreign-owned banks. He was never brought up on criminal charges, but the accusations achieved their objectives: Pou was sacked on April 25, and Cavallo was able to replace him with a hand-picked successor, Roque Maccarone, who would do Cavallo's bidding.

The pressure brought to bear on the central bank achieved its intended result. Just before Pou was replaced, the central bank approved a measure allowing banks to hold short-term government bonds to satisfy their liquidity requirements. The government leaned on the banks to buy $2 billion of these bonds, and the banks went along because, with their high interest rates, the bonds would be very profitable *if* the government avoided default. (And, even if a default did occur, the government might provide a bailout.) Under Maccarone, bank regulations were weakened, making it even easier for banks to increase their holdings of government bonds, so that, by the end of 2001, the banks' holdings of government debt had increased to 20% of their assets, from 10% in 1994 and 15% at the end of 2000.

Despite the barrier to the central bank printing money to finance government deficits from the Convertibility Plan, the federal and provincial governments were still able to, in effect, print money to finance their deficits. They issued small-denomination bonds (*lecops* for the federal government and *patacones* for the province of Buenos Aires, for example) that could be used to make payments. By the end of 2001, these *quasi-monies* exceeded 25% of the pesos in circulation, and by March 2002 they accounted for nearly 40%.[24] The appearance of such quasi-monies further illustrates the inability of the Convertibility Plan to enforce fiscal responsibility.

Cavallo also used his special powers to revise the charter of the central bank to remove limits on its ability to inject liquidity into the economy. This further weakened the currency board arrangement of convertibility because it allowed the central bank, now effectively controlled by the government, to pursue a discretionary expansionary policy, which it eventually did. These actions compromised the independence of the central bank and opened the door for policies that would bring the currency board down. Confidence in the peso and in the ability of the government to pay back its debt was thus dealt another blow.

Confidence in the health of the banking system was also deteriorating. The banks' rising exposure to defaults on their holdings of government debt created doubts about their soundness. Because government deposit insurance was limited in Argentina, depositors started to pull their deposits out of the banks. From December 2000 to March 2001, deposits at Argentine banks fell by 2.8%; they fell by another 6% from March to July 2001. What had once been considered one of the best-supervised and strongest banking systems among emerging market countries was now under attack.[25]

Despite the government's announcement in July that it would pursue a "zero deficit" policy, the spread between interest rates on Argentine debt and U.S. Treasuries remained well above 1000 basis points. The Argentine government then sought a fresh infusion of funds from the IMF. Even though there was little hope of a successful bailout and even though the action was highly controversial internally, the IMF announced another $6 billion loan to Argentina in August. It was unable to stem the tide. In October negotiations between the central government and the provinces to improve the fiscal situation broke down, and tax revenues continued to fall as the economy declined. Interest rates on Argentine sovereign bonds now climbed to over 2000 basis points above those on U.S. Treasuries. Cavallo made a last-ditch effort to arrange a debt restructuring at the end of October, but default was now inevitable. As a result, a full-fledged bank panic began in November, with deposit outflows running nearly $1 billion a day. At the beginning of December, the government was forced to close the banks temporarily and impose a restriction called the *corralito* (small fence), under which depositors could withdraw only $250 in cash per week. The corralito was particularly devastating for the poor, who were more dependent on cash to conduct their daily transactions.

The social fabric of Argentine society began to unravel. Nearly thirty people died in violent riots. On December 19 Cavallo and all other government ministers resigned, followed the next day by President de la Rúa. He was followed by a series of temporary presidents until Eduardo Duhalde was chosen as the new president by the legislative assembly on December 30, 2001.

Stage Three: Currency Crisis and the Collapse of the Currency Board

The bank panic signaled that the government could no longer allow interest rates to remain high in order to prop up the value of the peso and preserve the currency board, because this would destroy the already weakened banks. The public now recognized that the peso would have to decline in value in the near future, and so they began selling pesos for dollars, thus using up the central bank's foreign currency reserves. In addition, the dire fiscal position of the government meant that it would not be able to pay back its debt, providing another reason for the investors to pull money out of the country, leading to further peso sales.

On December 23 the government announced the inevitable: a suspension of external debt payments for at least sixty days. With this default and a continuing loss of foreign exchange reserves (which had dropped to $15 billion, just enough to cover the amount of domestic currency in circulation), the currency board could no longer be maintained. After assuming power on January 2, President Duhalde announced the abandonment of convertibility. The peso was devalued to 1.4 to the dollar on January 6, 2002; subsequently it was allowed to float.

Final Stage: Currency Crisis Triggers Full-Fledged Financial Crisis

The peso went into free fall, falling from a value of $1.00 to less than $0.30 by June 2002 and then stabilizing at around $0.33 thereafter. As in Mexico, the devaluation led to a surge of inflation, which at its peak reached an annual rate of around 40%. Because the rise in actual inflation was accompanied by a rise in expected inflation, interest rates went to even higher levels. The higher interest payments led to a decline in the cash flow of both households and businesses, which now had to seek external funds if they wanted to finance their investments. Given the uncertainty in financial markets, asymmetric information problems were particularly severe, and this meant that investment could not be funded. Households and businesses drastically cut back on their spending.

Because Argentina had a higher percentage of debt denominated in dollars than any of the other crisis countries, the effects of the peso depreciation on balance sheets were even more devastating. Indeed, this may explain why

Argentina's crisis was so much more severe, despite its success in achieving institutional reforms of the financial sector before the crisis. With the peso falling to one-third of its value before the crisis, all dollar-denominated debt tripled in peso terms. Since Argentina's tradable sector was small, most businesses' production was priced in pesos. If they had to pay back their dollar debt, almost all firms would become insolvent. In this environment, financial markets could not function, because net worth would not be available to mitigate adverse selection and moral hazard problems.

Given the losses on the defaulted government debt and the rising loan losses, Argentine banks found their balance sheets in a precarious state. This, combined with the run on the banks, which led to huge deposit outflows, meant that they did not have the resources to make new loans and so could no longer solve adverse selection and moral hazard problems. The government bond default and conditions in Argentine financial markets also meant that foreigners not only were unwilling to lend, but were actually pulling their money out of the country.

With the financial system on the ropes, financial flows came to a grinding halt and the economy tanked. The corralito may have also played an important role in weakening the economy. By making it more difficult to get cash, it may have caused a sharp slowdown in the underground economy, which is large in Argentina and runs primarily on cash. In the first quarter of 2002, output was falling at an annual rate of more than 15% and unemployment shot up to near 20%. The increase in poverty was dramatic: the percentage of the Argentine population in poverty rose to almost 50% in 2002.[26] Argentina was experiencing the worst depression in its history, one every bit as bad as, and maybe even worse than, the one the United States faced in the 1930s.

Destruction of Property Rights

Given the state of households' and firms' balance sheets, the government knew it had to do something. It chose "pesofication," the forcible conversion of all domestic dollar debt into peso debt. This was clearly a violation of property rights, because dollar contracts could no longer be enforced by Argentine individuals and businesses. Despite the ramifications of pesofication, the abrogation of contracts may not do a huge amount of harm if it is seen to be a one-time event in an emergency situation, and if it is seen to be carried out in a nonarbitrary fashion that treats all creditors equally.[27] But this was not how it was done in Argentina, which pursued a politically motivated, asymmetric pesofication.

Dollar debt was converted into peso debt at a one-to-one rate, but, to curry favor with the Argentine public, bank deposits were converted at a higher rate of 1.4 pesos per dollar. This meant that banks got one peso per dollar of loans but had to pay 1.4 pesos per dollar of deposits, thus leaving them in the hole for 0.4 peso. Banks were subjected to huge losses from this asymmetric pesofication. Their situation was even worse because they had dollar debt obligations to foreigners, which could not be pesofied with a domestic decree. The banks thus had obligations to pay the foreign loans back at the even higher exchange rate of around 3 pesos per dollar. Given that over 70% of bank assets were held by foreign banks, it is not surprising that the political support for taking resources from the banks through asymmetric pesofication was high. When the government realized that pesofication was in effect bankrupting all the banks, it offered them a "compensation bond." What the government had taken away with one hand, it had given back with the other. Because the compensation was arbitrary, however, it did not encourage a belief that the government was committed to upholding property rights.

This destruction of property rights was compounded by additional government policies. Some pesofied loans and deposits, which were indexed to the consumer price index, were deindexed while others were not, and the corporate bankruptcy code was weakened to assist ailing firms. The deposit freeze, an abrogation of property, was made permanent. The maturity of time deposits was forcefully restructured by an involuntary lengthening. The Argentine government broke contracts to grab resources from the recently privatized utilities, which were generally owned by foreigners. The government converted utility rates, denominated in dollars, into the sharply depreciated pesos on a one-to-one basis and then froze these rates. The utilities could not pass through to their customers their higher costs, which were based on dollar prices for energy in world markets. Although the freezing of rates was originally an emergency measure, the freeze was kept in place. The Argentine government also played hardball with foreign creditors who owned government bonds with a face value of close to $90 billion, agreeing to pay only $.25 to $.30 on the dollar of the face value of these bonds.[28] The lack of respect for property rights exhibited by the government was not out of line with what it had done in the past. The Argentine government has had a sorry history of expropriating assets from the public.

Recovery

In 2003 the Argentine economy began to recover, both because of the inevitable bounceback after a sharp economic downturn and because there was a fortuitous increase in foreign demand for its agricultural products. By the end of the year, economic growth was running at an annual rate of around 10% and unemployment had fallen to below 15%. Were Argentina's problems over?

In some areas of the economy, Argentina had made great strides in the 1990s. The reforms engineered in the early part of President Menem's term had brought Argentina a long way. Property rights and the infrastructure of the financial system had been improved dramatically, and this encouraged financial deepening. Prudential regulation and supervision had been brought up to the standards of advanced countries, which promoted safety and soundness in the financial industry. State-owned businesses were privatized, and this drove them to be more efficient. Significant steps had been made in opening up Argentine markets and the financial system to foreign competition. The result was that, from 1991 to 1998, the Argentine economy had average growth rates that were among the highest in its history. Argentina had embraced globalization and was the darling of both the IMF and the markets.

Unfortunately all this gold turned to dross when the peso became overvalued and fiscal policy spun out of control. Although the growth-debt trap was driven by a considerable amount of bad luck, other factors played a role. When confronted with bad outcomes, Argentina's political institutions made it easy for the politicians to destroy their country's carefully built institutions without a second thought.

Today confidence in property rights in Argentina is at a low ebb. Why would domestic residents or foreigners make large investments when they know that their property rights can be violated on a politician's whim? The current political climate is depressing. The government has been slow to restructure its once proud banking system to get it back on its feet.[29] I see little willingness on the part of Argentina's politicians to rebuild the institutions that they so blithely destroyed.

Under these conditions, we should not expect that funds will be channeled to their most productive uses. The willingness to further open up their markets internationally to promote competition and to achieve the flexibility needed to promote rapid growth does not appear to be strong. Argentina may be growing rapidly, but its long-run prospects are not good. Until the 1930s, Argentina had one of the highest standards of living in the world. Then it lost sixty years, and fell far behind countries with which it had once been an economic equal. Given the current environment, Argentina faces the prospect of losing another sixty years.

What Do the Case Studies Tell Us?

The case studies we have looked at in this chapter and the preceding two illustrate how damaging it can be to get financial globalization wrong and why there is no clear-cut relationship between financial globalization and economic growth. The case studies give us clues as to how financial globalization should be managed to make it a force for good, which is the topic to which we turn in the next chapter. They suggest that good prudential regulation and supervision of the financial system, as well as responsible fiscal policy, are crucial to successful financial globalization. The studies also illustrate the dangers of pegged-exchange-rate regimes when they interact with liability dollarization. They warn us that merely taking policies that work in advanced countries and applying them to emerging market countries is often a mistake. They suggest that policies that sweep problems under the rug often promote more disastrous financial crises, while policies that focus on establishing a solid institutional foundation for the economy not only have long-run benefits but also can restore the confidence that can stimulate a more rapid recovery from a financial crisis.

Part Three

How Can Disadvantaged Nations Make Financial Globalization Work for Them?

Eight

Ending Financial Repression: The Role of Globalization

Good investments make people productive, and greater productivity is the road to riches. But good investments can occur only if funds are channeled to those with good investment opportunities via an effective financial system. To achieve this goal, disadvantaged nations must end financial repression and promote financial deepening. How exactly can they do this?

The key to ending financial repression is the development of institutions that enable the financial system to work well. If the development of such institutions is so important to improving poorer countries' well-being, why doesn't it happen? As we have seen, setting up the infrastructure for an efficient financial system is by no means easy: it takes time for institutions to evolve and adapt to local circumstances, to particular cultural and historical conditions. In addition, powerful elites in disadvantaged countries often oppose the necessary reforms because such changes will weaken their power or allow others to cut into their profits. How can poorer countries overcome these obstacles? How can they redistribute power so there is the political will to promote institutional reform? The answer is globalization.

Developing Institutional Infrastructure

The basic principles for developing an institutional infrastructure that fosters financial development were developed in detail earlier in the book. Let's review them briefly here.

1. Develop strong property rights. Because investments will not be undertaken if the fruits of the investment are likely to be taken away by the government or others, strong property rights are needed to encourage productive investment. Enforceable property rights are also necessary to create collateral. With collateral, lenders become confident that they can cope with asymmetric information problems (adverse selection and moral hazard) when providing funds to borrowers. In *The Mystery of Capital,* Hernando De Soto sees the inability of the poor in developing countries to acquire property rights as a key reason they are unable to gain access to capital and so remain mired in poverty.

2. Strengthen the legal system. An essential step in supporting strong property rights is a legal system that enforces contracts quickly and fairly. Such a legal system reduces moral hazard problems and encourages lending. For example, lenders write restrictive covenants into loan contracts to prevent borrowers from taking on too much risk, but such covenants have value only if they can be legally enforced. An inefficient legal system in which loan contracts cannot be enforced will preclude productive lending. If it is too expensive to set up legal businesses or to obtain legal title to property, the poor will never have access to the legal system and will be cut off from the lending that could help them open small businesses and escape poverty.

3. Reduce corruption. Eliminating corruption is essential to strengthening property rights and the legal system. When a corrupt official demands a bribe, she reduces the incentives for entrepreneurs to make investments. The ability to buy off judges weakens enforcement of the legal contracts that enable the financial system to function smoothly.

4. Improve the quality of financial information. High-quality financial information is essential to well-functioning financial markets. If lenders cannot figure out what is going on in a firm, they will be unable to screen out good credit risks from bad or to monitor the firm to ensure that it does not take on too much risk at the lender's expense. In other words, if information is too asymmetric, the adverse selection and moral hazard problems will prevent profitable lending, and productive investment will not take place. To make reliable and accurate information easier to access, accounting standards must be high enough that prospective lenders can make sense of what is in a business's books. Setting up standards for credit reporting will encourage the establishment of credit registries or bureaus, which gather and share information about the credit history of prospective borrowers. These can be especially beneficial in increasing lending to households and small business borrowers, a practice that encourages financial deepening.[1] Rules that require businesses to disclose information must be enforced, so that prospective investors can make sensible decisions about whether the business deserves their hard-earned money.

5. Improve corporate governance. The purchase of stocks is another way to channel funds to business. For people to be willing to buy stocks, there must be rules to ensure that corporate managers act in the stockholders' interest. If managers find it easy to steal from the company, or to use funds for their own personal gain rather than for the benefit of the company, no one will want to invest.

6. Get the government out of the business of directing credit. Too much government involvement in allocating credit hinders the flow of funds to productive uses. State-owned financial institutions do not have incentives to make profits and so are often willing to make loans to those who are politically connected rather than those whose investments will increase productivity. Similarly, when governments allocate credit directly, it is likely to go to politicians' cronies or to business interests that support their campaigns.

The Role of Globalization

One of the most powerful weapons to stimulate institutional development is globalization. Poorer countries must let go of the idea that financial infrastructure and wealth can be built up when the countries remain closed off to the rest of the world. Poorer countries must embrace globalization: they must open up their financial markets and their markets for goods and services to other nations so that funds, goods, and, often, the ideas that accompany them can flow in and help them achieve the reforms that build productivity and wealth.

Opening Up Financial Markets to Foreigners: Externally Oriented Financial Liberalization

Globalizing the domestic financial system by pursuing externally oriented financial liberalization encourages financial development and growth in wealth in two ways. Opening up to foreign capital directly increases liquidity and lowers the cost of capital for those with productive investments to make.[2] Opening up to foreign financial institutions promotes reforms to the financial system that make it work better. Allowing foreign financial institutions to operate in an emerging market country brings in expertise developed abroad. Bringing in best practices from other nations—in such areas as screening good from bad credit risks and monitoring borrower activities to reduce the amount of risk they take on—directly improves the functioning of financial markets.[3] Because of their familiarity with more advanced financial systems, foreign financial firms are also likely to increase the pressure on the domestic government to make reforms that will enable the financial system to work more effectively.

As domestic financial institutions start to lose business to better-run and more trustworthy foreign institutions, they realize the need for an improved legal and accounting infrastructure that will make it easier for them to minimize adverse selection and moral hazard problems as they seek out new customers. They will thus be far more likely to advocate and support the reforms to make this happen.

Opening Up Domestic Markets to Foreign Goods: Trade Liberalization

Although not as immediately obvious, opening up domestic markets to foreign goods, known as *trade liberalization,* can also be a key driver of financial development. Trade liberalization can weaken the political power of entrenched business interests who might otherwise block institutional reforms, a point made emphatically by Raghuram Rajan and Luigi Zingales in their book *Saving Capitalism from the Capitalists.* By promoting a more competitive environment, trade liberalization will lower the revenues of entrenched firms so that they will need greater access to external sources of capital. They will thus be more likely to support reforms that promote a more efficient financial system and financial deepening. This is why a deeper financial sector is positively associated with greater trade openness.[4]

Free trade also promotes financial deepening by reducing corruption. High tariffs breed corruption because importers have incentives to pay off customs officials to look the other way when the importers avoid tariffs by smuggling in goods. Not surprisingly, countries that restrict international trade are found to be more corrupt.[5]

Focusing Domestic Markets on International Trade: Export Orientation

Many developing countries have been unwilling to tear down all their barriers to imports and so have not embraced trade liberalization. Nonetheless, they can still generate incentives for institutional reform by encouraging their domestic markets to focus on international trade. Encouraging an export orientation in domestic markets creates a greater need for a well-functioning financial system because, to compete effectively in the international arena, firms need better access to capital. If they can't get capital, they won't be able to make the investments they need to increase productivity and price their goods competitively. In this way, international trade creates a demand for reforms that will make the financial system more efficient.

We are seeing how the globalization of trade is driving financial reform in China. As Chinese enterprises have increasingly entered international markets, China's hybrid system, combining communism with semi-capitalist property rights (the town and village enterprises), has worked less and less well in enabling businesses to grow.[6] China's exports have grown from $9.7 billion in 1978, when Deng Xiaoping came into power, to $430 billion today.[7] The exploding export sector now needs access to ever-greater amounts of capital, and it needs a better financial system to achieve this. Although it has taken time, globalization is finally generating the demand for an improved financial system, which is driving the reform process in China.

The communist leadership recognizes that the old development model has to change. The government has announced that state-owned banks are being put on the path to be privatized and has allowed foreign investment in China's banking system, amounting to $20 billion in 2005 alone.[8] In addition the government is instituting legal reforms to make financial contracts more enforceable. New bankruptcy laws will give lenders the ability to take over the assets of firms that default on their loan contracts.[9]

Governments Often Discourage Exports

Given the clear-cut benefits of an export orientation, it is surprising that governments in many developing countries not only do not encourage an export orientation but actually take active steps to discourage it. This has been an especially serious problem in Latin America and Africa, and it helps explain why their growth performance has been so disappointing.

The primary way in which governments discourage exports is by imposing large taxes on them. Because high export taxes are one method of obtaining revenue, governments may be attracted to them to solve their budget problems. They may also use these taxes to punish their political opponents, who are often involved in a particular export industry. The government can then distribute the resulting revenue to its supporters.

The most pernicious export taxes are those that are hidden. The government sets an official exchange rate that artificially keeps the domestic currency at a value well above what it would be in foreign currency (say, dollars) in a free market. It then makes it illegal to sell dollars for the larger amount of domestic currency that could be obtained on the black market. (You might have experienced this as a tourist in certain poorer countries, when shady individuals approach you and offer to give you a much better rate for your local currency than you could get from a bank.)

The difference between the official exchange rate and the freely established, black market rate (often called the black market premium) imposes a tax on exporters because they are forced to sell the dollars they earn to the government or to the central bank at the official rate, thus yielding them a much lower price for their goods in terms of the domestic currency. In some countries the tax from the black market premium is confiscatory. In 1982, for example, Ghana had a black market premium of over 1000%, so that exporters of cocoa (primarily from a different tribe than members of the ruling government party) were getting only 6% of the world price. With a tax rate so high, cocoa exports—which accounted for 19% of Ghana's GDP in the 1950s—had fallen to 3% by 1982.[10] During the twenty years when the black market premium was so high, the average income of Ghanaians fell by 30%.

High black market premiums also breed corruption, with all its negative effects, because there are such strong incentives to bribe officials or to smuggle goods to avoid paying the tax. (Indeed, one of the reasons governments in poorer countries often use this method of taxation, rather than an explicit tax, is that it allows government officials to get rich from the bribes they receive.)

High black market premiums that hurt exports are damaging to economic growth. Countries with a black market premium above 40% had average annual income growth per person of 0.1% (in contrast to 1.7% for countries without such a premium), while countries with a black market premium above 1000% had an annual growth rate of –3.1%.[11] Government policies that discourage exports are disastrous and have been a major source of continuing poverty throughout the world.

Trade Globalization Has Other Benefits

Although we have been focusing on how globalization promotes financial deepening, we should not forget that trade globalization, which involves both trade liberalization and an export orientation, is a key driver of economic growth for additional reasons.[12]

Additional Benefits of Trade Liberalization

The first economics course that college students take always teaches the concept of comparative advantage: by trading with another country, you can focus your production on what you are really good at, so that your productivity will be high. This higher productivity then leads to higher economic welfare.

Trade liberalization, more importantly, promotes competition in domestic markets, which in turn forces domestic firms to increase productivity and make better products, thus driving economic growth. If a foreigner produces a superior product that can be imported, domestic firms must make a better product at a lower price to remain competitive at home. One graphic example of how trade promotes competition occurred in India, which up until 1991 protected its tool industry with a 100% tariff (a tax on imports). After the Indian government cut the tariff sharply, Taiwanese firms initially grabbed a third of the Indian market. Over the next decade, however, Indian firms boosted their productivity almost to Taiwanese levels, thus winning back the domestic market. Eventually Indian tool firms became so efficient that they were able to start selling their goods abroad and become substantial exporters.[13]

Decreasing trade barriers helps promote exports. Increased competition from imports lowers the profits firms can earn by focusing solely on the domestic market, and so they naturally concentrate more of their energy on exporting. Trade liberalization helps developing countries to access markets in advanced countries; as an illustration, the United States, through free trade agreements, has been more willing to lower tariffs for countries such as Mexico and Chile if they do the same.

Empirical evidence indicates that trade liberalization has positive effects on productivity and economic growth for both importing and exporting countries;[14] it has even been found to be associated with more rapid increases in life expectancy and a reduction in infant mortality.[15] In addition, as a survey published in the American Economic Association's *Journal of Economic Literature* concludes, "Concerns that trade liberalization has generally adverse effects on the employment or wages of poor people, or on government spending on the poor due to falling fiscal revenues, are not well founded, even though specific instances of each of these problems can be identified."[16]

Yet, as is often the case in economics, empirical evidence is never completely clear-cut: there is some skepticism as to whether the evidence strongly supports a positive link between trade liberalization and growth.[17] Nonetheless the logic of the benefits of trade liberalization and the preponderance of the evidence supporting its positive effects lead most members of the economics profession, including me, to the following conclusion: not only is trade liberalization highly beneficial to the overall economy, but the resulting economic growth is an important tool for poverty alleviation.

Additional Benefits of an Export Orientation

But even if trade liberalization is not adopted, encouraging domestic markets to sell goods to rich countries is an incredibly important engine for growth in poorer countries. Because foreigners don't have a natural predilection to buy your goods, you have to be supercompetitive—your goods have to be better and cheaper than goods made in the foreign country. Domestic firms have to focus even more on being highly productive, and boosting productivity will lead to rapid economic growth.

Japan's postwar experience shows what focusing on exporting can accomplish. In the immediate aftermath of World War II, Japan was a poor country. Its economic infrastructure had been destroyed by the war, and Japanese goods were considered to be shoddy. (I can remember when "made in Japan" was a derogatory statement about the quality of a product.) Furthermore, Americans had just come out of a war with Japan, and many Americans refused to buy Japanese goods, just as many refused to buy German goods.

To convince Americans to buy their products, Japanese firms had to produce goods that were cheaper and better than their American-made counterparts.

Selling Japanese products such as cars in America meant that Japanese companies had to produce a superb product at low cost, and this is what they did. Eventually, Japanese cars took over a huge percentage of the American market; companies like Toyota and Honda grew to be household names, becoming far more profitable than the once-dominant General Motors and Ford.

The export industries in Japan became enormously productive and supercompetitive. Productivity grew and, three decades after World War II, Japan was one of the richest countries in the world. From the 1990s until recently, Japan's economy did not fare so well because of mismanagement of the domestic economy and the financial sector by the government. The Japanese export sector, however, continued to have extremely high productivity growth.

Some countries have been highly successful without fully embracing trade liberalization. South Korea, one of the great Asian success stories even with its crisis in the late 1990s, had very high barriers to trade up until the 1990s, and its early development strategy did not include opening up its domestic market to foreign goods. However, through its export sector South Korea has participated fully in global markets, and this participation has been a key to its success. South Korea's development strategy focused on promoting its export sector, and that sector led the country to high productivity and economic growth. Indeed, all successful growth stories in less-developed economies (Chile, China, India, Japan, Singapore, South Korea, Taiwan) have been export driven, and some of these countries have also pursued trade liberalization.

Only by embracing global markets can less-developed countries get rich.[18] Trade globalization has a key role to play in economic growth by directly stimulating domestic firms to become more productive. Along with financial globalization, it also encourages emerging market economies to develop the institutions that foster financial development and end financial repression. Even Dani Rodrik of Harvard University, a prominent skeptic on globalization, has admitted that "No country has developed successfully by turning its back on international trade and long-term capital flows."[19]

Globalization must be one of the highest priorities for developing countries. But how can globalization be pursued successfully, avoiding the financial crises that often follow it? This is the subject to which we turn next.

Nine

Preventing Financial Crises

In a now famous, but initially ignored, paper published in 1985, "Good-Bye Financial Repression, Hello Financial Crash," Latin American economist Carlos Diaz-Alejandro was way ahead of his time in warning of the dangers of financial globalization.[1] As the recent experiences of Mexico, South Korea, Argentina, and many other countries have shown, financial globalization does not always work for emerging market countries. Without proper implementation and management, financial liberalization can lead to financial crises with disastrous and often long-term consequences for the economy. Can emerging market countries avoid these crises and reap all the potential benefits that financial globalization has to offer? Our understanding of how globalization can go wrong suggests a number of basic principles for financial reform that can promote stability while avoiding crises.

Prudential Regulation and Supervision

Banks are the main institutions that gather and process information about the financial state of businesses and households and that solve the asymmetric information problems (moral hazard and adverse selection) in the financial markets. Deterioration in banks' balance sheets, caused by the proliferation of bad loans and declines in net worth, can lead to banking crises in which banks cut back sharply on lending, financial information is not collected, and asymmetric information problems intensify. Banking crises, if severe, bring on financial crises. Problems in the banking sector also make a foreign exchange crisis more likely. Through harmful effects on the balance sheets of nonfinancial and financial firms, a foreign exchange crisis leads to a full-blown, downward-spiraling financial crisis.

Since financial institutions like banks are at the core of what can trigger a financial crisis, prevention of financial crises must start with a government providing effective prudential regulation and supervision of the financial system. To do so requires implementation of several types of reforms. In discussing these reforms, we draw on the experiences of many countries with prudential supervision. We must not forget, however, that reforms in one country do not always work well in another. Because the details of the reforms may require substantial modification to fit a particular nation's circumstances, the reforms discussed here should not be viewed as a checklist to be followed exactly by every country. Instead, they point out the overall direction in which emerging market countries need to move to make financial globalization work for them.

1. Limit Currency Mismatch

Emerging market countries almost always suffer from *currency mismatch:* many firms have debt denominated in a foreign currency like the U.S. dollar (*liability dollarization*), while the value of their production and assets is denominated in the domestic currency. In countries with a currency mismatch, currency crises and devaluations will trigger full-fledged financial crises by decimating the balance sheets of nonfinancial and financial firms. As an IMF study has put it, "almost all recent crisis episodes were marked by currency mismatch exposures."[2] Currency mismatch does not usually happen in industrialized countries, because their debt is generally denominated in the domestic currency. This is why insufficient attention has been paid to risks from liability dollarization in the international banking standards developed by advanced countries, such as the Basel Accord.

An economy would be far less prone to financial crises if the issuance of foreign-denominated debt was discouraged, especially for firms that sell their production primarily in domestic markets.[3] Although reducing foreign-denominated debt is not an unmixed blessing, because it might prevent some firms from borrowing,[4] there are strong reasons to believe that excessive liability dollarization is detrimental to the health of developing economies. Governments are more likely to bail out firms and banks when they all fail together, and this mass failure is exactly what happens when firms have borrowed heavily in a foreign currency and the currency depreciates. Thus a government safety net encourages financial and nonfinancial firms to borrow in foreign currencies, even though this leaves the economy more vulnerable to financial crises.[5]

Because so much foreign-denominated debt is intermediated through the banking system, regulation and supervision to force banks to acknowledge and reduce the risk posed by currency mismatches could greatly limit liability dollarization and thus enhance financial stability.[6] Similarly, restrictions on corporate borrowing in foreign currency or tax policies to discourage such borrowing could help an economy withstand a currency depreciation without undergoing a financial crisis. Anne Krueger, the first deputy managing director of the IMF, has even suggested that emerging market countries should make foreign-currency debt incurred by domestic firms unenforceable in domestic courts and that restrictions should be placed on lending to emerging market countries by financial institutions in industrialized countries.[7] However, blanket restrictions like these or tax policies to discourage borrowing in foreign currencies may be too draconian: firms that price their production in a foreign currency *should* be borrowing in that currency to limit their exchange rate risk.[8] A more nuanced approach—one that focuses on systemic risk to the economy from currency mismatch, rather than on the amount of liabilities denominated in foreign currency—makes more sense.

Another reason that residents in emerging market economies denominate debt in currencies from industrialized countries is that these currencies have more stable purchasing power and therefore less inflation risk than their domestic currencies. If domestic residents had access to debt indexed to inflation, they would have an alternative way to lower their inflation risk, and liability dollarization would be less likely.[9] With indexation, debt contracts would be denominated in an index unit tied to a price level index like the Consumer Price Index (CPI), so that, when the price level rose, the nominal value of debt would rise one for one. With indexation, the real value of the debt in terms of goods and services would remain unchanged. In the 1960s Chile developed an indexing unit (the Unidad de Fomento), and indexation of debt and other contracts became widespread. As a result Chile was able to avoid liability dollarization, despite having high and variable inflation rates similar to those in other Latin American countries that had significant liability dollarization.[10]

2. Without Proper Institutional Backup, Be Wary of Adopting Deposit Insurance

Deposit insurance, which protects depositors from losses when banks go broke, originated in the United States. As of 1960 only six countries had emulated the United States and adopted deposit insurance. This began to change in the late 1960s, and the trend accelerated in the 1990s, by which time over seventy countries had adopted deposit insurance.[11]

Despite its popularity, deposit insurance is a mixed blessing. The positive effect: By decreasing the incentive for depositors to withdraw their money if a bank gets into trouble, it can prevent bank panics; depositors will be less likely to run on the bank.

The negative effect: Deposit insurance increases moral hazard incentives for banks to take on excessive risk. Without adequate prudential regulation and supervision to reduce banks' incentives to take on too much risk, deposit insurance can increase, rather than decrease, the likelihood of a banking crisis. This is exactly what has occurred in many emerging market countries. Research done primarily at the World Bank has found that, on average, the adoption of explicit government deposit insurance is associated with greater instability in the banking sector and a higher incidence of banking crises. Furthermore, the adoption of deposit insurance seems to retard financial development.[12] However, these negative effects occur only in countries with weak institutional environments: an absence of rule of law, ineffective regulation and supervision of the financial sector, and rampant corruption. Thus deposit insurance policies that work in advanced countries may not work in developing countries, and they may even be counterproductive.

3. Restrict Connected Lending and Prevent Commercial Enterprises from Owning Financial Institutions

The financial sectors of many developing countries are rife with *connected lending:* loans made by financial institutions to their owners or managers, or to their business associates, friends, and families.[13] This practice helped lead to the 1994–95 collapse of Mexico's financial system. Financial institutions have less incentive to monitor loans to their owners or managers, a situation that increases the moral hazard incentive for the borrowers to take on excessive risk. These risky loans expose the institution to potential losses. In addition, connected lending in which large loans are made to one party can result in a lack of diversification for the institution, further increasing its risk exposure.

Restrictions on connected lending can take several forms.[14] Most countries have regulations limiting connected lending, and many developing countries have limits on the books that are stricter than those in industrialized countries, although these limits are often not enforced effectively. An IMF study published in 1995, before the East Asian crisis, found that bank examiners in Asia were often unable to assess the amount of connected lending because they lacked the authority to trace to whom loans were made and because banks hid such loans in dummy accounts.[15] Strong efforts to increase disclosure of connected lending and to increase the authority of bank examiners to verify the accuracy of loan information are essential in controlling this moral hazard.

Allowing commercial businesses to own large shares of financial institutions also increases the incentives for connected lending. The Korean financial crisis of 1997 was caused in part by the chaebols' ownership of merchant banks, which were virtually unsupervised. The merchant banks supplied the chaebols with large amounts of money by borrowing abroad and lending the proceeds. As a result of the merchant banks' high-risk lending to the chaebols, most of the banks became insolvent, and their insolvency was a key factor in the Korean financial crisis. Regulations preventing commercial enterprises from owning financial institutions are crucial for promoting financial stability in emerging market countries.

4. Ensure That Banks Have Plenty of Capital

Requiring that banks have sufficient equity capital (that their assets are greater than their liabilities) is another way to encourage them to take on less risk. When a bank is forced to hold a large amount of equity capital, it has more to lose if it fails and is thus more likely to pursue safer investments.[16]

Bank capital requirements can take two forms. The simplest type, *the leverage ratio,* is the amount of capital divided by the bank's total assets. To be classified as well capitalized in the United States, for example, a bank's leverage ratio must exceed 5%; a lower leverage ratio, especially one below 3%, triggers increased regulatory restrictions.

A more complicated system of capital requirements is that codified under the Basel Accord, which requires banks to hold a certain amount of capital depending on the type of assets the bank holds and an assessment of how risky they are. These are referred to as *risk-based capital requirements.*

Although the Basel Accord does encourage banks to reduce risk by making them hold more capital when they hold higher-risk assets, it was designed for advanced countries' banking systems and is not as effective for emerging market economies. For example, the accord classifies government bonds as having the lowest risk of all bank assets. This classification may make sense in the United States, where U.S. Treasury bonds are extremely unlikely to ever experience a default, but it makes little sense for government bonds issued by emerging market countries. In fact, a major factor in the banking crisis in Argentina was the sharp fall in the value of banks' holdings of Argentine government bonds when these bonds went into default. In addition, emerging market economies are subjected to much greater economic shocks than advanced economies, and the increased risk that banks in these countries face suggests that the amount of capital they hold should be even larger. Thus bank capital requirements in emerging market economies need to be even more stringent than the international standards adopted by bank supervisors in advanced countries.[17]

5. Focus on Risk Management

The traditional approach to bank supervision has focused on the quality of a bank's balance sheet at a given point in time and on whether the bank complies with capital requirements. Although this traditional focus is important in reducing excessive risk taking, it may no longer be adequate by itself. Financial innovation has produced new markets and instruments that make it easy for financial institutions and their employees to quickly take on huge amounts of risk. In this new financial environment, an institution that is healthy today can be rapidly driven into insolvency from trading losses tomorrow. This point was forcefully demonstrated by the failure of Barings Bank in 1995. Although it was initially well capitalized, Barings was brought down in a matter of months by the losses incurred by a rogue trader. An auditor's examination that focuses only on a financial institution's balance sheet position at one point in time may not be an effective indicator of whether the bank will be taking on excessive risk in the near future.

Bank examiners in developing countries can help promote a safer and sounder financial sector by evaluating how banks manage risk. Such an evaluation should look at the following variables: (1) the quality of risk measurement and monitoring systems, (2) the adequacy of policies to limit activities that present significant risks, (3) the adequacy of internal controls to prevent fraud or unauthorized activities on the part of employees, and (4) the quality of oversight of risk management procedures by the board of directors and senior management.[18] Once its assessment is completed, the bank supervisory agency should make sure that this information is disclosed to the public. By giving poor rankings to banks that are not up to par on risk management, banking supervisors can make sure that best practices for risk management will spread throughout the banking industry in their country.[19]

6. Encourage Disclosure and Market-Based Discipline

There are two problems with relying solely on supervisors to control risk taking by financial institutions. First, financial institutions have incentives to keep information hidden from bank examiners so that they are not restricted in their activities. Even if supervisors are conscientious, they may not be able to stop institutions from engaging in risky activities. Second, supervisors may give in to political pressure or be corrupt and not do their jobs properly.

To eliminate these problems, it would be better to allow the impartial market to discipline financial institutions when they take on too much risk. Disclosure by financial institutions of the state of their balance sheets encourages them to hold more capital, because individual depositors and creditors will be unwilling to put their money into an institution that is thinly capitalized.

Disclosure requirements have one important advantage over capital requirements. If bank capital requirements are set too low, they will have little impact. If they are set too high, banks may try to evade them. Disclosure of a bank's true balance sheet position can help the market discipline the bank by withholding funds if it does not have an adequate amount of capital. Similarly, disclosure of the extent of a bank's lending in foreign currency can help limit the degree of currency mismatch. Depositors and other creditors will be more wary of putting their money into a bank if it is has lent extensively in dollars to firms that have their products denominated in the domestic currency, so that a currency depreciation will result in a surge in bad loans. In addition, disclosure about the risk level of banks' other activities allows individual depositors or other creditors to monitor the institutions and withdraw their money if the institutions take on too much risk.

Because financial institutions are able to take on more risk than many conventional businesses and because they are typically provided with a government safety net, disclosure requirements must go beyond the simple public issuance of conventional balance sheet and income statements. Governments need to hold bank directors and managers responsible for timely and accurate disclosure of a wide range of information on the quality of their assets, the amount of risk they are exposed to, and the procedures they use to manage risk. Recent evidence indicates that disclosures of this type are the most effective tool in promoting a sound banking system.[20]

Insisting that financial institutions have credit ratings is another useful measure to help increase market discipline. Part of the supervisory system implemented in Argentina in December 1996 was the requirement that every bank have an annual rating provided by an agency registered with the central bank.[21] Institutions with more than $50 million in assets were required to have ratings from two agencies. As part of this scheme, the Argentinean central bank was responsible for performing an after-the-fact review of the credit ratings to confirm that the rating agencies were doing a proper job. In addition, banks were required to post these credit ratings in their branches, on all deposit certificates, and on all other publications intended to solicit funds from the public.[22] The lack of a credit rating or a poor rating would make depositors and other creditors reluctant to put their funds into a bank, thus giving the bank incentives to reduce its risk taking and boost its credit rating.[23] The elements of the Argentine regulatory system that focused on disclosure worked extremely well in promoting a healthy banking system; it was the failure of the regulatory system to deal effectively with currency mismatch and the large holdings of government bonds that led to the destruction of the country's banking system.[24]

Making Prudential Supervision Work

We would like to think that politicians and government officials (the *agents*) work on behalf of the public (the *principals*), but this view doesn't take human nature into account. The principal-agent problem occurs because agents have incentives to act in their own interest rather than in the principals' interest.

To act in the public's interest, prudential regulators and supervisors have to limit currency mismatch, restrict connected lending, ensure that banks have enough capital, make sure that banks don't take on too much risk, and encourage disclosure. They also must not engage in regulatory forbearance by allowing financial institutions that are broke to continue to operate, because such an approach creates enormous incentives for banks with almost nothing to lose to take on even more risk. Because of the principal-agent problem, however, prudential supervisors have incentives to do just the opposite. Bankers in developing countries may bribe these government officials to allow banks to skirt prudential regulations, or persuade politicians to pressure the supervisors to weaken regulations or look the other way when banks are not complying with them. The principal-agent problem, and the inadequate prudential supervision that results, has been the source of financial crises in emerging market countries (such as Mexico and South Korea), and it has also has led to banking crises in most advanced countries, including the United States.[25]

What reforms can limit the principal-agent problem and ensure that prudential supervision will work?

1. Implement Prompt Corrective Action

To avoid financial crises, it is essential for prudential supervisors to quickly stop undesirable activities by financial institutions and, even more importantly, to avoid regulatory forbearance and close down institutions that do not have sufficient capital. An important way to ensure that bank supervisors do not engage in regulatory forbearance is to implement *prompt corrective action provisions* which require supervisors to intervene earlier and more vigorously either to force financial institutions to make necessary changes or to close them down if they are near insolvency.[26] Prompt corrective action is crucial to preventing problems in the financial sector because it creates incentives for institutions to take on less risk in the first place: they know that, if they assume too much risk, they will be closed down quickly when they get into trouble.

For corrective action to be effective, supervisors must have an accurate assessment of banks' condition. Such accuracy is achieved by examining banks frequently and ensuring that they recognize their bad loans, so that they are subtracted from the amount of capital on hand. It is particularly important to prohibit banks from evergreening, a practice common in developing countries in which banks extend new loans to troubled borrowers, who then use the new loans to pay back the old loans plus interest.[27] In this way the banks take the old loans, which would otherwise be classified as nonperforming, off their books and so do not have to record the loss and lower the value of their capital.

Not only must weak institutions be closed down, but such closures must be done properly. Funds must not be supplied to weak or insolvent institutions to keep them afloat. The correct way to recapitalize a banking system is to close down all insolvent and weak institutions and sell off their assets to healthy institutions. If healthy institutions cannot be persuaded to buy these assets, a public corporation—like the Resolution Trust Corporation in the United States or the Korea Asset Management Corporation in South Korea—can be created which will have the responsibility of selling off the assets of the defunct banks. In order to put these assets quickly into productive use by the private sector, and so limit the losses, they must be sold off as promptly as possible, as was the case in both the United States and South Korea.

The government must also make clear that stockholders, managers, and large creditors will suffer significant losses when financial institutions are closed and public funds are injected into the financial system. If these entities expect to be bailed out by the government (and this is often the case in developing countries), they will have tremendous moral hazard incentives to take on risk. If their bets pay off, they win big; if the bets fail, the government will cover (at least partially) their losses.

Punishing the managers and owners of insolvent financial institutions is necessary to generate public support for committing sufficient funds to clean up the financial sector. In the United States, for example, owners of insolvent banking institutions such as savings and loans did incur substantial financial losses when they failed; some were even jailed. Such actions helped provide political support for the full cleanup of the savings and loan and banking industries in the late 1980s and early 1990s. Such a thorough housecleaning is rare in developing countries, and even in certain advanced countries, like Japan. As a result the public is often unwilling to support the injection of public funds into the banking system to get it back on its feet. In Japan the public was outraged that owners of failed banking institutions (some of whom were criminal figures) got off free. The lack of political support for cleaning up its banking mess has been disastrous for Japan, and it was an important cause of the country's economic stagnation.[28]

2. Limit "Too Big to Fail" Policies

Because the failure of a large financial institution makes it more likely that a major, systemic financial disruption will occur, banking supervisors are naturally reluctant to allow such an institution to fail and cause losses to depositors. As a result most countries either explicitly or implicitly have a *"too big to fail" policy* under which all depositors (insured and uninsured) at a big bank are fully protected if the bank fails.[29] The problem with such a policy is that it increases the moral hazard incentives for big banks to take on excessive risk. Once large depositors know that a financial institution is too big to fail, they have no incentive to monitor the bank or pull out their deposits when it takes on too much risk. No matter what the bank does, large depositors will not suffer any losses. And as monitoring of banks by depositors declines, banks are more likely to take on even bigger risks, making failures all the more likely.[30]

This problem is even more severe in emerging market countries, because their financial systems are typically smaller than those in developed countries.

These systems tend to be dominated by fewer institutions, which are large relative to the overall size of the economy, increasing the likelihood that they will be considered too big to fail.

Government officials, particularly in less-developed countries, are also reluctant to close banks that are "too politically connected to fail." In Indonesia before its financial crisis in 1997, it was widely expected that the government of President Suharto would bail out the banks owned by his children and cronies, and this is exactly what happened, despite the protests of the IMF. The government connections and political power of large financial institutions are typically much greater in emerging market countries, making it more likely that they will be bailed out if they experience difficulties. Indeed, in many such countries, other creditors, stockholders, and uninsured depositors have been protected when large institutions have been subject to failure.

Limiting the moral hazard that arises when financial institutions are too big or too politically connected to fail is a critical part of prudential supervision in emerging market countries. To discourage large institutions from taking on excessive risk, supervisors need to scrutinize them even more rigorously and allow large depositors, and especially shareholders and managers, to suffer losses when these institutions are insolvent.[31]

The same incentives clearly apply to nonfinancial companies if they are considered by the government to be too big or too politically connected to fail. Lenders, knowing that they are unlikely to be subjected to losses if a company gets into trouble, will not monitor the company and call in its loans if it is taking on excessive risk. In many emerging market countries, governments have propped up large and politically connected companies when they suffered financial distress; this support has only led to increased risk taking by these companies, especially when they faced difficult times. As we have seen, the "too big to fail" policy for the chaebols was a key factor behind the South Korean financial crisis.

To eliminate incentives for the corporate sector to take on too much risk, "too big to fail" policies must be eliminated, as in the financial sector. This reform implies a greater separation between the corporate sector and the government, necessitating a change in the business cultures of many emerging market countries.

3. Give Adequate Resources to Prudential Regulators and Supervisors

In many emerging market countries, prudential regulators and supervisors are not given sufficient resources to do their jobs effectively. In close to 40% of developing countries, supervisors can be held personally liable for their actions in civil lawsuits.[32] In addition their salaries are generally low relative to those paid in the private sector. In India, for example, bank supervisors in the late 1990s typically had an annual salary of $3000 (plus housing benefits), while a comparable assistant vice president position in a private sector bank was paying $75,000.[33] While the problem of low public sector pay relative to the private sector also exists in rich countries, it is far less severe. When I was an executive at the Federal Reserve Bank of New York, I worried that employees could often double or triple their salaries by moving to the private sector—not increase their income by a factor of twenty-five!

Without sufficient resources and incentives, supervisors will not adequately monitor the activities of banks and their managers. Indeed, proper monitoring of banking institutions has been absent in both emerging market countries *and* industrialized countries. For example, the U.S. Congress's resistance to providing the savings and loan supervisory agencies with the resources to hire an adequate number of bank examiners was a key factor in worsening the savings and loan crisis in the 1980s.

Giving supervisors the resources to do their jobs is critical to promoting a financial system that is resistant to financial crises. Ruth de Krivoy, who was the president of Venezuela's central bank during that country's banking crisis in 1994 and witnessed the supervisory process from the inside, has put it nicely: supervisors in emerging market countries must be given not merely adequate compensation but also respect.[34] If they are paid poorly, they will be more easily bribed, either directly or through promises of high-paying jobs, by the institutions they supervise. Allowing supervisors to be held personally liable in legal suits for carrying out their responsibilities makes it less likely that they will take the appropriate actions, for fear of such suits. And if they do not have sufficient resources to monitor financial institutions, particularly in terms of information technology, they will be unable to spot excessive risk taking.

Adequate government funding to enable supervisors to close down insolvent institutions is also essential if prompt corrective action is to work. When a banking system is in trouble, politicians and regulatory authorities often engage in wishful thinking, hoping to avoid a large injection of public funds to save the system. Such regulatory forbearance only allows insolvent institutions to keep operating and invites even more disastrous consequences.

4. Give Independence to Regulatory and Supervisory Agencies

Because politicians often pressure prudential supervisors to discourage them from doing their jobs, the bank regulatory or supervisory agency must be sufficiently independent from the political process that it will not be encouraged to sweep problems under the rug.[35] Providing supervisory agencies with adequate resources will help promote their independence. If supervisory agencies must come hat in hand to the government for the funds to close down insolvent institutions, they will be subject to political pressure to engage in regulatory forbearance.

5. Make Supervisors Accountable

Giving independence to prudential supervisors is not an unmixed blessing. The principal-agent problem shows that they will not always act in the public's interest. They have incentives not only to do the bidding of bankers and politicians in not enforcing regulations to restrain bank risk taking, but also to engage in regulatory forbearance, hiding the problems of insolvent banks and hoping the situation will improve—a behavior that Edward J. Kane, an expert on banking, has characterized as "bureaucratic gambling."[36]

To improve incentives for them to do their jobs properly, supervisors must be held accountable if they engage in regulatory forbearance.[37] Opening up the actions of bank supervisors to public scrutiny makes this course less attractive to them, thereby reducing the principal-agent problem. In addition, politicians will be less likely to influence supervisors to relax their supervision of banks when the reasons for supervisory actions are visible to the public. To encourage supervisors to do their jobs, they must also be subject to criminal prosecution (but not civil lawsuits) if they are caught taking bribes, and they must be subject to censure and penalties if they take jobs with institutions that they have recently supervised. In many emerging market countries, supervisors are allowed to get too close to the institutions they supervise and go to work for them almost immediately after leaving the public sector.

6. Strong Discretionary Supervisory Powers May Backfire

The new Basel Accord for bank supervision (known as Basel II), which is to go into effect in 2007 and 2008, has strengthening of official supervision as one of its three pillars. (The other two are institution of minimum capital requirements and strengthening of market discipline.) Basel II suggests that supervisors be given stronger statutory, discretionary powers such as the legal ability to issue cease and desist orders to force a bank to change its internal organizational structure, suspend dividends, stop bonuses, decrease management fees, remove and replace managers and directors, and so on. These powers provide supervisors with a stick to force banks to comply with regulations and to restrain them from engaging in risky behavior.

However, giving supervisors these powers is beneficial *only* if they are acting in the public interest, that is, only if the principal-agent problem is not severe. In countries with a strong rule of law, an active free press that holds supervisors accountable for their actions, and relatively high wages for supervisors, supervisory powers are far more likely to be used in the public interest. What works well in rich countries with strong institutional environments, however, may not work in the weaker institutional environments of developing countries. Instead of acting in the public interest as a helping hand, supervisors may instead act in their own interest as a grabbing hand. An important new book, *Rethinking Bank Regulation and Supervision: Till Angels Govern*, uses a unique database on bank supervisory practices throughout the world compiled by the World Bank to see whether supervisors act as a helping hand or a grabbing hand.[38] In rich countries supervisors generally help; in developing countries they generally grab. The statistical evidence suggests that strengthening the discretionary powers of supervisors in developing countries has led to lower levels of bank development, greater corruption in lending, and banks that are less sound.

The possibility that supervisors in developing countries will act as a grabbing hand suggests that giving them strong statutory authority to implement prudential measures like prompt corrective action, limiting connected lending, focusing on risk management, and limiting "too big to fail" policies may not work well. This is one reason why making supervisors accountable by increasing the transparency of their actions is so important: it makes it less likely that they will grab and more likely that they will help. If institutional development is so weak in a country that this cannot be done, then following the Basel II recommendation of strengthening supervisory powers may do more harm than good.

Should we just throw up our hands and give up on prudential supervision in developing countries with weak institutional environments? Clearly not. Measures to make prudential supervision effective should be high on policymakers' agendas. But since instituting effective and accountable prudential supervision takes time, stronger statutory powers for supervisors may have to be phased in. For countries with weak institutional development, prudential supervision may need to focus less on telling banks what to do and more on encouraging market discipline by making sure banks comply with disclosure requirements, that is, making sure that information provided by financial institutions is both accurate and sufficient. Only when the institutional environment has improved to the point that supervisors are accountable for doing their jobs properly should they be given discretionary statutory powers.

7. Get the Government Out of the Banking Business

Governments in developing countries often set up banking systems dominated by state-owned banks which do not have the incentives to allocate credit to productive uses. The resulting poor allocation of capital leads to less efficient investment and slower growth.[39] State-owned banks also weaken the banking system. The absence of a profit motive means that they are less likely to manage risk properly and operate efficiently. State-owned banks typically have larger loan losses than private institutions, and the countries with the largest share of state-owned banks, on average, are also the ones with a higher percentage of nonperforming loans and higher operating costs.[40]

The inefficiency of state-owned banks and their higher loan losses strongly argue for privatization of the banking sector. However, even privatization must be managed properly or it can lead to disaster. If purchasers of banks are those who are likely to engage in excessive risk taking or even fraud, banking problems will arise. If purchasers are allowed to put very little of their own capital into the bank (as in Mexico), they may also have strong incentives to engage in risky activities at the depositors' and taxpayers' expense. If corporations are allowed to purchase banking institutions (as in South Korea), they are more likely to make connected loans, which in turn are more likely to end in default. The potential downsides of privatization do not suggest that it should be avoided altogether, but rather that the chartering or licensing process be sufficiently stringent to screen out bad owners and ensure that bank ownership goes to individuals who will improve bank performance relative to that under the previous government managers.

Opening Up the Financial System to Foreigners

Opening up the financial system to foreigners, a key element of financial globalization, encourages financial and economic development by lowering the cost of capital directly and by increasing the support for domestic reforms that will make the system operate more efficiently. It also has the potential benefit of making financial crises less likely.

1. Allow Entry of Foreign Banks

Many developing countries have laws that prevent foreign banks from establishing branches or affiliates in the country. Instead of seeing foreign banks as a threat, developing countries should see their entry as an opportunity to increase the stability of the financial system in general and the efficiency of the banking system in particular.[41]

Foreign banks have more diversified portfolios and often have access to sources of funds from all over the world through their parent companies. This diversification means that these foreign banks are exposed to less risk and are less affected by negative shocks to the home country's economy. Because many emerging market and transition economies are more volatile than industrialized countries, having a large foreign component to the banking sector is especially valuable because it can help insulate the banking system from domestic shocks. Encouraging the entry of foreign banks is thus likely to lead to a banking and financial system that is substantially less fragile and far less prone to crisis. In fact, data show that countries that allow foreign bank entry have more stable financial systems and fewer episodes of financial crisis.[42]

The entry of foreign banks can also encourage adoption of best management and prudential supervisory practices. Foreign banks come with expertise in areas like risk management and are typically more efficient than domestic banks.[43] For example, when bank examiners see better practices in risk management, they can encourage the spread of these practices throughout their country's banking system by downgrading banks that do not adopt them. Having foreign banks demonstrate the latest risk management techniques can thus lead to improved control of risk in the home country's banking system.[44]

Foreign bank entry can redistribute economic power to encourage institutional reforms. Foreign banks know firsthand of the benefits of screening and monitoring credit risks from the institutional frameworks in the advanced countries where they originate; therefore they have incentives to encourage the domestic government to take steps to improve the quality of the financial system. As domestic financial institutions lose business to foreign banks, they too will recognize the need for reforms to improve the legal system and the quality of information in financial markets, so that they can make profitable loans to new customers. Foreign bank entry can have the added benefit of turning domestic financial institutions into supporters of institutional reform.

Encouraging the entry of foreign banks makes it more likely that a failed bank's uninsured depositors and creditors will not be bailed out.[45] Governments are far less likely to bail out the banking sector if a large number of banks are foreign owned because such a move will be politically unpopular.[46] Thus uninsured depositors and other creditors will have greater incentives to monitor a bank's practices and performance and will withdraw their funds if it takes on too much risk. The resulting increase in market discipline is likely to encourage more prudent behavior by banking institutions: foreign banks have higher amounts of funds set aside to cover potential loan losses (loan loss provisions) and have higher recovery rates for loans that go into default.[47]

Are there disadvantages to foreign bank entry? Two concerns about the entry of foreign banks seem unfounded. The first is that the entry of foreign banks might hurt small customers because it may cause the demise of the small domestic banks that specialize in lending to small businesses and individuals. A similar concern was expressed in rich countries like the United States when large banks from one state were allowed to open branches in other states, and the fear that small businesses would suffer from interstate branching was generally unfounded.[48] When domestic banks in Argentina were first acquired by foreign banks, they did not initially focus on consumer, mortgage, or property lending, but over time they began to enter these businesses aggressively, thereby lowering interest rates for consumers.[49]

A second concern is that foreign banks may be more likely to cut and run (close their branches and stop lending) during a crisis and thus could exacerbate the crisis. However, the opposite seems to be the case in emerging market countries like Argentina and Mexico, where the presence of foreign banks has stabilized credit flows during crises.[50]

In recent years, the benefits of foreign entry of banking institutions have been more widely recognized in emerging market countries, with the result that the foreign share of emerging market banking markets has grown. Today in Argentina, Chile, Mexico, and Peru, more than 50% of the assets in the banking system are in foreign banks, compared with less than 30% in 1995.[51] A major study done by the Inter-American Development Bank, *Unlocking Credit: The Quest for Deep and Stable Bank Lending*, concludes that the benefits of foreign bank entry greatly outweigh its potential costs.[52]

However, there *are* possible downsides to allowing foreign bank entry. Entry of foreign banks will only generate benefits if it increases competition in the financial system. If foreign banks are allowed to create monopolies, they may not have the incentives to be efficient and to bring in best practices. If they earn monopoly profits, they are also less likely to support institutional reform. Ensuring that foreign bank entry will in fact make the banking system more competitive may require rules—along the lines of the antitrust regulations that we see in many advanced countries like the United States—that make it difficult for foreign banks and domestic banks to unfairly squeeze out their competition.

Foreign bank entry may have another downside if it leads to a banking system with too large a share of foreign banks. Because foreign banks are unlikely to have a domestic political constituency, if a banking crisis occurs they can be a convenient scapegoat for the government. The government may blame them for causing the crisis and expropriate some of their resources. This happened in Argentina just after its currency board collapsed in 2002: banks, because they were mostly foreign, were required to pay their depositors a larger number of pesos per dollar than they were allowed to collect on their loans; they suffered large losses.[53] The lack of political protection for foreign banks is both good and bad. They are less likely to be bailed out and so have less incentive to take on too much risk. On the other hand, they are more likely to be subjected to large losses if a country experiences a crisis—and this may deter them from entering an emerging market country in the first place.

2. Only Use Capital Controls as Part of Prudential Supervision

In the aftermath of recent financial crises in which countries experienced large capital inflows before the crisis and large capital outflows afterward, much attention has been focused on whether international capital movements are a major source of financial instability and should therefore be controlled.

The case for capital controls. The pattern of financial crises suggests that international capital movements play an important role in producing financial instability when a government safety net and inadequate supervision of banking institutions encourage capital inflows which lead to a lending boom and excessive risk taking by banks.[54] Controls on capital inflows of the type implemented in Chile in the early 1990s have received support from prominent policymakers, economists, and media sources—including Robert Rubin, former secretary of the U.S. Treasury, Stanley Fischer, former first deputy managing director of the IMF, and the *Economist* magazine—because they are seen as a way to cut off the fuel for a lending boom that can trigger a financial crisis.[55]

Capital outflows have also been cited as a cause of the foreign exchange crises that have promoted financial instability in emerging market countries: foreigners pull their capital out of a country, and the resulting capital outflow forces the country to devalue its currency. Controls on capital outflows may thus lessen the severity of the crisis, and this strategy has been endorsed by such economists as Paul Krugman, Dani Rodrik, and Joseph Stiglitz.[56]

The case against capital controls. Capital controls that interfere with the free operation of financial markets also have many undesirable consequences. Controls on capital inflows may block the entrance of funds that could be used for productive investments.[57] In addition, opening up the financial sector to foreign capital can promote beneficial reforms, and capital controls on inflows interfere with this process. Although these controls may limit the fuel supplied to lending booms, over time they produce substantial distortions and misallocation of resources, as households and businesses try to get around them.[58] Controls on capital inflows can lead to corruption, with government officials getting paid off to look the other way when firms are trying to bring capital into the country. There are serious doubts about whether capital controls can be effective in today's environment, in which trade is open and so many financial instruments make it easier to circumvent these controls. There is little evidence that controls on capital inflows actually make crises less likely: to the contrary, the evidence suggests that capital controls probably make financial crises more likely.[59]

This analysis of why financial crises occur certainly does not make a case for control of capital outflows as a solution to financial crises. We have seen that a key factor in foreign exchange crises is problems in the domestic economy (such as weak banks or irresponsible fiscal policy) that lead to speculative attacks and subsequent capital outflows. In this view, the capital outflow associated with the foreign exchange crisis is a symptom of underlying fundamental domestic problems rather than the cause of the crisis. This observation is borne out by empirical evidence that the first people to pull their money out of a country are not foreigners but domestic residents.[60] The consensus from many empirical studies provides support for this view: changes in capital flows or the current account do not predict foreign exchange crises, but fundamentals, such as problems in the banking sector, do.[61]

Capital controls on outflows of the type put in place by Malaysia in the immediate aftermath of the 1997 crisis suffer from several serious deficiencies. First, empirical evidence indicates that controls on capital outflows are seldom effective during a crisis, because the private sector eventually finds ingenious ways to evade them and ultimately has little difficulty moving funds out of the country.[62] This is a key reason why Malaysia instituted its controls for only a brief, temporary period. Second, the evidence suggests that capital flight may even increase after controls are put into place, because confidence in the government is weakened.[63] Third, controls on capital outflows are even more likely to lead to corruption than controls on capital inflows, because domestic residents will be desperate to get their funds out of the country during a crisis and so will pay even greater bribes. Fourth, controls on capital outflows may lull governments into thinking they do not have to take steps to reform their financial systems to deal with the crisis, with the result that opportunities are lost to improve the economy.[64] Fifth, putting controls on capital outflows, even temporarily, may discourage capital from flowing into the country by suggesting that it may be difficult to take out the proceeds from investments in the future.[65]

Paul Krugman, Dani Rodrik, and Joseph Stiglitz have taken the position that Malaysia performed better than other East Asian countries after the crisis, suggesting that Malaysia's capital controls did help lessen the severity of the crisis.[66] I take a different position, one that I believe is more consistent with the facts.[67] That Malaysia was in a far better position than other East Asian countries at the onset of its troubles explains why its crisis was less severe. Before the crisis, Malaysia had a smaller lending boom and a smaller problem with nonperforming loans because its central bank did a much better job of supervising the banking system than did the central banks in the other crisis countries.[68] Instead, it was the anti-market policies and statements of the Mahathir government that caused the Malaysian crisis to be as severe as it was. The primary impact of the Malaysian capital controls was to give the government greater scope to assist politically connected firms and to engage in cronyism. The fact that politically connected firms saw a relative rise in their stock market value when the capital controls were imposed supports the negative impact of these controls.[69]

The case for prudential controls. There is a strong case for improving bank regulation and supervision so that capital inflows are less likely to produce a lending boom and excessive risk taking by banking institutions. For example, if banks were restricted in how fast their foreign borrowing could grow, the impact of capital inflows might be dampened. These prudential controls could be thought of as a form of capital control, but they are different from the typical controls because they focus on the sources of financial fragility rather than the symptoms. Supervisory controls of this type can enhance the efficiency of the financial system rather than hamper it.

The controls on capital inflows implemented in Chile, so often cited by proponents of capital controls as a success, were not designed to restrict the overall inflow of capital but were instead intended to restrict only *short-term* capital inflows ("hot money") that might destabilize the financial system. The controls were not set up as an outright ban but as a tax on capital inflows that would only be in effect for a short time. They look less like restrictions on capital flows and more like a form of prudential control. Indeed, the evidence is strong that the overall flow of capital into Chile was unaffected by the controls, but that the composition of the flows was more long term than short term.[70] Chile eventually decided that these controls were unproductive, and in April 2001 Chile's capital account was completely liberalized with the elimination of all restrictions on capital flows.

Managing the Overall Economy

So far I have outlined reforms that focus on the details of how to develop a financial system that is less prone to crises. But there is a bigger picture: the overall economy must be managed to prevent financial crises.

1. Financial Liberalization Should Be Sequenced

Although deregulation and liberalization are highly desirable objectives, the analysis of financial crises indicates that, if this process is not managed properly, it can be disastrous. A crash program of immediate deregulation and liberalization can have negative consequences that may be difficult to predict. If the proper bank regulatory/supervisory structure, accounting and disclosure requirements, restrictions on connected lending, and well-functioning legal and judicial systems are not in place when liberalization occurs, the appropriate constraints on risk-taking behavior will be far too weak. Bad loans will be likely, with potentially disastrous consequences for bank balance sheets in the future.

In addition, before liberalization occurs, banks may not have the expertise to make loans wisely, and so opening them up to new lending opportunities may also lead to loan portfolios of poor quality. Opening up to foreign capital inflows often leads to a lending boom, because of increased opportunities for bank lending and because of financial deepening in which more funds flow into the banking system. Although financial deepening is a positive development for an economy in the long run, in the short run the lending boom may outstrip the available information resources and promote a financial collapse.

The dangers of financial deregulation and liberalization do not imply that countries would be better off by rejecting liberalization. To the contrary, financial liberalization and globalization are critical to the efficient functioning of financial markets. Getting funds to those with the most productive investment opportunities is especially critical in emerging market countries, because these investments can have especially high returns, thereby stimulating rapid economic growth.

To avoid financial crises, policymakers need to put in place the proper institutional structure before liberalizing their financial systems, especially if there are no restrictions on financial institutions seeking funds abroad or issuing foreign-denominated debt.[71] Crucial to avoiding financial crises is implementation of the policies outlined earlier: limits on currency mismatch, restrictions on connected lending and ownership by commercial enterprises, requirements for adequate bank capital, an appropriate focus on risk management, adequate disclosure and encouragement of market-based discipline, adoption of prompt corrective action, limits on "too big to fail" policies, provision of adequate resources to bank supervisors, shielding of bank regulators and supervisors from short-run political pressure, increased accountability of bank supervisors, elimination of state-owned banks, and encouragement of the entry of foreign banks.

There is an important counterargument to the view that these reform measures must be fully in place before financial liberalization can take place.[72] Because, as we have seen, powerful elites in emerging market countries often oppose reforms intended to improve the working of the financial system, many countries do not pursue reforms before they undertake financial liberalization. Instead, the opening up of the financial system itself provides an important impetus for reform. Indeed, in one study of financial liberalizations, the rule of law improved before financial liberalization in only 18% of countries, while it improved after liberalization in 64%.[73] This same study also found that financial liberalization is followed by greater volatility in business cycles but leads to more stability in the long run.[74]

Because financial liberalization may still be worth pursuing even if the necessary reforms are not already in place and because of the stresses that rapid expansion of the financial sector puts on both managerial and supervisory resources, restricting the growth of credit when financial liberalization is put into place makes a lot of sense. Such restrictions can take the form of putting upper limits on loan-to-value ratios or, for consumer credit, setting maximum repayment periods and minimum downpayment percentages. Restrictions can also be placed on how fast certain types of loans in banks' portfolios are allowed to grow. In addition, at the beginning of the liberalization process, restrictions on foreign-denominated debt and prudential controls that might limit capital inflows may be necessary to reduce the vulnerability of the newly liberalized financial system. As the appropriate infrastructure is put into place, these restrictions can be reduced.

Although a complete financial liberalization is a worthy goal, it may have to be phased in over time, with some restrictions imposed along the way.

The arguments for phasing in financial liberalization have important lessons for China. The Chinese authorities have recognized that the development of an efficient financial system is a high priority. However, they are still a long way from this goal. Many of the recommendations listed earlier have not yet been implemented. Prudential regulation of the banking system is still in a primitive state, while the state-owned banking sector, which dominates Chinese financial markets, has a huge problem with bad loans. Although the government is making some progress on dealing with these problems (for example, it has pumped nearly $250 billion into recapitalizing the largest four banks and has allowed over sixty foreign banks to set up shop in China),[75] pushing financial liberalization and globalization too quickly would almost surely lead to disaster. Indeed, Chinese officials have been very concerned recently about the continued rapid growth of lending and have been trying to rein it in.[76] At this juncture, full-scale financial liberalization and opening up completely to foreign capital flows would further fuel the lending boom, sharply increase the percentage of nonperforming loans, and eventually lead to a financial crisis. Nevertheless, officials from the advanced countries, and particularly the United States, have been pressuring the Chinese to rapidly liberalize their capital markets and fully integrate them with the world market.[77] This pressure may be ill advised, and the Chinese have wisely not caved in to it. They do need to pursue a process of financial liberalization and globalization, but they must do it at a measured pace.

2. Fiscal Policy Should Be Reformed to Prevent Excessive Budget Deficits

Although most financial crises in recent years have been triggered by deficiencies in the financial system, the Argentine crisis of 2001–02 demonstrates that even a prudential regulatory and supervisory system that effectively restricts risk taking may not be enough to prevent devastating crises if fiscal policy spins out of control. Fiscal reform is thus another key to preventing financial crises in emerging market countries, and it takes several forms.

First, provincial or state governments must not be bailed out by the central government when they cannot pay their bills. Knowing that the central government will come to the rescue, the provinces or states have every incentive to overspend, because they can put the burden onto the taxpayers in other provinces. This is just another manifestation of moral hazard and the free-rider problem, but in this case it applies to governments and not the private sector. When provinces spend far more than they take in and turn to the central government to fund their deficits, the government will print money to pay the bills. This practice leads to high inflation or to a default on the government debt, which triggers a financial crisis. Both outcomes occurred in Argentina.

Americans take it for granted that state budgets have little impact on what happens to federal government debt. Indeed, no one worries that profligate spending by any state or local government will lead to a ballooning federal deficit. Instead Americans focus on what the federal government spends relative to its revenue, and they realize that state and local governments must sink or swim on their own.

As a native New Yorker, I will never forget the full-page headline in the *New York Daily News* on October 30, 1975: "Ford to City: Drop Dead." This quintessential New York–style banner ran when President Gerald Ford turned down a request from local politicians to bail out the city when it was facing a budget crisis. Without the bailout, New York was forced to restructure its debt and cut spending, actions that sent the city into a downward spiral from which it has recovered only in recent years. Although I (along with millions of other New Yorkers) was pained by the consequences for the city, President Ford did exactly the right thing. If the federal government had bailed out New York, then state and local governments would have realized they had license to be fiscally irresponsible, and the United States might have ended up a bit more like Argentina.

Think of what would have happened in California during its recent budget crisis if New York had been bailed out in the 1970s. California would also have expected a federal bailout, and its spending would have spun out of control, with a huge impact on the federal deficit.

A "no bailout" rule for state and local governments is a critical reform for any country, but especially for emerging market countries in which significant government fiscal imbalances can trigger a financial crisis. Alternatively, budget rules can be set up for state and local governments that prevent them from running large deficits. The members of the European Monetary Union have followed this approach with their Stability and Growth Pact, which limits member states to maximum budget deficits of 3% of GDP. However—as has become clear recently when France and Germany violated this limit—enforcing budget rules of this type may not be easy.

Another reform necessary to keep fiscal imbalances from triggering crises is the establishment of budget rules that increase transparency. Fiscal policy gets out of control in emerging market countries because the government's fiscal accounts are nontransparent. If the public has no idea what the government is spending—a clear-cut information asymmetry—then it is hard for them to restrain politicians from spending money on projects that reward their families and friends or the constituents who will fill their campaign coffers. Such pork barrel spending is not restricted to emerging market countries; it occurs in advanced countries as well. There is typically far less transparency in emerging market countries, however, and this is why their fiscal problems are generally far worse.

Increasing transparency by eliminating special accounts and consolidating all fiscal activities under one bottom-line measure that summarizes the total government budget situation is one step in this direction. Giving more power to chief executives or finance ministers to control spending can constrain the tendencies of different parts of the government to push their pet spending projects, which might lead to large budget deficits.[78] In addition, measures requiring balanced budgets can be put in place to ensure fiscal responsibility. However, rules of this type can be manipulated and thus require a high degree of budget transparency to work.

3. The Monetary Policy Framework Should Promote Price Stability

Monetary policy can play an important role in promoting financial stability. Price stability, which entails a low inflation rate, is a worthy goal in its own right. Not only do public opinion surveys indicate that the public is hostile to inflation, but there is also strong evidence that inflation is harmful to the economy. Inflation, particularly at high levels, is found to be negatively associated with growth, while at lower levels it decreases the level of economic activity, although not necessarily the growth rate.[79] Empirical evidence also indicates that price stability helps promote financial deepening, with all the benefits it brings, such as a lower cost of capital, a higher rate of economic growth, and reduction of poverty.[80]

Our understanding of the causes of financial crises provides additional reasons why price stability is so important. We have seen that, when countries have a past history of high inflation, debt contracts are often denominated in foreign currencies,[81] and this liability dollarization makes the financial system more fragile because currency depreciation can trigger a financial crisis. Achieving price stability is a necessary condition for having a sound currency, and with a sound currency it is far easier for banks, nonfinancial firms, and the government to raise capital with debt denominated in domestic currency. Israel, for example, went from over 50% dollarization of its bank deposits in the mid-1980s to less than 10% by the mid-1990s after a decade of achieving low and stable inflation and fiscal consolidation. The successful pursuit of price stability is another way to reduce an economy's dependence on foreign-denominated debt, reduce currency mismatches, and enhance financial stability.[82]

What reforms can help emerging market countries achieve price stability? Examining this topic could fill a book, so I will only touch on it here. The fiscal reforms mentioned earlier are key; if fiscal imbalances become too large, governments resort to printing money to finance their deficits, and inflation will take off. Indeed, the primary reason that emerging market countries often have such a bad historical experience with inflation is that they have so often pursued irresponsible fiscal policy. Central banks also need to be insulated from the political process, because politicians typically focus on the short-run creation of jobs and often push central banks to pursue an expansionary policy to create them. When this happens, inflation rises, which harms the economy in the long run and thus eventually hurts workers rather than helping them.[83] Granting the central bank independence so that it can set monetary policy without political interference can help it to focus on the longer-term goal of containing inflation. In addition, giving the central bank a mandate to pursue price stability as its overriding goal can provide more political support for measures to control inflation. As I have advocated in a number of articles and in my book *Inflation Targeting: Lessons from the International Experience*, which I wrote with Ben Bernanke (now the chairman of the Federal Reserve), Thomas Laubach, and Adam Posen, having the government and the central bank commit to achieving an explicit numerical goal for inflation (an *inflation target*) can help anchor inflation expectations and increase the probability that the central bank will seriously pursue the goal of price stability.[84] The resulting improved control of inflation and reduction of liability dollarization will promote financial stability.

4. Pegging the Exchange Rate Can Be Dangerous

Pegged-exchange-rate regimes, in which the domestic currency is pegged to a foreign currency like the U.S. dollar, have often been used by emerging market countries to promote price stability. Although often successful in bringing inflation down, such regimes have also been a common element in financial crises in emerging market countries. A pegged-exchange-rate regime appears to encourage liability dollarization, which makes the economy highly vulnerable to harmful effects from depreciation of the domestic currency.[85] By providing a more stable value for the currency, an exchange rate peg can lower the perceived risk for foreign investors and thus encourage capital inflows. Although these capital inflows might be channeled into productive investments and stimulate growth, the presence of a government safety net and weak bank supervision can lead instead to excessive lending. The capital inflow is then likely to lead to a lending boom, an explosion of nonperforming loans, and an eventual financial crisis.

A pegged-exchange-rate regime can also make it easier for a country to tap foreign markets for credit and, with access to additional markets for its debt, for the government to engage in irresponsible fiscal policy. Argentina again provides a graphic example of this problem: when its fiscal policy became unsustainable, it provoked a disastrous crisis that pushed it into a serious depression.

Pegged-exchange-rate regimes are subject to speculative attacks, and if these attacks are successful the collapse of the domestic currency is usually much larger, more rapid, and less anticipated than when a depreciation occurs under a floating-exchange-rate regime.[86] The pegged regime makes an emerging market economy especially vulnerable to twin crises, in which the currency collapse destroys firms' and households' balance sheets, thus provoking a financial crisis and a sharp economic contraction.

The hazards of pegged-exchange-rate regimes are evident in the case studies of financial crises in Chapters 5–7, and additional research confirms their dangers. Countries exiting from such regimes experience more serious financial crises and larger declines in output the longer the exchange rate peg has been in place.[87]

These hazards are so clear that most emerging market countries would be far better off avoiding exchange rate pegs and instead adopting a flexible regime in which the exchange rate is allowed to float on a daily basis. As Stanley Fischer, former first deputy managing director of the IMF, put it: "The adoption of flexible exchange rate systems by most emerging market countries is by far the most important emerging market crisis prevention measure."[88] Under a floating regime, exchange rate movements are much less nonlinear than in a pegged-exchange-rate regime. Indeed, the daily fluctuations in the exchange rate in a floating regime make clear to private firms, banks, and governments that there is substantial risk involved in issuing liabilities denominated in foreign currencies. Furthermore, a depreciation in the exchange rate may provide an early warning signal to policymakers to enable them to adjust their policies to limit the potential for a financial crisis.[89]

Floating-exchange-rate regimes do not avoid the negative consequences of exchange rate volatility, because liability dollarization does not disappear entirely and a currency depreciation can still damage balance sheets and harm the economy. Nevertheless, scorched fingers are better than death by fire.[90]

Thus a pegged-exchange-rate regime, which is backed only by a government's announcement of the peg and not by a firmer institutional commitment, is likely to increase financial instability in emerging market countries. This is why in my academic writings I have advocated the adoption of a floating-exchange-rate regime for most emerging market countries, but with a strong commitment to controlling inflation by means of an inflation target.[91]

Pegged exchange rates are not always inappropriate, however, and advocacy of floating-exchange-rate regimes can be taken too far. As Paul Volcker, a former chairman of the Federal Reserve, has put it, " We still hear the siren song that somehow floating exchange rates will solve the problem. That seems to me a strange and sad refrain."[92]

In emerging market countries whose political and monetary institutions are particularly weak and which therefore have a history of high inflation, fixing the exchange rate relative to a sound currency may be the only way to break inflationary psychology and stabilize the economy. This consideration has driven some economists to suggest that there are times when a strong commitment to a fixed exchange rate (either through a currency board or through full dollarization, in which the country abandons its currency and adopts a foreign currency like the dollar as its money) might be necessary.[93]

However, as I have argued earlier in this book and in a study I wrote with Guillermo Calvo, the chief economist of the Inter-American Development Bank, the choice of exchange rate regime, whether a fixed or a floating one, is likely to be of secondary importance compared with the development of sound financial, fiscal, and monetary institutions in producing economic success in emerging market countries.[94] When countries have placed their hopes for institutional development on adoption of a particular exchange rate regime—as the Argentineans did when they adopted the Convertibility Plan— they have been sorely disappointed. Placing too much emphasis on a particular choice of exchange rate regime can actually be harmful because it may reduce the focus on institutional reforms that is so critical to successful financial globalization—reforms such as improved bank and financial sector regulation, fiscal restraint, building consensus for a sustainable and predictable monetary policy, and increasing openness to trade.

5. Open Up to International Trade

Opening up to foreign trade is another measure that can make financial crises not only less likely but also, when they do occur, less severe. When a country experiences a sudden cessation of capital inflows, it can no longer finance its net purchases of foreign goods and services and so must increase its *net exports* (the difference between its exports and imports). The value of the currency must then fall to increase the domestic demand for exports by making them cheaper and decrease the demand for imports by making them more expensive. In this way net exports increase. When a country is more open to trade, exports and imports account for a larger percentage of GDP, and net exports can more easily adjust for a given change in the exchange rate. When there is a sudden stop in capital flows, a country that is more open to international trade will experience less downward pressure on its currency and will be more likely to avoid a currency crisis. In addition, an economy open to trade has more firms exporting goods and services that are priced in foreign currency. When a depreciation occurs, even if firms have debt denominated in foreign currency, the price of the goods and services they produce rises in terms of the domestic currency. When the currency depreciates, the resulting rise in the domestic-currency-denominated value of firms' assets offsets the increase in the foreign-currency-denominated value of their debt, and the depreciation has less impact on their balance sheets.

Trade openness therefore reduces the likelihood of a currency crisis and also makes it less likely that a currency crisis will trigger a severe financial crisis. Empirical research bears this out. Countries that are more open to trade are less likely to experience currency crises, and, when they experience sudden stops in capital flows, the size of the output contraction is smaller.[95] We have already seen that trade openness promotes financial development, which is so necessary for economic growth. The fact that trade openness also makes financial crises less likely and less severe should make achieving such openness a top priority for developing countries.

Building Support for Financial Globalization

The benefits of preventing financial crises are self-evident, but there is another compelling reason to institute reforms that make them less likely: building support for financial globalization. Although financial globalization can generate huge benefits for emerging market countries by encouraging development of the financial system, it also has a dark side. Because it has not always been managed well, it has often led to financial crises, which leave economic devastation in their wake, hitting hardest the poorest and most vulnerable in a society. Not surprisingly, financial crises give financial globalization a bad name and provide powerful ammunition to anti-globalizers. Reforms to prevent financial crises are an imperative. Without these reforms, support for financial globalization will erode and emerging market countries will never achieve the financial systems they need and deserve, and they will never reach their full potential.

The reforms outlined here are challenging to implement, and strong forces often block reform efforts. Business elites in emerging market countries benefit from such practices as connected lending, which provides their businesses with cheap sources of finance. They also want weak prudential regulation and supervision of the banks they own.

But, as we have seen, globalization can help overcome these opposition forces. It increases competition, which weakens domestic elites. It also promotes domestic industries that require more capital and thus have an interest in reforming the financial sector. The next chapters show how international organizations and those of us in the rich countries can create incentives to promote the reforms discussed here. The reforms needed to prevent financial crises are not easy to implement, but they must be given the highest priority if emerging market countries are ever to get rich.

Ten

Recovering from Financial Crises

The previous chapter identified the reforms
needed to realize the benefits of financial
globalization while avoiding the devastation brought on by financial crises. To
make financial globalization work, emerging market countries must have
institutions and policies in place that can not only help prevent financial
crises but also help them recover quickly and at minimal cost if such crises do
occur.

What steps can emerging market countries take to recover quickly from crises?

Restoring Confidence

The key to a rapid recovery is restoration of confidence. Only when confidence
in the system returns will participants return to the financial markets so that
the system will again be able to channel funds to those with productive investment opportunities. When the problems in the financial system are homegrown, the government must demonstrate that it is serious about reform, to
restore the confidence of its own citizens and of foreign partners. It must take
immediate steps to fully recapitalize the financial system,[1] and it must allow
the creditors and owners of banks to suffer large losses.[2] Furthermore, the government must quickly make a commitment to increase and strengthen prudential
regulation and supervision to promote a healthy financial system.

Speed is of the essence in recapitalizing the financial system and implementing financial sector reforms. The faster the government gets the reforms
under way, the quicker confidence will be restored and the recovery can

begin. Procrastination only allows the financial crisis to drive the economy further downward and makes it even harder to recover.

The aftermath of the South Korean crisis of 1997 (described in Chapter 6) provides a near-textbook example of how a recovery should be managed. The South Korean economy bounced back quickly (GDP had climbed to above its previous peak value by 1999) because the new government worked strenuously to restore confidence by pushing forward necessary financial reforms. In December 1997, just one month after the crisis reached its peak, thirteen financial reform bills were pushed through the South Korean National Assembly, including an act establishing a new financial supervisory authority. In addition, the government provided substantial resources to resolve nonperforming loans by purchasing them from troubled financial institutions. The central bank was given more independence from the government, and this made it easier for it to pursue price stability. And the government did not try to blame foreigners for its problems: it made clear that the crisis was a Korean problem that had to be fixed by Koreans. These policies bore fruit almost immediately. By early 1998 the Korean won had stabilized and interest rates began to decline, restoring the balance sheets of financial institutions and corporations and paving the way to a rapid recovery.

What Won't Work in Promoting a Recovery

Another approach to stimulating recovery after emerging market countries experience a financial crisis has been proposed by Joseph Stiglitz.[3] Stiglitz argues that these countries should pursue traditional expansionary monetary and fiscal policies. He (along with Jeffrey Sachs and Paul Krugman) has been extremely critical of the IMF, which advocated tight monetary and fiscal policies for Mexico and the East Asian countries when they were hit by their financial crises.[4] Who is right?

Recovery in Advanced Market Economies

At first blush, Stiglitz's call for expansionary policy in the face of a crisis makes sense, because it is exactly what *advanced* countries like the United States should do when they are faced with a possible financial crisis, and it is fairly easy for advanced countries to pursue such policies.[5] Traditional monetary and fiscal policies, however, only work in advanced economies, because they have institutional features very different from those of emerging market economies.

First, in contrast to emerging market countries, advanced countries do not have a history of defaulting on their debt, because the expansionary fiscal policy undertaken to stimulate economic activity is typically reversed at some point in the future so that the debt can be paid back. In an advanced economy, increases in government spending when the economy is depressed do not produce fears of default. Because people do not believe the government spending will lead to a default, the increase in demand for goods and services that spending creates will help stimulate the economy and promote recovery from depressed conditions.

Second, the structure of debt markets in advanced economies is entirely different from that in emerging market countries: debt contracts are almost solely denominated in domestic currency and, because inflation has tended to be moderate, many debt contracts are of fairly long duration. This debt structure is crucial to the efficacy of an expansionary monetary policy. When a central bank pursues such a policy by injecting liquidity into the financial system, more money chases goods and the price level rises. The higher price level, often referred to as *reflation* of the economy, causes the real debt burden of households and firms to fall, because they can pay back the debt with a smaller amount of labor or goods and services. Reflation induced by monetary policy thus increases the net worth of firms and households. Borrowers now have more collateral to offer lenders, and borrowers have incentives to take on less risk because they have more to lose. Reflation undoes some of the increase in adverse selection and moral hazard problems induced by a financial crisis and helps stimulate recovery. In addition, injecting liquidity into the economy raises the prices of assets, such as land and stocks, thus improving net worth and reducing adverse selection and moral hazard problems.

Expansionary monetary policy works through improving the ability of the financial system to fund investments by reducing asymmetric information problems. But it also operates through more conventional policy transmission mechanisms, which have been the subject of extensive research.[6] Injecting liquidity into the financial system leads to a reduction in interest rates, which, by lowering the cost of financing, stimulates both consumer spending and business investment. The higher asset prices that arise from expansionary monetary policy increase household and firm net worth and directly stimulate spending.

A second method by which a central bank can promote recovery from a financial crisis is to pursue the lender-of-last-resort role defined by Walter Bagehot in his famous book *Lombard Street*, in which he advocated that the central bank should stand ready to lend freely during a financial crisis.[7] Bagehot's prescription was intended as advice to the Bank of England in the nineteenth century, but it is equally valid today in advanced countries. For example, when faced with a possible banking panic, a central bank can provide liquidity to banks to prop them up, giving the government time to close them down in an orderly fashion. Indeed, this is exactly what the Federal Reserve did in 1984 when it lent $5 billion to Continental Illinois, one of the ten largest banks in the United States at the time. The loan gave the Federal Deposit Insurance Corporation time to take over Continental Illinois, thereby making sure that depositors did not suffer any losses.[8] No further runs on other banks occurred, and a bank and financial panic was avoided. The Fed took such action again in the late 1980s and early 1990s, when it extended credit to troubled banks during the banking crisis of that period.

Not only can a central bank in an advanced country act as a lender of last resort to banks, it can also play the same role for the financial system as a whole. Again the United States offers two recent examples: the Federal Reserve provided liquidity in the aftermath of the stock market crash of October 19, 1987, in which stock prices fell by over 20% in one day, and following the September 11, 2001, attack on the World Trade Center.[9]

After the 1987 crash, securities firms needed to extend massive amounts of credit (nearly $2 billion) on behalf of their customers to cover their margin calls, in order to keep the stock market and the related index futures market functioning in an orderly fashion. Understandably enough, banks were growing nervous about the financial health of securities firms and were reluctant to lend to them at the time when they most needed the funds. A spreading collapse of securities firms and a further market meltdown were real possibilities. To prevent this collapse, Alan Greenspan, who had been appointed Fed chairman only a few months before, announced before the opening of the market on Tuesday, October 20, the Federal Reserve's "readiness to serve as a source of liquidity to support the economic and financial system."[10] In addition, the Fed made clear that it would provide liquidity to any bank that would make loans to the securities industry, although this step did not prove necessary. As a result of the Fed's extremely quick intervention, the impact of the stock market crash on the economy was negligible, and the amount of liquidity that the Fed actually needed to supply to the economy was not very large.[11]

An even more dramatic lender-of-last-resort operation was carried out in the aftermath of the destruction of the World Trade Center on September 11, 2001. The collapse of the twin towers destroyed much of the infrastructure that banks and other financial institutions relied on to transfer funds to one another. As a result, the liquidity needs of the financial system skyrocketed. To satisfy these needs and to keep the financial system from seizing up, within a few hours of the incident the Fed made an announcement similar to the one it had made after the crash of 1987: "The discount window [the Fed's lending facility] is available to meet liquidity needs."[12] The Fed then proceeded to provide $45 billion to banks through its discount window, a two-hundred-fold increase over the lending activity during the previous week. As a result of this action, along with the injection of $80 billion of reserves through open-market purchases of government bonds, the financial system kept functioning.

What's Right for Advanced Countries
Is Wrong for Most Emerging Market Countries

All three of these incidents demonstrate the effectiveness of lender-of-last resort operations in an advanced country like the United States in extricating an economy from a financial crisis. The injection of liquidity under an expansionary monetary policy stimulates recovery. That fears of default on government debt are less prevalent in advanced countries makes it more likely that such a policy will stimulate recovery. Thus Joseph Stiglitz's recommendation for promoting recovery from a financial crisis is exactly *right* for advanced economies.

But Stiglitz's prescription is exactly *wrong* for most emerging market economies, because their institutional features are so different.

Emerging market economies differ from advanced economies in several basic ways: much of their debt is denominated in foreign currency; most debt contracts are of very short duration because of the countries' past histories of very high inflation; and expansionary monetary policy is likely to cause expected inflation to rise dramatically. In an economy with these characteristics, a central bank cannot use expansionary monetary policy to promote recovery from a financial crisis.

Think what would happen if expansionary monetary policy and reflation of the economy were pursued in an emerging market country with a large amount of foreign-denominated debt. Given the past record on inflation, the policy would likely arouse a loss of confidence in the central bank and inspire fears that inflation would spiral out of control. In this case, the policy would likely cause the domestic currency to depreciate sharply. This depreciation would raise the burden of firms' indebtedness and lower banks' and firms' net worth: because much of their debt was denominated in foreign currency, balance sheets would deteriorate. In addition, the jump in expected inflation would be likely to cause interest rates to rise because lenders must be protected from the loss of purchasing power when they lend. The resulting rise in interest rates would cause interest payments to soar and the cash flow of households and firms to decline. Household and firm balance sheets would further deteriorate, and banking institutions would potentially suffer greater loan losses. In addition, because debt contracts were of very short duration, the rise in the price level would not appreciably affect the value of households' and firms' debts, so the balance sheet benefit seen in advanced countries would not be seen.

For similar reasons, lender-of-last-resort activities by a central bank in an emerging market country with substantial foreign-denominated debt would be likely to do more harm than good and would not be as beneficial as in advanced countries. In the wake of a financial crisis, central bank lending to the financial system (which expands domestic credit) would be likely to arouse fears that inflation would spiral out of control and cause a substantial depreciation of the domestic currency. This is what happened to South Korea during its crisis in 1997: after financial market participants found out that the Korean central bank was extending credit to troubled financial institutions, the currency collapsed and the financial system imploded.

The net result of injecting liquidity to conduct a lender-of-last operation or to pursue expansionary monetary policy in an emerging market country with a large amount of foreign-denominated debt is damage to the balance sheets of households, firms, and banks. Thus its effect is just the opposite of that found in industrialized countries: it causes a deterioration in balance sheets and amplifies the adverse selection and moral hazard problems in financial markets, rather than dampening them.

If expansionary monetary policy cannot be used in emerging market countries in crisis, can they turn to expansionary fiscal policy to promote recovery? Again the different structure of emerging market economies means that expansionary fiscal policy will work in the wrong direction. Because of past defaults on government debt, expanding government spending during a financial crisis will almost surely make markets more nervous about the ability of the government to pay back its debt. Interest rates on government debt will then shoot through the roof, as happened in Argentina, and interest rates on private debt will rise with them. The resulting rise in interest payments will cause a sharp decline in cash flow, which will exacerbate adverse selection and moral hazard problems in the financial markets. In addition, fears of government default will cause a collapse of the currency, which will destroy balance sheets and make the financial crisis even worse.

What works for advanced countries when they are embroiled in a financial crisis—the pursuit of expansionary monetary and fiscal policies—just won't work in emerging market countries. In these countries, expansionary policies destroy confidence and exacerbate the crisis; they do not offer an easy way out. On the other hand, the tight monetary and fiscal policies recommended by the IMF may not by themselves boost confidence during a crisis, because of the weakened state of the economy.[13] The only way to restore confidence and recover rapidly from a financial crisis is the hard way. The government has to convince the markets that it will pursue serious financial reforms and recapitalize the financial system. This is the route that South Korea took, and its success in recovering from its crisis (even though its reform process has recently stalled) points the way for emerging market countries.

Why the Policies Needed to Stimulate Recovery Are Often Not Implemented

Unfortunately South Korea's response to its financial crisis is the exception rather than the rule. Why have so many countries found it hard to pursue policies that would help their economies recover faster?

One possibility is simple ignorance. Policymakers don't know what to do to facilitate recovery. Yet my experience in the policy world tells me that this is only a small part of the problem. When I began my career as a professor in 1976, I was very idealistic; I believed that understanding the "right" policies would be the key to solving many of the world's problems. Of course this view was extremely naive, and as I became older and wiser I realized that the world was more complicated. Just how complicated arriving at the right policies can be became even clearer to me when I visited Ecuador at the request of the Banco Central del Ecuador in March 1999, shortly after a major financial crisis had begun there. In my meetings with the top officials of the central bank and the ministry of finance, they expressed their fears that the crisis might destabilize the country, an outcome that truly scared them. At the time, Colombia and Peru, their immediate neighbors, had active and dangerous guerilla movements, which might have turned any weakness in Ecuador to their advantage. When we discussed what policy measures were needed to restore confidence, there seemed to be general agreement that reforms along the lines I have presented here were needed. When I asked them what they were going to do, however, the officials indicated that they were unwilling to push hard for the reforms because powerful interests would oppose them. Even in a time of national crisis that could destabilize their society, the officials were telling me that the country would not pull together to solve the problem.

This behavior is, of course, exactly what we might expect, given that reforms to promote recovery from a crisis have benefits that are dispersed widely across a country's citizenry, while the costs are often borne by narrower interests—interests that will fight bitterly to block the reforms.[14] This phenomenon is not restricted to emerging market countries. As we saw in Chapter 4, by the end of 1986, the crisis in the U.S. savings and loan (S&L) industry had reached epidemic proportions. The Federal Home Loan Bank Board, the federal government's deposit insurance agency for the savings and loans, did not have enough funds to close down insolvent S&Ls. President Reagan and the U.S. Congress, faced with intense lobbying by the S&L industry, were unwilling to provide adequate funds, and the crisis was worsening. Only after the new administration of George H. W. Bush took office at the beginning of 1989 was a serious attempt made to clean up the S&L mess. Legislation enacted in 1989 (the Financial Institutions Reform, Recovery and Enforcement Act) and 1991 (the Federal Deposit Insurance Corporation Improvement Act) finally recapitalized the S&Ls and put prudential regulation and supervision of them and commercial banks on a sounder footing. If insolvent institutions had been closed down more promptly, the cost of the bailout would have been "only" $50 billion instead of the more than $150 billion, or 3% of GDP, eventually required.[15]

The Japanese government was even slower to deal with the banking crisis in its country, which started in the mid-1990s. Active lobbying by the banking industry kept the Japanese government from closing down insolvent banks, and it is only recently that the banking industry has begun to return to health. The cost of the crisis to the Japanese taxpayer dwarfs the cost borne by U.S. taxpayers; it is estimated to be 20% of GDP.[16]

If advanced countries like the United States and Japan are unwilling to quickly take the measures necessary to put their financial systems on a solid footing, this problem is likely to be far worse in emerging market countries with lower levels of transparency and a less educated public. But there is hope, as the example of South Korea suggests. Furthermore, international financial institutions like the IMF and the World Bank might be able to help, as we will see in the next chapter.

Part Four

How Can the International Community Promote Successful Globalization?

Eleven

What Should the International Monetary Fund Do?

An overriding theme in previous chapters is that the blame for the failure of globalization usually rests with the emerging market countries themselves. Indeed, taking responsibility for policy failures, as South Korea did in the late 1990s, is a crucial step in putting in place the reforms that can set a country on the path to wealth. Often international institutions such as the IMF step in to help countries in crisis. As often as not, however, the IMF doesn't help matters as much as it could—and sometimes it makes bad situations even worse. Have some IMF policies contributed to globalization failures? Can these policies be reoriented to help emerging market countries make globalization work?

The role of the IMF in coping with financial crises in emerging market countries in recent years has been highly controversial. Indeed, it has come under attack, sometimes quite viciously, by those in both developing and advanced countries. Does the world economy need an IMF?[1] If so, what should be its mission and how should it operate? How can the IMF promote successful financial globalization?

This chapter is not intended to provide an exhaustive examination of the IMF, a topic well beyond the scope of this book.[2] However, the financial crisis framework developed in earlier chapters does have something to say about what the IMF should do and how it should do it.

What Is the International Monetary Fund?

As their victory in World War II was becoming certain in 1944, the Allies met in Bretton Woods, New Hampshire, to develop a new international monetary system to promote world trade and prosperity after the war. The Bretton Woods agreement created two institutions headquartered in Washington, D.C.: the International Monetary Fund, which had 30 original member countries in 1945 and currently has over 180, and the World Bank, whose member countries are the same. The IMF and the World Bank are headquartered just across the street from each other in Washington, and their buildings are in fact connected by underground passageways.

The IMF was given the task of promoting the growth of world trade by setting rules for the maintenance of pegged exchange rates (under the Bretton Woods agreement, countries had their exchange rates pegged to the U.S. dollar) and by making loans to countries that were experiencing balance-of-payments difficulties. IMF lending is funded by contributions (called *quotas*) from the member countries. The World Bank (its more formal name is the International Bank for Reconstruction and Development) was given the role of providing long-term loans that would contribute to economic development and help eradicate poverty. These loans are primarily funded by issuing World Bank bonds, which are sold principally in the capital markets of the developed countries.

As part of its role in monitoring the compliance of member countries with its rules (a function referred to as *surveillance,* although it has nothing to do with spying), the IMF took on the job of collecting and standardizing international economic data. Since the collapse of the Bretton Woods system of pegged exchange rates in 1971, the IMF has assumed new roles. It continues to collect data, and it also provides technical assistance to its member countries and monitors their exchange rate policies. Its role as an international lender to governments increased in importance during the third world debt crisis in the 1980s, when the IMF assisted developing countries, particularly in Latin America, in repaying their loans. This role expanded further during the financial crises in Mexico in 1994–95, East Asia in 1997–98, and Argentina in 2001–02, when the IMF made huge loans to these and other affected countries to help them recover and to prevent the crises from spreading to other countries. This role, in which the IMF acts as an international lender to help governments cope with financial instability, is highly controversial.[3]

Do We Need the IMF as an International Lender of Last Resort?

When a financial crisis occurs, the seizing up of information gathering in the financial system leads to disastrous consequences for a nation and its economy.

The country's financial system must be restarted so that it can resume its job of channeling funds to those with productive investment opportunities. Government can intervene to help put the financial system back on its feet and prevent a financial crisis from spinning out of control through its role as a lender of last resort. This role involves emergency lending by the government or a government agency to companies or financial institutions facing a liquidity squeeze.

In advanced economies, domestic central banks have the ability to prevent financial crises by acting as a lender of last resort to troubled domestic banks and financial institutions. In the United States, as we saw in Chapter 10, the Federal Reserve has acted successfully to prevent two possibly devastating financial seizures over the past twenty years: after the stock market crash of October 19, 1987, and after the terrorist attacks of September 11, 2001.

The necessity for a lender of last resort is just as strong, and arguably stronger, in emerging market countries, because they are especially vulnerable to financial instability. Despite the greater need for a lender of last resort, central banks in these countries often cannot undertake this role because of the nature of their financial systems: the injection of liquidity into the financial system that comes with a lender-of-last-resort action will actually make the financial crisis worse. Why? Because such an injection will cause the domestic currency to depreciate. With a debt structure characterized by short-term debt denominated in foreign currency, this depreciation causes a deterioration of balance sheets and pushes the economy further down in the financial death spiral.

If a domestic central bank cannot conduct a lender-of-last-resort operation to stop a financial crisis or promote a recovery when one occurs, is there someone else who can come to the rescue? The answer comes not from within, but from without: liquidity provided by foreign sources can help emerging market countries cope with financial crises, yet it does not lead to any of the undesirable consequences that result from the provision of liquidity by the domestic central bank. Foreign liquidity assistance does not lead to increased inflation, higher interest rates, and a depreciation of the domestic currency, because it gives the government international reserves which can then be used to stabilize the value of the domestic currency. Indeed, foreign liquidity assistance helps lower interest rates (which improves firms' cash flow) and increase the value of the domestic currency. The resulting strengthening of domestic balance sheets helps undo the asymmetric information problems created by a financial crisis.

Because emerging market countries need help to manage a financial crisis in the absence of a domestic lender of last resort, there is a strong argument for having an international organization serve as that lender.[4] Another possible rationale for having an international lender of last resort exists if there is contagion from one emerging market country to another during a financial crisis.[5]

An international lender of last resort has the ability to stop contagion by providing international reserves to emerging market countries threatened by speculative attacks. This assistance can keep currencies from plummeting and therefore prevent financial crises from spreading.

That there is a need for an international lender of last resort is clear. But what institution is best suited to perform this role?

Traditionally national central banks have acted as lenders of last resort because they can create the necessary liquidity at will and have successfully performed this role. These facts would argue for the creation of a world central bank to act as an international lender of last resort.[6] But creation of such a bank is pie in the sky. It is highly unlikely that nations would give up control of their domestic monetary policy to an international organization.[7]

The only international organization that can currently perform the international lender-of-last-resort role is the IMF.[8] It has plenty of money and a staff of over 2500 economists. It has assumed the role by default, by lending to emerging market governments during recent crises.

One objection to the IMF's performing a lender-of-last-resort role is that it cannot create unlimited liquidity by printing money, as can a central bank.[9] But, as persuasively argued by Stanley Fischer, former first deputy managing director of the IMF, it is not necessary that an international lender of last resort have unlimited resources to create liquidity. It needs just enough to do the job at hand.[10] The IMF's resources might limit its abilities to manage certain crises, but in recent situations they were probably sufficient. Furthermore, if the IMF requires greater resources to adequately deal with financial crises, member nations' quotas could be raised to increase its funds (although the question of whether the IMF should have access to more resources is highly controversial).[11]

The IMF's role as an international lender of last resort does, however, suffer from a major disadvantage relative to the lender-of-last-resort role of a national central bank. The IMF does not provide funds directly to financial markets or institutions to avert financial crises because it does not supervise these institutions; it does not know them well enough to decide whether it makes sense to lend to them. Instead, it lends to domestic governments, who can then use the funds to provide assistance to financial institutions or to meet international financial obligations.[12] The IMF therefore has less control of how the liquidity it provides is used when it conducts a lender-of-last-resort operation than would a central bank.

How Should the IMF Operate as an International Lender of Last Resort?

Although there is a strong need for the IMF to be ready to act as an international lender of last resort so that the benefits of financial globalization can be realized, getting it to do this well will not be easy. And the IMF does have other important duties, derived from its original mandate, that are unrelated to its lender-of-last-resort role, such as making sure that countries maintain exchange rate arrangements that promote international trade. Yet because these other duties are so far removed from the IMF's lending operations, measures to improve the IMF's performance as an international lender of last resort would not interfere with the performance of those duties.

Our understanding of why financial crises occur immediately suggests three general principles for how the IMF can operate effectively as an international lender of last resort.

1. Restore Confidence to the Financial System by Quickly Providing Liquidity

When a financial crisis occurs, the lender of last resort's most crucial task is to restore confidence in the financial system. Without confidence, participants will pull out of the financial markets and the system will not be able to channel funds to those with productive investment opportunities. Confidence is essential to an efficiently operating financial system, and it is key to promoting recovery from or forestalling a financial crisis. Promoting and restoring confidence are easier said than done, however, and they require several measures.

The first measure is to provide ample liquidity so that markets can operate effectively. It is critical that this liquidity be provided as quickly as possible. Experience shows that the faster the lending, the lower the amount that actually must be lent.[13]

The Federal Reserve's lender-of-last-resort operation in the aftermath of the stock market crash in October 1987 illustrates the benefits of acting quickly. What is remarkable about this episode is that the Fed did not need to lend directly to the banks to encourage them to lend to the securities firms who needed funds to clear their customers' accounts. Because the Fed acted so quickly (within a day) and reassured banks that the financial system would not seize up, banks knew that lending to securities firms would be profitable. They saw that it was in their interest to make these loans immediately, even without borrowing from the Fed. Banks thus began lending freely to securities firms, with the result that confidence was restored and the fear of crisis diminished almost immediately. The Fed did not have to increase its lending to the banking system by one penny, and the actual amount of liquidity that the Fed injected into the banking system through open-market operations in the immediate aftermath of the crash was less than $2 billion—a small amount relative to IMF bailouts, which typically run into many billions of dollars. Furthermore, the Fed was able to remove this liquidity almost immediately, within weeks after the crash.

The resolution of and recovery from a financial crisis require a restoration of the balance sheets of financial and nonfinancial firms. Restoration of balance sheets requires several measures: the closing down of insolvent financial institutions, the injection of public funds so that healthy financial institutions can buy up the assets of insolvent institutions, and a well-functioning bankruptcy law that enables the balance sheets of nonfinancial firms to be cleaned up quickly so they can regain access to the credit markets.

Crucial to the successful resolution of a financial crisis is that a nation commit to necessary reforms and not go only halfway. Allowing weak financial institutions to continue to operate may encourage them to take on excessive risk because they have little to lose. Because the continued presence of excessive risk diminishes confidence in the future health of the financial system, insolvent financial institutions must be put out of their misery.

The IMF and other international financial institutions can help restore confidence in a crisis country's financial system by providing liquidity quickly, but also by sharing their expertise and encouraging the government to take steps to create a better resolution process for failed financial institutions (as it did in South Korea).

2. Limit Moral Hazard by Encouraging Adequate Prudential Supervision and by Acting as a Lender of Last Resort Infrequently

When the IMF acts as an international lender of last resort, the funds it provides to governments are often used indirectly to protect depositors and other creditors of banking institutions from losses. This safety net means that depositors and other creditors have little incentive to monitor these banking institutions and withdraw their deposits if the institutions are taking on too much risk. As a result these institutions are encouraged to take on excessive risks, which make financial crises more likely.

To limit the moral hazard problem created by its acting as a lender of last resort, the IMF needs to adopt several additional measures. First, it must encourage governments to punish the owners, if not also the managers, of insolvent institutions. In emerging market countries (and often in advanced countries, Japan being a prominent example), governments frequently provide insolvent institutions with funds to keep them from failing, and they leave the existing owners and managers in charge. Bailing out the owners and managers in this way leads to an even larger moral hazard problem. Knowing that a bailout will occur, they have incentives to take on huge risks because they have so little to lose. Furthermore, the owners and managers of these institutions often take the rescue funds for their own personal gain and send them out of the country before the institution fails.

Because a lack of consequences for the owners of poorly run financial institutions makes a financial crisis more likely, the IMF and other international organizations must limit this moral hazard by insisting that the governments to whom they lend punish owners and managers of insolvent institutions. They must not be allowed to keep their institutions operating, and, when the institutions are closed down, the owners must suffer substantial losses and the managers must lose their jobs. Allowing large creditors of risk-taking financial institutions to incur losses will further reduce moral hazard incentives, because the creditors will have strong incentives to monitor the institutions and pull out their funds if they are taking on excessive risk.

The moral hazard problem created by the existence of a safety net for financial institutions can also be limited by the usual elements of a well-functioning prudential regulatory and supervisory system: adequate disclosure and capital requirements, limits on currency mismatch and connected lending, prompt corrective action, careful monitoring of an institution's risk management procedures, close supervision of financial institutions to enforce compliance with the regulations, and sufficient resources and accountability for supervisors so they are likely to act as a helping hand rather than a grabbing hand. Often, however, strong political forces resist putting these kinds of measures into place. This resistance has been a problem in industrialized countries (it was, for example, an important factor in the U.S. savings and loan debacle of the 1980s),[14] but the problem is far worse in many emerging market countries, where the political will to adequately regulate and supervise financial institutions has been especially weak because powerful special interests act to prevent it.

Because it has so much leverage over the emerging market countries to whom it lends or who might want to borrow from it in the future, the IMF is particularly well suited to encourage adoption of prudential regulatory and supervisory measures to limit moral hazard.[15] Only with this kind of pressure can the moral hazard problem arising from lender-of-last-resort operations be contained.

Because there is a tradeoff between the benefits of a lender-of-last-resort role in preventing financial crises and the moral hazard that it creates, such a role is best undertaken only when absolutely necessary. The IMF should not provide funds to countries not in crisis or ones that are truly insolvent because they have an unsustainable amount of debt.[16] Furthermore, once a crisis is over, the liquidity that has been injected into the financial system must be removed so that financial markets do not become dependent on it. In other words, the IMF will be more successful as a guardian of the international financial system if it provides funds infrequently and for short periods of time.

3. Just Say No: Act as a Lender of Last Resort Only for Countries That Are Serious about Implementing Necessary Reforms

The IMF knows that, if it doesn't come to the rescue, an emerging market country in a financial crisis will suffer extreme hardship and possible political instability. Politicians in the crisis country may exploit these concerns and engage in a game of chicken with the IMF, resisting necessary reforms in the hope that the IMF will cave in. Elements of this game were present in the Mexico crisis of 1994–95 and in the Indonesia crisis of 1997.

The IMF will produce better outcomes if it makes it clear that it will not play this game. It will be more successful if it does not give in to short-run humanitarian concerns and let emerging market countries avoid necessary reforms. It will improve its performance by being willing to walk away from a country that is not willing to help itself. Indeed, if the IMF caves in to one country's government during a financial crisis, politicians in other countries will see that they can get away with not implementing needed reforms, and it will become difficult if not impossible for the IMF to encourage governments in emerging market countries to develop effective financial systems as well as limit moral hazard.

Where Has the IMF Gone Wrong?

The IMF has become an organization that many people love to hate. It is often portrayed by critics as incompetent or as an agent for greedy capitalists in the advanced countries. In 2000 I had the opportunity to see the workings of the IMF up close when I was appointed by its executive board to chair a committee of independent experts charged with evaluating the IMF's research activities.[17] For close to six months I spent two days a week visiting the IMF, interviewing its staff and reading a slew of its internal and external documents. Because the IMF's research activities are spread throughout almost all departments of the institution, I not only saw how research was conducted but was also privileged to get an inside look into how the IMF operated. Despite some critics' portrayal of it as an "evil" organization, I found the IMF's staff to be dedicated, incredibly hard working, and very smart.

Yet even with a large and experienced staff, the IMF does not operate effectively. Keeping in mind the principles outlined in the previous section, we can better understand where things have gone wrong at the IMF and can evaluate some of the more prominent proposals for its reform.

The IMF's Agenda and Lending Policies

Although the IMF was originally set up in 1944 to provide short-term liquidity to cope with balance-of-payments imbalances after the Latin American debt crisis of 1982 it began to broaden its policy agenda, a trend that has continued. Going beyond its primary role as an emergency lender, the IMF has now been given an explicit policy goal of reducing poverty, which it does by lending to poor countries.[18] The role of providing long-term loans to poor countries to help alleviate poverty was traditionally assigned to the World Bank. However, after sixty years and billions of dollars in loans, the World Bank has not made effective headway in achieving its main goal. The IMF has stepped in to fill this perceived void. It has also begun to venture into labor and environmental issues. With this change in its agenda, the nature of the IMF's lending has expanded, and it now regularly engages in frequent, longer-term lending to poor countries.[19] Even the IMF's "emergency" lending has become astoundingly frequent. Seventy countries have received "emergency" credit under IMF programs for twenty or more years.[20] As of May 31, 2005, sixty-two countries had outstanding long-term loans for poverty reduction of over $60 billion, and the amount of these loans accounted for 73% of all IMF lending as of that date.[21]

Why the Broadening of the IMF's Agenda and Its Long-Term and Frequent Lending Policies Are a Problem

The broadening of the IMF's agenda, which some have referred to as "nefarious mission creep,"[22] and the expansion of the IMF's lending activities beyond emergency lending have interfered with its ability to act as an effective international lender of last resort. They are at odds with all three principles for the success of a lender of last resort. They make it harder to inject liquidity quickly into the financial system, violate the principle that lending should be performed infrequently and only for short periods of time, and make it harder for the IMF to just say no. If the IMF is to serve as an effective lender of last resort, it must make funds available quickly and then take them away just as quickly after the crisis is over. Having long-term, poverty alleviation loans outstanding greatly hampers the IMF.

Why It's Hard for the IMF to Inject Liquidity Quickly

Because the IMF lends only to governments, it has a disadvantage relative to central banks in its ability to inject liquidity quickly: it can do so only at the request of a government. When the IMF engages in long-term and continuous lending, it necessarily takes on the mindset of a commercial bank, rather than a lender of last resort. Commercial banks impose restrictive covenants (conditions) on their loans to reduce risk taking on the part of borrowers. Similarly, when the IMF makes a long-term loan or makes frequent loans as part of its lending program, it has to impose *conditionality*, a set of wide-ranging limits on the financial behavior of the country to whom it is lending. By incorporating conditionality into its loans, the IMF tries to ensure that its funds are used for the appropriate purposes. Unfortunately, designing conditionality takes time, and yet, as the first principle indicates, the success of a lender-of-last-resort operation depends on providing liquidity as fast as possible.

For example, it took up to two months to put together the rescue packages during the recent financial crises in Mexico and East Asia. During those months the crises worsened, and much larger sums (over $100 billion) were ultimately needed to shore up the financial systems. If funds could have been made available more quickly, a much smaller amount would have been needed to turn things around, as was the case in the lender-of-last-resort operation performed by the Federal Reserve in the aftermath of the 1987 stock market crash.

The broader IMF agenda and the wide-ranging insistence on conditionality result in a lack of focus in IMF programs. Conditionality was extreme during the Indonesian crisis, in which the IMF imposed 140 separate conditions on its lending program, effectively micromanaging the Indonesian economy. For example, the IMF insisted that Indonesia end government-granted monopolies in cloves and plywood, which were unrelated to the causes of the crisis.[23] As the analysis of financial crises in this book indicates, microeconomic factors in goods markets have *not* been a fundamental driving factor behind most of the recent crises, although microeconomic problems in the *financial* sector have been. For this reason, the IMF should focus on encouraging reforms that will ensure a safe and sound financial system. Because high and variable inflation encourages liability dollarization that makes the financial system more fragile and because fiscal imbalances can trigger financial crises, the IMF should also encourage fiscal and monetary policy reforms to reduce the likelihood of financial crises.

IMF programs for crisis countries often have conditions that require financial sector, fiscal, and monetary policy reforms, but, with so many other microconditions imposed, politicians in crisis countries may pick and choose the conditions they wish to follow. They are then likely to drag their feet on reforms which could run contrary to their interests and those of their cronies. In the 1997 Indonesian crisis, for example, Suharto was willing to accede to some IMF conditions but balked at others, such as closing a number of insolvent banks, some of which were owned by his friends and family members. In one notorious case, a bank owned by Suharto's son Bambang was closed and then allowed to reopen three weeks later under a different name.

Furthermore, wide-ranging conditionality frequently imposes conditions that no government in an advanced country would tolerate, such as ending subsides for agricultural products. The IMF's conditions for the loan to Indonesia, for example, included the elimination of subsidies on sugar, wheat flour, corn, soybean meal, and fish meal. Many of these reforms may be beneficial, and the IMF (and technocrats in these countries) may see a window of opportunity, but pushing for them during a crisis is likely to backfire. Such conditions smack of hypocrisy and enable governments in emerging market countries to claim violation of their sovereignty to garner political support for avoiding the necessary reforms of the financial sector.

Another problem with wide-ranging conditionality has been raised by Martin Feldstein, an eminent Harvard economist and the president of the National Bureau of Economic Research.[24] Because these conditions are often considered onerous, their possible imposition may discourage countries from coming to the IMF in the early stages of a financial crisis. Thus it becomes more likely that IMF lending will be slow in coming, and the financial crisis will worsen and require an even larger amount of funds.

To deal with the problem of delays, the IMF established a Contingent Credit Line (CCL) facility in 1999, which allowed preapproved countries that had adopted policies to promote safety and soundness in their financial systems to receive credit immediately without having to negotiate the conditions for the loans. However, no countries applied, and the facility was allowed to expire at the end of November 2003. Qualified countries were no doubt concerned that applying for this facility would be interpreted as a source of weakness rather than strength. In addition, they were worried that being dropped from the preapproved list would send strong negative signals that would cause sharp capital outflows, possibly precipitating the very financial crises they were trying to avoid.

Why IMF Lending Increases Moral Hazard

Long-term lending is obviously inconsistent with the principle that loans should be made for short periods of time, while continuous lending to the same countries over and over again is inconsistent with the principle that lender-of-last-resort operations should be infrequent. The habit of frequent, continuous lending makes it more likely that the IMF will engage in "crisis" lending when it might not be absolutely necessary, thereby increasing the expectation by countries and financial institutions that they will be bailed out. This, as we have seen, increases the moral hazard problem and makes it more likely that financial crises will occur.

How much moral hazard is created directly by IMF lending is the subject of much debate. Some argue that the loans do not create moral hazard for governments borrowing from the IMF because governments pay a high penalty when they approach the IMF for loans to avert crises: they frequently find themselves thrown out of office shortly afterwards because they have had to agree to politically unpopular policy measures. IMF loans also do not involve subsidies to the countries that receive them, even if they carry below-market interest rates, because they have seniority over other debt (that is, they are paid back first) and actually pose a low risk for the lender, the IMF.[25] Because IMF loans are almost always paid back, borrowing countries, especially their taxpayers, eventually bear the full cost of the loans, but this does not mean that the government does. IMF loans often enable governments to gamble on resurrection and pursue risky policies that postpone the inevitable but have high costs later. We saw exactly this kind of moral hazard at work in Argentina, when IMF loans allowed Domingo Cavallo to adopt disastrous policies which weakened fundamental institutions and made the eventual financial crisis far worse.

Moral hazard can also be a potentially serious problem for foreign creditors, because IMF loans might make it more likely that they will be paid back even when countries have pursued inappropriate policies. The empirical evidence on whether foreign creditor moral hazard is a significant factor is far from clear-cut,[26] but there are suggestions that it could be minimized if the IMF were to engage in not only bailouts but also "bail-ins," that is, if it would encourage foreign creditors to provide funds to crisis countries along with the IMF.[27]

Most importantly, IMF loans create moral hazard by giving the governments of emerging market countries the resources to bail out their financial sectors. Knowing that they are more likely to be bailed out makes it easier for banking institutions to get funds even if they are taking on excessive risk. This makes banking crises and a bailout of the banking system more likely. Even if the IMF does not lose any money, the taxpayers of the country receiving the loans do. IMF bailouts are at the expense of these countries' taxpayers, not the international taxpayers who ultimately provide the funding for the IMF.[28] Making bank bailouts easier can also encourage foreign lending to banks, because they are more likely to be protected by a government safety net.

Why Continuous IMF Lending Makes It Hard to Say No

Continuous lending produces a culture of "pushing money out the door" and creates incentives within the IMF to lend. (These incentives to push money out the door are just as strong, if not stronger, at the World Bank.) As a result the IMF finds it hard to resist lending to countries that are not sufficiently committed to financial, fiscal, and monetary reform. After all, continuing lending implies an ongoing, close relationship with a country's authorities, making it harder to cut them off. In addition, when a new government (or even a new finance minister) enters office, the new officials argue that it was previous officials who pursued the policies that got the country into trouble and that they should be given a clean slate in requesting loans.[29] The willingness to give new governments a clean slate and close relationships with a country's authorities explain why the IMF (and the World Bank) often provides new loans to countries that have not complied with conditions in previous agreements and continue to pursue bad policies. Ecuador and Pakistan received one IMF loan after another for over two decades, even though they did not meet the conditions specified in past loans. (They have, however, recently complied with the conditions for the loans for the first time.)[30] Furthermore, none of the twenty countries receiving repeated lending during the period 1980–99 achieved higher economic growth or succeeded in controlling their macroeconomic imbalances.[31] Continuous lending lowers the likelihood that a country will pursue reforms to make financial crises less likely, and it also results in less encouragement for the reforms that will eventually make the financial system work efficiently, and which are so critical to rapid economic growth.

A particularly egregious case of the IMF's inability to say no to lending occurred during the Argentinean crisis in 2001–02, discussed in Chapter 7. In the run-up to the crisis, Domingo Cavallo, the economy minister, engineered the resignation of Pedro Pou, the president of the central bank, to weaken prudential regulations so that the government could sell more of its debt to the banks. At this point, it was clear that the government's commitment to sound financial institutions was diminishing. In addition, Argentina's fiscal imbalances were spinning out of control.

Michael Mussa, the former chief economist of the IMF, argues that by August 2001 it was clear that the IMF would be throwing good money after bad if it gave another loan to Argentina's government—yet it did.[32] The Argentine government was in the process of dismantling whatever sound institutions it still had, and by giving it a loan at this juncture the IMF was condoning the government's behavior. This provided misguided incentives for the Argentine authorities and created a bad precedent: other governments in emerging market countries saw that the IMF would continue to give them funds even if they were not pursuing the policies necessary to avoid or get out of a financial crisis. Finally, in December 2001 the IMF recognized that there was no hope for Argentina and refused to supply another requested loan. This refusal to lend was, however, the exception that proves the rule: it demonstrated that the IMF would stop lending only when the situation had deteriorated to such an extent that nothing could be done to save a country.

In the aftermath of its crisis, the Argentine government kept looking for quick fixes and did not implement the fundamental reforms needed to get the economy back on a sound footing. The government has also been accused of acting in bad faith in settling with its international creditors.

In September 2003 Argentina had an IMF loan coming due. It could not repay the loan unless the IMF provided it with a new loan to pay off the old one. Even though Argentina was *not* complying with IMF conditions calling for a primary budget surplus of at least 4.5% and an increase in the prices that utilities could charge for energy, the IMF gave in and made the new loan.[33] This sequence of events looked just like "evergreening," the making of new loans to hide older, nonperforming loans. As part of its recommendations to emerging market countries, the IMF has stipulated that evergreening should be prohibited—and yet it was engaging in the practice itself! (Argentina was able to pay back all its IMF loans at the beginning of 2006. It did so, however, only with some help, both from Venezuela's Hugo Chávez, whose government bought $1 billion in Argentine bonds, and from high commodity prices, which increased the value of the country's exports.)[34]

Because the IMF has given in to Argentina, emerging market countries now believe it is likely to give in again. Thus this episode creates bad incentives for Argentina, sends exactly the wrong signal to other emerging market countries, and flies in the face of the third principle enunciated earlier: that the IMF should make loans only to countries that are willing to implement reforms.

Why the IMF Has Gone Wrong

To understand why the IMF has broadened its agenda and expanded its lending in directions that make it less effective, we need to look at how it is governed and how its hierarchy works.

IMF Governance

At the very top of the IMF sit the managing director, the first deputy managing director, and two other deputy managing directors (who together are referred to as the management). The IMF's staff reports to the management. The overall authority for overseeing the IMF resides in its board of governors, which consists of the finance ministers and the heads of the central banks of the over 180 countries that are members of the IMF. More direct oversight of the IMF is provided by the International Monetary and Financial Committee, which meets twice a year and is made up of the finance ministers or heads of central banks from twenty-four countries. Ongoing decisions are made by the executive board, which consists of twenty-four executive directors: eight executive directors each represent a single country (China, France, Germany, Japan, Russia, Saudi Arabia, the United Kingdom, and the United States) and the remaining sixteen each represent several countries. Votes by the executive board are not determined by a one man–one vote rule but are proportional to the importance of a country in the world's economy, with the United States' vote having the largest weight (17.1%). Particularly important is that key decisions of the executive board require an 85% vote, effectively giving veto power to the United States.

The expansion of the IMF's lending activities and its frequent unwillingness to deny loans to governments unwilling to pursue serious reforms may be the result of its governance structure. Decisions at the IMF are frequently driven by political considerations within the governments of the member countries, particularly the United States. One often-cited example occurred when the IMF continued to provide funds to Russia until shortly before that country entered its financial crisis in August 1998, even though there was strong evidence that the Russian government was not adopting the necessary economic and financial reforms. Boris Fedorov, a former Russian deputy prime minister and minister of finance, even felt compelled to write, in an open letter dated July 9, 1999, to Michel Camdessus, then the managing director of the IMF:

> In August 1993, as Deputy Prime Minister and Minister of Finance, I wrote a letter to you refusing to take the second tranche of the STF [Systemic Transformation Facility, an IMF loan program for transition countries] since Russia was not on track with reform. Still, the IMF in 1994–98 provided billions of dollars and this helped to stall and compromise reforms. *Not a single agreement with Russia was ever implemented. . . .* I strongly believe that IMF money injections in 1994–1998 *were detrimental to the Russian economy* and interests of Russian people. Instead of speeding up reforms they slowed them.[35]

Reports on this episode suggest that the U.S. government (at the urging of the State Department) pushed for the Russian bailout because it wanted to prop up the government of President Boris Yeltsin and was concerned that an economic collapse might destabilize Russia, possibly putting nuclear weapons into the hands of extremists.[36] Russia was "too strategic to fail." The IMF did say no to further lending when the financial crisis eventually hit, and Russia was not bailed out. But it was too late: the damage had already been done. Political pressures may explain the IMF's reluctance to say no to lending to a country that has the support of powerful member countries like the United States, and they may also have led to the expansion of the IMF's policy agenda to engage in longer-term lending to poor countries.

The decisionmaking process at the IMF also has flaws. Meetings of the executive board normally take place three times a week, with the agenda set by the management. These meetings revolve around reports and papers prepared by the staff, most of whom are Ph.D. economists. Executive directors complain that they are overwhelmed by the massive amount of detailed information and find it hard to hold the management and staff accountable to them or to the member countries.[37] I experienced this firsthand: Although my committee's report on the IMF's research activities (a document of over 40,000 words) had been ready a month earlier, it was circulated by the management only days before the meeting in which it was to be discussed. Many executive directors at the meeting expressed their frustration about the short time they had had to digest the report, and I and the other members of my committee felt that the discussion was severely hampered as a result.[38]

The Hierarchical Structure of the IMF

The IMF is a hierarchical organization. When I was interviewing IMF staff as part of my committee's work, many of the staffers compared the IMF to the Catholic Church. Each department was a fiefdom, with the most important one, the Policy Development and Review Department (PDR), being the Vatican. The

PDR reviews all documents produced by the staff and imposes coherence on the positions adopted by the staff. It is the keeper of the faith.

The IMF's hierarchical structure has some important advantages. It helps establish common positions, which in turn enable different parts of the IMF to coordinate their actions and move relatively quickly for a large bureaucracy. Like an army, the IMF gets things done.

Its sister institution, the World Bank, is completely different organizationally. It is far more decentralized, and strikingly different views are often held in different parts of the organization. When I spent the academic year 2000–01 at the World Bank, the openness of debate about ideas was indeed refreshing. But its decentralization does have a major drawback. The World Bank has no internal agreement on what needs to be done to accomplish its core mission of eliminating poverty. Should the priority be on eradicating debilitating diseases, boosting education, promoting efficient financial systems, or achieving a sustainable environment? This disagreement on priorities makes it difficult for the World Bank to move quickly or have coherent policies. When I asked a high official at the IMF, who had also worked at the World Bank, why the IMF had gotten into poverty reduction lending (which I have argued is a bad idea), he responded that the IMF had to do so because the World Bank just couldn't get anything done. Morris Goldstein, a former deputy director of the research department at the IMF, points out that, because of the IMF's reputation in official circles for being able to act quickly, it is continually asked to expand its mission—and it has rarely said no to those requests.[39]

The "One Size Fits All" Syndrome and the Mexican and East Asian Crises

The downside of the IMF's hierarchical structure is that it frequently fixates on one way of thinking about policy problems. While I was investigating IMF research activities in 2000, many of the staff told me that there was far too great a focus on fiscal issues and not enough on the financial sector. Indeed, the in-joke was that the organization's initials stood for "It's Mostly Fiscal." As pointed out by Edwin Truman, who was a high official in both the Federal Reserve System and the U.S. Treasury, this excessive focus on fiscal issues stems in part from the fact that the "culture and work of the IMF is dominated by macroeconomists."[40]

The Latin American debt crisis of the early 1980s—in which capital flew out of the region, currencies collapsed, and severe economic contractions occurred— was the direct result of irresponsible fiscal policies that led to a default on government debt. After the crisis, the IMF became committed to the view that poor fiscal management was the trigger for capital flight and hence the source of currency crises. However, many crises originate in the financial sector, not in government fiscal policies. For example, the Mexican crisis of 1994–95 was due to problems in the banking sector, not fiscal irresponsibility: the government's budget deficit was very small before the crisis. Yet, despite the facts, the IMF was unable to change its "one size fits all" view that all crises were fiscal in origin. This inflexibility led to serious policy mistakes when the East Asian crises hit in 1997. The IMF recommended that the governments of the crisis countries pursue the austerity policy of balancing their budgets, which my colleague Joseph Stiglitz has criticized as being the wrong medicine at the wrong time.[41] Asking the government to cut spending or raise taxes is a contractionary policy that could make the economic downturn resulting from a financial crisis even worse. The IMF did reverse this policy quickly, and the damage from contractionary fiscal policy was not a major source of the economic contraction in those countries.[42] The IMF has also subsequently acknowledged that recommending a balanced government budget was a mistake.[43]

The fact that the IMF's pursuit of balanced budgets was the wrong policy choice in East Asia does not necessarily mean that Stiglitz's recommendation is the right one: expansionary policy, particularly monetary policy, destroys confidence that the central bank will be able to control inflation. Uncontrolled inflation (or expectations of uncontrolled inflation) makes currency depreciation more likely. In turn, currency depreciation makes firms' balance sheets worse, thereby exacerbating the financial crisis.

The "one size fits all" mentality according to which the IMF focused too narrowly on fiscal issues made it harder for its officials to learn from the Mexican crisis and to understand the key role that weakness in the financial sector would be likely to play in future crises. When the East Asian crisis began, this lack of understanding led the IMF to neglect the important principle that the key to recovering from a financial crisis is restoring confidence in the financial system. Joseph Stiglitz and Jeffrey Sachs have bitterly criticized the IMF's policy of insisting on the closure of sixteen banks in Indonesia without setting up an adequate safety net for the rest of the banking system, and I strongly agree with them.[44] These closures led to a weakening of confidence in the banking system, which led to a full-fledged bank panic and a further collapse of the Indonesian rupiah. The panic and collapse of the rupiah, through the mechanisms described earlier, further exacerbated the financial crisis.

There are other examples of mistakes made by the IMF because of its "one size fits all" thinking, recommending policies that made sense for advanced countries with solid financial institutions but which backfired in countries with weaker institutional environments. There is a general impression that the IMF strongly advocated capital account liberalization (opening up domestic financial markets to international capital flows) for emerging market countries without considering the quality of their regulatory and supervisory frameworks.[45] The outcome of the capital account liberalizations was the financial crises in, for example, Mexico, East Asia, and Russia. The IMF also advised transition countries to pursue privatization without paying sufficient attention to whether there were constraints on competition or to standards of corporate governance. This lack of attention left many countries with botched privatization programs and oligarchs that have been holding back economic growth.[46] In 2000 the IMF acknowledged its mistakes in these cases in its *World Economic Outlook*.[47]

The hierarchical nature of the IMF is not the only source of the "one size fits all" mentality. Another is the expansion of IMF activities. The IMF staff is stretched so thin that it has become less capable of acquiring the information and knowledge that would enable it to be more open minded. One finding of my research evaluation committee was that the IMF's research staff was so overburdened that the organization did not have the time to step back and do the necessary thinking to achieve a better understanding of the nature of the crises it was facing.[48]

Another organizational problem is that the IMF has a mobility requirement for its staff: to advance within the organization, a staffer must move from department to department. This jack-of-all-trades policy means that many staffers do not have time to become sufficiently expert in the countries they analyze, making it more likely that they will rely on "one size fits all" advice.

The Dangers of "One Size Fits All" Thinking

Unfortunately, the "one size fits all" syndrome lives on at the IMF. Stanley Fischer, the first deputy managing director from September 1994 to August 2001, was enormously influential owing to his brilliance, integrity, prodigious work ethic, and genuine kindness. (I am somewhat prejudiced: Stan was the primary advisor on my Ph.D. thesis at MIT and was incredibly helpful to me. But I can attest that my views are representative of those I heard from members of the IMF staff.) After the East Asian crisis, Fischer made it clear that he was highly skeptical of exchange rate regimes in which the value of the domestic currency was pegged at a fixed rate to a major currency like the U.S. dollar: "Each of the major international capital market–related crises since 1994—Mexico in 1994, Thailand, Indonesia and Korea in 1997, Russia and Brazil in 1998, and Argentina and Turkey in 2000—has in some way involved a fixed or pegged exchange rate regime. At the same time, countries that did not have pegged rates—among them South Africa, Israel in 1998, Mexico in 1998—avoided crises of the type that afflicted emerging market countries with pegged rates."[49] Fischer even went so far as to declare that adoption of a floating-exchange-rate system is the most important preventive measure that an emerging market country can take against crises.[50]

Given Fischer's influence, the view that pegged exchange rates are dangerous and that countries would be better off allowing their exchange rates to float has had a huge impact on IMF policies. It has survived even after his departure, despite the fact that there are opposing views within the organization about the desirability of various exchange rate regimes.[51] Fischer is not alone in his view; it is also held by such prominent organizations as the Council on Foreign Relations, which has made the following recommendation: "The IMF and the Group of Seven (G-7) should advise emerging economies against adopting pegged exchange rates and should not provide funds to support unsustainable pegs."[52]

In general I agree with this view. I pointed out in Chapter 9 the dangers of a pegged-exchange-rate regime and concluded that such a regime, which is backed only by a government announcement of the peg, is likely to increase financial instability in emerging market countries. Indeed, this is why in my writings I have advocated adoption of a floating-exchange-rate regime in most cases, but with a strong commitment to controlling inflation with an inflation target.[53] However, even if an emerging market country might be better served in the long run by adopting a floating-exchange-rate regime, abandoning a peg in the middle of a currency crisis can have disastrous consequences. When a speculative attack on the currency is in progress, the move to a float will lead to a sharp fall in the value of the domestic currency, which will raise the value of debt denominated in foreign currency. The resulting widespread destruction of corporate and household balance sheets will send the economy into a devastating downward spiral, triggering a financial crisis.

The "one size fits all" view on the benefits of floating exchange rates has led the IMF to commit policy mistakes. In 2002 Uruguay was hit by contagion from Argentina, and by June it was experiencing a bank panic and a run on its public debt. However, although Uruguay was losing international reserves at a rapid rate, it was able to maintain its exchange rate peg. Given its view on exchange rate regimes, the IMF told the Uruguayans that they would be able to receive loans only if they allowed their exchange rate to float. In an economy with as much liability dollarization as Uruguay had, the subsequent depreciation of the exchange rate would lead to a devastation of balance sheets and a full-fledged banking and financial crisis.

I have been told by Uruguayan officials that they pleaded with the IMF to let them maintain the peg, to give them time to set up a backstop for the banking system. On June 18, the day before the peg was abandoned, the central bank of Uruguay still held a substantial amount of international reserves, $1.3 billion, which was three times the amount of the monetary base and more than two times the monetary aggregate, M2.[54] Thus, while the peg could not have been maintained indefinitely, because the Uruguayans had $2 billion of debt service coming due within the next two years, it is possible that the commitment to the peg could have been maintained in the short run, particularly with IMF assistance. This might have allowed the Uruguayans to shore up their banking system, which would in turn have made the subsequent crisis far less severe.[55]

Even though there was dissent within the IMF on whether abandoning the peg was the right thing to do because of its implications for the financial system, the IMF forced Uruguay to abandon the peg. As Uruguayan officials had feared, a disastrous financial crisis followed; they are still bitter about the episode. Their economy has suffered a great depression: it contracted at an annual rate of 11% from 2002 to 2003, and the unemployment rate soared to 17%. Most demoralizing is the fact that Uruguay's financial crisis has forced many young, highly educated people to leave the country; one out of every twenty-five urban households in the period from March to December 2002 had at least one family member going abroad.[56] The "one size fits all" syndrome can indeed be very costly.

Reforming the IMF

The need for the IMF to operate as an international lender of last resort is so great that, if we didn't have an IMF, we would have to invent it. But what can be done to reform the IMF so that its lending activities help promote a safer and healthier world economy?

Narrow the IMF's Focus

The expansion of the IMF's agenda and lending activities over time has led to calls for reform to narrow the organization's focus and put more emphasis on issues related to macroeconomic and financial stability.[57] Recent proposals for reform have come from many different sources, including the U.S. Treasury,[58] the Council on Foreign Relations Task Force,[59] the Overseas Development Council Task Force,[60] and the International Financial Institution Advisory Commission set up by the U.S. Congress and chaired by Allan Meltzer, a professor at Carnegie Mellon University.[61] What is striking is that all of them call for narrowing the IMF's focus and putting more emphasis on crisis management.[62] Furthermore, the U.S. Treasury, the Overseas Development Council Task Force, and the Meltzer Commission have all recommend that the IMF get out of the long-term lending business. The Meltzer Commission took a particularly extreme position: that liquidity loans should have a short maturity of 120 days with only one renewal allowed, be made at penalty (above-market) rates, and be collateralized by a clear priority claim on borrowers' assets. In addition, these loans would be made only to countries that met stringent preconditions, including soundness of their financial systems.

Although reforms intended to narrow the IMF's focus appear to have widespread support, the IMF itself has not been receptive to them. The report of the external evaluation committee for IMF surveillance, chaired by John Crow, the former governor of the Bank of Canada—which was produced at the same time that my committee was reporting on research activities— recommended a narrowing of focus for surveillance activities. Yet this prescription was opposed by the IMF's staff and was not supported by the IMF's executive board.[63]

Although I have been critical of the IMF here, it has been making some progress. It has admitted that wide-ranging conditionality was a mistake. In 2000 the then-new managing director, Horst Köhler, stated that the organization "has been overstretched in the past and needs to refocus" and expressed his concerns about "mission creep" and the need to streamline conditionality.[64] The number two official at the time, Stanley Fischer, stated in 2001 that the IMF "has adopted the view that structural conditions should be included only if they are essential to achieving the macroeconomic goals of the program."[65] In 2002 the IMF adopted revised conditionality guidelines that emphasized the need for fewer conditions.[66] Nevertheless, recent IMF lending programs have still had an average of twenty conditions (over thirty for some), which is far more than the two to three they had on average during the period 1987–89.[67]

Improve IMF Surveillance

To better its ability to function as an international lender of last resort, the IMF needs to be able to operate more in line with the principles outlined earlier: provide liquidity faster, limit moral hazard, and be able to say no when governments are following policies that are likely to lead to a crisis. To satisfy these three principles, improving IMF surveillance is crucial.[68]

IMF surveillance involves monitoring the economic and financial policies and performance of the member countries. Surveillance of member countries is conducted under Article IV of the IMF's statutes (the practice is known as Article IV consultations) and usually involves a visit (called a *mission*) to the country, usually on an annual basis. The mission is undertaken by a team of IMF economists, who meet with government and central bank officials and increasingly with representatives of the private sector. The IMF team analyzes the country's monetary, fiscal, financial, and exchange rate policies, as well as other policies, and then prepares a *staff report* that is reviewed by the IMF's executive board. The views of the executive board are recorded in a *summing up* of the Article IV consultation, which is transmitted to the country's government officials.

In recent years the IMF has made progress in improving its surveillance. It has increased its focus on financial sector issues by greatly expanding the staff of the Monetary and Financial Systems Department, which focuses on that sector. It has also implemented two joint IMF–World Bank programs, the Financial Sector Assessment Program (FSAP) and the Reports on the Observance of Standards and Codes (ROSCs).[69] Both produce reports on individual member countries using teams of experts from the IMF, the World Bank, and national authorities to evaluate the quality of financial regulation and supervision and the health of the financial sector. (ROSCs also examine standards and codes in other areas, including data dissemination, monetary and fiscal transparency, and money laundering and terrorist financing.) The FSAP and ROSCs not only provide incentives for countries to improve prudential supervision and regulation, they also supply the IMF with better information to help it determine whether a country is deserving of a loan and what conditions should be attached to that loan.

The IMF has also recognized the importance of institutions to economic growth, and these are a prominent focus of Article IV consultations. A staff paper presented to the IMF executive board in March 2003 notes that "There is accumulating evidence of the benefits of robust legal and supervisory frameworks, low levels of corruption, a high degree of transparency and good corporate governance."[70] Narrowing the IMF's focus to financial, monetary, and fiscal policy issues and deemphasizing social, labor, and environmental issues would help improve IMF surveillance. (Issues like legal and supervisory frameworks, corruption, transparency, and corporate governance fit with an emphasis on financial sector surveillance.) And eliminating mobility requirements, which require regular rotation of IMF staff to different departments, could help them to become more expert on the countries they analyze. Shifting more staff into surveillance of emerging market countries, those most vulnerable to currency and financial crises, would make the best use of the IMF's scarce resources.[71]

Because surveillance is conducted on a regular basis, it can provide the IMF with the information it needs to recognize if a government's policies will hurt the economy and enable it to make faster decisions about whether the country deserves a loan. Improved surveillance can help the IMF to operate "less as a fireman, and more as a policeman."[72] Instead of limiting moral hazard by imposing a large number of ex post conditions on an IMF lending program—which makes it extremely difficult for the IMF to act quickly as an international lender of last resort—IMF surveillance can be used to encourage countries to pursue policies that limit moral hazard *before* it provides loans.[73]

One way of limiting moral hazard on the part of both governments and domestic financial institutions is to publish FSAPs and staff reports for Article IV consultations and *public information notices* that include the summings up of the executive board discussion. Publication is in fact already the norm in most cases, but it remains at the discretion of the member country's government. Increased transparency of IMF surveillance provides incentives for governments to clean up their acts and pursue better policies to limit moral hazard. Transparency will subject those policies to outside scrutiny and ultimately enhance the ability of the country to borrow in international financial markets. The IMF has been moving toward increased transparency of its surveillance: in 2003 the executive board changed its policy from voluntary publication of Article IV staff reports to one of "presumed publication."[74] The IMF could go further in this direction and make all its surveillance documents public.[75]

The IMF can also limit moral hazard and strengthen the incentives for countries to pursue appropriate reforms by giving countries greater access to its lending programs when they have previously pursued appropriate policies.[76] The IMF's CCL facility was to provide such an incentive, but it was not a success. Using surveillance to decide whether a country qualifies for a loan overcomes the two objections that led potential applicants to shun the CCL: concern that applying for the facility would be seen as a sign of weakness and that being dropped from the facility would immediately precipitate a crisis. Because surveillance is applied to all member countries, there is no stigma attached to it, and no danger that a country will be dropped from surveillance.[77]

Using surveillance to decide whether countries qualify for IMF lending requires some flexibility, however. This kind of flexibility is already a feature of lender-of-last-resort operations by central banks, which decide on a case-by-case basis if such lending is justified. If a country were automatically ruled out from a lending program, this action could in and of itself precipitate a crisis. Setting firm rules for prequalification also requires that economists know for sure which policies are the most important in preventing crises. But our knowledge of what causes crises is continually evolving: we may simply not know enough.[78] Nonetheless, some guidelines for when a country would be entitled to emergency IMF lending would help contain moral hazard, and a requirement that the IMF report on whether a country had complied with these guidelines would help limit lending when countries pursue inappropriate policies.[79]

Improve IMF Governance

The IMF will be able to limit moral hazard on the part of governments and financial institutions only if it is able to refuse to provide loans. Unfortunately the IMF's current system of governance has led to politically motivated lending and the frequent inability to deny loans to countries that are pursuing inappropriate policies. To prevent this lending, the IMF could be made more independent, along the lines of what has happened in central banks in recent years: executive directors would be appointed for long terms and would not be allowed to take orders directly from their national governments.[80]

The central bank model of independence may not, however, work as well for an organization like the IMF. Unlike central banks, it does not have clearly defined objectives, such as the pursuit of price stability, and it is an inherently political organization, driven by the interests of its member countries.[81] Increased independence without adequate accountability could be dangerous;

executive directors might pursue their own private interests or the narrow interests of their countries rather than the public good. To prevent this, steps would be needed to increase the transparency of decisionmaking at the IMF by publishing detailed minutes of the executive board meetings and the votes by the executive directors.

Many developing countries feel that the IMF is overly influenced by the rich countries, particularly the United States, and that it is often used by them to further their own strategic ends. Not only was this a concern when Russia received IMF loans in the 1990s, but there are currently suspicions that the United States may encourage funds to be directed to those countries that help it pursue the war on terror. To regain the trust and respect of its member countries, the IMF must address the allocation of specific countries' voting power and their representation on the executive board.[82]

Promote a More Open Dialogue

Another major disadvantage of "one size fits all" thinking is that it causes great resentment in the emerging market world. The public and officials in emerging market countries know that their circumstances and institutional development are often very different from those in other countries. As we have seen, policies that are successful in other countries may not work well in their countries. In Uruguay the dollarization of almost all debt meant that a float during the crisis led to disaster: during a less turbulent period (or in a more advanced country), a float would not have caused a problem. The capital requirements set forth in the Basel Accord are inadequate for many emerging market countries because they do not take account of the special risks that emerging financial systems face. Putting into place standard advanced-country legal protections of property rights during the early development of the market economy in communist China in the 1980s would have resulted in corruption and an intractable and unsettling inconsistency with communist ideology.

When the IMF or other international financial institutions impose a standard reform program that ignores emerging market countries' special circumstances, and then ignore the views of the countries themselves, it smacks of arrogance, and the countries in crisis rightfully resent it. This resentment in turn makes the IMF's job far more difficult. Even when the conditions for IMF loan programs in an emerging market country are completely appropriate, politicians in the pocket of powerful interests can still play to the public's dislike of the IMF, promoting either active or passive resistance. We have seen this ploy time and time again in the emerging market world, and it is one reason why so many countries with IMF programs do not comply with IMF conditions in either letter or spirit.

How can this dynamic change? The IMF needs to become more open and to engage in a dialogue with its member countries. It needs to learn to listen. It needs to admit that it doesn't know all the answers.

This change in IMF attitude would have enormous benefits. If IMF programs for emerging market countries were designed after greater consultation with both officials and segments of the public in these countries, resentment of the IMF would decrease, the quality of IMF surveillance would likely improve, the countries would feel a greater sense of ownership of these programs, and they would be much more likely to try to live up to the programs' conditions. And there are success stories. My conversations with officials involved in designing the financial sector reforms that South Korea adopted in the aftermath of its crisis made clear that there was an open dialogue with the IMF and that the Koreans felt that they had ownership of the program. This made it easier for them to buy into it, a key reason for its success.

An open dialogue does not mean that the IMF or other international financial institutions like the World Bank should give in to whatever officials in emerging market countries want. We have already seen that officials in these countries are often influenced by business interests who resist necessary institutional reform because of its likely effect on their pocketbooks. Indeed, the key role of the IMF and other institutions should be to provide incentives that will help overcome the influence of special interests and put needed reforms into place. Often the institutions will have to veto policies put forward by officials in these countries if they think such policies are not in the public's interest. Nor should they completely ignore these officials. The key to an effective dialogue is give-and-take.

As Dani Rodrik has emphasized, "There is no unique correspondence between the functions that good institutions perform and the form that such institutions take. Reformers have substantial room for creatively packaging these principles into institutional designs that are sensitive to local constraints and take advantage of local opportunities."[83]

Organizations like the IMF and the World Bank have tremendous expertise in their staffs and can provide valuable technical assistance to emerging market countries. Despite their critics, they can be an important force for good. They can help emerging market countries design and implement more effective institutions that would make globalization work for them, but they need to cultivate a more open attitude, one that shuns "one size fits all" solutions to these countries' problems.

Twelve

What Can the Advanced Countries Do?

Outlining the reforms that poor countries must take to harness the power of globalization and achieve rapid economic growth is easy—all it takes is ink and paper. Implementing these reforms, however, is very, very difficult. Not impossible, but difficult. As success stories like Singapore, Hong Kong, Taiwan, and Chile suggest, it *can* be done. International financial institutions like the IMF can help (particularly if it narrows its focus, improves its governance, and promotes a more open dialogue with developing countries), but the rich nations of the world also have a role to play. We in the affluent nations have a moral responsibility to help make globalization a force for good in the poorer countries. Yet it is not just altruism that should motivate us to help poorer countries. Helping them to develop economically and to grow will promote world stability and make our lives safer.

But what can we do? How can citizens in rich countries help poorer countries to get rich?

Is International Financial Architecture the Answer?

The financial crises in emerging market countries in recent years have sent economists and policymakers scrambling to discover a magic bullet to prevent them from occurring or to lessen their devastating impact. This search has led to calls for reform of the international financial architecture, that is, the institutions and rules that govern the flow of capital between countries. The amount of ink spilled on this topic is immense, and numerous proposals for reform by academics and government leaders have appeared. These proposals include suggestions for the development of codes of practice for prudential regulation and supervision, accounting principles, corporate governance, and information disclosure;[1] changes in the rules governing international debt contracts;[2] and the creation of an international bankruptcy court or an international lender of last resort.[3] The hope of all the authors of these proposals is that, if the international financial architecture can be fixed properly, devastating financial crises in emerging market countries may become a thing of the past.[4]

Many of these proposals are highly controversial,[5] and evaluating them would be the subject of another book.[6] Adopting some of them may help international financial markets work better. In this book, however, I have argued strongly that the financial-sector problems of emerging market countries arise *primarily* from within the countries themselves and not from outside agents such as other countries or international institutions. Thus, while shocks from outside emerging market countries can trigger financial crises in those countries,[7] their vulnerability to financial crises from these shocks results from the flawed policies of the countries themselves. The only way to make financial crises less likely in emerging market economies and for those countries to enjoy the full benefits of financial globalization is for them to adopt fundamental reforms. The reform of international financial architecture, no matter how worthwhile, is not the answer to helping these countries harness the power of globalization to help them grow.

Establishing institutions to make the financial globalization process beneficial for emerging market countries is hard work. It requires overcoming vested interests and corruption, and it is fraught with technical difficulties. After all, it took hundreds of years for advanced countries to develop the successful institutions that govern their financial systems and to make them work efficiently and effectively. There is a danger that the focus on international architecture may diminish the efforts of international organizations (such as the IMF and the World Bank) to establish incentives and provide the technical assistance that will help emerging market countries develop the institutions they need. Economists, policymakers, and citizens of developed and developing nations must realize that reform of the international financial architecture alone will not solve the problem.

Aid or Trade?

Another popular, widely disseminated view on how to make poorer countries rich is that rich countries should increase the amount of aid they direct to poorer countries. After all, the percentage of GDP that rich countries currently give to foreign countries in aid for economic development is paltry: foreign aid as a percentage of gross national income is 0.04% in the United States, 0.04% in Japan, 0.07% in Canada, 0.10% in Germany, 0.12% in the United Kingdom, and

0.16% in France.[8] Prominent economists like Jeffrey Sachs and his colleagues at the UN Millennium Project have argued that a "big push" in public investments funded by a doubling of foreign aid would enable African countries to escape their poverty trap.[9] In his book *The End of Poverty*, Sachs even argues that, if rich countries would increase their foreign aid budgets to between $135 and $195 billion over the next decade, they could eliminate extreme global poverty (defined as income of less than $1 per day).[10] (Sachs, along with rock stars like Bono, has also campaigned for aid in the form of debt relief for the poorest countries, arguing that only when they escape from their debt burden will these countries be able to put resources into the areas that will stimulate development. This campaign by Sachs, Bono, and many others culminated in the June 2005 agreement to let eighteen impoverished countries stop making payments on over $50 billion of debt owed to the World Bank, the African Development Bank, and the International Monetary Fund.) Is increased foreign aid the answer to lifting nations out of poverty?

The Problem with Aid: Why Giving More Money to Poor Countries Won't Work

The answer is no.[11] Despite its good (and grandiose) intentions, Sachs's plan to end poverty by increasing aid is almost surely doomed to failure. From 1960 to 2003, over $500 billion of aid (in today's dollars) was poured into Africa with little to show for it.[12] In his superb analysis of why economic development often doesn't occur, *The Elusive Quest for Growth*,[13] William Easterly explains that foreign aid usually doesn't work because it does not provide the right incentives.[14] Aid is almost always given to governments in poor countries, and, as we have seen repeatedly throughout this book, these governments often do not have incentives to act in the interest of their people. Instead the political elites use the funds to line their own or their friends' pockets, or to cement their power. Indeed, aid to poor countries may even make things worse. A particularly notorious case is that of Zaire (Congo) under the rule of President Mobutu Sese Seko. For twenty-five years Zaire received one loan after another from several international institutions—eleven (totaling nearly $2 billion) from the IMF alone. Zaire received $20 billion in foreign aid during Mobutu's rule, while he looted the country, leaving a resource-rich nation one of the poorest in the world.[15] With access to increased resources, bad governments are even more likely to stay in power.

We see this over and over again when governments in poor countries receive windfalls from their oil exports. Would Saddam Hussein have survived as long as he did without his country's oil wealth? Would Hugo Chavez continue to stay in power without the recent rise in oil prices, which has propped up the Venezuelan economy despite his disastrous policies? Both Saddam and Chavez have bankrupted their countries, and the considerable resources placed at their disposal by oil exports have allowed them to do so. Economic analysis shows that foreign aid can have the same negative impact, and more formal empirical evidence finds that kleptocratic policies are more likely when foreign aid and natural resources provide rulers with the means to buy off their opponents and reward their allies.[16]

Even if it is not stolen outright, giving aid to governments may not be the answer because they can divert it from productive uses; sadly this has often been the case in developing countries.[17] This outcome also provides an argument against doling out aid in the form of loans, which is the way development banks like the World Bank work. In many cases loans necessarily have to go to governments because many nongovernmental organizations (NGOs), charitable organizations, and private agencies with worthwhile programs do not have credit ratings and so could not qualify for these loans. An alternative would be to give foreign aid in the form of outright grants, which could go to NGOs; this is one recommendation of the report of the International Financial Institutions Advisory Commission (the Meltzer Commission).[18]

This is not to say that all foreign aid is counterproductive. Foreign aid to stop the spread of diseases like AIDS or malaria is likely to have high returns.[19] Studies suggest that, if a poor country has good governance, foreign aid does help alleviate poverty—although other studies dispute this conclusion.[20] One of the most successful instances of foreign aid was the Marshall Plan, which helped achieve the reconstruction of Europe after World War II. The plan worked not because it handed over large amounts of money to Europe but because it created incentives for the European countries to eliminate price controls, pursue fiscal consolidation, and liberalize trade.[21] (The example of the Marshall Plan may not be completely applicable to today's foreign aid climate. The plan was aimed at reconstructing economies that were already advanced and had good institutional frameworks, whereas foreign aid is today directed at countries with poor institutional frameworks.)

The Benefits of Trade: Why Opening Up Advanced Countries' Markets to Poor Countries' Goods Will Help

Although foreign aid can be made more effective, getting it to provide the right incentives to help poor countries get rich is no easy matter. Rich countries need to take an alternative approach that will help poor countries help themselves, and this alternative approach is trade. By opening up their markets to goods and services from emerging market countries, rich countries can provide exactly the right incentives for poorer countries to put their financial houses in order and get rich. If firms in emerging market countries have access to foreign markets, the profit motive will provide them with the incentives to become more productive. The resulting push for higher productivity then becomes an engine for growth.

These firms will also have stronger incentives to promote institutional reforms that will improve the functioning of their countries' financial markets. Their increased need for capital will lead them to demand that the legal system enforce property rights and the financial contracts that will enable them to borrow. These growing export firms will also want to see improvements in the availability and quality of information, because the fewer are the problems with asymmetric information, the easier it will be for them to get loans. They will also be more supportive of improvements in prudential regulation and supervision because a more efficient banking system can be a rich source of credit. Opening up the markets in advanced countries to emerging market countries can be a powerful stimulus to encourage these countries to reform their financial systems. In turn, financial reforms can increase financial deepening and help allocate capital to its most productive uses.

More open trade with emerging market firms can also help reduce the likelihood and severity of financial crises by increasing the size of the export sector in emerging market countries.[22] Having debt denominated in foreign currency makes firms more vulnerable to currency depreciations if the goods they produce are sold primarily in domestic markets and are priced in the local currency. Under these circumstances, a domestic currency depreciation increases the value of their foreign-currency-denominated debt in terms of the local currency, while the domestic currency value of their output remains unchanged. The discrepancy between the increase in what they have to pay on their debt (liabilities) and what their product sales will bring in (which determines the value of their assets) destroys their balance sheets. However, if firms are selling their goods abroad, when there is a depreciation the demand for the goods they produce rises in terms of local currency, so that the value of their production goes up, thus compensating for the increased value of the debt. When an emerging market country's export sector is larger, it is less vulnerable to a financial crisis because a currency depreciation will do less damage to the firms' balance sheets. Indeed, one of the reasons why Argentina was hit so hard by the collapse of its currency in 2001 was that it had such a small export sector.

As we have seen throughout our analysis, opening up advanced countries' markets to goods and services from emerging markets is a powerful force to help poorer countries get rich and to insulate them from devastating financial crises.

The Hypocrisy of Rich Countries

If we in the advanced countries really care about poverty in the rest of the world, we must be in favor of encouraging poor countries to send us their goods. But we often do the opposite.

Advanced countries, including the United States, impose higher barriers to imports from poor countries than to those from rich ones. While rich countries impose average tariffs on all manufactured goods of 3%, tariffs on labor-intensive manufactured imports from poor countries are far higher at 8%, while tariffs on agricultural products from poor countries average 14%.[23] The fact that rich countries make it hard for poor countries to sell goods to them has led Oxfam, a prominent international charitable organization, to hand out awards for double standards in trade policy, with first prize going to the European Union, second prize to the United States, third prize to Canada, and fourth prize to Japan.[24]

The political left in most rich countries, including the United States, has often been against trade liberalization, even as it claims to care deeply about eliminating poverty in the rest of the world. Those who hold these opposing positions must recognize their inconsistency. Trade liberalization by advanced countries is one of the most effective ways of eradicating poverty in the less-developed world. If supporters of the left really do care about the poor, they must encourage the opening of our markets to those who are less fortunate.

Why Doing Good Is Also Doing Well

The standard argument for trade liberalization is that it improves economic efficiency. By trading with another country you can focus your production on what you are really good at, so that your productivity will increase. Estimates of gains from trade are indeed high. A recent study for the Institute for International Economics estimates that further trade liberalization could raise GDP in the United States by as much as $1 trillion, or $10,000 per U.S. household.[25]

These benefits come not only with trade in goods but also with trade in services. One type of trade in services that has become controversial lately is *outsourcing*, in which domestic firms have services done for them abroad. For example, you can buy a Linksys wireless network router that costs less than $100 and enables you to have a wireless network in your house. When the router goes on the blink, you call up Linksys customer service and talk to a technician who may be in New Delhi or Manila. Linksys uses Indians and Filipinos to provide this service cheaply because their wages are lower than those of similar workers in advanced nations, such as the United States, Canada, or the United Kingdom. If Linksys could use only residents of rich countries, where most of their routers are sold, to provide this service, it would be too expensive. With outsourcing, Linksys can provide this technical service to you for free and still make a profit on selling their routers. Indeed, if Linksys did not provide this technical support, the wireless router might be worthless because you might not be able to get it to work on your own. The outcome of this trade in a service, technical support, allows you to be far more efficient, and it benefits India and the Philippines because they now have workers who hold more productive jobs with higher-than-average rates of pay.

Because it makes advanced countries more productive, outsourcing can actually create more jobs than it sends abroad.[26] The outcry over the outsourcing of white-collar jobs is unfounded.[27] In fact, foreign companies outsource more office and white-collar work to the United States than American companies send abroad. The Commerce Department reported that the value of U.S. exports of legal work, computer programming, telecommunications, banking, engineering, management consulting, and other private services was $131 billion in 2003 while imports of private services (outsourcing) were far smaller at $77 billion.[28]

If open trade is such a good idea, why are so many people against it, not only in industrialized countries like the United States but also in many emerging market countries? The answer is that the benefits of open trade are spread widely, while the costs are often concentrated: individual firms lose profitable business or individual people lose their jobs because of trade, and so they lobby hard against it. For example, when Linksys outsources its technical support to India, computer technicians in the United States lose their jobs. When Americans buy steel made in Korea, American steelworkers may also find themselves out of well-paying jobs. On the other hand, the benefits of having better services for computers or cheaper steel are more subtle: Americans as a whole can buy these goods and services more cheaply, and they will have access to goods and services that will help them be more productive. Even if the society as a whole benefits by being more efficient in the long run, does this mean that that efficiency should be paid for by American computer technicians and steelworkers? Is this fair?

One response to this dilemma is to restrict trade through protectionism: imports can be reduced by adding an additional tax (a *tariff*) to their cost or can be prevented altogether by setting a *quota* that fixes the maximum amount of a good that can be brought in. In the case of outsourcing, protectionism could be achieved by passing laws against companies having services done for them overseas or by taxing them if they do. Clearly protectionism has a cost: it will make Americans on average less efficient and productive. But perhaps we should be willing to pay this cost if the cost to particular workers who lose as a result of free trade would be too high.

Even if you believe that it is worth helping these workers, protectionism is not the way to do it. Instead of using protectionism to prevent imports or outsourcing, we can devise schemes to compensate displaced workers who lose directly from trade, either with direct payments or with programs to help them retrain themselves to get better jobs.[29] This strategy can be described as protecting people, not firms. Protecting businesses by restricting imports is a costly way to protect workers who are hurt by imports because it leads to higher prices for all Americans. The tariff on luggage in the United States, for example, was found to protect only 226 jobs at a cost to consumers of $211 million, for a cost of $934,000 per job. If, instead of the tariff, each one of those workers had been compensated with a Rolls Royce or its cash equivalent, the U.S. government would still have saved a lot of money.[30]

Providing displaced workers with a social safety net if they are hurt by trade, but still allowing the trade to continue, helps deal with the fairness issue but also enables firms and workers in both advanced and developing countries to concentrate on engaging in the most productive activities. Even if compensation schemes or retraining programs for displaced workers are not completely efficient, it still may be worthwhile to put them in place because they encourage political support for trade liberalization, which in the end strengthens the economy.

Trade liberalization is important in all countries because it promotes competition, which, in turn, raises productivity and improves the quality of domestically produced products. This is just as true for rich countries like the United States as for poor countries. When I bought my first car thirty years ago, I bought a new Toyota because it was far more reliable at a lower price than equivalent American cars. For fifteen years I bought only Japanese cars because their reliability and price remained so much better than those of American cars, but this eventually changed. Competition from Japan had a huge impact on American car makers, who were forced to improve their cars or go out of business. Now American cars have better reliability ratings at lower prices than German cars and are not far behind Japanese cars in reliability.

The bottom line is that opening up markets to products from developing countries improves not only life and the economy in those countries but also life and the economy in rich countries. It is not just the right thing to do; it actually improves the quality of our lives as well.

Part Five

Where Do We Go from Here?

Thirteen

Getting Financial Globalization Right

Promoting economic growth and alleviating poverty in so many disadvantaged
countries is one of the greatest challenges the world faces today. How can these
countries safely get on the path to riches?

What Have We Learned?

The chapters in this book contain a lot of information, a lot of data, a lot of economic reasoning, and a lot of advice. Here are six lessons we can draw from
it all.

1. Financial Globalization Is Not the Answer,
but It Is an Important Part of the Answer

An economy's ability to allocate capital to its most productive uses enables it
to reach its full potential in terms of growth, high income per person, and all
the benefits that come with achieving these goals. Developing this ability
takes dedication, hard work, commitment, and time. It also takes the development of institutions that promote strong property rights and a well-
functioning financial system that moves funds to support productive investments. Institutional development is a complex process, and the "one size fits
all" approach of taking institutions from advanced countries and plopping them
down in poor countries has not worked.[1] Institutional frameworks must be
homegrown.

Strong forces, however, are often lined up against financial development. By keeping property rights and the financial system underdeveloped, powerful, entrenched business and political interests are able to restrict competition and prevent entrepreneurs in poor countries from accessing the funds they need to put their ideas into practice. The special interests thus keep the markets to themselves and continue to earn high profits. The economy remains unproductive, and, no matter how hard the average person in the society is willing to work, the country remains poor.

What is the solution? There are no easy answers, but the key is incentives.

As it opens the economy up to foreign capital and financial institutions, financial globalization creates incentives for institutional development by increasing demands within a country for the institutional reforms that promote financial development. When domestic firms can borrow from abroad or from foreign financial institutions, domestic financial institutions will start to lose business. They will need to seek out new customers to whom they can profitably lend. To do this they will require high-quality information to screen out good credit risks from bad and to monitor new borrowers to make sure they don't take on excessive risk. They will now have incentives to encourage the institutional reforms that will make it easier for them to acquire the information they need to make profitable loans. Instead of blocking financial development, they will become supporters of it; they will begin to push for institutional reforms to improve accounting standards and disclosure of financial information. To make loans less risky, they will support reforms of the legal system to enhance the enforcement of contracts that protect property rights, thereby making it easier to establish title to assets and avoid the "tyranny of collateral."

Opening up financial markets to the outside world does not magically or automatically make a country rich. Financial globalization will help promote institutional development only if it is managed to promote greater competition in financial markets. Financial globalization will promote growth only if the process is not perverted and does not lead to destructive blowups of the financial system.[2] Financial crises in the aftermath of financial liberalization and globalization have, unfortunately, been a fact of life for many emerging market countries, and they have led to depressions that have increased poverty and have stressed the social fabric. *Successful* financial globalization, which avoids these crises, requires effective prudential regulation and supervision, responsible fiscal policy, and strong monetary policy institutions.

2. Throwing Money at the Problem Won't Work

One objection to focusing on financial development and globalization as key factors in economic growth is that it is far from clear that emerging market countries are finance constrained. In other words, they often do not have trouble getting money for investments. The discussion in this book supports the view that a lack of money flowing to investments is often not the problem in emerging market countries, and it demonstrates that randomly throwing money at investments does not work. Indeed, as the recent financial crises indicate, too much money flowing into emerging market countries often resulted in bad loans and investments, which led to disastrous financial crises. The argument for the importance of financial development is not that it increases investment, but that it promotes the allocation of investment funds to where they can do the most good for the economy. Research finds that financial development primarily increases growth not by increasing the amount of investment, but by ensuring that investment is allocated to uses that increase productivity.[3]

Throwing money at countries through foreign aid also does not work. William Easterly, in his *The Elusive Quest for Growth* and *The White Man's Burden: Why the West's Efforts to Aid the Rest Have Done So Much Ill and So Little Good*, documents numerous instances of why foreign aid has failed to aid economic development.[4] Throwing money at poor countries can actually make them worse off. Foreign aid often props up corrupt regimes and makes it easier for governments to avoid undertaking the institutional reforms so necessary to economic growth.

3. Disadvantaged Countries Must Take Responsibility for Their Own Fates

The ultimate responsibility for the success or failure of poor countries is theirs. Emerging market countries need to build the political will to promote institutional development. This is not the view that is heard when anti-globalization protestors rally in the streets. They see a cabal of sinister institutions —particularly those based in Washington, D.C.: the International Monetary Fund (IMF), the World Bank, and the U.S. Treasury Department—as the source of the poor countries' woes.

And this view is held not only in the streets but also by some leading academics. The most prominent critic of the IMF is Nobel Prize winner Joseph Stiglitz, who titled one of the chapters in his book *Globalization and Its Discontents* "The East Asia Crisis: How IMF Policies Brought the World to the Verge of a Global Meltdown."[5] Those who believe that Washington-based institutions are the reason why the developing countries stay mired in poverty are just plain wrong. Developing countries are poor because they have not developed the institutions needed to foster economic growth.

4. International Financial Institutions and Citizens in Advanced Countries Can Make a Difference

International financial institutions, like the IMF and the World Bank, and government agencies in advanced countries, like the U.S. Treasury Department, have made mistakes in the past, but they can create incentives to promote institutional development in poor countries. The IMF, the World Bank, and the U.S. Treasury Department can admit that they don't know all the answers and can recognize that the answers to promoting institutional development often reside within the emerging market countries themselves. They can give greater ownership of policies to these countries by designing them jointly through a process of give-and-take. They can also provide the right incentives for institutional development by providing funds to countries only when they are serious about putting in place the kinds of reforms needed to establish strong property rights and an efficient and effective financial system. If special interests block these reforms, then institutions like the IMF and the World Bank have to pull back their funds and just say no, thereby providing incentives to overcome the powerful forces that oppose the reforms needed for successful financial globalization.

Can we as individuals in the advanced countries help? Yes—by supporting the opening of our markets to goods and services from emerging market countries. By encouraging these countries to expand their export sectors, we create exactly the right incentives for them to implement the hard measures that will enable them to grow rich. Exporters have strong incentives to be productive so that they can take advantage of access to our markets, and they will thus make the investments needed for growth. They will also push for the institutional reforms to make financial markets more efficient and promote financial deepening. By getting financial markets to work well, exporters will have access to the capital they need to expand their businesses. A larger export sector in emerging market countries also helps make financial crises less likely and less severe. Firms that sell their goods in foreign markets find that declines in the value of the domestic currency help raise the demand for their goods, and this outcome compensates for the higher value of their liabilities denominated in foreign currency.

Opening up markets to emerging market countries is an important way that we in the advanced countries can help them become successful. Although providing more aid to poor countries seems like a good way to eradicate poverty, it rarely works, because it usually does not create the right incentives to promote economic growth. A handout is almost never as effective as a hand up. Do you really care about world poverty? If you do, you need to support free entry of goods and services from poor countries to our shores. Economists and celebrities who gallivant around the world advocating an end to poverty should campaign for free trade, not more aid. Americans used to say, "Give me your tired, your poor."[6] Now they need to say, "Give me your goods and services."

Arguing that we need to keep jobs in rich countries like the United States, and that we therefore have to bar imports or limit outsourcing, is just another way of saying that we want to keep workers in less fortunate countries poor. Should we care only about the poor in Detroit and not the even poorer in the favelas of Rio de Janeiro?[7] This doesn't mean that those who lose their jobs in advanced countries don't deserve our sympathy and our support in finding new jobs. But displaced workers can be taken care of in ways other than imposing trade restrictions. In the long run, free trade raises productivity in advanced countries like the United States and so eventually provides *better* jobs.

5. It's the Politics, Stupid

It is not easy to make financial globalization work for emerging market countries. It requires the development of institutions, a process that takes considerable time and effort. Furthermore it requires building the political will in poor countries to support institutional reform. This is a difficult task, but it is not an insurmountable one—as the successes of Chile, Hong Kong, Singapore, South Korea, and Taiwan have all demonstrated.

The example of South Korea, which opened this book, is particularly instructive. South Korea has over the years pursued many different strategies to promote growth. When it started to focus on economic development after the Korean War, the South Korean government did not implement reforms to develop an efficient financial system. The government was heavily involved in allocating capital, financial markets were highly regulated, and the domestic financial system was completely closed off from the rest of the world. Then, when the government liberalized its financial system and opened the economy to flows of foreign capital, it did so in a particularly perverse way that culminated in a financial crisis of massive proportions. The Korean government, however, learned from its mistakes. After the financial crisis, it actively pushed for reforms to make the country's financial system work better and leave it less prone to crises. South Korea was rewarded with a far stronger recovery than the other countries in the region that suffered crises.

South Korea still has a long way to go in the reform process, which slowed and sometimes even reversed once the economy recovered. Yet I believe that Korean policymakers understand that, if their country is to reach the next stage of development, it must develop a first-class financial system. If it does, South Korea will surely reach its goal and take its rightful place as one of the richest countries in the world.

6. There Is No Simple Answer

This book argues that institutional development that promotes strong property rights and a financial system that directs capital to its most productive uses are crucial to achieving high economic growth and the eradication of poverty. This does not mean that other factors, such as health, education, and income equality, are not important to economic growth.[8] I have simply pointed out that the importance of developing a well-functioning financial system has not received sufficient attention in discussions about economic growth.

This book does not offer ten easy ways to get financial globalization right. Globalization requires hard work on the part of emerging market countries. All that advanced nations can do is provide incentives that encourage policy-makers, politicians, and citizens to support the kind of institutional development that will promote economic growth in poor countries. Getting governments to work in the interest of the public, so that the right kind of reform occurs, is one of the toughest problems facing development economists and political scientists today.[9]

Epilogue: Harnessing Globalization—Chile, 1980–2006

Putting in place the institutional reforms to make financial globalization work is a daunting task. Are these reforms unrealistic? Is it possible for emerging market countries to develop them?

The answer is yes. Hong Kong, Singapore, and Taiwan have completely embraced globalization and have developed the institutions to make it work. They have established efficient and healthy financial systems that are well regulated and well supervised, they have responsible fiscal policies, and they have monetary policy institutions that have achieved price stability. Since its 1997 crisis, South Korea has also made huge progress in its reform process, although it needs to go further. Can emerging market countries elsewhere in the world make globalization work for them?

Chile has shown that it can be done, even in Latin America, a region which in general has had a disappointing experience with globalization over the past twenty years.

Globalization and the Chilean
Financial Crisis of 1982–1983

From the end of World War II until the 1980s, Chile seemed to have all the problems of other Latin American countries. It had an inward-looking economy with extensive barriers to free trade, was substantially poorer than neighboring countries like Argentina, had a low growth rate, and had experienced high and variable inflation rates, reaching an annual rate of over 600% in 1973. After the government of Augusto Pinochet took power in 1973, it pursued an ambitious policy of financial liberalization, opening up markets to foreign capital and allowing banks to engage in new types of lending without controls on the interest rates they could charge. Unfortunately this financial liberalization was carried out without putting into place the necessary prudential regulatory and supervisory safeguards. The result was a lending boom from the mid-1970s until the early 1980s, just like those in Mexico and South Korea, an increase in non-performing loans, and then a currency collapse and financial crisis that were actually far worse than Mexico's or South Korea's. Output in the economy declined almost 14% in 1982 and another 3% in 1983, with inflation increasing to above 20%.[10] The cost to the Chilean taxpayer for bailing out the country's banking system was over 40% of GDP, as compared with around 20% for Mexico and 30% for South Korea.[11]

Recovery and Triumph

In the aftermath of the crisis, the Chileans recognized that they had made serious policy mistakes; they were determined not to make them again.[12] After rapidly recapitalizing the banking system using taxpayers' money (with some assistance from the IMF), the Chilean government completely overhauled its prudential regulation and supervision of the financial system with a new banking law in 1986 (very much along the lines suggested in Chapter 12). The law increased the role of the supervisory agency in rating banks' risk using loan classifications, required more disclosure of information to the public, and imposed strict enforcement of restrictions on connected lending. These efforts have resulted in bank regulatory and supervisory practices that a World Bank study cites as among the best in the emerging market world and that are comparable to those in advanced countries.[13] As a result, even during the Mexican crisis of 1995, the Russian meltdown of 1998, and the current difficulties in Latin America, the soundness of Chile's financial system has never faltered. The controls on short-term capital inflows adopted by the government have also been cited as an important factor behind the Chilean success story, but they were more an element of prudential regulation than capital controls, and research suggests they were not important to Chile's subsequent economic success.[14]

Chile pursued a series of major fiscal reforms: giving enhanced power to the executive branch to manage spending and tax decisions, introducing a value-added tax (in effect a national sales tax), closing tax loopholes, and privatizing public companies. This process culminated in an administrative decision by the new government in 2000 to implement a flexible, balanced-budget rule (Regla del Balance Estructural or Structural Balance Rule for the Central Government), which has strong elements of transparency, including provision for committees of outside experts to set the key parameters of the budget rule.[15] As a result of these reforms, during the period 1991–2003 Chile's budget was actually in surplus by some 1% of GDP. This is a record that most advanced countries would love to have.

The government has worked on developing strong monetary institutions. In 1989 it passed new central bank legislation (which took effect in 1990) that gave independence to the central bank and mandated price stability as its primary objective. In 1991 the Chilean central bank adopted an inflation-targeting regime; at first the announced inflation objectives were interpreted more as official inflation projections rather than formal or "hard" targets.[16] Only after the central bank had some success with disinflation, bringing inflation down from over 20% to under 12% by 1994, did the inflation projections become hard targets, with the central bank held accountable for meeting them. In May 2000 Chile finally adopted a full-fledged inflation-targeting regime, including most of the features seen in advanced countries like the United Kingdom.[17] Since 2001 inflation in Chile has been close to 3%, a figure at the center of the central bank's target range.

Chile also pursued trade liberalization. From one of the most closed economies in the world in the 1970s, Chile has transformed itself into one of the most open: average tariff rates fell from 105% in 1973 to 6% today. In addition, there are no tariffs on products from countries that have signed free-trade agreements with Chile, so that the average actual tariff rate on Chilean imports is close to 2.5%. The country has also dropped all restrictions on the entry of foreign capital.

All of these institutional reforms paid off. From 1991 to the present, Chile has been able to lower inflation rates from above 20% to around 3%, the central bank's stated goal. Over the same period, output growth has been high, averaging over 5% per year since 1991. Chile's success has gained it the nickname the "Latin Tiger," putting it on equal footing with the fast-growing "Asian Tigers."

The Future

Chile is not without its problems. It still has unequal income distribution. Reforms have so far been largely unable to raise the educational attainment of the general population to levels closer to those in industrialized countries. Because Chile is in a bad neighborhood (Argentina, Bolivia, and Peru sit on its borders), it is subject to the shocks that periodically hit the region, such as the withdrawal of foreign capital that occurred after the East Asian crisis and the Russian meltdown in 1997–98. However, Chile's performance continues to be outstanding compared with that of other Latin American nations, with a growth rate that is the envy of the region. And Chile's vibrant democracy is fully committed to the globalization process, because the public rightfully sees globalization as the way for them to get rich.

Not every emerging market country has the political will of Chile, Hong Kong, Singapore, and Taiwan to adopt the reforms needed to make financial globalization work. But globalization will work when a country's political and business leadership is committed to improving the lot of its citizens. These countries prove that the next great globalization should be financial. I hope this book provides some guidance on how it can be done right.

Notes

Chapter One   The Next Great Globalization: A Force for Good?

1. The share of exports and imports in its gross domestic product was a minuscule 3.1% and 12.2%, respectively; International Monetary Fund, *Direction of Trade Statistics* (Washington, D.C.: International Monetary Fund, 2004).

2. In 2001, the net flow of foreign debt, foreign direct investment, portfolio equity, and grants was over $9 billion, while the comparable figure in 1960 was $400 million. The source for this data is World Bank, *Global Development Finance* (Washington, D.C.: World Bank, 2003).

3. For excellent surveys of the globalization debate, see François Bourguignon et al., *Making Sense of Globalization: A Guide to the Economic Issues,* CEPR Policy Paper (July 2002); Stanley Fischer, "Globalization and Its Challenges," *American Economic Review* 93 (2003): 1–30; Johan Norberg, *In Defense of Global Capitalism* (Washington, D.C.: Cato Institute, 2003); and Martin Wolf, *Why Globalization Works* (New Haven, Conn.: Yale University Press, 2004).

4. The data reflect world exports plus imports. The source of this data is the International Monetary Fund, *Direction of Trade Statistics* (Washington, D.C.: International Monetary Fund, 2004). The 1960 numbers have been converted into today's dollars using the GDP implicit price deflator for the United States found in *Economic Report of the President* (Washington, D.C.: United States Government Printing Office, 2005).

5. International capital flows in 1975 were $165 billion in today's dollars ($57 billion in 1975 dollars). The source of this data is the Bank for International Settlements, *47th Annual Report* (Basel: Bank for International Settlements, June 1976). The more recent data are from Bank for International Settlements, *74th Annual Report* (Basel: Bank for International Settlements, June 2004).

6. There is some arbitrariness as to when to date the start of the First Age of Globalization. The rapid drop of transportation costs starting in the 1820s is often cited as starting the First Age (Richard E. Baldwin and Philippe Martin, "Two Waves of Globalisation: Superficial Similarities, Fundamental Differences," NBER Working Paper 6904 [January 1999]). The 1870 date is the most commonly used starting date, however.

7. GDP is defined as the market value of all final goods and services produced in a country during the course of the year and is the most commonly reported measure of aggregate output. The international trade data are from Alan Taylor, "Globalization, Trade and Development: Some Lessons from History," NBER Working Paper 9326 (November 2002), while the GDP data are from Angus Maddison, *The World Economy: A Millennial Perspective* (Paris: Development Centre of the Organisation for Economic Co-operation and Development, 2001). The capital flow data are from Maurice Obstfeld and Alan M. Taylor, "Globalization and Capital Markets," NBER Working Paper 8846 (March 2002).

8. John Maynard Keynes, *The Economic Consequences of the Peace* (New York: Harcourt, Brace and Howe, 1920), 11–12. Note that this citation is to the 1920 edition, even though the book was first published in 1919.

9. Angus Maddison, *The World Economy,* 94, Table 3-1a.

10. See Peter Lindert and Jeffrey Williamson, "Does Globalization Make the World More Unequal?" NBER Working Paper 8228 (April 2001).

11. Fernand Braudel, *Civilisation and Capitalism, 15th–18th Century: The Perspective of the World,* vol. 3 (New York: Harper and Row, 1984); Paul Bairoch, *Economics and World History* (London: Harvester-Wheatsheaf, 1993); and Richard E. Baldwin and Philippe Martin, "Two Waves of Globalisation."

12. The data are also from Angus Maddison, *The World Economy.* Note that the data for income per person throughout this book are in real purchasing power parity–adjusted terms (2005 dollars).

13. Maurice Obstfeld and Alan M. Taylor, "Globalization and Capital Markets."

14. See Richard Lukas, *The Forgotten Holocaust: The Poles under German Occupation, 1939–44* (New York: Hippocrene, 1997) for estimates of the deaths from the Holocaust.

15. Raghuram Rajan and Luigi Zingales, "The Great Reversals: The Politics of Financial Development in the 20th Century," *Journal of Financial Economics* 69, no. 1 (2003): 5–50.

16. Fanz Estevadeordal and Alan M. Taylor, "The Rise and Fall of World Trade 1870–1939," *Quarterly Journal of Economics* 118 (2003): 359–407.

17. World Bank, *World Development Indicators* (Washington, D.C.: World Bank, 2004).

18. Angus Maddison, *The World Economy.*

19. See Angus Maddison, *The World Economy.*

20. See Paul Collier and David Dollar, *Globalization, Growth and Poverty: Building an Inclusive World Economy* (New York: Oxford University Press, 2002).

21. See David Dollar and Aart Kraay, "Growth Is Good for the Poor," *Journal of Economic Growth* 7, no. 3 (2002): 195–225; and Alan Winters et al., "Trade Liberalization and Poverty: The Evidence So Far," *Journal of Economic Literature* 42, no. 1 (2004): 72–115. How-

ever, wage inequality may have increased because there has been a fall in the wages of unskilled workers relative to skilled workers throughout the world, including developing countries that have actively entered global markets. The leading explanation for this phenomenon is that trade-induced technical change has been biased against the wages of unskilled labor. Thus the jury is still out on whether trade liberalization has increased income inequality within developing countries.

22. For example, see Dani Rodrik, *Has Globalization Gone Too Far?* (Washington, D.C.: Institute for International Economics, 1997) and William Cline, *Trade and Wage Inequality* (Washington, D.C.: Institute for International Economics, 1997).

23. See Xavier Sala-i-Martin, "The Disturbing 'Rise' of Income Inequality," NBER Working Paper 8904 (April 2002); Peter Lindert and Jeffrey Williamson, "Does Globalization Make the World More Unequal?"; Lant Pritchett, "Divergence Big Time," *Journal of Economic Perspectives* 11 (1997): 3–17; François Bourguignon and Christian Morrison, "Inequality among World Citizens," *American Economic Review* 92 (2002): 727–44.

24. United Nations, *Common Database* (New York: United Nations Statistics Division, 2004).

25. World Bank, *World Development Indicators.*

26. Peter Lindert and Jeffrey Williamson, "Does Globalization Make the World More Unequal?"

27. Maurice Obstfeld and Alan M. Taylor, *Global Capital Markets: Integration, Crisis and Growth* (Cambridge: Cambridge University Press, 2004).

28. This is documented in Maurice Obstfeld and Alan M. Taylor, *Global Capital Markets,* and in Laura Alfaro et al., "Capital Flows in a Globalized World: The Role of Policies and Institutions," NBER Working Paper 11696 (October 2005).

29. Robert Lucas, "Why Doesn't Capital Flow from Rich to Poor Countries?" *American Economic Review* 80 (1990): 92–96.

30. As we will see, the main reason why capital does not flow from rich to poor countries is because of the weaker institutional environment in poor countries. Empirical evidence supports this view: Laura Alfaro et al., "Why Doesn't Capital Flow from Rich to Poor Countries? An Empirical Investigation," NBER Working Paper 11901 (December 2005); and Laura Alfaro et al., "Capital Flows in a Globalized World."

31. Institute for International Finance, "Update of Capital Flows to Emerging Market Economies," March 31, 2005, http://www.iif.com/verify/data/report_docs/cf_0305.pdf.

32. See Maurice Obstfeld and Alan M. Taylor, *Global Capital Markets,* and Alan M. Taylor, "External Dependence, Demographic Burdens and Argentine Economic Decline after the *Belle Epoque," Journal of Economic History* 52 (1992): 907–36.

33. In 2003, foreign portfolio investment in bonds and equity, plus net flows of foreign domestic investment, were a little over 5% of gross capital formation in Argentina, and this percentage has been below 10% since 2001. However, for a short period in the late 1990s, the percentage of gross capital formation supplied by foreigners was far higher, reaching a peak of over 40% in 1999. The data for these calculations come from the online database World Bank, *2005 World Development Indicators Online* (Washington, D.C.: World Bank, 2005).

34. See Figure 7.5 in Maurice Obstfeld and Alan M. Taylor, *Global Capital Markets*, 242.

35. For example, in James R. Kearl et al., "A Confusion of Economists," *American Economic Review Papers and Proceedings* 69, no. 2 (1979): 28–37, 97% of economists agreed (generally or with some provisions) with the statement "Tariffs and import quotas reduce general economic welfare."

36. The importance of finance to economic growth has also frequently been ignored by economists. For example, the leading undergraduate textbook on economic growth, David N. Weil, *Economic Growth* (Boston: Addison-Wesley, 2005) does not discuss the link between finance and growth at all.

37. Quote from A. Edward Alden and Alan Beattie, "Comment and Analysis— Keeping the Faith," *Financial Times*, London edition, May 6, 2002, p. 16.

38. M. Ayhan Kose et al., "The Macroeconomic Implications of Financial Globalization: A Reappraisal and Synthesis," IMF mimeo (November 2005) come to a similar conclusion that, although financial globalization has many benefits, it can go very wrong because it can lead to financial crises.

39. This figure is cited in James R. Barth et al., *Rethinking Bank Regulation and Supervision: Til Angels Govern* (New York: Cambridge University Press, 2006).

40. Joseph E. Stiglitz, *Globalization and Its Discontents* (New York: W. W. Norton, 2002).

41. Jagdish Bhagwati, *In Defense of Globalization* (New York: Oxford University Press, 2004).

42. Jagdish Bhagwati, "The Capital Myth: The Difference between Trade in Widgets and Dollars," *Foreign Affairs* 77, no. 3 (1998): 7. Also see Jagdish Bhagwati, *The Winds of the Hundred Days: How Washington Mismanaged Globalization* (Cambridge, Mass.: MIT Press, 2002), and "The Perils of Gung-ho International Financial Capitalism," in Jagdish Bhagwati, *In Defense of Globalization*, 199–208.

43. George Soros, *On Globalization* (New York: Public Affairs, 2002). George Soros is often viewed by the media as being hostile to financial globalization. However, reading his book closely suggests that he supports financial globalization if steps are taken to make it work well, a theme that is consistent with the views expressed in my book. An exception to popular books that criticize financial globalization is Martin Wolf's superb *Why Globalization Works* (New Haven, Conn.: Yale University Press, 2004). Also see Charles Calomiris, *A Globalist Manifesto for Public Policy* (London: Institute of Economic Affairs, 2002).

44. This wonderful phrase was coined by the great American philosopher Yogi Berra.

45. World Bank, *World Development Indicators*.

46. In 1930, the income per person in Argentina in 1990 dollars was $4080, which was more than that for the average for Western Europe (twenty-nine countries) of $4014. The source is Angus Maddison, *The World Economy: Historical Statistics* (Paris: Organisation for Economic Co-operation and Development, 2003), 143, Table 4c.

47. William Easterly, *The Elusive Quest for Growth: Economists' Adventures and Misadventures in the Tropics* (Cambridge, Mass.: MIT Press, 2001), 203.

48. Associated Press, "Argentina Exports Suspension Now in Effect," March 10, 2006.

49. Andrew Higgins, "Liberté, Precarité: Labor Law Ignites Anxiety in France," *Wall Street Journal*, March 29, 2006, p. A8.

50. Gregg Ip and Neil King, Jr., "Ports Deal Shows Roadblocks for Globalization," *Wall Street Journal*, March 11, 2006, p. A1.

51. For research showing that health is extremely important to economic growth, see David N. Weil, "Accounting for the Effect of Health on Economic Growth," NBER Working Paper 11455 (July 2005). However, see William Easterly, *The Elusive Quest for Growth*, for a skeptical view that spending on health and education promotes economic growth. David Dollar and Aart Kraay, "Growth Is Good for the Poor," also find that public spending on health and education is not positively associated with declines in poverty.

52. There is now a large literature that shows the importance of good institutions to economic growth. See, for example, Douglas C. North and Robert P. Thomas, *The Rise of the Western World: A New Economic History* (Cambridge: Cambridge University Press, 1973); Robert Hall and Chad I. Jones, "Why Do Some Countries Produce So Much More Output per Worker than Others?" *Quarterly Journal of Economics* 114, no. 1 (1999): 83–117; Daron Acemoglu et al., "The Colonial Origins of Comparative Development: An Empirical Investigation," *American Economic Review* 91 (2001): 1369–401; William Easterly and Ross Levine, "It's Not Factor Accumulation: Stylized Facts and Growth Models," *World Bank Economic Review* 15 (2001): 177–219; Dani Rodrik et al., "Institutions Rule: The Primacy of Institutions over Geography and Integration in Economic Development," NBER Working Paper 9305 (November 2002); William Easterly and Ross Levine, "Tropics, Germs and Crops: How Endowments Influence Economic Development," *Journal of Monetary Economics* 50 (2003): 3–40; Edward Glaeser et al., "Do Institutions Cause Growth?" NBER Working Paper 10568 (June 2004); and the recent survey by Daron Acemoglu et al., "Institutions as the Fundamental Cause of Long-Term Growth," in Philippe Aghion and Steven N. Durlauf, eds., *Handbook of Economic Growth*, vol. 1, part A (Amsterdam: North-Holland, 2005), 385–472.

53. William Easterly, *The Elusive Quest for Growth*, 69.

54. The data for this fact are from 2003 and were obtained from World Bank, *World Development Indicators*.

55. Institutional development can refer to a broader definition that includes political institutions. Edward Glaeser et al., "Do Institutions Cause Growth?", argue that many measures of institutional development are flawed because they reflect conceptually ambiguous assessment of institutional outcomes. Their results, for example, do not support the idea that democracy and constraints on government are necessary for economic development, because security of property rights can be established by dictators. See also Stephen Haber et al., *The Politics of Property Rights: Political Instability, Credible Commitments, and Economic Growth in Mexico, 1876–1929* (Cambridge: Cambridge University Press, 2003), who show that the Porfirio Diaz government in Mexico did establish a form of property rights that promoted economic growth.

56. The phrase "Wall Street–Treasury Department complex" has been used by Jagdish Bhagwati in "The Capital Myth," 7–12.

57. This figures is for official development assistance for 2003 and comes from the United Nations Common Database, United Nations Statistics Division, New York, 2004.

58. William Easterly, *The Elusive Quest for Growth*.

59. William Easterly expands on this theme in his book *The White Man's Burden: Why*

the West's Efforts to Aid the Rest Have Done So Much Ill and So Little Good (New York: Penguin, 2006).

60. From remarks at an UNCTAD conference in February 2000, as quoted in Johan Norberg, *In Defense of Global Capitalism,* 155.

Chapter Two   How Poor Countries Can Get Rich: Strengthening Property Rights and the Financial System

1. Douglass North, *Institutions, Institutional Change, and Economic Development* (Cambridge: Cambridge University Press, 1990), 3.

2. See David O. Beim and Charles W. Calomiris, *Emerging Financial Markets* (Boston: McGraw-Hill Irwin, 2001).

3. See Rafael La Porta et al., "Legal Determinants of External Finance," *Journal of Finance* 52, no. 3 (1997): 1131–50, and Rafael La Porta et al., "Law and Finance," *Journal of Political Economy* 106 (1998): 1113–55.

4. The inefficiency of the legal system in many developing countries often leads to the use of social arrangements to substitute for formal business contracts. For example, many societies compensate for weak legal systems by placing a greater emphasis on "trust" and "honor" or familial relationships in economic transactions. Because these social arrangements lead to cronyism and make it more difficult to conduct transactions with strangers, they are much less efficient than a well-functioning legal system.

5. Douglass North, *Institutions, Institutional Change,* 54.

6. World Bank, *Doing Business in 2005: Removing Obstacles to Growth* (Washington, D.C.: World Bank, International Finance Corporation, and Oxford University Press, 2005).

7. Jonathan Karp, "India's Laws a Mixed Blessing for Investors—U.S. Firms Struggle in Court but Copyright Laws Improve," *Wall Street Journal,* Eastern edition, July 11, 1997, p. A10.

8. Matt Moffett and Geraldo Samor, "Opportunity Cost: In Brazil, Thicket of Red Tape Spoils Recipe for Growth," *Wall Street Journal,* May 24, 2005, pp. A1, A9.

9. Since taxation also takes part of the value of your property, why isn't it as readily associated with a violation of property rights? There are two answers. First, if it is administered equitably, taxation does not create uncertainty, while corruption and other violations of property rights do. You know exactly what the tax rate is before you make decisions and can act accordingly. Second, under a democracy, the decision of how high taxes should be is determined by politicians who are elected by the public. In addition, the public has some say, through its elected officials, over how tax revenues are spent. If tax revenues are spent well—say, on good public infrastructure (e.g., highways, port facilities, police, education)—the taxation can make a society better off. If the public has no say over tax rates or how tax revenue is spent, however, taxation can be considered a violation of property rights: hence the rallying cry for American independence, "No taxation without representation." Taxes can also violate property rights if they are confiscatory or if the tax to be paid is set at the whim of the tax collector and so is arbitrary. This is why making sure that the tax system is applied fairly can be thought of as an element of strong property rights.

10. Paolo Mauro, "Corruption and Economic Growth," *Quarterly Journal of Economics* 110 (1995): 681–712, and Paolo Mauro, "The Effects of Corruption on Growth, Investment and Government Expenditures," in Kimberly Ann Elliott, ed., *Corruption and the Global Economy* (Washington, D.C.: Institute for International Economics, 1997), 83–107. Shang-Jin Wei, "How Taxing Is Corruption on International Investors," NBER Working Paper 6030 (May 1997), finds that corruption also significantly reduces foreign direct investment, which is usually beneficial to growth.

11. Hernando De Soto, *The Mystery of Capital: Why Capitalism Triumphs in the West and Fails Everywhere Else* (New York: Basic Books, 2000), 18–28.

12. World Bank, *Doing Business in 2005*, 19.

13. See Simeon Djankov et al., "The Regulation of Entry," NBER Working Paper 7892 (September 2000).

14. The World Bank considers the cost of setting up businesses to be so important that it now produces an annual publication that estimates the time and cost of setting up a business for 145 countries. The latest one is World Bank, *Doing Business in 2005*. It uses a somewhat different methodology than does De Soto, and reports that the time and cost of setting up businesses in Peru takes 98 days at a cost of $783 in official fees (which do not include bribes).

15. In 1990, Zimbabwe exported 742,000 tons of corn, but exported only 10,674 tons in 2000. United Nations, *Trade Statistics* (New York: United Nations Statistics Division, 2005).

16. Andrei Shleifer and Robert W. Vishny, *The Grabbing Hand: Government Pathologies and Their Cures* (Cambridge, Mass.: Harvard University Press, 1998).

17. For example, see Raghuram Rajan and Luigi Zingales, *Saving Capitalism from the Capitalists: Unleashing the Power of Financial Markets to Create Wealth and Spread Opportunity* (New York: Crown Business, 2003), and Daron Acemoglu et al., "Institutions as the Fundamental Cause of Long-Term Growth," in Philippe Aghion and Steven N. Durlauf, eds., *Handbook of Economic Growth*, vol. 1, part A (Amsterdam: North-Holland, 2005), 385–472.

18. See "The Missing Lessons of U.S. History," in Hernando De Soto, *The Mystery of Capital*, 105–51.

19. See Yingyi Qian, "How Reform Worked in China," in Dani Rodrik, ed., *In Search of Prosperity: Analytic Narratives of Economic Growth* (Princeton, N.J.: Princeton University Press, 2003).

20. This theme has been emphasized by Dani Rodrik, a prominent development economist at Harvard University. See Dani Rodrik, "Growth Strategies," NBER Working Paper 10050 (October 2003).

21. The actual figure for 1970–2000 is 56%, and it is found in Andreas Hackethal and Reinhard H. Schmidt, "Financing Patterns: Measurement Concepts and Empirical Results," Johann Wolfgang Goethe–Universität Working Paper 125 (January 2004). The figure is even higher in Canada, 73% (Apostolos Serletis and Karl Pinno, "Corporate Financing in Canada," University of Calgary, mimeo, February 2004), while in Germany and Japan, it is over 80% (Andreas Hackethal and Reinhard H. Schmidt, "Financing Patterns").

22. Note that by making private loans, financial intermediaries cannot entirely eliminate the free rider problem. Knowing that a financial intermediary has made a loan to a particular company reveals information to other parties that the company is more likely to be creditworthy and will be undergoing monitoring by the financial institution. Thus some of the benefits of information collection produced by the financial institution will accrue to others.

23. See Table 4 in Frederic S. Mishkin, *The Economics of Money, Banking, and Financial Markets*, 8th edition (Boston: Addison-Wesley, 2007), 41.

24. Andreas Hackethal and Reinhard H. Schmidt, "Financing Patterns"; and Apostolos Serletis and Karl Pinno, "Corporate Financing in Canada."

25. For example, see Liliana Rojas-Suarez and Steven R. Weisbrod, "Financial Market Fragilities in Latin America: From Banking Crisis Resolution to Current Policy Challenges," IMF Working Paper WP/94/117 (October 1994).

26. Another example of screening to avoid the adverse selection problem occurs when rich people hire private detectives to investigate the background of potential spouses. (Although this does seem to be pretty heartless, it makes perfect financial sense.)

27. For a discussion of how banks establish long-term customer relationships, see "Banking and the Management of Financial Institutions," in Frederic S. Mishkin, *The Economics of Money, Banking, and Financial Markets*, 219–46. One way banks institutionalize long-term customer relationships is via loan commitment arrangements in which a bank makes a commitment (for a specified future period of time) to provide a firm with loans up to a given amount at an interest rate that is tied to some market interest rate. The majority of commercial and industrial loans in advanced countries are made under the loan commitment arrangement.

28. Douglas W. Diamond, "Financial Intermediation and Delegated Monitoring," *Review of Economic Studies* 51 (1984): 393–414, provides a theoretical model that demonstrates why banks are lower-cost monitors than individuals.

29. See Joseph E. Stiglitz and Andrew Weiss, "Incentive Effects of Terminations: Applications to Credit and Labor Markets," *American Economic Review* 73 (1983): 912–27.

30. See Franklin Edwards and Frederic S. Mishkin, "The Decline of Traditional Banking: Implications for Financial Stability and Regulatory Policy," *Federal Reserve Bank of New York Economic Policy Review* 1, no. 2 (1995): 27–45.

31. Alan Greenspan, "Global Challenges," remarks at the Financial Crisis Conference, Council on Foreign Relations, New York, July 12, 2000, http://www.federalreserve.gov/boarddocs/speeches/2000/20000712.htm.

32. Andrew Crockett et al., *Conflicts of Interest in the Financial Services Industry: What Should We Do about Them?* Geneva Reports on the World Economy 4 (Geneva and London: International Center for Monetary and Banking Studies and Centre for Economic Policy Research, 2003), refer to this as socialization of information production and argue that it is a poor solution to producing sufficient information.

Chapter Three   Financial Development, Economic Growth, and Poverty

1. The term *financial repression* is often used more narrowly to indicate an environment in which the government directs credit and interest rates are not allowed to be

set by markets and thus have an allocative role. An excellent nontechnical survey of the extensive empirical evidence on this topic can be found in World Bank, *Finance for Growth: Policy Choices in a Volatile World* (Oxford: World Bank and Oxford University Press, 2001). See also Ross Levine, "Finance and Growth," in Philippe Aghion and Steven N. Durlauf, eds., *Handbook of Economic Growth,* vol. 1, part A (Amsterdam: North-Holland, 2005), 865–934, and Sergio L. Schmukler, "Financial Globalization: Gain and Pain for Developing Countries," *Federal Reserve Bank of Atlanta Review* 89, no. 2 (2004): 39–66. For a recent paper that also finds that financial deepening is crucial to economic growth for developing countries, see Philippe Aghion et al., "The Effect of Financial Development on Convergence: Theory and Evidence," *Quarterly Journal of Economics* 120 (2005): 173–222.

2. Abdul Abiad et al., "The Quality Effect: Does Financial Liberalization Improve the Allocation of Capital?" paper presented at the Journal of Banking and Finance/World Bank Conference on Globalization and Financial Services in Emerging Market Countries, June 20–21, 2005, Washington, D.C., find that financial liberalization, which improves the institutional framework of the financial sector, does lead to higher economic growth and is far more important to economic growth than just expansion of the financial sector.

3. Robert King and Ross Levine, "Finance and Growth: Schumpeter Might Be Right," *Quarterly Journal of Economics* 108 (1993): 717–37. One concern with this result is that high economic growth before 1960 could have led to high financial development and to further high economic growth, so that causality might not run from financial development to growth. To rule this possibility out, later papers have used instrumental variables techniques in which the origin of the legal system (British, French, German, or Scandinavian), which was determined typically hundreds of years ago, well before recent growth, is used as an instrument for financial development at the beginning of the period. The result is the same: economic growth is positively related to financial development. For example, see Ross Levine et al., "Financial Intermediation and Growth: Causality and Causes," *Journal of Monetary Economics* 46, no. 1 (2000): 31–77; Ross Levine and Sara Zervos, "Stock Markets, Banks, and Economic Growth," *American Economic Review* 88, no. 3 (1998): 537–58; and Thorsten Beck et al., "Finance and the Sources of Growth," *Journal of Financial Economics* 58, no. 1–2 (2000): 261–300.

4. See Ross Levine et al., "Financial Intermediation," and Aubhik Khan, "The Finance and Growth Nexus," *Business Review of the Federal Reserve Bank of Philadelphia,* no. 1 (2000): 3–14.

5. See Raghuram Rajan and Luigi Zingales, "Financial Dependence and Growth," *American Economic Review* 88, no. 3 (1998): 559–86, and Asli Demirguc-Kunt and Vojislav Maksimovic, "Law, Finance and Firm Growth," *Journal of Finance* 53 (1998): 2107–37.

6. This is particularly true in industries that depend more on external finance. See Raghuram Rajan and Luigi Zingales, "Financial Dependence and Growth."

7. Evidence on the link between financial development and growth in overall productivity (more formally referred to as *total factor productivity*) can be found in Thorsten Beck et al., "Finance and the Sources of Growth"; William Easterly and Ross Levine, "It's Not Factor Accumulation: Stylized Facts and Growth Models," *World Bank Economic Review* 15 (2001): 177–219; and Ross Levine, "Finance and Growth."

8. Patrick Honohan, "Financial Development, Growth and Poverty: How Close Are the Links?" World Bank Policy Working Paper 3203 (February 2004), 2. Case studies, such as Hyeok Jeong and Robert M. Townsend, "Sources of TFP Growth: Occupational Choice and Financial Deepening," University of Chicago mimeo (April 2005), also support the importance of financial deepening to economic growth.

9. See Hongyi Li et al., "Explaining International and Intertemporal Variations in Income Inequality," *Economic Journal* 108 (2001): 26–43; Thorsten Beck et al., "Finance, Inequality and Poverty: Cross-Country Evidence," World Bank, mimeo (April 2004); and Patrick Honohan, "Financial Development, Growth and Poverty."

10. Rajeev H. Dehejia and Roberta Gatti, "Child Labor: The Role of Income Variability and Access to Credit in a Cross Section of Countries," World Bank Policy Research Paper 2767 (January 2002).

11. See Abhijit Banerjee and Andrew Newman, "Occupational Choice and the Process of Development," *Journal of Political Economy* 101 (1993): 274–98; Oded Galor and J. Zeira, "Income Distribution and Macroeconomics," *Review of Economic Studies* 60 (1993): 35–52; and Philippe Aghion and Patrick Bolton, "A Trickle-Down Theory of Growth and Development with Debt Overhang," *Review of Economic Studies* 64 (1997): 151–72.

12. Hernando De Soto, *The Mystery of Capital: Why Capitalism Triumphs in the West and Fails Everywhere Else* (New York: Basic Books, 2000), 20–28.

13. The World Bank in its annual publication, *Doing Business,* updates De Soto's numbers on the time and cost of registering property using a somewhat different methodology. The World Bank's numbers are substantially lower than De Soto's, but they still show that the time and cost of registering property in poor countries are much greater than in rich countries.

14. Hernando De Soto, *The Mystery of Capital,* 35.

15. Inter-American Development Bank, *Unlocking Credit: The Quest for Deep and Stable Bank Lending, 2005 Report, Economic and Social Progress in Latin America* (Washington, D.C.: Inter-American Development Bank and Johns Hopkins University Press, 2004), 209.

16. Raghuram Rajan and Luigi Zingales, *Saving Capitalism from the Capitalists: Unleashing the Power of Financial Markets to Create Wealth and Spread Opportunity* (New York: Crown Business, 2003).

17. See Rafael La Porta et al., "Legal Determinants of External Finance," *Journal of Finance* 52, no. 3 (1997): 1131–50; Rafael La Porta et al., "Law and Finance," *Journal of Political Economy* 106, no. 6 (1998): 1113–55; and Stijn Claessens and Leora Klapper, "Bankruptcy around the World: Explanations of Its Relative Use," *American Law and Economic Review* 7, no. 1 (2005): 253–83.

18. See Rafael La Porta et al., "Legal Determinants of External Finance"; Rafael La Porta et al., "Law and Finance"; and the recent survey in Thorsten Beck and Ross Levine, "Legal Institutions and Financial Development," NBER Working Paper 10417 (April 2004).

19. One notorious example was how the Belgian Congo was run under King Leopold of Belgium, as is discussed in Daron Acemoglu et al., "The Colonial Origins

of Comparative Development: An Empirical Investigation," *American Economic Review* 91, no. 5 (2001): 1369–1401, and Bogumil Jewsiewicki, "Rural Society and the Belgian Colonial Economy," in David Birmingham and Phylis M. Martin, eds., *The History of Central Africa*, vol. II (New York: Longman, 1983), 95–126. Belgian policy in the Congo was so exploitive and ruthless that it led to an international protest movement in the early twentieth century.

20. Daron Acemoglu et al., "The Colonial Origins of Comparative Development." David Albouy, "The Colonial Origins of Comparative Development: A Reexamination Based on Improved Settler Mortality Data," University of California, Berkeley, mimeo (February 2005), questions the strength of the results of Daron Acemoglu et al. on methodological grounds, arguing that the settler mortality data used by them are flawed. However, other papers, using very different methodological approaches that do not make use of settler mortality data, do support the conclusion of Daron Acemoglu et al. that institutional development is a key driving factor behind economic development. For example, see William Easterly and Ross Levine, "Tropics, Germs and Crops: How Endowments Influence Economic Development," *Journal of Monetary Economics* 50 (2003): 3–40; Dani Rodrik et al., "Institutions Rule: The Primacy of Institutions over Geography and Integration in Economic Development," NBER Working Paper 9305 (November 2002); and Edward Glaeser et al., "Do Institutions Cause Growth?" NBER Working Paper 10568 (June 2004).

21. See Daron Acemoglu et al., "The Colonial Origins of Comparative Development." In addition, when legal systems were transplanted to a country with an unreceptive environment, they also did not seem to work very well: David Berkowitz et al., "Economic Development, Legality and the Transplant Effect," Harvard University, Center for International Development Working Paper 39 (March 2000). For a recent survey of this literature, see Ross Levine, "Law, Endowments, and Property Rights," NBER Working Paper 11502 (August 2005).

22. For example, see Edward Kane, "Good Intentions and Unintended Evil: The Case against Selective Credit Allocation," *Journal of Money, Credit and Banking* 9, no. 1 (1977): 55–69, and World Bank, *Finance for Growth*.

23. Inter-American Development Bank, *Unlocking Credit*. Chapter 10 of that report finds that state-owned banks are less efficient, have higher numbers of nonperforming loans, higher overhead, and lower returns than do private sector banks.

24. Rafael La Porta et al., "Government Ownership of Banks," *Journal of Finance* 57, no. 1 (2002): 265–301. Also see James R. Barth et al., "Banking Systems around the Globe: Do Regulation and Ownership Affect Performance and Stability?" in Frederic S. Mishkin, ed., *Prudential Regulation and Supervision: What Works and What Doesn't* (Chicago: University of Chicago Press, 2001), 31–97.

25. Gerard Caprio, Jr., and Maria Soledad Martinez-Peria, "Avoiding Disaster: Policies to Reduce the Risk of Banking Crises," World Bank mimeo and Egyptian Center for Economic Studies Working Paper 47 (2000); Rafael La Porta et al., "Government Ownership of Banks"; and James R. Barth et al., "Bank Regulation and Supervision: What Works Best?" *Journal of Financial Intermediation* 13, no. 2 (April 2004): 205–48.

26. World Bank, *Finance for Growth*, 123.

27. This figure is adjusted for purchasing power. World Bank, *World Development Indicators* (Washington, D.C.: World Bank, 2004). At current exchange rates, the income per person of China is less than one-twentieth that of the United States.

28. World Bank, *World Development Indicators*.

29. See Patrick Honohan, "Financial Development, Growth and Poverty."

30. Genevieve Boyreay-Debray and Shang-Jin Wei, "Pitfalls of a State-Dominated Financial System: The Case of China," CEPR Discussion Paper 4471 (July 2004), show that the state-dominated financial system in China has favored inefficient state firms, resulted in low capital mobility across regions, and moved capital away from more productive regions toward the less productive ones.

31. See Martin Weitzman, "Soviet Postwar Economic Growth and Capital Labor Substitution," *American Economic Review* 60, no. 4 (1970): 676–92.

32. See "The Taming of the Government" in Raghuram Rajan and Luigi Zingales, *Saving Capitalism from the Capitalists*, 129–56, for a description of this process in England.

33. For a feel for how actively aggressive the free press was even in the colonial period before the United States was founded, see Walter Isaacson, *Benjamin Franklin: An American Life* (New York: Simon and Schuster, 2003).

34. The principal-agent analysis also explains the result found in Rafael La Porta et al., "Government Ownership of Banks," that the negative effect of state ownership of banks on financial development and growth is found to be larger for poorer countries. In poorer countries where there is less transparency, it is easier for politicians to persuade state-owned banks to channel funds to themselves, their cronies, or to business interests that support them. In rich countries with a strong free press, this is far more difficult because the press is more likely to expose such practices.

35. Raghuram Rajan and Luigi Zingales, *Saving Capitalism from the Capitalists*.

36. The history of Latin America illustrates many examples of incumbents' encouragement of financial repression. For example, see Stephen Haber, ed., *How Latin America Fell Behind: Essays on the Economic Histories of Brazil and Mexico, 1800–1914* (Stanford, Calif.: Stanford University Press, 1997), and Stephen Haber, "Political Institutions and Financial Development: Evidence from the Economic Histories of Mexico and the United States," Stanford University mimeo (October 2005).

37. Raghuram Rajan and Luigi Zingales, *Saving Capitalism from the Capitalists*, provides a graphic example in which incumbent financial institutions in Japan were able to repress the financial system with government help. In 1933, the Japanese banks were able to get the approval of the Ministry of Finance to set up a Bond Committee that decided which firms could issue corporate bonds and on what terms. As a result, the Japanese banks were able to limit the issuance of corporate bonds. With the opening up of the global financial markets in the late 1970s, this system broke down and corporate bond issuance skyrocketed. The Rajan and Zingales view is backed up by a substantial body of research. The survey by Randall Morck et al., "Corporate Governance, Economic Entrenchment and Growth," *Journal of Economic Literature* 53 (2005): 655–720, summarizes this literature as follows:

> Many countries effectively entrust substantial parts of their corporate sectors to the large pyramidal groups of a few extremely wealthy families. This

can potentially magnify poor governance by a few family patriarchs into inefficient economywide capital allocation, reduced investment in innovation and retarded economic growth. Moreover, such elite families understandably value the status quo. They sometimes, but not always appear to influence public policies to curtail private property rights development, capital market development, economic openness, and other threats to the status quo. Much existing work points to this *economic entrenchment* as a significant issue in many countries.

38. These restrictive regulations were actually not fully eliminated until the 1990s.

39. Raghuram Rajan and Luigi Zingales, *Saving Capitalism from the Capitalists,* and World Bank, *Finance for Growth.*

40. Trade openness also weakens the effectiveness of capital controls because firms engaged in international trade can avoid them by over- and underinvoicing exports and imports. With less effective capital controls due to openness of trade, it is more likely they will be abandoned, thereby promoting financial globalization. See Joshua Aizenman, "On the Hidden Links between Financial and Trade Opening," NBER Working Paper 9906 (August 2003).

41. Raghuram Rajan and Luigi Zingales, "The Great Reversals: The Politics of Financial Development in the 20th Century," *Journal of Financial Economics* 69 (2003): 5–50, and H. Svalaeryd and J. Vlachos, "Market for Risk and Openness to Trade: How Are They Related?" *Journal of Public Economics* 57, no. 2 (2002): 364–95.

42. See Jose De Gregorio, "Financial Integration, Financial Development, and Economic Growth," University of Chile mimeo (July 1998); Jeannine Bailliu, "Private Capital Flows, Financial Development, and Economic Growth in Developing Countries," Bank of Canada Working Paper 2000-15 (July 2000); and Michael Klein and Giovanni Olivei, "Capital Account Liberalization, Financial Depth and Economic Growth," NBER Working Paper 7384 (October 1999), for evidence linking capital account liberalization to higher financial development.

43. For example, see Ross Levine, "Foreign Banks, Financial Development and Economic Growth," in Claude E. Barfield, ed., *International Financial Markets: Harmonization versus Competition* (Washington, D.C.: American Enterprise Institute Press, 1996), 224–55; Stijn Claessens et al., "The Role of Foreign Banks in Domestic Banking Systems," in Stijn Claessens and Marion Jansen, eds., *The Internationalization of Financial Services: Issues and Lessons for Developing Countries* (Boston: Kluwer Academic, 2000); Stijn Claessens et al., "How Does Foreign Bank Entry Affect Domestic Banking Markets," *Journal of Banking and Finance* 25, no. 5 (2001): 891–911; Adolfo Barajas et al., "The Impact of Liberalization and Foreign Investment in Colombia's Financial Sector," *Journal of Development Economics* 63, no. 1 (2000): 157–96; George Clarke et al., "The Effect of Foreign Entry on Argentina's Banking System," in Stijn Claessens and Marion Jansen, eds., *The Internationalization of Financial Services;* and Angelo Unite and Michael Sullivan, "The Effect of Foreign Entry and Ownership Structure on the Philippine Domestic Banking Market," *Journal of Banking and Finance* 27, no. 12 (2003): 2323–45.

44. See Linda Goldberg, "Financial Sector FDI and Host Countries: New and Old Lessons," Federal Reserve Bank of New York Staff Reports 183 (April 2004).

45. Frederic S. Mishkin, "Financial Policies and the Prevention of Financial Crises in Emerging Market Countries," in Martin Feldstein, ed., *Economic and Financial Crises in Emerging Market Countries* (Chicago: University of Chicago Press, 2003), 93–130.

46. Financial development also helps promote competition because it enables new firms to acquire firms so that they can compete with established ones. Increased competition is also a critical element in producing growth because it encourages efficiency and adoption of superior technology. Indeed, an important reason why developing countries like those in Latin America have done so poorly are their barriers to competition, among which is financial repression. For a discussion of how barriers to competition have stunted economic growth, see Harold L. Cole et al., "Latin America in the Rearview Mirror," NBER Working Paper 11008 (December 2004).

47. These figures are from Peter Blair Henry, "Capital Account Liberalization, the Cost of Capital and Economic Growth," *American Economic Review* 93, no. 2 (2003): 91–96. For additional evidence, see Ross Levine and Sara Zervos, "Capital Control Liberalization and Stock Market Development," *World Development* 26 (1998): 1169–84; Geert Bekaert and Campbell R. Harvey, "Foreign Speculators and Emerging Equity Markets," *Journal of Finance* 55 (2000): 562–613; Geert Bekaert et al., "Dating the Integration of World Equity Markets," NBER Working Paper 6724 (September 1998); Geert Bekaert et al., "Does Financial Liberalization Spur Growth?" NBER Working Paper 8245 (September 2001); Peter Blair Henry, "Equity Prices, Stock Market Liberalization, and Investment," *Journal of Financial Economics* 58, no. 1–2 (2000): 301–34; Peter Blair Henry, "Stock Market Liberalization, Economic Reform, and Emerging Market Equity Prices," *Journal of Finance* 55 (2000): 529–64; International Monetary Fund, *World Economic Outlook* (Washington, D.C.: International Monetary Fund, October 2001); and E. Han Kim and Vijay Singal, "Stock Market Opening: Experience of Emerging Market Economies," *Journal of Business* 73 (2000): 25–66. Michael Klein and Giovanni Olivei, "Capital Account Liberalization, Financial Depth and Economic Growth," and Jeannine Bailliu, "Private Capital Flows," however, find that these benefits are less clear for the poorest countries.

48. Peter Blair Henry, "Capital Account Liberalization, the Cost of Capital and Economic Growth."

49. See Michael Klein and Giovanni Olivei, "Capital Account Liberalization, Financial Depth, and Economic Growth"; Menzie D. Chinn, "The Compatibility of Capital Controls and Financial Development: A Selective Survey and Empirical Evidence," in Gordon DeBrouwer and Yunjong Wang, eds., *Financial Governance in East Asia: Policy Dialogue, Surveillance, and Cooperation* (London: Routledge Curzon, 2004), 216–38; Menzie D. Chinn and Hiro Ito, "Capital Account Liberalization, Institutions and Financial Development: Cross Country Evidence," NBER Working Paper 8967 (June 2002); and Barry Eichengreen, "Financial Instability," in Bjorn Lomborg, ed., *Global Crises, Global Solutions* (Cambridge: Cambridge University Press, 2004).

50. Michael Klein, "Capital Account Openness and the Varieties of the Growth Experience," NBER Working Paper 9500 (January 2003), finds that capital account lib-

eralization only has favorable effects when a country has an annual income per person in excess of $2000.

51. For example, see the surveys in Ross Levine, "Financial Development and Economic Growth: Views and Agenda," *Journal of Economic Literature* 35, no. 2 (1997): 688–72; Barry Eichengreen, "Capital Account Liberalization: What Do Cross-Country Studies Tell Us?" *World Bank Economic Review* 15, no. 3 (2001): 341–65; Stanley Fischer, "Globalization and Its Challenges," *American Economic Review* 93 (2003): 1–30; Hali J. Edison et al., "Capital Account Liberalization and Economic Performance: Survey and Synthesis," *IMF Staff Papers* 51, no. 2 (2004): 26–62; and Eswar Prasad et al., "Effects of Financial Globalization on Developing Countries: Some Empirical Evidence," International Monetary Fund mimeo (March 2003). Prasad et al. summarize this literature by stating (p. 31): "Table 3 summarizes the 14 most recent studies on this subject. Three out of the fourteen papers report a positive effect of financial integration on growth. However, the majority of the papers tend to find no effect or a mixed effect for developing countries. This suggests that, if financial integration has a positive effect on growth, it is probably not strong or robust." In a later paper (Eswar Prasad et al., "Financial Globalization Growth and Volatility in Developing Countries," NBER Working Paper 10942 [December 2004], p. 17), they have a more positive slant on financial globalization, stating that "we do find that financial globalization can be beneficial under the right circumstances. Empirically, good institutions and quality of governance are crucial in helping developing countries derive the benefits of globalization." Some of the most cited papers in this literature are Alberto Alesina et al., "The Political Economy of Capital Controls," in Leonardo Leiderman and Assaf Razin, eds., *Capital Mobility: The Impact on Consumption, Investment and Growth* (Cambridge: Cambridge University Press, 2004); Dennis P. Quinn, "The Correlates of Change in International Financial Regulation," *American Political Science Review* 91 (1997): 531–51; Aart Kraay, "In Search of the Macroeconomic Effects of Capital Account Liberalization" (Washington, D.C.: World Bank, Development Research Group, 1998); Dani Rodrik, "Who Needs Capital-Account Convertibility?" in Stanley Fischer et al., *Should the IMF Pursue Capital-Account Convertibility?* Essays in International Finance 207, Department of Economics, Princeton University (May 1998); Aaron Tornell et al., "The Positive Link between Financial Liberalization, Growth and Crises," NBER Working Paper 10293 (February 2004); C. Arteta et al., "When Does Capital Account Liberalization Help More Than It Hurts?" NBER Working Paper 8414 (August 2001); Sebastian Edwards, "Capital Mobility and Economic Performance: Are Emerging Economies Different?" NBER Working Paper 8076 (January 2001); and Hali J. Edison et al., "International Financial Integration and Economic Growth," *Journal of International Money and Finance* 21 (2002): 749–76. More recent evidence in Michael Klein, "Capital Account Liberalization, Institutional Quality and Economic Growth: Theory and Evidence," NBER Working Paper 11112 (February 2005), however, suggests that capital account liberalization in countries with better institutions does indeed lead to higher growth. Barry Eichengreen and David Leblang, "Capital Account Liberalization and Growth: Was Mr. Mahathir Right?" *International Journal of Finance and Economics* 8 (2003): 205–24, find that capital account liberalization is good

for growth when it is undertaken by countries that are not crisis prone but is bad for growth when they are.

52. Aaron Tornell et al., "The Positive Link Between Financial Liberalization, Growth and Crises," documents the empirical relationship between financial liberalization and the increased incidence of financial crises.

53. However, Graciela Kaminsky and Sergio Schmukler, "Short-Run Pain, Long-Run Gain: The Effects of Financial Liberalizations," World Bank Working Paper 2912 (October 2002), take the view that the short-run pain from financial crises resulting from financial globalization may still result in long-run gains in growth.

Chapter Four   When Globalization Goes Wrong: The Dynamics of Financial Crises

1. See Nora Lustig, "Crises and the Poor: Socially Responsible Macroeconomics," forthcoming in *Economia;* François Bourguignon et al., "Crisis and Income Distribution: A Micro-Macro Model for Indonesia," World Bank mimeo (June 2001); and Jed Freidman and James Levinsohn, "The Distributional Impacts of Indonesia's Crisis on Household Welfare: A 'Rapid Response' Methodology," *World Bank Economic Review* 16, no. 3 (2002): 397–423. Emanuele Baldacci et al., "Financial Crises, Poverty and Income Distribution," *Finance and Development* 39, no. 2 (June 2002): 24–27, find this result holds generally in the sixty-five financial crises they study. Marina Halac and Sergio L. Schmukler, "Distributional Effects of Crises," World Bank mimeo (June 2004), show that one mechanism that increases income inequality during financial crises occurs by redistributions through the financial sector.

2. See Emanuele Baldacci et al., "Financial Crises, Poverty and Income Distribution," and Francisco H. G. Ferreira et al., "Protecting the Poor from Macroeconomic Shocks: An Agenda for Action in a Crisis and Beyond," World Bank Policy Research Working Paper 2160 (August 1999).

3. Marina Halac and Sergio L. Schmukler, "Distributional Effects of Crises."

4. Michael D. Bordo and Barry Eichengreen, "Crises Now and Then: What Lessons from the Last Era of Globalization?" NBER Working Paper 8716 (January 2002), document that financial crises in emerging market economies have been increasing in recent years.

5. Although not as well known, Chile went through a similar crisis in 1982–83. GDP declined almost 14% in 1982 and 3% in 1983, with inflation increasing to above 20%. See Carlos Diaz-Alejandro, "Good-Bye Financial Repression, Hello Financial Crash," *Journal of Development Economics* 19, no. 1–2 (1985): 1–24.

6. See Graciela L. Kaminsky and Carmen M. Reinhart, "The Twin Crises: The Causes of Banking and Balance of Payments Problems," *American Economic Review* 89 (1999): 473–500. Similar findings are found in Reuven Glick and Michael Hutchison, "Banking and Currency Crises: How Common Are Twins?" in Reuven Glick et al., eds., *Financial Crises in Emerging Markets* (New York: Cambridge University Press, 1999); Asli Demirguc-Kunt and Enrica Detragiache, "Financial Liberalization and Financial Fragility," IMF Working Paper 98/83 (June 1998); and John Williamson and M. Mahar, *A Survey of Financial Liberalization,* Princeton Essays in International Finance 211 (Princeton, N.J.: Princeton University, November 1998).

7. See Frederic S. Mishkin, "Global Financial Instability: Framework, Events, Issues," *Journal of Economic Perspectives* 13, no. 4 (1999): 11, Table 2.

8. Frederic S. Mishkin, "Global Financial Instability," 11, Table 2.

9. As Milton Friedman and Anna J. Schwartz, *A Monetary History of the United States 1867–1960* (Princeton, N.J.: Princeton University Press, 1963), have emphasized, another negative effect on the economy can occur through the effect of a banking panic on the money supply. Because a banking panic also results in a movement from deposits to currency, the usual money multiplier analysis indicates that the money supply will fall. The resulting decline in the money supply then leads to higher interest rates, which increase adverse selection and moral hazard problems in financial markets and cause a further contraction in economic activity.

10. Paul Krugman, "What Happened to Asia?" M.I.T. mimeo (January 1998), and Michael Dooley, "A Model of Crises in Emerging Markets," *Economic Journal* 110 (2000): 256–72, emphasize that the government safety net was a key factor in producing lending booms and subsequent financial crises.

11. Asli Demirguc-Kunt and Enrica Detragiarche, "The Determinants of Banking Crises: Evidence from Developed and Developing Countries," *IMF Staff Papers* 45, no. 1 (1998): 81–109, find that greater competition from financial liberalization also lowers bank franchise value and hence bank net worth, which increases bank's incentives to take on excessive risk. This provides another reason why financial liberalization may promote a lending boom.

12. Ronald McKinnon and Huw Pill, "Exchange Rate Regimes for Emerging Markets: Moral Hazard and International Overborrowing," *Oxford Review of Economic Policy* 15, no. 3 (1999): 19–38.

13. See David Folkerts-Landau et al., "Effect of Capital Flows on the Domestic Financial Sectors in APEC Developing Countries," in Moshin S. Khan and Carmen M. Reinhart, eds., *Capital Flows in the APEC Region* (Washington, D.C.: International Monetary Fund, 1995), 31–57.

14. This phenomenon of being starved for resources has also occurred for other regulators in the United States. The SEC clearly did not have enough resources to adequately police the securities industry during the frothy years of the late 1990s, an important factor behind the explosion of conflicts of interest scandals in recent years (e.g., see Andrew Crockett et al., *Conflicts of Interest in the Financial Services Industry: What Should We Do about Them?* Geneva Reports on the World Economy 4 [Geneva and London: International Center for Monetary and Banking Studies and Centre for Economic Policy Research, 2003]). One of the reasons that the SEC was short of funds to carry out its business was that the financial services industry did not support an increase, which would have subjected them to more scrutiny.

15. Edward J. Kane, "Zombies on the Loose: The S&L Insurance Mess," *Financier: The Journal for Private Sector Policy* 15 (July 1991): 9–19.

16. Quoted in Tom Morganthau et al., "The S&L Scandal's Biggest Blowout," *Newsweek*, November 6, 1989, p. 35.

17. Morganthau et al., "The S&L Scandal's Biggest Blowout."

18. For a more extensive discussion of the savings and loan crisis in the United States, see Edward J. Kane, *The S&L Insurance Mess: How Did It Happen?* (Washington, D.C.:

Urban Institute Press, 1989), and Frederic S. Mishkin, *The Economics of Money, Banking and Financial Markets,* 8th edition (Boston: Addison-Wesley, 2007).

19. For the costs of bailing out banks after crises, see Daniela Klingebiel and Luc Laewen, *Managing the Real and Fiscal Effects of Banking Crises,* World Bank Discussion Paper 428 (2002).

20. Edward J. Kane, *The S&L Insurance Mess.*

21. Although Brazil underwent a fiscal and currency crisis in 1999, it did not undergo a financial crisis because its banking system was hedged against foreign exchange rate risk, in contrast to the other countries discussed here.

22. The analysis here is the same as that used by Joseph E. Stiglitz and Andrew Weiss to explain credit rationing, in which some borrowers are denied loans even when they are willing to pay a higher interest rate. Joseph E. Stiglitz and Andrew Weiss, "Credit Rationing in Markets with Imperfect Information," *American Economic Review* 71 (1981): 393–410. The Stiglitz-Weiss model was first applied to explain how interest rate increases can lead to a financial collapse in N. Gregory Mankiw, "The Allocation of Credit and Financial Collapse," *Quarterly Journal of Economics* 101 (1986): 455–70.

23. Note that this effect of higher interest rates is due to a contraction of the supply of loans, and that it operates over and above the usual demand story of why higher interest rates lead to an economic contraction. In that story, the demand for investment and borrowing falls when interest rates rise because the cost of financing investment projects has risen.

24. For empirical evidence that cash flows affect investment, see Steven M. Fazzari et al., "Financial Constraints and Corporate Investment: New Evidence on Financing Constraints," *Brookings Papers on Economic Activity* 1 (1988): 141–95; Mark Gertler and Simon Gilchrist, "Monetary Policy, Business Cycles, and the Behavior of Small Manufacturing Firms," *Quarterly Journal of Economics* 109 (1994): 309–40; and the surveys in R. Glenn Hubbard, "Is There a 'Credit Channel' for Monetary Policy?" *Federal Reserve Bank of St. Louis Review* 77 (1995): 63–74, and Ben S. Bernanke and Mark Gertler, "Inside the Black Box: The Credit Channel of Monetary Transmission," *Journal of Economic Perspectives* 9, no. 4 (1995): 27–48.

25. For a theoretical treatment and empirical evidence on net worth effects on investment and output fluctuations, see Ben S. Bernanke and Mark Gertler, "Agency Costs, Net Worth and Business Fluctuations," *American Economic Review* 79 (1989): 14–31; Charles W. Calomiris and R. Glenn Hubbard, "Price Flexibility, Credit Availability and Economic Fluctuations: Evidence from the United States, 1894–1909," *Quarterly Journal of Economics* 104 (1989): 429–52; Charles W. Calomiris and R. Glenn Hubbard, "Firm Heterogeneity, Internal Finance, and 'Credit Rationing,' " *Economic Journal* 100 (1990): 90–104; and the surveys mentioned in the previous note.

26. One factor that leads to financial instability in industrialized economies but not in emerging market economies (and so is not discussed in the text) is the debt-deflation phenomenon described in Irving Fisher, "The Debt-Deflation Theory of Great Depressions," *Econometrica* 1 (1933): 337–57. In economies in which inflation has been moderate (as in most industrialized countries), many debt contracts are typically of fairly long duration. In this institutional environment, an unanticipated decline in the price

level leads to a decrease in the net worth of firms. When the price level falls, it lowers the value of the assets, but since debt payments are contractually fixed in nominal terms, the unanticipated decline in the price level lowers firms' net worth. (Alternatively, you could think of the result of the price level falling as raising the value of firms' liabilities in *real* terms—the decrease in the price level increases the real burden of the debt, but does not raise the real value of the assets. The result is that net worth in real terms—the difference between assets and liabilities in real terms—declines.) An unanticipated deflation therefore causes a substantial decline in real net worth and an increase in adverse selection and moral hazard problems facing lenders. The resulting increase in adverse selection and moral hazard problems (of the same type that were discussed in assessing the effect of declines in net worth earlier) will also work to cause a decline in investment and economic activity. The debt-deflation phenomenon is what the United States experienced during the Great Depression, and it is what Japan has been experiencing recently, though to a lesser extent.

27. Craig Burnside et al., "On the Fiscal Implications of Twin Crises," NBER Working Paper 8277 (May 2001), point out that banking crises can also create fiscal imbalances because the government bailout of the banking system requires the government to run future budget deficits. This provides an additional channel for the deterioration of bank balance sheets that can lead to speculative downward pressure on the domestic currency and thus lead to a currency crisis.

28. Barry Eichengreen and Ricardo Hausmann, "Exchange Rates and Financial Fragility," in *New Challenges for Monetary Policy* (Kansas City, Mo.: Federal Reserve Bank of Kansas City, 1999), 329–68, and Barry Eichengreen et al., "The Mystery of Original Sin," in Barry Eichengreen and Ricardo Hausmann, eds., *Other People's Money: Debt Denomination and Financial Instability in Emerging-Market Economies* (Chicago: University of Chicago Press, forthcoming), argue that an additional reason countries are unable to issue debt denominated in domestic currency is the lack of liquidity for markets in this type of debt. They call this phenomenon *original sin*. This view is, however, highly controversial. See Morris Goldstein and Philip Turner, *Controlling Currency Mismatches in Emerging Markets* (Washington, D.C.: Institute for International Economics, 2004).

29. The percentage of liabilities that are dollarized is close to 40% in both Latin America and low and middle income countries. See Inter-American Development Bank, *Unlocking Credit: The Quest for Deep and Stable Bank Lending. 2005 Report, Economic and Social Progress in Latin America* (Washington, D.C.: Inter-American Development Bank and Johns Hopkins University Press, 2004), 50, Figure 4.1. Figure 4.7 on page 53 shows that firms in nontradable sectors are highly leveraged in foreign currency debt in countries with high levels of dollarization.

30. The much larger, more rapid, and more unanticipated decline in the exchange rate when a country has a pegged exchange rate and suffers a currency crisis provides a powerful argument against fixed exchange rate regimes. See Frederic S. Mishkin, "The Dangers of Exchange Rate Pegging in Emerging-Market Countries," *International Finance* 1 (1998): 81–101.

31. See Eduardo Levy-Yeyati, "Financial Dollarization: Where Do We Stand?"

paper presented at the IDB/World Bank Conference, Financial Dedollarization: Policy Options, December 1–2, 2003, Washington, D.C., and Christian Broda and Eduardo Levy-Yeyati, "Endogenous Deposit Dollarization," Federal Reserve Bank of New York Staff Reports 160 (February 2003).

32. A. Suryahadi et al., "The Evolution of Poverty in Indonesia, 1996–99," World Bank mimeo (September 2000), find that the poverty rate climbed from 7–8% just before the crisis to 18–20% in September 1998.

33. See Guillermo A. Calvo et al., "Sudden Stops, the Real Exchange Rate, and Fiscal Sustainability: Argentina's Lessons," NBER Working Paper 9828 (July 2003), which documents that countries are more vulnerable to sudden stops if they have (1) a low degree of openness, (2) a high degree of liability dollarization, or (3) high debt levels. Using the methodology in Jeffrey Frankel and David Romer, "Does Trade Cause Growth," *American Economic Review* 89 (1999): 379–99, Jeffrey Frankel, "Contractionary Currency Crashes in Developing Countries," NBER Working Paper 11508 (July 2005), also finds evidence that vulnerability to sudden stops is higher when trade openness is low.

34. See Graciela L. Kaminsky and Carmen M. Reinhart, "The Twin Crises." Crises, in many cases, come in triplets, because the currency and financial crises are often accompanied by a sovereign-debt crisis in which the government defaults on its debt or has to go through a painful restructuring.

35. The share of liabilities denominated in dollars in Argentina in 2001 was over 70%. See Inter-American Development Bank, *Unlocking Credit*, 50, Figure 4.1.

36. An important point is that even if banks have a matched portfolio of foreign-currency denominated assets and liabilities and so appear to avoid foreign-exchange market risk, a devaluation can cause substantial harm to bank balance sheets. The reason is that when a devaluation occurs, the offsetting foreign-currency denominated assets are unlikely to be paid off in full because of the worsening business conditions and the negative effect that these increases in the domestic-currency value of these foreign-currency denominated loans have on the balance sheet of the borrowing firms. In other words, when there is a devaluation, the mismatch between foreign-currency denominated assets and liabilities on borrowers balance sheets can lead to defaults on their loans, thereby converting a market risk for borrowers to a credit risk for the banks that have made the foreign-currency denominated loans.

37. The term "sudden stop" first appeared in the academic literature in Rudiger Dornbusch et al., "Currency Crises and Collapses," *Brookings Papers on Economic Activity* 2 (1995): 219–93. For a discussion of the sudden stop phenomenon in which capital inflows abruptly switch to capital outflows, see Guillermo A. Calvo and Carmen M. Reinhart, "When Capital Inflows Come to a Sudden Stop: Consequences and Policy Options," in Peter Kenen and Alexander Swoboda, eds., *Reforming the International Monetary and Financial System* (Washington, D.C.: International Monetary Fund, 2000), 175–201.

38. One of the earliest papers to test for contagion is Barry Eichengreen et al., "Contagious Currency Crises: First Tests," *Scandanavian Journal of Economics* 98 (1996): 463–84. For surveys that discuss the extensive theoretical and empirical literature on

contagion, see Graciela L. Kaminsky et al., "The Unholy Trinity of Financial Contagion," NBER Working Paper 10061 (October 2003), and Stijn Claessens et al., "Contagion, Why Crises Spread and How This Can Be Stopped," in Stijn Claessens and Kristin J. Forbes, eds., *International Financial Contagion* (Boston: Kluwer Academic, 2001), 9–41.

39. For a description of the spillover of the Argentine financial crisis to Uruguay, see Gerardo Licandro and Jose Antonio Licandro, "Building the Dollarization Agenda: Lessons from the Uruguayan Case," Central Bank of Uruguay mimeo (September 2003).

40. All four major credit rating agencies—Standard and Poor's, Moody's, Duff & Phelps, and Fitch—had given Uruguayan government bonds an investment grade in the first half of 1997.

41. Uruguay's share of liabilities denominated in dollars was even greater than in Argentina, exceeding 80%, as reported in Inter-American Development Bank, *Unlocking Credit*, 50, Figure 4.1.

42. See Frederic S. Mishkin, "Asymmetric Information and Financial Crises: A Historical Perspective," in R. Glenn Hubbard, ed., *Financial Markets and Financial Crises* (Chicago: University of Chicago Press, 1991), 69–108.

43. The Finnish twin crises of the early 1990s is an exception. However, Finland, like many emerging market countries, did have substantial amounts of foreign-denominated debt.

44. Frederic S. Mishkin, "The Causes and Propagation of Financial Instability: Lessons for Policymakers," in Federal Reserve Bank of Kansas City, *Maintaining Financial Stability in a Global Economy* (Kansas City, Mo.: Federal Reserve Bank of Kansas City, 1997), 55–96.

Chapter Five   Mexico, 1994–1995

1. Michelle Camdessus, "Drawing Lessons from the Mexican Crisis: Preventing and Resolving Financial Crises—The Role of the IMF," address given at the 25th Washington Conference of the Council of the Americas on "Staying the Course: Forging a Free Trade Area in the Americas," Washington D.C., May 22, 1995.

2. See Carlos Diaz-Alejandro, "Good-Bye Financial Repression, Hello Financial Crash," *Journal of Development Economics* 19, no. 1–2 (1985): 1–24, which describes the Chilean crisis and was a precursor to the analysis described in this and the previous chapter.

3. In one sense, the fiscal situation was not solid because the government had an implicit liability: it had a commitment to bail out private banks and state-owned development banks if they went broke. This meant that government debt would balloon if a banking crisis occurred, which is indeed what transpired. The analysis here does not view this as a problem of macroeconomic fundamentals, as conventionally defined, because the source of the problem was the weak banking system, which the chapter emphasizes as a key element driving the crisis.

4. See Stephen Haber, "Mexico's Experiment with Bank Privatization and Liberalization, 1991–2002," *Journal of Banking and Finance* 29 (2005): 2325–53.

5. For example, during the rule of the Mexican dictator Porfirio Diaz from 1876 to 1911, Mexico's major financiers were allowed to write the rules for the banking system.

As a result, severe barriers to competition were created, and bankers were provided with monopolies that enabled them to earn high rates of return. The quid pro quo for the Porfirian government was that it received large amounts of credit from the largest bank in the system, Banamex. See Stephen Haber et al., *The Politics of Property Rights: Political Instability, Credible Commitments, and Economic Growth in Mexico, 1876–1929* (Cambridge: Cambridge University Press, 2003). Also see Stephen Haber, "Banking without Deposit Insurance: Mexico's Banking Experiments, 1884–2004," Stanford University mimeo (August 2005), for a discussion of the relationship between the Mexican government and the banking system over a longer historical time span.

6. See Stephen Haber, "Mexico's Experiment with Bank Privatization and Liberalization."

7. See Frederic S. Mishkin, *The Economics of Money, Banking and Financial Markets*, 8th edition (Boston: Addison-Wesley, 2007), 244, Table 2.

8. The first restrictions on foreign banks were put in place in 1884 by the Mexican government under Porfirio Diaz, which required that foreign-owned banks had to be incorporated in Mexico. In 1964, as part of a general push toward "Mexicanization," retail banks had to have majority ownership from Mexicans. It is only in recent years that Mexico has opened its banking system to foreigners.

9. See Unal Haluk and Miguel Navarro, "The Technical Process of Bank Privatization in Mexico," *Journal of Financial Services Research* 16 (1999): 61–83.

10. The lack of market discipline is reflected in the fact that various measures of a bank's risk had no impact on its deposit growth from 1991 to 1995; Maria Soledad Martinez Peria and Sergio L. Schmukler, "Do Depositors Punish Banks for Bad Behavior? Market Discipline, Deposit Insurance and Banking Crisis," *Journal of Finance* 56 (2001): 1029–51.

11. Rafael La Porta et al., "Related Lending," *Quarterly Journal of Economics* 118 (2003): 231–68.

12. See the discussion in Stephen Haber, "Mexico's Experiment with Bank Privatization and Liberalization." Mexico did not even have a law allowing credit bureaus until 1993. Mexican banks did not have credit departments because they made very few loans to private enterprises in the 1980s, when they were under government control. I thank Steve Haber for these insights.

13. Stephen Haber, "Mexico's Experiment with Bank Privatization and Liberalization."

14. In the nineteenth and early twentieth centuries, the shoe was on the other foot when the United States was not the superpower it is today. Increases in interest rates in Great Britain, the financial superpower of its time, were the source of sharp rises in U.S. interest rates that often were a factor in the many financial crises that we experienced in that era. See Frederic S. Mishkin, "Asymmetric Information and Financial Crises: A Historical Perspective," in R. Glenn Hubbard, ed., *Financial Markets and Financial Crises* (Chicago: University of Chicago Press, 1991), 69–108.

15. Rudiger Dornbusch and Andrew Warner, "Mexico: Stabilization, Reform and No Growth," *Brookings Papers on Economic Activity* 1 (1994): 253–315, estimated that the Mexican peso was overvalued by 20%; this was also the view inside the Federal

Reserve (J. Bradford DeLong and Barry Eichengreen, "Between Meltdown and Moral Hazard: The International Monetary and Fiscal Policies of the Clinton Administration," NBER Working Paper 8443 (August 2001). The overvalued exchange rate also had political advantages for the ruling PRI party in Mexico because it made imported goods cheaper, helping the PRI to win the 1994 presidential election.

16. See Burnside, Eichenbaum, and Rebelo, "Prospective Deficits and the Asian Currency Crisis," *Journal of Political Economy* 109 (December 2001), 1155–97, for a model of how this would occur.

17. The data come from Frederic S. Mishkin, "Understanding Financial Crises: A Developing Country Perspective," in Michael Bruno and Boris Pleskovic, eds., *Annual World Bank Conference on Development Economics, 1996* (Washington, D.C.: World Bank, 1997), 29–62.

18. Anne O. Krueger and Aaron Tornell, "The Role of Bank Restructuring in Recovering from Crises: Mexico 1995–98," NBER Working Paper 7042 (March 1999).

19. Peter M. Garber and Subir Lall, "Derivative Products in Exchange Rate Crises," in Federal Reserve Bank of San Francisco, *Proceedings* (San Francisco: Federal Reserve Bank of San Francisco, 1996), 206–31, suggest that Mexican financial institutions in effect did not even have a matched book because of their use of undisclosed off-balance sheet and offshore derivatives contracts. These contracts left the banks exposed more directly to currency mismatch and may have played an important role in the crisis.

20. The rates for "pobreza alimentaria" are from Secretaría de Desarrollo Social con base en las Encuestas Nacionales de Ingresos y Gastos de los Hogares (1992, 1994, 1996, 1998, 2000, 2002), INEGI.

21. From 1994 to 1996, the crime rate in Mexico City rose by 53% (Mexico City Judicial Police website: http://www.pgjdf.gob.mx/estadisticas/index.asp).

22. See J. Bradford DeLong and Barry Eichengreen, "Between Meltdown and Moral Hazard."

23. Details of the package are: $20 billion from the ESF; $17.8 billion from the IMF, the largest loan amount ever given by the organization up to that time; $10 billion in loans from the Bank of International Settlements (BIS); $3 billion from U.S. commercial banks; and $2 billion from Canada and Latin American countries. Ngaire Woods, "International Financial Institutions and the Mexican Crisis," in Carol Wise, ed., *The Post-NAFTA Political Economy* (University Park: Pennsylvania State University Press, 1998).

24. For a discussion of the role of the export sector in Mexico's recovery, see Daniel Lederman et al., "Mexico: Five Years after the Crisis," in Boris Pleskovic and Nicholas Stern, eds., *Annual Bank Conference on Development Economics, 2000* (Washington, D.C.: World Bank, 2001), 263–83.

25. See Inter-American Development Bank, *Unlocking Credit: The Quest for Deep and Stable Bank Lending,* 2005 Report, Economic and Social Progress in Latin America (Washington, D.C.: Inter-American Development Bank and Johns Hopkins University Press, 2005), 76–77.

26. See Gerard Caprio, Jr., et al., *Banking Crises Data Base* (October 2003) at http://www1.worldbank.org/finance/html/database_sfd.html.

27. See Stephen Haber and Aldo Musacchio, "Foreign Banks and the Mexican Economy, 1997–2004," Stanford University mimeo (August 2005).

28. See Stephen Haber, "Mexico's Experiment with Bank Privatization and Liberalization."

29. See Aaron Tornell et al., "Nafta and Mexico's Less-than-Stellar Performance," NBER Working Paper 10289 (February 2004).

30. See Stephen Haber, "Mexico's Experiment with Bank Privatization and Liberalization," Table 15.

31. The 15% includes total bank lending, including loans to the government. The amount of bank lending to the private sector as a fraction of GDP is around 11%. See Stephen Haber, "Mexico's Experiment with Bank Privatization and Liberalization," Table 9.

Chapter Six   South Korea, 1997–1998

1. This number is adjusted for purchasing power parity (i.e., it is on a purchasing power parity basis) from Alan Heston et al., Penn World Table Version 6.1 (Philadelphia: Center for International Comparisons, University of Pennsylvania [CICUP], October 2002).

2. For example, see Alice Amsden, *Asia's Next Giant: South Korea and Late Industrialization* (Oxford: Oxford University Press, 1989); Yoon-Je Cho, "Finance and Development: The Korean Approach," *Oxford Review of Economic Policy* 5, no. 4 (1989): 88–102; Yoon-Je Cho and Joon-Hyung Kim, *Credit Policies and the Industrialization of Korea* (Seoul: Korea Development Institute Press, 1997); Dwight H. Perkins, "Structural Transformation and the Role of the State: Korea 1945–95," in D. S. Cha et al., *The Korean Economy 1945–1995: Performance and Vision for the 21st Century* (Seoul: Korea Development Institute Press, 1997), 57–101; and Wonhyuk Lim, *The Origin and Evolution of the Korean Economic System* (Seoul: Korea Development Institute Press, 2000).

3. See Marcus Noland, "South Korea's Experience with International Capital Flows," Institute for International Economics Working Paper Wp 05-4 (June 2005), and Joseph E. Stiglitz, *Globalization and Its Discontents* (New York: W. W. Norton, 2002).

4. Makoto Abe and Mamoko Kawakami, "A Distributive Comparison of Enterprise Size in Korea and Taiwan," *Developing Economies* 35, no. 4 (1997): 382–400. The same top five chaebols produced value added of 8.4% of GDP.

5. Joon-Ho Hahm and Frederic S. Mishkin, "The Korean Financial Crisis: An Asymmetric Information Perspective," *Emerging Markets Review* 1, no. 1 (2000): 21–52. The source for the data on manufacturing sector I in the United States is http://www.bizstats.com/corpdecurrent.htm, originally collected from corporate federal income tax returns.

6. This tendency was even stronger for the bigger and older commercial banks, such as Korea First, Seoul, Hanil, and Commercial Bank of Korea. Naturally they were the worst hit by the 1997 crisis and had to be taken over by the government.

7. See Marcus Noland, "South Korea's Experience with International Capital Flows."

8. Stephen Haggard, *The Political Economy of the Asian Financial Crisis* (Washington, D.C.: Institute for International Economics, 2000).

9. Joon-Ho Hahm, "The Government, the Chaebol and Financial Institutions before the Economic Crisis," in Stephan Haggard et al., eds., *Economic Crisis and Corporate Restructuring in Korea* (Cambridge: Cambridge University Press, 2003), 79–101.

10. Figure 7 in Joon-Ho Hahm and Frederic S. Mishkin, "The Korean Financial Crisis: An Asymmetric Information Perspective."

11. Table 2 in Joon-Ho Hahm and Frederic S. Mishkin, "The Korean Financial Crisis: An Asymmetric Information Perspective."

12. Table 6 in Joon-Ho Hahm and Frederic S. Mishkin, "The Korean Financial Crisis: An Asymmetric Information Perspective."

13. To be more precise, the 20% export price decline described here is relative to import prices and is known as a terms of trade shock. This decline was the largest drop in the terms of trade since the first oil shock of 1974–75.

14. Joon-Ho Hahm and Frederic S. Mishkin, "The Korean Financial Crisis: An Asymmetric Information Perspective."

15. Sammi, the 25th largest, on March 19; Jinro, the 19th largest, on April 21 and July 15; KIA, the 8th largest, on July 15; Haitai, the 24th largest, on November 1; and New Core, the 28th largest, on November 4.

16. The Ministry of Finance recommended several years earlier that the Bank of Korea deposit foreign exchange reserves in Korean banks' overseas branches, but it was right before the crisis that these deposits sharply increased. At the end of 1996, these deposits totaled $3.8 billion, while at the end of 1997 they had risen to $11.3 billion.

17. For example, on August 26, 1997, the government announced that the Bank of Korea would provide emergency liquidity (a total of 4 trillion won) to Korea First Bank and merchant banks through repurchase transactions. A similar injection of liquidity by the central bank to troubled banks to prop them up without measures to fix the problem also occurred in Ecuador just before its financial crisis.

18. Derived from line 78bgd in International Monetary Fund, *International Financial Statistics* (Washington, D.C.: International Monetary Fund, 2004).

19. Shaohua Chen and Martin Ravallion, "How Did the World's Poorest Fare in the 1990s?" *Review of Income and Wealth* 47, no. 3 (2001): 283–300.

20. Joung-Woo Lee, "Social Impact of the Crisis," in Duck-Koo Chung and Barry Eichengreen, eds., *The Korean Economy Beyond the Crisis* (Cheltenham: Edward Elgar, 2004), 137–59.

21. The deal with Korea's major bank creditors was made on December 24, 1997, and it was broadened at the end of January to reschedule the short-term debt. See Jack Boorman et al., "Managing Financial Crises: The Experience in East Asia," *Carnegie-Rochester Conference Series on Public Policy* 53 (2000): 1–67, and Paul Bluestein, *The Chastening* (New York: Public Affairs, 2001) for more details on the eleventh-hour deal.

22. For a discussion of the political economy of the South Korean reform, see Joon-Ho Hahm and Wonhyuk Lim, "Turning a Crisis into Opportunity: The Political Economy of Korea's Financial Sector Reform," Yonsei University mimeo (August 2003).

23. Joon-Ho Hahm and Wonhyuk Lim, "Turning a Crisis into Opportunity."

24. Using the average won/dollar exchange rate for the period 1998–2001.

25. Joon-Ho Hahm and Wonhyuk Lim, "Turning a Crisis into Opportunity," and Table 4, which summarizes the financial restructuring.

26. Table 8.2 in Joon-Ho Hahm, "Financial Restructuring," in Duck-Koo Chung and Barry Eichengreen, *The Korean Economy Beyond the Crisis*, 172–93.

27. Table 6 in Joon-Ho Hahm and Wonhyuk Lim, "Turning a Crisis into Opportunity."

28. For a discussion of the slow restructuring and recapitalization of the banking sector in the United States, see Chapter 11 in Frederic S. Mishkin, *The Economics of Money, Banking and Financial Markets*, 8th edition (Boston: Addison-Wesley, 2007), 279–307.

29. For more discussion of these corporate reforms, see Junggun Oh et al., "Financial Crisis Management in Korea: Its Processes and Consequences," in Tran Van Hoa, ed., *Economic Crisis Management: Theory, Practice, Outcomes and Prospects* (Cheltenham: Edward Elgar, 2001), 112–46.

30. Footnote 25 in Joon-Ho Hahm, "Financial Restructuring," 193.

31. This assessment of the South Korean financial system is from International Monetary Fund, "Republic of Korea Financial System Stability Assessment," February 14, 2003, found on the IMF website at http://www.imf.org/external/pubs/ft/scr/2003/cr0381.pdf.

32. Ha-Sung Chang, "Korea Discount and Corporate Governance," *Corporate Governance Studies* 1 (2002): 56–71.

Chapter Seven   Argentina, 2001–2002

1. For other descriptions of how the Argentine crisis played out, see Michael Mussa, *Argentina and the Fund: From Triumph to Tragedy* (Washington, D.C.: Institute for International Economics, 2002); Jiri Jonas, "Argentina's Crisis and Its Implications for the Exchange Rate Regime Debate," IMF mimeo (June 2002); Augusto De la Torre et al., "Living and Dying with Hard Pegs: The Rise and Fall of Argentina's Currency Board," *Economia* 3, no. 1 (2003): 43–107; and Kathryn M. E. Dominguez and Linda L. Tesar, "International Borrowing and Macroeconomic Performance in Argentina," NBER Working Paper 11353 (May 2005).

2. The Convertibility Law did not put in place a pure currency board, which requires a 100% backing of the domestic currency by foreign currency. It allowed up to one-third of the foreign exchange reserves to be internationally traded, with Argentine sovereign bonds denominated in U.S. dollars. This practice allowed some flexibility for liquidity creation by the central bank, which could provide it by buying these bonds with pesos. The monetary policy regime in Argentina might thus be more appropriately referred to as a "quasi-currency board." See Steve H. Hanke, "On Dollarization and Currency Boards: Error and Deception," *Policy Reform* 5, no. 4 (2002): 203–22.

3. Ministerio de Economía y Producción, Argentina Economic Indicators, April 2004.

4. Ministerio de Economía y Producción, Argentina Economic Indicators, April 2004.

5. See Banco Central de la Republica Argentina, "Main Features of the Regulatory Framework of the Argentine Financial System," mimeo (April 1997), and Charles W. Calomiris and Andrew Powell, "Can Emerging Market Bank Regulators Establish Credible Discipline? The Case of Argentina, 1992–99," in Frederic S. Mishkin, ed.,

Prudential Supervision: What Works and What Doesn't (Chicago: University of Chicago Press, 2001), 147–97, for a description of the Argentine BASIC system.

6. Especially Article 35bis. See Augusto De la Torre, "Resolving Bank Failures in Argentina," World Bank Policy Research Working Paper 2295 (March 2000).

7. See Table 1 in Augusto De la Torre et al., "Living and Dying with Hard Pegs," 50.

8. See Table 1 in Augusto De la Torre et al., "Living and Dying with Hard Pegs," 50.

9. See World Bank, "Argentina: Financial Sector Review," Report 17864-AR (Washington, D.C.: World Bank, 1998), 39–61.

10. World Bank, "Argentina: Insolvency and Creditor Rights Systems," Report on the Observance of Standards and Codes (ROSC) (Washington, D.C.: World Bank, June 2002).

11. Figure 1 in Augusto De la Torre et al., "Living and Dying with Hard Pegs," 49.

12. Figure 3 in Augusto De la Torre et al., "Living and Dying with Hard Pegs," 54.

13. See Carmen M. Reinhart and Kenneth Rogoff, "Debt Intolerance," NBER Working Paper 9908 (August 2003).

14. Michael Mussa, *Argentina and the Fund.*

15. Fabio M. Bertranou et al., "From Reform to Crisis: Argentina's Pension System," *International Social Security Review* 56, no. 2 (2003): 103–14.

16. Miguel Kiguel, "Structural Reforms in Argentina: Success or Failure?" manuscript prepared for the Croatian National Bank Conference on Current Issues in Emerging Market Economies, Dubrovnik, June 28–30, 2001, documents that increased spending by the provinces was a major source of Argentina's deficit problems in the late 1990s. Also see Mariano Tommasi et al., "Fiscal Federalism in Argentina: Policies, Politics, and Institutional Reform," *Economia* 1, no. 2 (2001): 147–201.

17. See Guillermo A. Calvo and Frederic S. Mishkin, "The Mirage of Exchange Rate Regimes for Emerging Market Countries," *Journal of Economic Perspectives* 17, no. 4 (2003): 99–118.

18. The exchange rate index used to calculate the appreciation of the U.S. dollar is a broad trade-weighted index, TWEXB, which is published by the Board of Governors of the Federal Reserve.

19. The Argentine real exchange rate began appreciating even earlier in mid-1995, because the higher inflation rate in Argentina meant that its goods in dollar terms were rising in value.

20. Christian Broda and Cedric Tille, "Coping with Terms-of-Trade Shocks in Developing Countries," *Federal Reserve Bank of New York Current Issues in Economics and Finance* 9, no. 1 (2003): 1–7, estimate that Argentina's terms of trade declined by 6% in 1998 and 1999, and that this created a drag on economic growth averaging 1.4% per year between 1999 and 2001.

21. Relative to the U.S. dollar.

22. See Guillermo Perry and Luis Serven, "The Anatomy and Physiology of a Multiple Crisis: Why Was Argentina Special and What Can We Learn from It?" World Bank, Washington, D.C., mimeo (2002).

23. Blejer made this remark in a speech at the World Bank on October 22, 2003, titled "Argentina: Managing the Crisis." For the context of this remark, see Mario Blejer, "Managing Argentina's 2002 Financial Crisis," in Timothy Besley and Roberto Zahga, eds., *Development Challenges in the 1990s: Leading Policymakers Speak from Experience* (Washington, D.C.: World Bank and Oxford University Press, 2005), 167–77.

24. Augusto De la Torre et al., "Living and Dying with Hard Pegs," Table 9.

25. Eduardo Levy-Yeyati et al., "Market Discipline under Systemic Risk: Evidence from Bank Runs in Emerging Economies," World Bank mimeo (April 15, 2004), describe how systemic factors, such as heightened concerns about the viability of the currency board and the possibility of government debt default, helped promote the banking crisis.

26. Ignacio Franceschelli, "Poverty and Employability Effects of Workfare Programs in Argentina," Poverty Monitoring, Measurement and Assessment Network Paper, presented at the 4th PEP Research Network general meeting, Colombo, Sri Lanka, June 13–17, 2005.

27. Indeed, this occurred in the United States in 1933, when the U.S. government devalued the dollar by abandoning the dollar's peg to the price of gold at $35 per ounce and declared that gold could no longer be used in financial contracts. This meant that so-called gold clauses in the majority of bond contracts, which specified that the creditor could demand payment in gold, were no longer valid. The dispute over this abrogation of contracts went all the way to the Supreme Court, where it was upheld. To do otherwise would have exposed numerous firms to bankruptcy, because contracts paid in a fixed amount of gold would have required almost 60% more dollars at the new rate of $20 per ounce. This debt repudiation did not have serious negative consequences because, in contrast to Argentina's, all creditors were treated equally. In addition, the United States did not have a history of debt repudiation, which was not the case for Argentina, whose government had confiscated assets many times in the past. For a discussion of the episode, see Randall Kroszner, "Is It Better to Forgive Than Receive: An Empirical Analysis of the Impact of Debt Repudiation," University of Chicago mimeo (December 2003).

28. Argentina eventually arranged a debt swap with over a 75% acceptance rate on March 18, 2005, in which Argentina's $103 billion government debt was converted into bonds with a value of around 30% of the original face value. Note that by 2005, the amount of government debt had grown because of unpaid interest payments.

29. See Inter-American Development Bank, *Unlocking Credit: The Quest for Deep and Stable Bank Lending, 2005 Report, Economic and Social Progress in Latin America* (Washington, D.C.: Inter-American Development Bank and Johns Hopkins University Press, 2004), 78–82.

Chapter Eight   Ending Financial Repression: The Role of Globalization

1. See Tullio Japelli and Marco Pagano, "Information Sharing in Credit Markets: Theory and Evidence," in Marco Pagano, ed., *Defusing Default: Incentives and Institutions* (Washington, D.C.: Inter-American Development Bank, 2001); Tullio Japelli and

Marco Pagano, "Public Credit Information: A European Perspective," in Margaret J. Miller, ed., *Credit Reporting Systems and the International Economy* (Cambridge, Mass.: MIT Press, 2003); Chapter 13 in Inter-American Development Bank, *Unlocking Credit: The Quest for Deep and Stable Bank Lending, 2005 Report, Economic and Social Progress in Latin America* (Washington, D.C.: Inter-American Development Bank and Johns Hopkins University Press, 2004), 175–85; and World Bank, *Finance for Growth: Policy Choices in a Volatile World* (Oxford: World Bank and Oxford University Press, 2001), 65–71, for discussions of the benefits of credit registries. The empirical evidence finds that countries with credit registries have on average nearly 9% more financial development than countries that don't.

2. As documented in Ross Levine and Sara Zervos, "Capital Control Liberalization and Stock Market Development," *World Development* 26 (1988): 1169–84; Geert Bekaert et al. "Dating the Integration of World Equity Markets," NBER Working Paper 6724 (September 1988); Peter Blair Henry, "Equity Prices, Stock Market Liberalization, and Investment," *Journal of Financial Economics* 58, no. 1–2 (2000): 301–34; and Peter Blair Henry, "Stock Market Liberalization, Economic Reform, and Emerging Market Equity Prices," *Journal of Finance* 55, no. 2 (2000): 529–64, when stock markets in emerging market countries are opened to foreign capital, dividend yields fall, there is an increase in average stock prices, and liquidity goes up.

3. This argument is made in World Bank, *Finance for Growth,* and in Linda Goldberg, "Financial Sector FDI and Host Countries: New and Old Lessons," Federal Reserve Bank of New York Staff Reports 183 (April 2004).

4. See Raghuram Rajan and Luigi Zingales, "The Great Reversals: The Politics of Financial Development in the 20th Century," *Journal of Financial Economics* 69, no. 1 (2003): 5–50, and H. Svalaeryd and J. Vlachos, "Market for Risk and Openness to Trade: How Are They Related?" *Journal of International Economics* 57, no. 2 (2002): 364–95.

5. Alberto Ades and Rafael Di Tella, "Rents, Competition and Corruption," *American Economic Review* 89, no. 4 (1999): 982–94.

6. The view that a financial system that has worked well in the initial stages of development needs to move toward the model used in advanced countries is espoused by Raghuram Rajan and Luigi Zingales, "Financial Dependence and Growth," *American Economic Review* 88, no. 3 (1998): 559–86.

7. The source of this data is International Monetary Fund, *Direction of Trade Statistics* (Washington, D.C.: International Monetary Fund, 2004). The latest export data are for 2003.

8. The largest four state-owned banks, with 70% of China's bank deposits, are scheduled to be privatized in the following order: the Construction Bank, the Bank of China, the Industrial and Commercial Bank, and the Agricultural Bank.

9. See the speech by the governor of the central bank of China, Zhou Xiaochuan, "Improve Legal System and Financial Ecology," speech at the Forum of 50 Chinese Economists, December 2, 2004, Beijing.

10. See William Easterly, *The Elusive Quest for Growth: Economists' Adventures and Misadventures in the Tropics* (Cambridge, Mass.: MIT Press, 2001), 222.

11. William Easterly, *The Elusive Quest for Growth,* 223.

12. Indeed, almost all economists think that trade liberalization, a key element of globalization, is a good thing. For example, in James R. Kearl et al., "A Confusion of Economists," *American Economic Review Papers and Proceedings* 69, no. 2 (1979): 28–37, 97% of economists agreed (generally or with some provisions) with the statement "Tariffs and import quotas reduce general economic welfare." A typical view advocating trade liberalization is expressed by Jagdish Bhagwati, one of the most prominent trade theorists in the world, in his book, *In Defense of Globalization* (New York: Oxford University Press, 2004).

13. This example comes from David N. Weil, *Economic Growth* (Boston: Addison-Wesley, 2005), 322, and is described more extensively in David Dollar and Paul Collier, *Globalization, Growth and Poverty: Building an Inclusive World Economy* (Washington, D.C.: World Bank, 2001).

14. The literature on the effects of trade liberalization on growth and poverty is immense. See the surveys in Jonathan Temple, "The New Growth Evidence," *Journal of Economic Literature* 37, no. 1 (1999): 112–56; François Bourguignon et al., *Making Sense of Globalization: A Guide to the Economic Issues,* CEPR Policy Paper 8 (July 2002); Alan Winters et al., "Trade Liberalization and Poverty: The Evidence So Far," *Journal of Economic Literature* 42, no. 1 (2004): 72–115; and Martin Wolf, *Why Globalization Works* (New Haven, Conn.: Yale University Press, 2004). Earlier studies, such as David Dollar, "Outward-Oriented Developing Economies Really Do Grow More Rapidly: Evidence from 95 LDCs, 1976–85," *Economic Development and Cultural Change* 40 (1992): 523–44; Jeffrey D. Sachs and Andrew Warner, "Economic Reform and the Process of Global Integration," *Brookings Papers on Economic Activity* 1 (1995): 1–118; and Sebastian Edwards, "Openness, Productivity and Growth: What Do We Really Know?" *Economic Journal* 108 (1998): 383–98, found that trade openness was associated with higher growth rates. However, because the direction of causation from this evidence is difficult to establish, other researchers have used instrumental variable procedures to establish causality from trade liberalization to growth. See Jeffrey Frankel and David Romer, "Does Trade Cause Growth?" *American Economic Review* 89, no. 3 (1999): 379–99. Using a very different approach to identify the direction of causation, Ha Yan Lee et al., "Once Again, Is Openness Good for Growth?" *Journal of Development Economics* 75, no. 2 (2004): 451–72, also find that trade openness has a positive effect on growth.

15. Shang-Jin Wei and Yi Wu, "The Life-and-Death Implications of Globalization," paper presented at the NBER Inter-American Seminar on Economics, November 15–16, 2002, Monterey, Mexico.

16. Alan Winters et al., "Trade Liberalization and Poverty."

17. For example, see Ann Harrison, "Openness and Growth: A Time-Series, Cross-Country Analysis for Developing Countries," *Journal of Development Economics* 48, no. 2 (1996): 419–47, and particularly Francisco Rodriguez and Dani Rodrik, "Trade Policy and Economic Growth: A Skeptic's Guide to the Evidence," in Ben Bernanke and Kenneth Rogoff, eds., *NBER Macro Annual 2000* (Cambridge, Mass.: MIT Press, 2000), 261–325.

18. The finding in Benjamin F. Jones and Benjamin A. Olken, "The Anatomy of Start-Stop Growth," NBER Working Paper 11528 (July 2005), that growth takeoffs are primarily

associated with large and steady expansions in international trade provides further support for this view.

19. Dani Rodrik, *The Global Governance of Trade: As If Development Really Mattered* (New York: United Nations Development Programme, October 2001), 23.

Chapter Nine   Preventing Financial Crises

1. Carlos Diaz-Alejandro, "Goodbye Financial Repression, Hello Financial Crash," *Journal of Development Economics* 19, no. 1–2 (1985): 1–24.

2. Mark Allen et al., "A Balance-Sheet Approach to Financial Crisis," IMF Working Paper 02/210 (December 2002).

3. This is consistent with evidence in Guillermo A. Calvo et al., "On the Empirics of Sudden Stops: The Relevance of Balance-Sheet Effects," NBER Working Paper 10520 (May 2004), and Michael D. Bordo and Christopher M. Meissner, "The Role of Foreign Currency Debt in Financial Crises: 1880–1913 vs. 1972–1997," NBER Working Paper 11897 (December 2005), who find that more liability dollarization is associated with a higher probability of financial crises and more severe crises.

4. Augusto de la Torre and Sergio L. Schmukler, "Coping with Risk through Mismatches: Domestic and International Financial Contracts for Emerging Economies," World Bank mimeo (December 2003), suggest that liability dollarization and currency mismatch may be a sensible way for firms to reduce risk. Thus limiting liability dollarization may have costs as well as benefits, implying that doing this right may be more complex than many advocates for restricting the use of foreign-denominated debt recognize.

5. See Eduardo Levy-Yeyati, "Financial Dollarization: Where Do We Stand?" paper presented at the IDB/World Bank Conference, Financial Dedollarization: Policy Options, December 1–2, 2003, Washington, D.C., and Christian Broda and Eduardo Levy-Yeyati, "Endogenous Deposit Dollarization," Federal Reserve Bank of New York Staff Reports 160 (February 2003). Ricardo Caballero and Arvind Krishnamurthy, "Excessive Dollar Debt: Financial Development and Underinsurance," *Journal of Finance* 58, no. 2 (2003): 867–93, provide an additional reason for why liability dollarization may be excessive: because firms that can borrow abroad in foreign currencies do not recognize the social value in providing insurance to domestic firms that do not have access to foreign borrowing.

6. See Peter Kenen, *The International Financial Architecture: What's New? What's Missing?* (Washington, D.C.: Institute for International Economics, 2001), and Morris Goldstein and Philip Turner, *Controlling Currency Mismatches in Emerging Markets* (Washington, D.C.: Institute for International Economics, 2004), for recommendations on dealing with currency mismatches. The Goldstein and Turner monograph also has an excellent survey of the literature on currency mismatches.

7. Anne Krueger, "Conflicting Demands on the International Monetary Fund," *American Economic Review* 90, no. 2 (2000): 38–42.

8. Morris Goldstein and Philip Turner, *Controlling Currency Mismatches in Emerging Markets,* for example, disagree with the Krueger proposal as being too draconian because the concern should be with currency mismatches rather than liability dollarization per se. In addition, restricting dollarization may lead to a reduction of finan-

cial deepening, both directly and because financial intermediation would move offshore. See G. De Nicolo et al., "Dollarization of the Banking System: Good or Bad?" IMF Working Paper 03/146 (July 2003), and Inter-American Development Bank, *Unlocking Credit: The Quest for Deep and Stable Bank Lending. 2005 Report, Economic and Social Progress in Latin America* (Washington, D.C.: Inter-American Development Bank and Johns Hopkins University Press, 2004), 49–65.

9. The argument here is for the indexation of financial contracts only. The indexation of other contracts, especially labor contracts, may have negative consequences, as seen in Latin America in the 1980s. Indexed labor contracts, which are typically indexed to past inflation, have the undesirable consequence of putting substantial inertia into the wage-setting process, thereby making it harder to wring inflation out of an economy. Alain Ize and Eduardo Levy-Yeyati, "Financial Dollarization," *Journal of International Economics* 59, no. 2 (2003): 323–47, find that dollarization is significantly lower in countries where indexation of contracts is prevalent.

10. Private markets are rarely able to develop indexed debt contracts on their own, and so active government involvement to encourage indexation seems to be required to develop indexed debt markets. For example, see Robert J. Shiller, "Public Resistance to Indexation: A Puzzle," *Brookings Papers on Economic Activity* 1 (1997): 156–229. (This has been true in the United States, where markets in indexed debt did not start to develop until the U.S. Treasury began to issue Treasury Inflation Protection Securities [TIPS] in January 1997.) As has been carefully documented by researchers at the Central Bank of Chile, avoiding dollarization and the development of indexed debt markets in Chile was not easy: it was a long, slow process, which required both implementing regulations to encourage indexation and substantial issuance of indexed debt by the Chilean authorities. Luis O. Herrera and Rodrigo O. Valdes, "Dedollarization, Indexation and Nominalization: The Chilean Experience," Banco Central de Chile manuscript (November 2003).

11. World Bank, *Finance for Growth: Policy Choices in a Volatile World* (Oxford: World Bank and Oxford University Press, 2001), 105, Figure 2.7.

12. Asli Demirguc-Kunt and Enrica Detragiache, "Does Deposit Insurance Increase Banking System Stability?" *Journal of Monetary Economics* 49, no. 7 (2002): 1373–406; Robert Cull et al., "Deposit Insurance and Financial Development," World Bank Policy Research Paper 2682 (September 2001); World Bank, *Finance for Growth*, 104–18, Figure 2.7; and Asli Demirguc-Kunt and Edward J. Kane, "Deposit Insurance around the Globe: Where Does It Work?" *Journal of Economic Perspectives* 16, no. 2 (2002): 175–95.

13. Recall that, as mentioned in Chapter 5, 20% of all large loans outstanding from 1995 to 1998 in Mexico had gone to bank directors, while these insider loans had interest rates that were 4 percentage points lower than those on other loans, a 33% higher default rate, and a 30% lower recovery rate for collateral. Rafael La Porta et al., "Related Lending," *Quarterly Journal of Economics* 118, no. 1 (2003): 231–68.

14. Barry Eichengreen, *Financial Crises* (New York: Oxford University Press, 2002), argues that restrictions on connected lending can hinder financial transactions in emerging market countries because it may be the only effective way of structuring and enforcing financial contracts in countries where the information and contracting envi-

ronments are weak. There are informational and enforcement benefits that can accrue from family and other connections, which is why it often makes sense to have inter-family lending and family control of businesses in poorer countries. However, connected lending by banking institutions that have access to a government safety net leads to huge moral hazard and excessive risk-taking, which is very destructive, as we have seen: this is why it needs to be restricted.

15. David Folkerts-Landau et al., "Effect of Capital Flows on the Domestic Financial Sectors in APEC Developing Countries," in Moshin S. Khan and Carmen M. Reinhart, eds., *Capital Flows in the APEC Region* (Washington, D.C.: International Monetary Fund, 1995), 31–57.

16. Bank regulations that restrict banks from holding particular risky assets, such as common stocks or real estate, are another means of ensuring that banks do not take on too much risk. Risk can also be reduced by regulations that promote diversification and prevent banks from concentrating loans on one large borrower or on a particular class of borrowers.

17. A counter to the view here is provided by James R. Barth et al., *Rethinking Bank Regulation and Supervision: Til Angels Govern* (New York: Cambridge University Press, 2006). They find little evidence that capital regulations improve bank stability, although they are cautious in interpreting this result. However, they do take the stronger stance that regulatory restrictions have negative consequences for bank efficiency and stability in countries where property rights and political institutions are weak. Their evidence suggests that going too far in adopting regulatory restrictions in developing countries may be counterproductive.

18. This kind of assessment by bank examiners is now standard in advanced countries and is part of the overall rating that banks receive from bank examiners.

19. More controversial is whether bank supervisors should recommend approaches to risk management. James R. Barth et al., *Rethinking Bank Regulation and Supervision,* suggest that the answer is no because giving increased discretionary powers to supervisors has not led to safer and sounder banks, for the reasons discussed in the subsection on strong discretionary supervisory powers.

20. James R. Barth et al., *Rethinking Bank Regulation and Supervision.*

21. See Banco Central de la Republica Argentina, "Main Features of the Regulatory Framework of the Argentine Financial System," mimeo (April 1997); Charles W. Calomiris, "Evaluation of Argentina's Banking Sector, 1991–1998," Columbia University mimeo (1998), for detailed descriptions of the Argentine regulatory system.

22. This regulation did not take effect until January 1998.

23. For a favorable assessment of the Argentine bank regulatory system before the crisis, see Charles W. Calomiris and Andrew Powell, "Can Emerging Market Bank Regulators Establish Credible Discipline? The Case of Argentina, 1992–99," in Frederic S. Mishkin, ed., *Prudential Supervision: What Works and What Doesn't* (Chicago: University of Chicago Press, 2001), 147–97.

24. Another way to impose market discipline on banks is to require that they issue subordinated debt (uninsured debt that is junior to insured deposits, but senior to equity). Subordinated debt, particularly if it has a ceiling on the spread between its interest rate

and that on government securities, can be an effective disciplining device. If the bank is exposed to too much risk, it is unlikely to be able to sell its subordinated debt. Thus compliance with the subordinated debt requirement will be a direct way for the market to force banks to limit their risk exposure. Alternatively, deposit insurance premiums could be charged according to the interest rate on the subordinated debt. Not only would the issuance of subordinated debt directly help reduce incentives for banks to engage in risky activities, but it would also provide supplemental information to bank examiners that could help them in their supervisory activities. In addition, information about whether banks are successful in issuing subordinated debt and the interest rate on this debt can help the public evaluate whether supervisors are being sufficiently tough on a particular banking institution, thus reducing the scope of the principal-agent problem.

A subordinated debt requirement necessitates that an emerging market country have pretty sophisticated capital markets. However, Argentina did implement a subordinated debt requirement in its BASIC program, although without an interest rate cap, which took effect on January 1998. As reported in Charles W. Calomiris, "Evaluation of Argentina's Banking Sector," initially about half of the banks were able to comply with this requirement. Interestingly, as expected, it was the weakest banks that have had trouble issuing subordinated debt. Furthermore, banks that complied with the requirement had lower deposit rates and larger growth in deposits. Thus the subordinated debt requirement looks like it has had the intended effect of promoting discipline on the banks (Charles W. Calomiris and Powell, "Can Emerging Market Bank Regulators Establish Credible Discipline?").

25. Frederic S. Mishkin, *The Economics of Money, Banking and Financial Markets*, 8th edition (Boston: Addison-Wesley, 2007), Chapter 11, "The Economic Analysis of Banking Regulation," especially pages 292–98. For an excellent survey of how the banking crisis played out in the United States, see Edward J. Kane, *The S&L Insurance Mess: How Did It Happen?* (Washington, D.C.: Urban Institute Press, 1989).

26. The outstanding example of prompt corrective action is the provision in the Federal Deposit Insurance Corporation Improvement Act (FDICIA) legislation implemented in the United States in 1991. Banks in the United States are classified into five groups based on bank capital. Group 1, classified as "well capitalized," are banks that significantly exceed minimum capital requirements and are allowed privileges, such as the ability to underwrite some securities. Banks in group 2, classified as "adequately capitalized," meet minimum capital requirements and are not subject to corrective actions but are not allowed the privileges of the well-capitalized banks. Banks in group 3 are "undercapitalized"; that is, they fail to meet capital requirements. Banks in groups 4 and 5 are "significantly undercapitalized" and "critically undercapitalized," respectively, and are not allowed to pay interest on their deposits at rates that are higher than average. FDICIA mandates that regulators must require undercapitalized banks to submit an acceptable capital restoration plan within 45 days of notification and implement the plan. In addition, the regulatory agencies must take steps to close down critically undercapitalized banks by putting them into receivership or conservatorship within 90 days, unless the appropriate agency and the FDIC concur that some other action would

better achieve the purpose of prompt corrective action. If the bank continues to be critically undercapitalized, it must be placed in receivership, unless specific statutory requirements are met. For further discussion of FDICIA's prompt corrective action provisions, see Frederic S. Mishkin, "Evaluating FDICIA," in George Kaufman, ed., *Research in Financial Services: Private and Public Policy*, FDICIA: Bank Reform Five Years Later and Five Years Ahead 9 (Greenwich, Conn.: JAI Press, 1997), 17–33.

27. Although evergreening is more prevalent in developing countries, it has occurred in advanced countries like Japan and has been a serious impediment to the health of their banking systems. Japanese banks have kept on lending to nonproductive businesses and as a result have not been channeling resources to more productive sectors. The low productivity growth in Japan has been the result. Takeo Hoshi and Anil Kashyap, "Solutions to Japan's Banking Problems: What Might Work and What Definitely Will Fail," in Takatoshi Ito et al., eds., *Reviving Japan's Economy: Problems and Prescriptions* (Cambridge, Mass.: MIT Press, 2005), 147–95.

28. Takeo Hoshi and Anil Kashyap, "Solutions to Japan's Banking Problems."

29. For an excellent discussion of the too-big-to-fail problem, see Gary H. Stern and Ron J. Feldman, *Too Big to Fail: The Hazards of Bank Bailouts* (Washington, D.C.: Brookings Institution Press, 2004). Frederic S. Mishkin, "How Big a Problem Is Too Big to Fail?" NBER Working Paper 11814 (December 2005), forthcoming in the *Journal of Economic Literature*, indicates, however, that although the too-big-to-fail problem is important, it is not the dominant problem for bank supervisors, as the Stern and Feldman book seems to suggest.

30. See John H. Boyd and Mark Gertler, "U.S. Commercial Banking: Trends, Cycles and Policy," in Olivier Blanchard and Stanley Fischer, eds., *NBER Macroeconomics Annual* (Cambridge, Mass.: MIT Press, 1993), 319–68, for evidence that, even in advanced countries like the United States, larger banks take on riskier loans than do smaller banks.

31. While governments will want to closely monitor large institutions and to allow the possibility of losses to encourage depositors and other creditors to more closely monitor these institutions, governments do not want the failure of a large financial institution to destabilize the financial system. How can these goals be balanced?

One proposal that I have made, in "Financial Consolidation: Dangers and Opportunities," *Journal of Banking and Finance* 23, no. 2–4 (1999): 675–91, is for the supervisory agencies to announce that uninsured depositors will not be fully protected unless this is the cheapest way to resolve a banking institution's failure. It is important to recognize that although large banking institutions may be too big to liquidate, they can be closed with losses imposed on uninsured creditors. This proposal would fit in nicely with what the 1991 FDICIA legislation specifies: except under very unusual circumstances a least-cost (cheapest) resolution procedure will be used to close down the bank. The legislation also allows for a *systemic-risk exception* to the least-cost-resolution rule. The exception applies when a bank failure poses "serious adverse effects on economic conditions or financial stability," but invoking it requires a two-thirds majority of both the board of governors of the Federal Reserve System and the directors of the FDIC, as well as the approval of the secretary of the Treasury. (The systemic-risk exception has never been exercised.)

An important concern is that the systemic-risk exception will always be invoked when the failing bank is large enough and that too-big-to-fail problem will still be alive, with all its negative consequences. One way to cope with this problem is for the authorities to announce that although they are concerned about systemic-risk possibilities, the *first* large bank to fail will not be treated as too-big-to-fail, and that costs will be imposed on uninsured depositors and creditors when the bank is closed. Once the initial large bank fails, the authorities will stand ready to extend the safety net to the rest of the banking system if they perceive that there is a serious systemic-risk problem.

The advantage of announcing such a stance is that uninsured depositors and creditors will have to worry that if their bank is the first one to fail, they will not be bailed out. As a result, these depositors and creditors will have an incentive to withdraw their funds if they worry about the soundness of the bank. These worries will alter the incentives of the bank to avoid taking on too much risk. Clearly, moral hazard still remains in the system because the authorities stand ready to extend the safety net to the rest of the system after the initial large institution fails if its failure creates the potential for a banking crisis. However, the extent of moral hazard is greatly reduced by adopting this policy. Furthermore, the cost of this remaining moral hazard must be balanced against the benefits of preventing a banking crisis if the initial bank failure is likely to snowball into a systemic crisis.

32. James R. Barth et al., *Rethinking Bank Regulation and Supervision,* indicate that in their sample, supervisors in one-third of all countries are subject to lawsuits for doing their jobs, and that the percentage is higher for developing countries. In private correspondence, Gerard Caprio informed me that 50 of 105 developing countries have their supervisors subject to lawsuits (38%), while this is true for only 15 of 45 industrialized countries (33%).

33. These figures come from James R. Barth et al., *Rethinking Bank Regulation and Supervision,* Chapter 2.

34. See Ruth de Krivoy, "Reforming Bank Supervision in Developing Countries," in Eric S. Rosengren and John S. Jordan, eds., *Building on Infrastructure for Financial Stability,* Conference Series 44 (Boston: Federal Reserve Bank of Boston, 2000), 113–33.

35. As I have argued in "An Evaluation of the Treasury Plan for Banking Reform," *Journal of Economic Perspectives* 6, no. 1 (1992): 133–53, one way to ensure against regulatory forbearance is to give the bank supervisory role to a politically independent central bank. This has desirable elements, but some central banks might not want to have the supervisory task thrust upon them because they worry that it might increase the likelihood that the central bank would be politicized, thereby impinging on its independence. Alternatively, bank supervisory activities could be housed in a bank regulatory authority that is independent of the government.

36. Edward J. Kane, *The S&L Insurance Mess.*

37. For example, an important but very often overlooked part of the FDICIA legislation that has helped make it effective is the mandatory report that the supervisory agencies must produce if the bank failure imposes costs on the FDIC. See Frederic S. Mishkin, "Evaluating FDICIA." The mandatory report is made available to any member of Congress and to the general public upon request, and the General Accounting Office must do an annual review of these reports.

38. James R. Barth et al., *Rethinking Bank Regulation and Supervision*. Also see Thorsten Beck et al., "Bank Supervision and Corruption in Lending," NBER Working Paper 11498 (July 2005).

39. Chapter 3 discussed why state-owned banks hurt economic growth. For additional arguments on why governments should get out of the banking business, see Gerard Caprio, Jr., and Patrick Honohan, "Finance in a World of Volatility," World Bank mimeo (2000), and James R. Barth et al., *Rethinking Bank Regulation and Supervision*.

40. For example, see Morris Goldstein and Philip Turner, "Banking Crises in Emerging Economies: Origins and Policy Options," BIS Economic Paper 46 (October 1996), and Gerard Caprio, Jr., and Patrick Honohan, "Finance in a World of Volatility."

41. Also see Ross Levine, "Foreign Banks, Financial Development, and Economic Growth," in Claude E. Barfield, ed., *International Financial Markets: Harmonization versus Competition* (Washington, D.C.: American Enterprise Institute Press, 1996), 224–55, for a general discussion of the benefits of foreign bank entry.

42. See Asli Demirguc-Kunt, Ross Levine, and Hong G. Min, "Opening to Foreign Banks: Issues of Efficiency, Stability, and Growth" in Seongtae Lee, ed., *The Implications of Globalization of World Financial Markets* (Seoul: Bank of Korea, 1998), and James R. Barth et al., *Rethinking Bank Regulation and Supervision*.

43. Foreign banks have lower overhead costs than domestic banks and are thus able to operate with lower net interest margins (net interest income relative to assets) and still earn similar returns on assets. See Figure 10.5 in Inter-American Development Bank, *Unlocking Credit*, 133.

44. See Ross Levine, "Foreign Banks, Financial Development and Economic Growth"; Gerard Caprio, Jr., and Patrick Honohan, "Restoring Banking Stability: Beyond Supervised Capital Requirements," *Journal of Economic Perspectives* 13, no. 4 (1999): 43–64; and Frederic S. Mishkin, "Financial Policies and the Prevention of Financial Crises in Emerging Market Countries," in Martin Feldstein, ed., *Economic and Financial Crises in Emerging Market Countries* (Chicago: University of Chicago Press, 2003), 93–130. There are also benefits from the increased competition that foreign bank entry brings to the banking industry in the home country, because it leads to improved management techniques and a more efficient banking system. See Ross Levine, "Foreign Banks, Financial Development and Economic Growth," and Gerard Caprio, Jr., and Patrick Honohan, "Restoring Banking Stability."

45. In addition, because foreign banks do not have the same political connections as domestic banks have, foreign bank entry seems to reduce political influence peddling in the financial sector. See Charles W. Calomiris et al., "A Taxonomy of Financial Crisis Restructuring Mechanisms: Cross-Country Experience and Policy Implications," in Luc Laeven, ed., *Systemic Financial Distress* (New York: Cambridge University Press, 2005), 25–76, and Randall Kroszner, "On the Political Economy of Banking and Financial Regulatory Reform in Emerging Markets," *Research in Financial Services* 10 (1998): 33–51.

46. Edward J. Kane, "How Offshore Financial Competition Disciplines Exit Resistance by Incentive-Conflicted Bank Regulators," *Journal of Financial Services Research* 17, no. 1 (2000): 265–91.

47. Jennifer S. Crystal et al., "Does Foreign Ownership Contribute to Sounder Banks in Emerging Markets? The Latin American Experience," in Robert Litan et al.,

eds., *Open Doors: Foreign Participation in Financial Systems in Developing Countries* (Washington, D.C.: Brookings Institution Press, 2001), 217–66.

48. See Phillip E. Strahan and James Weston, "Small Business Lending and Bank Consolidation: Is There Cause for Concern?" *Federal Reserve Bank of New York Current Issues in Economics and Finance* (March 1996): 1–6, and Frederic S. Mishkin, "Bank Consolidation: A Central Banker's Perspective," in Yakov Amihud and Geoffrey Miller, eds., *Mergers of Financial Institutions* (Boston: Kluwer Academic, 1998), 3–19.

49. George R. Clarke et al., "On the Kindness of Strangers? The Impact of Foreign Entry on Domestic Banks in Argentina," in Stijn Claessens and Marion Jansen, eds., *The Internationalization of Financial Services: Issues and Lessons for Developing Countries* (The Hague: Kluwer Law International, 2000), 331–35.

50. See Linda Goldberg et al., "Foreign and Domestic Bank Participation in Emerging Markets: Lessons from Mexico and Argentina," Federal Reserve Bank of New York, *Economic Policy Review* 6, no. 3 (2000): 17–36, and George Clarke et al., "Does Foreign Bank Penetration Reduce Access to Credit in Developing Countries? Evidence from Asking Borrowers," World Bank Policy Research Working Paper 2716 (November 2001).

51. Figure 10.4 in Inter-American Development Bank, *Unlocking Credit*, 131.

52. Inter-American Development Bank, *Unlocking Credit*, 137.

53. Later the banks did receive some compensation in the form of government bonds to offset these losses, but foreign banks were nevertheless treated as scapegoats during the crisis.

54. For a formal model of this process, see Guillermo A. Calvo et al., "The Capital Inflows Problem: Concepts and Issues," *Contemporary Economic Policy* 12, no. 3 (1994): 54–66.

55. For example, see Robert Rubin and Jacob Weisberg, *In an Uncertain World* (New York: Random House, 2003); Stanley Fischer, "Exchange Rate Regimes: Is the Bipolar View Correct?" *Journal of Economic Perspectives* 15, no. 2 (2001): 3–24; and *Economist*, "A Slightly Circuitous Route," May 3, 2003, p. 25. Also see three reports published in October 1998 from the Group of Twenty-Two, which is made up of officials from central banks and finance ministries from twenty-two major countries: *Report of the Working Group on Transparency and Accountability, Report of the Working Group on Strengthening Financial Systems*, and *Report of the Working Group on International Financial Crises*. They can be found on the IMF's website at http://www.imf.org/external/np/g22/index.htm. Note that support for Chilean-type capital controls by these individuals and entities is cautious rather than unqualified.

56. Paul Krugman, "Saving Asia: It's Time to Get Radical" *Fortune*, September 7, 1998, p. 74–81; Ethan Kaplan and Dani Rodrik, "Did the Malaysian Capital Controls Work?" in Sebastian Edwards and Jeffrey A. Frankel, eds., *Preventing Currency Crises in Emerging Markets* (Chicago: University of Chicago Press, 2002), 393–440; and Joseph E. Stiglitz, *Globalization and Its Discontents* (New York: W. W. Norton, 2002), argue that the Malaysian controls on capital outflows that were adopted in the immediate aftermath of its currency crisis helped Malaysia recover faster than did other crisis countries in East Asia.

57. Kristin Forbes, "One Cost of the Chilean Capital Controls: Increased Financial Constraints for Smaller Traded Firms," NBER Working Paper 9777 (June 2003), and Fran-

cisco Gallego and Leonardo Hernandez, "Microeconomic Effects of Capital Controls: The Chilean Experience during the 1990s," Central Bank of Chile mimeo (2002), suggest that the capital controls in Chile made it harder for smaller firms to obtain financing for productive investments.

58. See the surveys in Kristin J. Forbes, "Capital Controls: Mud in the Wheels of Market Discipline," in William Hunter et al., eds., *Market Discipline across Countries and Institutions* (Cambridge, Mass.: MIT Press, 2004), 187–211, and Kristin J. Forbes, "The Microeconomic Evidence on Capital Controls: No Free Lunch," NBER Working Paper 11372 (May 2005).

59. Reuven Glick and Michael Hutchinson, "Capital Controls and Exchange Rate Instability in Developing Countries," *Journal of International Money and Finance* 24, no. 3 (2005): 387–412; Reuven Glick et al., "Currency Crises, Capital Account Liberalization, and Selection Bias," Federal Reserve Bank of San Francisco Working Paper 2004-15 (June 2005); and Sebastian Edwards, "Capital Controls, Sudden Stops and Current Account Reversals," NBER Working Paper 11170 (March 2005), find that capital controls are not associated with a higher incidence of currency and financial crises, but rather tend to be associated with a lower probability of crises. However, once a crisis occurs, countries with higher capital mobility do experience more severe economic downturns. Sebastian Edwards and Roberto Rigobon, "Capital Controls, Exchange Rate Volatility and External Vulnerability," NBER Working Paper 11434 (June 2005), find that capital controls are associated with heightened vulnerability of the currency value to external shocks and greater volatility of the exchange rate.

60. Evidence that this occurred in Mexico can be found in Jeffrey Frankel and Sergio Schmukler, "Country Fund Discounts and the Mexican Crisis of 1994: Did Mexican Residents Turn Pessimistic before International Investors?" *Open Economies Review* 7 (Fall 1996): 511–34, and in Korea in Stephen J. Brown et al., "Hedge Funds and the Asian Currency Crisis of 1997," NBER Working Paper 6427 (February 1998), Hyuk Cho et al., "Do Foreign Investors Destabilize Stock Markets? The Korean Experience in 1997," NBER Working Paper 6661 (July 1998).

61. Lending booms are a better predictor of financial crises than are capital inflows. See Michael Gavin and Ricardo Hausman, "The Roots of Banking Crises: The Macroeconomic Context," in Ricardo Hausman and Liliana Rojas-Suarez, eds., *Banking Crises in Latin America* (Baltimore: Inter-American Development Bank, distributed by Johns Hopkins University Press, 1996), 27–63; Graciela L. Kaminsky and Carmen M. Reinhart, "The Twin Crises: The Causes of Banking and Balance of Payments Problems," *American Economic Review* 89, no. 3 (1999): 473–500; and the excellent survey in Graciela L. Kaminsky et al., "Leading Indicators of Currency Crises," IMF Working Paper WP/97/79 (July 1997). Reuven Glick et al., "Currency Crises, Capital Account Liberalization, and Selection Bias," find that capital account liberalization actually lowers the probability of a currency crisis when country characteristics that affect the tendency to liberalize are controlled for.

62. See Sebastian Edwards, "How Effective Are Capital Controls?" *Journal of Economic Perspectives* 13, no. 4 (2000): 65–84.

63. Leonardo Bartolini and Allan Drazen, "Capital Account Liberalization as a Signal," *American Economic Review* 87, no. 1 (1997): 138–54, point out that easing controls

on capital outflows are perceived as a government's commitment to sound macro-economic policies. Imposition of controls on capital outflows may thus weaken confidence in government policies and lead to capital outflows, exactly what they are trying to avoid.

64. For example, Michael D. Bordo et al., "Financial Crises: Lessons from the Last 120 Years," *Economic Policy* 16, no. 32 (2001): 53–82, find that currency crises are more likely to occur in countries that have capital controls. See also James R. Barth et al., *Rethinking Bank Regulation and Supervision*.

65. Indeed, the removal of capital controls can provide a positive signal to potential foreign investors and so can lead to an increase in capital inflows (Leonardo Bartolini and Alan Drazen, "Capital Account Liberalization as a Signal"); this is exactly what has happened in such countries as Colombia, Egypt, Italy, New Zealand, Mexico, Spain, Uruguay, and the United Kingdom. See Donald J. Mathieson and Liliana Rojas Suarez, "Liberalization of the Capital Account: Experience and Issues," IMF Occasional Paper 103 (Washington, D.C.: International Monetary Fund, 1993), and Raul M. Laban and Felipe B. Larrain, "Can a Liberalization of Capital Outflows Increase Net Capital Inflows?" *Journal of International Money and Finance* 16, no. 3 (1997): 415–31.

66. Ethan Kaplan and Dani Rodrik, "Did the Malaysian Capital Controls Work?"; Paul Krugman, "Balance Sheets, the Transfer Problem and Financial Crises," in P. Isard, A. Razin, and A. Rose, eds., *International Finance and Financial Crises* (Dordrecht: Kluwer Academic, 1999), 31–45; Paul Krugman, "Depression Economics Returns," *Foreign Affairs* 78, no. 1 (1999): 56–75; and Joseph E. Stiglitz, *Globalization and Its Discontents.*

67. Peter Kenen, *The International Financial Architecture*, makes the same point. Also see Rudiger Dornbusch, "Malaysia's Crisis: Was It Different?" in Sebastian Edwards and Jeffrey A. Frankel, eds., *Preventing Currency Crises in Emerging Markets*, 441–60, who is skeptical of the Kaplan and Rodrik results mentioned in the previous note, finding that the Malaysian capital controls had no significant impact on the economy's performance.

68. See Frederic S. Mishkin, "Global Financial Instability: Framework, Events, Issues," *Journal of Economic Perspectives* 13, no. 4 (1999): 3–20.

69. Simon Johnson and Todd Milton, "Cronyism and Capital Controls: Evidence from Malaysia," *Journal of Financial Economics* 67, no. 2 (2002): 351–82.

70. Jose DeGregorio et al., "Controls on Capital Inflows: Do They Work?" *Journal of Development Economics* 61, no. 1 (2000): 59–83; Sebastian Edwards, "Exchange Rate Regimes, Capital Flows and Crisis Prevention," NBER Working Paper 8529 (October 2001); and the survey in Nadal de Francisco Simone and Piritta Sorsa, "A Review of Capital Account Restrictions in Chile in the 1990s," IMF Working Paper 99/52 (April 1999).

71. Morris Goldstein, *The Asian Financial Crisis: Causes, Cures, and Systemic Implications* (Washington, D.C.: Institute for International Economics, 1998), provides a strong argument for sequencing.

72. Gregor Irwin et al., "How Should the IMF View Capital Controls?" in David Vines and Christopher L. Gilbert, eds., *The IMF and Its Critics: Reform of Global Financial Architecture* (Cambridge: Cambridge University Press, 2004), 181–206, make a similar argument. A staged approach may provide policymakers with an excuse for

prolonging bad policy. Politicians who benefit from the status quo are willing to agree in principle to reforms, but emphasize practical difficulties. Sequencing arguments then may be little more than a ploy for attracting assistance without implementing difficult policies.

73. Graciela L. Kaminsky and Sergio L. Schmukler, "Short-Run Pain, Long-Run Gain: The Effects of Financial Liberalization," NBER Working Paper 9787 (June 2003).

74. This result is also found in Roman Ranciere et al., "Systemic Crises and Growth," NBER Working Paper 11076 (January 2005).

75. James R. Barth et al., "Institute View," *Milken Institute Review* 2002, no. 2 (2004): 83–92.

76. See Su Bei "Investment Growth Splits Opinion," *China Daily*, May 20, 2005; "Beijing's Fight to Cool Economy Gets Harder," Bloomberg News, May 20, 2005; Kevin Yao and Tamora Vidaillet, "Fast China Investment Shows Tough Rebalancing Task," Reuters, May 19, 2005.

77. Ashraf Laidi, "China Answers Back, Yen Soars," *Forex News*, April 24, 2005.

78. Evidence that giving more power to chief executives or finance ministers to control spending produces better fiscal outcomes can be found in Alberto Alesina et al., "Budget Institutions and Fiscal Performance in Latin America," NBER Working Paper 5586 (May 1996), and Jurgen von Hagen and Ian J. Harden, "National Budget Processes and Fiscal Performance," *European Economy Reports and Studies* 3 (1994): 311–408. For further discussion of fiscal reforms, see James Poterba and Jurgen von Hagen, eds., *Fiscal Institutions and Fiscal Performance* (Chicago: University of Chicago Press, 1999).

79. See the survey in Palle Anderson and David Gruen, "Macroeconomic Policies and Growth," in Palle Anderson et al., eds., *Productivity and Growth* (Sydney: Reserve Bank of Australia, 1995), 279–319, and Stanley Fischer, "The Role of Macroeconomic Factors in Growth," *Journal of Monetary Economics* 32, no. 3 (1993): 485–512, one of the most cited papers in this literature.

80. See John H. Boyd et al., "The Impact of Inflation on Financial Sector Performance," *Journal of Monetary Economics* 47, no. 2 (2001): 221–48, and Kevin Cowan, Herman Kamil, and Alejandro. Izquierdo, "Macroeconomic Determinants of Dollarization: A New Look at the Evidence," Inter-American Development Bank mimeo (2004).

81. For evidence showing that a major source of dollarization is the lack of monetary credibility, see G. De Nicolo et al., "Dollarization of the Banking System: Good or Bad?"; Inter-American Development Bank, *Unlocking Credit,* 49–65; and Adam Honig, "Dollarization, Exchange Rate Regimes and Government Myopia," Columbia University mimeo (March 2003).

82. Arturo Galindo and Leonardo Leiderman, "Living with Dollarization and the Route to Dedollarization," paper prepared for IDB/World Bank Conference, Financial Dedollarization: Policy Options, Washington, D.C., December 1–2, 2003.

83. For why this happens, see "What Should Central Banks Do? Monetary Policy, Goals, Strategy, and Tactics," in Frederic S. Mishkin, *The Economics of Money, Banking and Financial Markets,* 8th edition (Boston: Addison-Wesley, 2007), 393–432.

84. Frederic S. Mishkin, "International Experiences with Different Monetary Policy Regimes," *Journal of Monetary Economics* 43, no. 3 (1999): 579–606; Frederic S. Mishkin,

"Inflation Targeting in Emerging Market Countries," *American Economic Review* 90, no. 2 (2000): 105–9; Frederic S. Mishkin, "What Should Central Banks Do?" *Federal Reserve Bank of St. Louis Review* 82, no. 6 (2000): 1–13. Frederic S. Mishkin and Miguel Savastano, "Monetary Policy Strategies for Latin America," *Journal of Development Economics* 66, no. 2 (2001): 415–44; Frederic S. Mishkin and Klaus Schmidt-Hebbel, "One Decade of Inflation Targeting in the World: What Do We Know and What Do We Need to Know?" in Norman Loayza and Raimundo Soto, eds., *Inflation Targeting: Design, Performance, Challenges* (Santiago: Central Bank of Chile, 2002), 171–219; Frederic S. Mishkin and Jiri Jonas, "Inflation Targeting in Transition Countries: Experience and Prospects," in Michael Woodford, ed., *Inflation Targeting* (Chicago: University of Chicago Press, 2005), 353–413; Frederic S. Mishkin, "Can Inflation Targeting Work in Emerging Market Countries?" in Carmen M. Reinhart et al., eds., *A Festschrift for Guillermo Calvo*, forthcoming; and Ben S. Bernanke et al., *Inflation Targeting: Lessons from the International Experience* (Princeton, N.J.: Princeton University Press, 1999).

85. See Eduardo Levy-Yeyati, "Financial Dollarization: Where Do We Stand?" and Christian Broda and Eduardo Levy-Yeyati, "Endogenous Deposit Dollarization."

86. Frederic S. Mishkin, "The Dangers of Exchange Rate Pegging in Emerging-Market Countries," *International Finance* 1, no. 1 (1998): 81–101.

87. Joshua Aizenman and Reuven Glick, "Pegged Exchange Rate Regimes— A Trap?" NBER Working Paper 11652 (September 2005); Barry Eichengreen, "Kicking the Habit: Moving from Pegged Exchange Rates to Greater Exchange Rate Flexibility," *Economic Journal* 109 (1999): C1–C14; and Barry Eichengreen and Paul Masson, "Exit Strategies: Policy Options for Countries Seeking Greater Exchange Rate Flexibility," IMF Occasional Paper 98/168 (Washington, D.C.: International Monetary Fund, 1998).

88. Stanley Fischer, "Globalization and Its Challenges," *American Economic Review* 93, no. 2 (2003): 1–30. Also see Stanley Fischer, "Exchange Rate Regimes: Is the Bipolar View Correct?"

89. For criticisms of pegged exchange rate regimes, see Maurice Obstfeld and Kenneth Rogoff, "The Mirage of Fixed Exchange Rates," *Journal of Economic Perspectives* 9, no. 4 (1995): 73–96; Barry Eichengreen, *Globalizing Capital: A History of the International Monetary System* (Princeton, N.J.: Princeton University Press, 1996), 1; Eduardo Levy-Yeyati and Federoci Sturzenegger, "To Float or to Fix: Evidence on the Impact of Exchange Rate Regimes on Growth," *American Economic Review* 93, no. 4 (2003): 1173; Martin Wolf, "Exchange Rates in a World of Capital Mobility," *Annals of the American Academy of Political and Social Science* 579, no. 1 (2002): 38–52.

90. This phrase was suggested to me by David Archer.

91. See, for example, Frederic S. Mishkin, "The Dangers of Exchange Rate Pegging in Emerging-Market Countries," and Frederic S. Mishkin, "Inflation Targeting in Emerging Market Countries." I lean to the position taken by Morris Goldstein in his monograph, *Managed Floating Plus*, Policy Analyses in International Economics 66 (Washington, D.C.: Institute for International Economics, 2002), who advocates flexible exchange rates, inflation targeting, and prudential measures to limit currency mismatch.

92. Paul Volcker, "Can We Bounce Back?", remarks at the Institute for International Finance, Washington, D.C., October 10, 1998.

93. For example, see Frederic S. Mishkin, "The Dangers of Exchange Rate Pegging in Emerging-Market Countries"; Frederic S. Mishkin and Miguel Savastano, "Monetary Policy Strategies for Latin America"; Guillermo A. Calvo and Carmen M. Reinhart, "Fixing for Your Life," NBER Working Paper 8006 (November 2000); Ronald McKinnon and Gunther Schnabl, "The East Asian Dollar Standard, Fear of Floating and Original Sin," *Review of Development Economics* 8, no. 3 (2004): 331–60.

94. Guillermo A. Calvo and Frederic S. Mishkin, "The Mirage of Exchange Rate Regimes for Emerging Market Countries," *Journal of Economic Perspectives* 17, no. 4 (2003): 99–118; see also Frederic S. Mishkin and Miguel Savastano, "Monetary Policy Strategies for Latin America." For a similar view that more focus needs to be on improving fundamental institutions rather than on exchange rate regimes, see Augusto de la Torre et al., "Financial Globalization: Unequal Blessings," *International Finance* 5, no. 3 (2002): 335–57.

95. Guillermo A. Calvo et al., "Sudden Stops, the Real Exchange Rate, and Fiscal Sustainability: Argentina's Lessons," NBER Working Paper 9828 (July 2003); Jeffrey Frankel and Eduardo A. Cavallo, "Does Openness to Trade Make Countries More Vulnerable to Sudden Stops or Less? Using Gravity to Establish Causality," NBER Working Paper 10957 (December 2004); Jeffrey Frankel, "Contractionary Currency Crashes in Developing Countries," NBER Working Paper 11508 (July 2005); Sebastian Edwards, "Financial Openness, Sudden Stops and Current Account Reversals," NBER Working Paper 10277 (February 2004); Sebastian Edwards, "Capital Controls, Sudden Stops and Current Account Reversals"; Mihir Desai et al., "Capital Controls, Liberalizations and Foreign Direct Investment," NBER Working Paper 10337 (March 2005).

Chapter Ten   Recovering from Financial Crises

1. The literature on banking crises emphasizes the importance of prompt resolution to limiting the overall costs. For example, Jose De Luna-Martinez, "Management and Resolution of Banking Crises: Lessons from the Republic of Korea and Mexico," World Bank Discussion Paper 413 (March 2000); Edward J. Kane and Daniela Klingebiel, "Alternatives to Blanket Guarantees for Containing a Systemic Crisis," *Journal of Financial Stability* 1, no. 1 (2004): 31–63; and Patrick Honohan and Daniela Klingebiel, "Controlling Fiscal Costs of Banking Crises," World Bank Policy Research Paper 2441 (September 2000).

2. For a detailed discussion of what works in responding to financial crises, see Charles W. Calomiris et al., "A Taxonomy of Financial Crisis Restructuring Mechanisms: Cross-Country Experience and Policy Implications," in Luc Laeven, ed., *Systemic Financial Distress* (New York: Cambridge University Press), 25–76.

3. See Joseph E. Stiglitz, *Globalization and Its Discontents* (New York: W. W. Norton, 2002).

4. Jason Furman and Joseph E. Stiglitz, "Economic Crises: Evidence and Insights from East Asia," *Brookings Papers on Economic Activity* 2 (1998): 1–114; Joseph E. Stiglitz, *Globalization and Its Discontents;* Jeffrey D. Sachs, "The Wrong Medicine for Asia," *New York Times,* November 3, 1997, p. 23; Jeffrey D. Sachs, "IMF Is a Power Unto Itself," *Financial Times,* December 11, 1997, p. 21; Steven Radelet and Jeffrey D. Sachs, "The East Asian

Financial Crisis: Diagnosis, Remedies and Prospects," *Brookings Papers on Economic Activity* 1 (1998): 1–74; and Paul Krugman, "The Confidence Game," *New Republic,* October 5, 1998, pp. 23–25.

5. For a discussion of how financial crises have played out in the United States over the past hundred and fifty years, see Frederic S. Mishkin, "Asymmetric Information and Financial Crises: A Historical Perspective," in R. Glenn Hubbard, ed., *Financial Markets and Financial Crises* (Chicago: University of Chicago Press, 1991), 69–108, and Robert Sobel, *Panic on Wall Street: A History of America's Financial Disasters* (London: Macmillan, 1968).

6. See Frederic S. Mishkin, "The Channels of Monetary Transmission: Lessons for Monetary Policy," *Banque de France Bulletin Digest* 27, no. 3 (1996): 33–44, for a discussion of these transmission mechanisms.

7. Walter Bagehot, *Lombard Street: A Description of the Money Market* (London: Smith, Elder and Co., 1915).

8. There were, however, problems in the way the Continental Illinois bailout was handled because not only depositors, but all creditors, were prevented from taking any losses. In addition, shortly afterward, the comptroller of the currency testified that eleven other banks were considered "too big to fail." This led to the "too big to fail" moral hazard problem because creditors of large banks had less incentive to monitor the bank and pull out their funds if the bank was taking on excessive risk. These problems, however, do not imply that the lender-of-last-resort operation wasn't the appropriate response. Instead, they suggest moral hazard needs to be limited when a government safety net is provided for the banking system.

9. I have described these episodes in Frederic S. Mishkin, "Asymmetric Information and Financial Crises," and Frederic S. Mishkin, *The Economics of Money, Banking and Financial Markets,* 8th edition (Boston: Addison-Wesley, 2007).

10. This episode is described in Frederic S. Mishkin, "Asymmetric Information and Financial Crises," and "Terrible Tuesday: How the Stock Market Almost Disintegrated a Day after the Crash," *Wall Street Journal,* November 20, 1987, p. 1.

11. See Frederic S. Mishkin, "Asymmetric Information and Financial Crises."

12. For more detail on this episode, see "Economic Front: How Policy Makers Regrouped to Defend the Financial System," *Wall Street Journal,* September 18, 2001, p. A1.

13. Not surprisingly, the literature on whether tight monetary policy promotes recovery or exacerbates the crisis is mixed. For example, see Jason Furman and Joseph E. Stiglitz, "Economic Crises"; Aart Kraay, "Do High Interest Rates Defend Currencies during Speculative Attacks?" *Journal of International Economics* 59, no. 2 (2003), 297–321; Taimur Baig and Ilan Goldfajn, "Monetary Policy in the Aftermath of Currency Crises: The Case of Asia," *Review of International Economics* 10, no. 1 (2002): 92–112; and Ilan Goldfajn and Poonam Gupta, "Does Tight Monetary Policy Stabilize the Exchange Rate?" *IMF Staff Papers* 50, no. 1 (2003): 90–114.

14. There are many other reasons why necessary reforms don't occur. The extensive literature on this subject is surveyed in Alan Drazen, *Political Economy in Macroeconomics* (Princeton, N.J.: Princeton University Press, 2000), and F. Sturzenegger and M. Tommasi, *The Political Economy of Reform* (Cambridge, Mass.: MIT Press, 1998).

15. See Frederic S. Mishkin, *The Economics of Money, Banking and Financial Markets,* for a discussion of the resolution of the S&L crisis in the United States.

16. Daniela Klingebiel and Luc LaeVen, "Managing the Real and Fiscal Effects of Banking Crises," World Bank Discussion Paper 428 (2002).

Chapter Eleven   What Should the International Monetary Fund Do?

1. Some prominent economists, like Anna J. Schwartz, say no: Anna J. Schwartz, "Time to Terminate the ESF and IMF," Cato Foreign Policy Briefing 48 (1998).

2. The amount of ink spilled on how the IMF should function is indeed immense. For recent thinking on how the IMF might be reformed, see Edwin M. Truman, ed., *Reforming the IMF for the Twenty-First Century* (Washington, D.C.: Institute for International Economics, 2006), and particularly the excellent background paper by Truman in that volume, "International Monetary Fund Reform: An Overview of the Issues." Because the framework in this book does not have a lot to say about them, there are many important issues about the IMF's operations that I ignore here. For example, I don't discuss such issues as the prevention of beggar-thy-neighbor exchange rate policies in which a country promotes an undervalued exchange rate that helps promote global imbalances; see Morris Goldstein, "Currency Manipulation and Enforcing the Rules of the International Monetary System," paper presented at the Institute for International Economics Conference on IMF Reform, September 23, 2005, Washington, D.C.

3. See Andres Velasco and Emre Deliveli, "The International Monetary Fund: Origins, Objectives, Controversies and Challenges," paper presented at the Plenary Meeting of the Club de Madrid, November 1–2, 2003, Madrid, for a brief summary of how the IMF's mission has changed over time.

4. See Stanley Fischer, "On the Need for an International Lender of Last Resort," *Journal of Economic Perspectives* 13, no. 4 (1999): 85–104.

5. For a recent survey on contagion, see Graciela L. Kaminsky et al., "The Unholy Trinity of Financial Contagion," NBER Working Paper 10061 (October 2003).

6. For example, see Jeffrey Garten, "In This Economic Chaos, a Global Central Bank Can Help," *International Herald Tribune,* September 25, 1998, p. 8.

7. One international financial institution that bears a resemblance to a central bank is the Bank for International Settlements (BIS). Because the BIS might be characterized as a central bank for central banks, the Shadow Open Market Committee, a group of prominent monetary economists, has advocated that the BIS take over the role of international lender of last resort; Shadow Open Market Committee, "Policy Statements and Position Papers, March 15–16, 1998," Bradley Policy Research Center Working Paper PPS 98-01 (March 1998). However, even though the BIS does hold substantial deposits from central banks of industrialized countries, it does not engage in traditional central banking functions like setting interest rates or injecting liquidity into the financial system. It is better to think of the BIS as an organization that allows central bankers to share information and coordinate their activities. For example, it has become a useful site for coordination of prudential regulations, such as those enacted by the Basel Committee for Bank Supervision, which meets under the auspices of the BIS.

If the BIS is a place that deals in information and if an international lender of last resort needs a lot of information to decide whether a lender-of-last-resort operation is actually needed, why doesn't the BIS fill this role? The BIS does not currently have the capability to gather the information a world central bank would need to act as an international lender of last resort. With just over five hundred employees (a staff smaller than many central banks), the BIS cannot perform, nor is it seeking to perform, the role of the world's central bank.

8. The Meltzer Commission, described later in the chapter (International Financial Institution Advisory Commission, *Report* [Washington, D.C.: International Financial Institution Advisory Commission, 2000]), also recommends that the IMF act as an international lender of last resort, but with some changes in its procedures. Stanley Fischer, "On the Need for an International Lender of Last Resort," also argues that the IMF should be an international lender of last resort.

9. Anna J. Schwartz, "Is There a Need for an International Lender of Last Resort?" Shadow Open Market Committee Report, March 7–8, 1999, Bradley Policy Research Center, Rochester University, http://www.somc.rochester.edu/archive1999.htm.

10. Stanley Fischer, "On the Need for an International Lender of Last Resort." Fischer points out that under the gold standard, central banks in reality did not have an unlimited capability to create liquidity and yet were able to perform the role of lender of last resort, and so the situation for the IMF in this regard is not all that different.

11. For example, see Ariel Buira, "Does the IMF Need More Financial Resources?" and Desmond Lachman, "How Should IMF Resources be Expanded?", papers presented at the Institute for International Economics Conference on IMF Reform, September 23, 2005, Washington, D.C., www.iie.com/prog_imf_reform.cfm.

12. Michael Mussa, "Reflections on the Function and Facilities for IMF Lending," paper presented at the Institute for International Economics Conference on IMF Reform, September 23, 2005, Washington, D.C., www.iie.com/prog_imf_reform.cfm, prefers to use the term "lender of final resort" because the IMF does not have the role of providing general liquidity to global financial markets to avoid a world-wide financial crisis. Instead, the IMF provides liquidity to individual countries to help them cope with international financial obligations. I use the term "international lender of last resort" to apply to the IMF because it directs liquidity to individual countries to help them stabilize their financial systems.

13. Frederic S. Mishkin, "Asymmetric Information and Financial Crises: A Historical Perspective," in R. Glenn Hubbard, ed., *Financial Markets and Financial Crises* (Chicago: University of Chicago Press, 1991), 69–108.

14. For example, see Edward J. Kane, *The S&L Insurance Mess: How Did It Happen?* (Washington, D.C.: Urban Institute Press, 1989).

15. Morris Goldstein, *The Asian Financial Crisis: Causes, Cures, and Systemic Implications* (Washington, D.C.: Institute for International Economics, 1998).

16. Morris Goldstein, "The International Financial Architecture," in C. Fred Bergston, ed., *The United States and the World Economy: Foreign Economic Policy for the Next Decade* (Washington, D.C.: Institute for International Economics, 2005), 373–407, argues that the IMF surveillance needs to increase its focus on debt sustainability.

17. The report I produced with my fellow committee members, Francesco Giavazzi and T. N. Srinivasan, can be found on the IMF website: International Monetary Fund,

External Evaluation of IMF Research Activities: Report by a Group of Independent Experts (Washington, D.C.: International Monetary Fund, 2000).

18. See International Monetary Fund, *The Poverty Reduction and Growth Facility (PRGF)—Operational Issues* (Washington, D.C.: International Monetary Fund, 1999), for a description of the mandate in poverty reduction and growth facility. Note that the funds for PRGF financing come from voluntary loans to an IMF-administered trust fund with the interest subsidy being covered largely by grants. The funds are not from quota resources, and so they are not like the loans to crisis countries, such as Argentina. For a discussion of the evolution of the IMF's agenda over time, see J. Boughton, "From Suez to Tequila: The IMF as Crisis Manager," *Economic Journal* 110, no. 460 (2000): 273–91; Anne O. Krueger, "Whither the World Bank and the IMF?" *Journal of Economic Literature* 36, no. 4 (1998): 1983–2021; and John W. Sewell, Nancy Birdsall, and Kevin Morrison, "The Right Role for the IMF in Development," ODC Policy Brief (May 2000).

19. Lending to poor countries at preferred rates was originally done under the Enhanced Structural Adjustment Facility (ESAF), which has been replaced by the Poverty Reduction and Growth Facility (PRGF).

20. See I. Vasquez, "The International Monetary Fund: Challenges and Contradictions," paper presented to the International Financial Advisory Commission, September 28, 1999, Washington, D.C.

21. Edwin M. Truman, "International Monetary Fund Reform."

22. Edwin M. Truman, "International Monetary Fund Reform." Also see Michael D. Bordo and Harold James, "The International Monetary Fund: Its Present Role in Historical Perspective," NBER Working Paper 7724 (June 2000) for why this mission creep has happened.

23. Morris Goldstein, "IMF Structural Programs," in Martin Feldstein, ed., *Economic and Financial Crises in Emerging Market Economies* (Chicago: University of Chicago Press, 2003), 363–437.

24. M. Feldstein, "Refocusing the IMF," *Foreign Affairs* 77, no. 2 (1998): 20–33.

25. Olivier Jeanne and Jeronim Zettelmeyer, "International Bailouts, Moral Hazard, and Conditionality," *Economic Policy* 16, no. 33 (2001): 409–32; Michael Mussa, "Reflections on Moral Hazard and Private Sector Involvement in the Resolution of Emerging Market Financial Crises," in Andrew G. Haldane, ed., *Fixing Financial Crises in the Twenty-First Century* (London: Routledge, 2004), 33–56; and Michael Mussa, "Reflections on the Functions and Facilities for IMF Lending." These papers explain why claims that IMF lending is a U.S. taxpayer subsidy to emerging market countries (as in International Financial Institutions Advisory Commission, *Report*) is incorrect. However, as Michael Mussa points out, IMF lending does lead to "indirect moral hazard," in that it may encourage governments to pursue bad policies or gamble for resurrection.

26. See the survey in Olivier Jeanne and Jeronim Zettelmeyer, "The Mussa Theorem: And Other Results on IMF-Induced Moral Hazard," IMF Working Paper 04/192 (October 2004), who argue that empirical tests in the literature have not been able to determine whether IMF lending has led to indications of moral hazard on market variables.

27. Nouriel Roubini and Brad Setser, *Bailouts or Bail-Ins? Responding to Financial Crises in Emerging Economies* (Washington, D.C.: Institute for International Economics, 2004).

28. See the evidence in Olivier Jeanne and Jeromin Zettelmeyer, "International Bailouts, Moral Hazard, and Conditionality."

29. This additional argument for why the IMF and World Bank continue to give loans to countries with bad policies was suggested to me by William Easterly in private correspondence. He also makes this argument in his book *The White Man's Burden: Why the West's Efforts to Aid the Rest Have Done So Much Ill and So Little Good* (New York: Penguin, 2006).

30. See William Easterly, *The White Man's Burden*.

31. William Easterly, "What Did Structural Adjustment Adjust? The Association of Policies and Growth with Repeated IMF and World Bank Adjustment Loans," *Journal of Development Economics* 76, no. 1 (2005): 1–22.

32. Michael Mussa, *Argentina and the Fund: From Triumph to Tragedy* (Washington, D.C.: Institute for International Economics, 2002).

33. In this case, the staff of the IMF opposed giving Argentina the new loan, but they were overruled by the IMF executive board.

34. The bond deal with Chavez, which helped Argentina to pay off its IMF loans, has a particularly perverse element because Argentina will pay Venezuela an interest rate more than double the 4% or so that Argentina was paying the IMF. Although the deal did not make economic sense, it has raised Kirchner's political standing in Argentina.

35. Boris Fedorov, "Open Letter to Michel Camdessus, Managing Director of the International Monetary Fund," July 9, 1999. This episode is discussed in detail in David O. Beim and Charles W. Calomiris, *Emerging Financial Markets* (Boston: McGraw-Hill Irwin, 2001).

36. See Jose De Gregorio et al., *An Independent and Accountable IMF*, Geneva Reports on the World Economy 4 (Geneva and London: International Center for Monetary and Banking Studies and Centre for Economic Policy Research, 1999).

37. See Jose De Gregorio et al., *An Independent and Accountable IMF*, and Ngaire Woods, "Accountability, Governance and the Reform of the IMF," in David Vines and Christopher L. Gilbert, eds., *The IMF and Its Critics: Reform of Global Financial Architecture* (Cambridge: Cambridge University Press, 2004), 396–416.

38. In addition, as is documented R. J. Arriazu et al., *External Evaluation of IMF Surveillance: Report by a Group of Independent Experts* (Washington D.C.: International Monetary Fund, 1999), disagreements among the staff about what policies should be adopted are not shared with the executive board.

39. Morris Goldstein, "IMF Structural Programs," 424.

40. Edwin M. Truman, "International Monetary Fund Reform."

41. Joseph E. Stiglitz, *Globalization and Its Discontents* (New York: W. W. Norton, 2002).

42. International Monetary Fund Independent Evaluation Office, *Evaluation Report: The IMF and Recent Capital Account Crises: Indonesia, Korea, Brazil* (Washington, D.C.: International Monetary Fund, 2003).

43. Jack Boorman et al., "Managing Financial Crises: The Experience in East Asia," *Carnegie-Rochester Conference Series on Public Policy* 53, no. 1 (2000): 1–67, and also the International Monetary Fund Independent Evaluation Office, *Evaluation Report: The IMF and Recent Capital Account Crises*.

44. Jason Furman and Joseph E. Stiglitz, "Economic Crises: Evidence and Insights from East Asia," *Brookings Papers on Economic Activity* 2 (1998): 1–114; Joseph E. Stiglitz, *Globalization and Its Discontents;* Jeffrey D. Sachs, "The Wrong Medicine for Asia," *New York Times,* November 3, 1997, p. 23; Jeffrey D. Sachs, "IMF Is a Power Unto Itself," *Financial Times,* December 11, 1997, p. 21; and Steven Radelet and Jeffrey D. Sachs, "The East Asian Financial Crisis: Diagnosis, Remedies and Prospects," *Brookings Papers on Economic Activity* 1 (1998): 1–74. A deposit insurance scheme was set up for small depositors, but it was insufficient to stave off the banking crisis.

45. However, this view is disputed by the International Monetary Fund Independent Evaluation Office, *Evaluation of the IMF's Approach to Capital Account Liberalization* (Washington, D.C.: International Monetary Fund, 2005), which found no evidence that the IMF pushed countries to liberalize their capital accounts faster than these countries were willing to go.

46. See Morris Goldstein, "IMF Structural Programs."

47. International Monetary Fund, *World Economic Outlook* (Washington, D.C.: International Monetary Fund, 2000).

48. See R. J. Arriazu et al., *External Evaluation of IMF Surveillance.*

49. Stanley Fischer, "Exchange Rate Regimes: Is the Bipolar View Correct?" *Journal of Economic Perspectives* 15, no. 2 (2001): 3–24.

50. Stanley Fischer, "Globalization and Its Challenges," *American Economic Review* 93, no. 2 (2003): 1–30.

51. See Edwin M. Truman, "International Monetary Fund Reform," for a discussion of the different views inside the IMF about exchange rate regimes. Also see Michael Mussa and Miguel Savastano, "The IMF Approach to Economic Stabilization," in Olivier Blanchard and Stanley Fischer, eds., *NBER Macro Annual, 1999* (Cambridge, Mass.: MIT Press, 1999), 79–128.

52. Carla Anderson Hills et al., *Safeguarding Prosperity in a Global Financial System: The Future International Financial Architecture* (Washington, D.C.: Institute for International Economics, 1999), 5.

53. I thus lean to the positions taken by Morris Goldstein in his monograph, *Managed Floating Plus,* Policy Analyses in International Economics 66 (Washington, D.C.: Institute for International Economics, 2002), who advocates flexible exchange rates, inflation targeting, and prudential measures to limit currency mismatch. Also see Edwin M. Truman, *Inflation Targeting in the World Economy* (Washington, D.C.: Institute for International Economics, 2003).

54. Geraldo Licandro and Jose Antonio Licandro, "Building the Dedollarization Agenda: Lessons from the Uruguayan Case," Central Bank of Uruguay mimeo (September 2003).

55. See Julio De Brun and Gerardo Licandro, "To Hell and Bank. Crisis Management in a Dollarized Economy: The Case of Uruguay," Central Reserve Bank of Peru and International Monetary Fund mimeo (April 2005), for a critique of the IMF's policies and for a general description of the Uruguayan crisis.

56. Adela Pellegrino and Andrea Vigorito, "Emigration and Economic Crisis: Recent Evidence from Uruguay," Universidad de la Republica, Uruguay mimeo (undated).

57. A contrary position is taken by Graham Bird and Paul Mosley, "The Role of the

IMF in Developing Countries," in David Vines and Christopher L. Gilbert, *The IMF and its Critics*, 288–315. They argue against narrowing the focus of the IMF and advocate that the IMF continue to lend long term to poor countries because it is not clear that World Bank can do it as well. The problem with their argument is that, as is discussed here, not narrowing its focus has led to the IMF's poor performance.

58. Lawrence Summers, "The Right Kind of IMF for a Stable Global Financial System," speech at the London School of Business, December 14, 1999, London. The U.S. Treasury has continued to argue for a narrowing of focus in the George W. Bush administration; see John W. Snow, *Statement on Behalf of the United States of America to the International Monetary and Financial Committee* (Washington, D.C.: International Monetary Fund, 2004).

59. Council on Foreign Relations, *Safeguarding Prosperity in a Global Financial System: The Future International Financial Architecture*. Report of an Independent Task Force Sponsored by the Council on Foreign Relations (Washington, D.C.: Institute for International Economics, 1999).

60. Overseas Development Council, "The Future Role of the IMF in Development."

61. International Financial Institutions Advisory Commission, *Report*.

62. Morris Goldstein, "IMF Structural Programs," 382, points out that narrowing the IMF's focus to crisis management "would be similar to the increasing popular practice of national central banks to announce that their primary objective is price stability."

63. See R. J. Arriazu et al., *External Evaluation of IMF Surveillance*, especially 96, 99, 100.

64. Horst Kohler, "Toward a More Focused IMF," address at the International Monetary Fund Conference, May 30, 2000, Washington, D.C.

65. Stanley Fischer, "The International Financial System: Crises and Reform," Robbins Lecture, London School of Economics, October 29–31, 2001, London, mimeo. Also see International Monetary Fund Independent Evaluation Office, *Evaluation Report: The IMF and Recent Capital Account Crises*, and Jack Boorman et al., "Managing Financial Crises."

66. See International Monetary Fund, *Review of the 2002 Conditionality Guidelines* (Washington, D.C.: International Monetary Fund, 2005).

67. Ariel Buira, "Does the IMF Need More Financial Resources?"

68. For an excellent discussion of how IMF surveillance can be improved, see Peter Isard, *Globalization and the International Financial System: What's Wrong and What Can Be Done* (Cambridge: Cambridge University Press, 2005).

69. For a discussion of FSAP, see International Monetary Fund, *Financial Sector Assessment Program—Review, Lessons, and Issues Going Forward* (Washington, D.C.: International Monetary Fund, 2003). For a discussion of ROCs, see International Monetary Fund, *International Standards—Background Paper on Strengthening Surveillance, Domestic Institutions, and International Markets* (Washington, D.C.: International Monetary Fund, 2003).

70. Eswar Prasad et al., "Effects of Financial Globalization on Developing Countries: Some Empirical Evidence," IMF mimeo (March 2003).

71. Eliminating mobility requirements and providing a greater focus on emerging market countries were recommendations in the committee I chaired with Francesco

Giavazzi and T. N. Srinivasan: International Monetary Fund, *External Evaluation of IMF Research Activities.*

72. This phrase has been paraphrased from Barry Eichengreen, *Toward a New International Architecture* (Washington, D.C.: Institute for International Economics, 1999), 16, and is consistent with the call by Morris Goldstein, *The Asian Financial Crisis*, for IMF surveillance to have more punch.

73. This point is also made in Olivier Jeanne and Jeromin Zettelmeyer, "International Bailouts, Moral Hazard, and Conditionality"; Council of Foreign Relations, *Safeguarding Prosperity in a Global Financial System;* and Peter Isard, *Globalization and the International Financial System.* Jonathan D. Ostry and Jeromin Zettelmeyer, "Strengthening IMF Crisis Prevention," IMF Working Paper 05/206 (November 2005), outline a specific proposal for how IMF surveillance can provide stronger incentives for countries to follow good policies. It involves a surveillance rating on the quality of a country's policies, which would be made publicly available, and a link between this rating and the availability of IMF funds.

74. International Monetary Fund, *The Fund's Transparency Policy—Issues and Next Steps* (Washington, D.C.: International Monetary Fund, 2003).

75. This is advocated by Jose De Gregorio et al., *An Independent and Accountable IMF;* Barry Eichengreen, "Financial Stability," paper prepared for the International Task Force on Global Public Goods (December 2004); and the International Monetary Fund Independent Evaluation Office, *The IMF and Recent Capital Account Crises*, among others.

76. This is the approach recommended by the International Financial Institutions Advisory Commission, *Report.*

77. This point comes from Peter Isard, *Globalization and the International Financial System.*

78. See Edwin M. Truman, "International Monetary Fund Reform."

79. Along these lines, Peter B. Kenen, *The International Financial Architecture: What's New? What's Missing?* (Washington, D.C.: Institute for International Finance, 2001), suggests that the IMF and World Bank would negotiate contracts with governments that would describe in detail the financial sector reforms to be completed over, say, a period of five to seven years. The IMF and the World Bank would monitor the country's progress, and if the country was in compliance, it would be promised easier access to IMF loans if the need arose. In addition, the contract and the progress made on it would be published, so market participants would be able to provide incentives for successful completion.

80. Jose De Gregorio et al., *An Independent and Accountable IMF.*

81. Timothy Lane, "Tension in the Role of the IMF and Directions for Reform," *World Economics* 6, no. 2 (2005): 47–66; Miles Kahler, "Internal Governance and IMF Performance," paper presented at the Institute for International Economics Conference on IMF Reform, September 23, 2005, www.iie.com/prog_imf_reform.cfm, and Daniel K. Tarullo, "The Role of the IMF in Sovereign Debt Restructuring," *Chicago Journal of International Law* 6, no. 1 (2005): 289–311.

82. Edwin M. Truman, "Rearranging IMF Chairs and Shares," in Edwin M. Truman, ed., *Reforming the IMF for the Twenty-First Century.* In a controversial recent speech, Mervyn King, the governor of the Bank of England (Mervyn King, "Reform of the International

Monetary Fund," speech made at the Indian Council for Research on International Economic Relations [ICRIER], New Delhi, February 20, 2006), has suggested that greater representation be given to emerging market countries and that IMF surveillance be more focused. He also suggested that the IMF be made more independent by converting the executive board into a nonresident board overseeing the IMF's management, which would be given more autonomy.

83. Dani Rodrik, "Growth Strategies," NBER Working Paper 10050 (October 2003), 3.

Chapter Twelve   What Can the Advanced Countries Do?

1. For example, these include the IMF's *Special Data Dissemination Standard, General Data Dissemination Standard, Code of Good Practices on Fiscal Transparency, Code of Good Practices on Transparency in Monetary and Financial Policies;* the Basel Committee on Bank Supervision's *Core Principles of Effective Banking Supervision;* the International Organization of Securities Commission's *Objectives and Principles for Securities Regulation;* the International Association of Insurance Supervisor's *Insurance Supervisory Principles;* the Committee on Payments and Settlements Systems' *Core Principles for Systematically Important Payment Systems;* the Organisation for Economic Co-operation and Development's *Principles of Corporate Governance;* the International Accounting Standard Committee's *International Accounting Standards;* and the International Federation of Accountants' *International Standards on Auditing.*

2. For example, see Barry Eichengreen and Richard Portes, *Crisis? What Crisis? Orderly Workouts for Sovereign Debtors* (London: Centre for Economic and Policy Research, 1995) and Barry Eichengreen, *Financial Crises and What to Do about Them* (New York: Oxford University Press, 2002).

3. Jeffrey D. Sachs, "Do We Need an International Lender of Last Resort?", presented as the Frank D. Graham Lecture, Princeton University, Princeton, N.J., April 20, 1994; Anne O. Krueger, "International Financial Architecture for 2002: A New Approach to Sovereign Debt Restructuring," address given at the National Economists Club Annual Members' Dinner, American Enterprise Institute, Washington, D.C., November 26, 2001; George Soros, *George Soros on Globalization* (New York: Public Affairs Books, 2002).

4. See "Appendix: A Chronology of Official Initiatives," in Barry Eichengreen, *Financial Crises and What to Do about Them,* 159–73, for a discussion of the numerous initiatives on international financial architecture.

5. For example, see Barry Eichengreen, *Financial Crises and What to Do about Them,* and Andrei Shleifer, "Will the Sovereign Debt Market Survive?" *American Economic Review* 93, no. 2 (2003): 85–90, for a critique of proposals for an international bankruptcy court.

6. For useful discussion of reforms to international financial architecture, see Barry Eichengreen's two books, *International Financial Architecture* (Washington, D.C.: Institute for International Economics, 1999) and *Financial Crises and What to Do about Them;* Carla Anderson Hills, Morris Goldstein, Peter G. Petersen, and Council on Foreign Relations, *Safeguarding Prosperity in a Global Financial System: The Future International Financial Architecture* (Washington, D.C.: Institute for International Economics, 1999); Peter

Kenen, *The International Financial Architecture: What's New? What's Missing?* (Washington, D.C.: Institute for International Economics, 2001); and Peter Isard, *Globalization and the International Financial System: What's Wrong and What Can Be Done* (Cambridge: Cambridge University Press, 2005).

7. See Guillermo A. Calvo and Carmen M. Reinhart, "When Capital Inflows Come to a Sudden Stop: Consequences and Policy Actions," in Peter Kenen and Alexander Swoboda, eds., *Reforming the International Monetary System* (Washington, D.C.: International Monetary Fund, 2000), 175–201.

8. These figures are for official development assistance for 2003 and come from the United Nations *Common Database,* United Nations Statistics Division, New York, 2004.

9. John W. McArthur, Guido Schmidt-Traub, Margaret Kruk, Chandrika Bahadur, Michael Faye, and Gordon McCord, "Ending Africa's Poverty Trap," *Brookings Papers on Economic Activity* 1 (2004): 117–216.

10. Jeffrey D. Sachs, *The End of Poverty: Economic Possibilities of Our Time* (New York: Penguin Press, 2005).

11. For an excellent nontechnical survey of the effectiveness of aid, see William Easterly, *The White Man's Burden: Why the West's Efforts to Aid the Rest Have Done So Much Ill and So Little Good* (New York: Penguin, 2006).

12. William Easterly, "Tone Deaf on Africa," Week in Review, *New York Times,* July 3, 2005, p. 10.

13. William Easterly, *The Elusive Quest for Growth: Economists' Adventures and Misadventures in the Tropics* (Cambridge, Mass.: MIT Press, 2001).

14. Easterly has also been directly critical of Sachs's book *The End of Poverty.* See William Easterly, "A Modest Proposal," *Washington Post,* March 13, 2005, p. BW3. Also see the amusing exchange of letters between Easterly and Sachs: Jeffrey D. Sachs, "Up from Poverty," *Washington Post,* March 27, 2005, p. BW12, and William Easterly, "Reply," *Washington Post,* March 27, 2005, p. BW12.

15. William Easterly, *The White Man's Burden.* Easterly also points out that the IMF and the World Bank knew about Mobutu's stealing, having sent a German banker, Erwin Blumenthal, to check the books of the Central Bank of Zaire in 1978–79; he documented and reported back on the amounts of Mobuto's theft.

16. Daron Acemoglu, James A. Robinson, and Thierry Verdier, "Kleptocracy and Divide-and-Rule: A Model of Personal Rule," National Bureau of Economic Research Working Paper 10136 (December 2003).

17. William Easterly, *The Elusive Quest for Growth;* William Easterly, "Can Foreign Aid Buy Growth?" *Journal of Economic Perspectives* 17, no. 3 (2003): 23–48; Jakob Svensson, "Why Conditional Aid Does Not Work and What Can Be Done about It," *Journal of Development Economics* 70 (2003): 381–402; Robert Lensink and Howard White "Are There Negative Returns to Aid?" *Journal of Development Studies* 37, no. 6 (2001): 42–65.

18. International Financial Institutions Advisory Commission, *Report* (Washington, D.C.: International Financial Institution Advisory Commission, 2000).

19. See Jeffrey D. Sachs, "Can Extreme Poverty Be Eliminated?" *Scientific American,* September 2005, pp. 55–66; Jeffrey D. Sachs, "Four Easy Pieces," *New York Times,* June 25, 2005, p. 15; and Xavier Sala-i-Martin and Elsa V. Artadi, "The Economic Tragedy of

the XXth Century: Growth in Africa," in Ernesto Hernandes-Cata, ed., *The African Competitiveness Report, World Economic Forum, Geneva*, March 2004, 1–19.

20. See Craig Burnside and David Dollar, "Aid, Policies, and Growth," *American Economic Review* 90, no. 4 (2000): 847–68. William Easterly, Ross Levine, and David Rodman, "New Data, New Doubts: A Comment on Burnside and Dollar's 'Aid, Policies, and Growth' (2000)," National Bureau of Economic Research Working Paper 9846 (July 2003), and Raghuram Rajan and Arvind Subramanian, "Aid and Growth: What Does the Cross-Country Evidence Really Show?" National Bureau of Economic Research Paper 11513 (July 2005), however, find that Burnside and Dollar's results are not robust.

21. Barry Eichengreen and Marc Uzan, "The Marshall Plan: Economic Effects and Implications for Eastern Europe and the Former USSR," *Economic Policy* 14 (1992): 13–77.

22. See Guillermo Calvo, Alejandro Izquierdo, and Luis-Fernando Mejia, "On the Empirics of Sudden Stops: The Relevance of Balance-Sheet Effects," National Bureau of Economic Research Working Paper 10520 (May 2004); Guillermo A. Calvo, Alejandro Izquierdo, and Ernesto Talvi, "Sudden Stops, the Real Exchange Rate, and Fiscal Sustainability: Argentina's Lessons," National Bureau of Economic Research Working Paper 9828 (July 2003); Guillermo A. Calvo and Ernesto Talvi, "Sudden Stop, Financial Factors and Economic Collapse in Latin America: Learning from Argentina and Chile," National Bureau of Economic Research Working Paper 11153 (February 2005); Sebastian Edwards, "Thirty Years of Current Account Imbalances, Current Account Reversals and Sudden Stops," National Bureau of Economic Research Working Paper 10276 (January 2004); Sebastian Edwards, "Financial Openness, Sudden Stops and Current Account Reversals," National Bureau of Economic Research Working Paper 10277 (January 2004); and Jeffrey A. Frankel and Eduardo A. Cavallo, "Does Openness to Trade Make Countries More Vulnerable to Sudden Stops or Less? Using Gravity to Establish Causality," National Bureau of Economic Research Working Paper 10957 (December 2004).

23. Martin Wolf, *Why Globalization Works* (New Haven, Conn.: Yale University Press, 2004), 213.

24. Oxfam, *Rigid Rules and Double Standards: Trade Globalization and the Fight Against Poverty* (Oxford: Oxfam International, 2002). Cited in Wolf, *Why Globalization Works*, 213.

25. Scott C. Bradford, Paul L. E. Grieco, and Gary Clyde Hufbauer, "The Payoff to America from Global Intergration," in C. Fred Bergsten, ed., *The United States and the World Economy: Foreign Economic Policy for the Next Decade* (Washington, D.C.: Institute for International Economics, 2005), 65–109.

26. An excellent nontechnical discussion of the myths surrounding outsourcing can be found in Martin N. Baily and Dianna Farrell, "Is Your Job Headed for Bangalore? The Myths and Realities of Outsourcing," *Milken Institute Review* 4 (2004): 33–41.

27. In his campaign for president in 2004, Senator John Kerry called the heads of American companies who outsource jobs "Benedict Arnold CEOs."

28. Michael M. Phillips, "More Work Is Outsourced to U.S. Than Away from It, Data Show," *Wall Street Journal*, March 15, 2004, pp. A2, A4.

29. For a discussion of programs to assist workers who are displaced by trade liberalization, see Lori G. Kletzer and Howard Rosen, "Easing the Adjustment on U.S. Workers," in C. Fred Bergsten, ed., *The United States and the World Economy*, 313–43.

30. These estimates are from Gary Clyde Hufbaur and Kimberly Ann Elliott, *Measuring the Costs of Protection in the United States* (Washington, D.C.: Institute for International Economics, 1994).

Chapter Thirteen   *Getting Financial Globalization Right*

1. William Easterly, in his book *The White Man's Burden: Why the West's Efforts to Aid the Rest Have Done So Much Ill and So Little Good* (New York: Penguin, 2006), points out that when Eastern European countries adopted Western-drafted laws as part of the conditions to receive foreign aid, the new laws often did not work well. For example, Albania passed a bankruptcy law in 1994, yet only one case ever made it to the Albanian courts, even after a Ponzi scheme led to horrendous losses for Albanian investors in the mid-1990s.

2. Pierre-Olivier Gourinchas and Olivier Jeanne, "Capital Mobility and Reform," University of California, Berkeley mimeo (October 2005), provide a theoretical model that is consistent with the arguments in this book. It shows that capital mobility encourages institutional reform because it enhances the benefits of good policies and helps lock in political support for reforms. However, capital mobility also makes it more likely that there would be capital flight, which could trigger a financial crisis that destroys the support for reform.

3. Thorsten Beck et al., "Finance and the Source of Growth," *Journal of Financial Economics* 58, no. 1–2 (2000): 261–300; William Easterly and Ross Levine, "It's Not Factor Accumulation: Stylized Facts and Growth Models," *World Bank Economic Review* 15, no. 2 (2001): 177–219; and Ross Levine, "Finance and Growth: Theory and Evidence," in Philippe Aghion and Steven Durlauf, eds., *Handbook of Economic Growth*, vol. 1, part A (Amsterdam: North-Holland, 2005), 865–934.

4. William Easterly, *The Elusive Quest for Growth: Economists' Adventures and Misadventures in the Tropics* (Cambridge, Mass.: MIT Press, 2001), and Willliam Easterly, *The White Man's Burden.*

5. Joseph E. Stiglitz, *Globalization and Its Discontents* (New York: W. W. Norton), 89–132.

6. The quote from Emma Lazarus's famous poem, which is emblazoned on the Statue of Liberty, is: "Give me your tired, your poor, Your huddled masses yearning to breathe free, The wretched refuse of your teeming shore. Send these, the homeless, tempest-tost to me, I lift my lamp beside the golden door."

7. Jerry Caprio in personal correspondence suggested this way of expressing this point.

8. Income inequality can also play an important role in hindering institutional development, which this book argues is key to economic growth. For example, see Stanley L. Engerman and Kenneth L. Sokoloff, "Factor Endowments, Institutions, and Differential Paths of Growth among New World Economies: A View from Economic Historians of the United States," in Stephen Haber, ed., *How Latin America Fell Behind: Essays on the Economic Histories of Brazil and Mexico, 1800–1914* (Stanford, Calif.: Stanford University Press, 1997), 260–304. For an excellent nontechnical discussion of the other factors behind economic growth see David N. Weil, *Economic Growth* (Boston: Addison-Wesley, 2005).

9. For a discussion of the recent literature on the politics of institutional development, see Daron Acemoglu et al., "Institutions as the Fundamental Cause of Long-Term Growth," in Philippe Aghion and Steven N. Durlauf, eds., *Handbook of Economic Growth*, vol. 1, part A (Amsterdam: North-Holland, 2005), 385–472, and Randall Morck et al., "Corporate Governance, Economic Entrenchment and Growth," *Journal of Economic Literature* 43, no. 3 (2005): 655–720.

10. See Carlos Diaz-Alejandro, "Good-Bye Financial Repression, Hello Financial Crash," *Journal of Development Economics* 19, no. 1–2 (1985): 1–24. For a more recent discussion and postmortem of the Chilean financial crisis, see Kevin Cowan and Jose De Gregorio, "International Borrowing, Capital Controls and the Exchange Rate: Lessons from Chile," NBER Working Paper 11382 (May 2005).

11. These data are from Gerard Caprio, Jr., et al., *Banking Crises Data Base* (October 2003) at http://www1.worldbank.org/finance/html/database_sfd.html.

12. For an excellent discussion of Chilean reforms and the political economy behind the reform process, see Romulo Chumacero et al., "Understanding Chilean Reforms," Banco Central de Chile mimeo (September 2004).

13. Gerard Caprio, Jr., "Banking on Crises: Expensive Lessons from Recent Financial Crises," World Bank Working Paper 1979 (September 1998).

14. Jose De Gregorio et al., "Controls on Capital Inflows: Do They Work?" *Journal of Development Economics* 61, no. 1 (2000): 59–83, and Sebastian Edwards, "How Effective Are Controls on Capital Inflows? An Evaluation of Chile's Experience," University of California, Los Angeles, mimeo (June 1999).

15. The rule specifies that the budget should have a surplus of 1% of GDP when GDP and the price of copper, a major export for Chile, are at their trend levels, but allows the budget balance to reflect deviations of GDP and copper prices from their trend. As a result, the Chilean government budget surplus has ranged between –1.5% and an estimated 4% of GDP in recent years.

16. Oscar Landerretche et al., "Inflation Targets and Stabilization in Chile," Central Bank of Chile Working Paper 55 (December 1999).

17. Frederic S. Mishkin and Miguel Savastano, "Monetary Policy Strategies for Emerging Market Countries: Lessons from Latin America," *Comparative Economic Studies* 44, no. 2 (2002): 45–83.

References

Abe, Makoto, and Mamoko Kawakami. 1997. "A Distributive Comparison of Enterprise Size in Korea and Taiwan." *Developing Economies* 35(4): 382–400.

Abiad, Abdul, Nienke Oomes, and Kenichi Ueda. 2005. "The Quality Effect: Does Financial Liberalization Improve the Allocation of Capital?" Paper presented at the Journal of Banking and Finance/World Bank Conference on Globalization and Financial Services in Emerging Market Countries, June 20–21, Washington, D.C.

Acemoglu, Daron, Simon Johnson, and James A. Robinson. 2001. "The Colonial Origins of Comparative Development: An Empirical Investigation." *American Economic Review* 91(5): 1369–1401.

Acemoglu, Daron, James A. Robinson, and Thierry Verdier. 2003. "Kleptocracy and Divide-and-Rule: A Model of Personal Rule." NBER Working Paper 10136 (December).

Acemoglu, Daron, Simon Johnson, and James A. Robinson. 2005. "Institutions as the Fundamental Cause of Long-Term Growth." In Philippe Aghion and Steven N. Durlauf, eds. *Handbook of Economic Growth,* vol. 1, part A. Amsterdam: North-Holland, 385–472.

Ades, Alberto, and Rafael Di Tella. 1999. "Rents, Competition and Corruption." *American Economic Review* 89(4): 982–94.

Aghion, Philippe, and Patrick Bolton. 1997. "A Trickle-Down Theory of Growth and Development with Debt Overhang." *Review of Economic Studies* 64(219): 151–72.

Aghion, Philippe, Peter Howitt, and David Mayer-Foulkes. 2005. "The Effect of Financial Development on Convergence: Theory and Evidence." *Quarterly Journal of Economics* 120(1): 173–222.

Aizenman, Joshua. 2003. "On the Hidden Links between Financial and Trade Opening." University of Santa Cruz mimeo (August).

Aizenman, Joshua, and Reuven Glick. 2005. "Pegged Exchange Rate Regimes—A Trap?" NBER Working Paper 11652 (September).

Albouy, David. 2005. "The Colonial Origins of Comparative Development: A Re-examination Based on Improved Settler Mortality Data." University of California, Berkeley, mimeo (February).

Alden, A. Edward, and Alan Beattie. 2002. "Comment and Analysis—Keeping the Faith." *Financial Times,* London edition, May 6, p. 16.

Alesina, Alberto, Ricardo Hausmann, Rudolf Hommes, and Ernesto Stein. 1996. "Budget Institutions and Fiscal Performance in Latin America." NBER Working Paper 5586 (May).

Alesina, Alberto, Vittorio Grilli, and Gian Maria Milesi-Ferretti. 2004. "The Political Economy of Capital Controls." In Leonardo Leiderman and Assaf Razin, eds., *Capital Mobility: The Impact on Consumption, Investment and Growth.* Cambridge: Cambridge University Press.

Alfaro, Laura, Sebnem Kalemli-Ozcan, and Vadym Volosovych. 2005. "Capital Flows in a Globalized World: The Role of Policies and Institutions." NBER Working Paper 11696 (October).

———. 2005. "Why Doesn't Capital Flow from Rich to Poor Countries? An Empirical Investigation." NBER Working Paper 11901 (December).

Allen, Mark, Christopher Rosenberg, Christian Keller, Brad Setser, and Nouriel Roubini. 2002. "A Balance-Sheet Approach to Financial Crisis." IMF Working Paper 02/210 (December).

Amsden, Alice. 1989. *Asia's Next Giant: South Korea and Late Industrialization.* Oxford: Oxford University Press.

Anderson, Palle, and David Gruen. 1995. "Macroeconomic Policies and Growth." In Palle Anderson, Jacqui Dwyer, and David Gruen, eds., *Productivity and Growth.* Sydney: Reserve Bank of Australia, 279–319.

Anderson Hills, Carla, Morris Goldstein, Peter G. Petersen, and Council on Foreign Relations. 1999. *Safeguarding Prosperity in a Global Financial System: The Future International Financial Architecture.* Washington, D.C.: Institute for International Economics.

Arriazu, R. J., John Crow, and N. Thygesen. 1999. *External Evaluation of IMF Surveillance: Report by a Group of Independent Experts.* Washington D.C.: International Monetary Fund.

Arteta, C., Barry Eichengreen, and Charles Wyplosz. 2001. "When Does Capital Account Liberalization Help More Than It Hurts?" NBER Working Paper 8414 (August).

Associated Press. 2006. "Argentina Exports Suspension Now in Effect" (March 10).

Bagehot, Walter. 1915. *Lombard Street: A Description of the Money Market.* London: Smith, Elder and Co.

Baig, Taimur, and Ilan Goldfajn. 2002. "Monetary Policy in the Aftermath of Currency Crises: The Case of Asia." *Review of International Economics,* vol. 10(1): 92–112.

Bailliu, Jeannine. 2000. "Private Capital Flows, Financial Development, and Economic Growth in Developing Countries." Bank of Canada Working Paper 2000-15 (July).

Baily, Martin N., and Dianna Farrell. 2004. "Is Your Job Headed for Bangalore? The Myths and Realities of Outsourcing." *Milken Institute Review* 4: 33–41.

Bairoch, Paul. 1993. *Economics and World History.* London: Harvester-Wheatsheaf.

Baldacci, Emanuele, Luiz de Melo, and Gabriela Inchauste. 2002. "Financial Crises, Poverty and Income Distribution." *Finance and Development* 39(2): 24–27.

Baldwin, Richard E., and Philippe Martin. 1999. "Two Waves of Globalisation: Superficial Similarities, Fundamental Differences." NBER Working Paper 6904 (January).

Banco Central de la Republica Argentina. 1997. "Main Features of the Regulatory Framework of the Argentine Financial System." Banco Central de la Republica Argentina mimeo (April).

Banerjee, Abhijit, and Andrew Newman. 1993. "Occupational Choice and the Process of Development." *Journal of Political Economy* 101(2): 274–98.

Bank for International Settlements. 1976. *47th Annual Report.* Basel: Bank for International Settlements (June).

———. 2004. *74th Annual Report.* Basel: Bank for International Settlements (June).

Barajas, Adolfo, Roberto Steiner, and Natalia Salazar. 2000. "The Impact of Liberalization and Foreign Investment in Colombia's Financial Sector." *Journal of Development Economics* 63(1): 157–96.

Barth, James R., Gerard Caprio, Jr., and Ross Levine. 2001. "Banking Systems around the Globe: Do Regulation and Ownership Affect Performance and Stability?" In Frederic S. Mishkin, ed., *Prudential Regulation and Supervision: What Works and What Doesn't.* Chicago: University of Chicago Press, 31–97.

Barth, James R., Gerard Caprio, Jr., and Ross Levine. 2004. "Bank Regulation and Supervision: What Works Best?" *Journal of Financial Intermediation* 13, no. 2 (April): 205–248.

Barth, James R., Gerard Caprio, Jr., and Ross Levine. 2006. *Rethinking Bank Regulation and Supervision: Til Angels Govern.* New York: Cambridge University Press.

Barth, James R., Rob Koepp, and Zhongfei Zhou. 2004. "Institute View" *Milken Institute Review* 2002(2): 83–92.

Bartolini, Leonardo, and Allan Drazen. 1997. "Capital Account Liberalization as a Signal." *American Economic Review* 87(1): 138–54.

Beck, Thorsten, and Ross Levine. 2004. "Legal Institutions and Financial Development." NBER Working Paper 10417 (April).

Beck, Thorsten, Ross Levine, and Norman Loayza. 2000. "Finance and the Sources of Growth." *Journal of Financial Economics* 58(1–2): 261–300.

Beck, Thorsten, Asli Demirguc-Kunt, and Ross Levine. 2004. "Finance, Inequality and Poverty: Cross-Country Evidence." World Bank mimeo (April).

———. 2005. "Bank Supervision and Corruption in Lending." NBER Working Paper 11498 (July).

Beim, David O., and Charles W. Calomiris. 2001. *Emerging Financial Markets.* Boston: McGraw-Hill Irwin.

Bekaert, Geert, and Campbell R. Harvey. 2000. "Foreign Speculators and Emerging Equity Markets." *Journal of Finance* 55(2): 562–613.

Bekaert, Geert, Campbell R. Harvey, and Robin L. Lumsdaine. 1998. "Dating the Integration of World Equity Markets." NBER Working Paper 6724 (September).

Bekaert, Geert, Campbell R. Harvey, and R. Lundblad. 2001. "Does Financial Liberalization Spur Growth?" NBER Working Paper 8245 (September).

Berkowitz, David, Katharina Pistor, and Jean-François Richard. 2000. "Economic Development, Legality and the Transplant Effect." Harvard University Center for International Development Working Paper 39 (March).

Bernanke, Ben S., and Mark Gertler. 1989. "Agency Costs, Net Worth and Business Fluctuations." *American Economic Review* 79(1): 14–31.

———. 1995. "Inside the Black Box: The Credit Channel of Monetary Transmission." *Journal of Economic Perspectives* 9(4): 27–48.

Bernanke, Ben S., Thomas Laubach, Frederic S. Mishkin, and Adam Posen. 1999. *Inflation Targeting: Lessons from the International Experience.* Princeton, N.J.: Princeton University Press.

Bertranou, Fabio M., Rafael Rofman, and Carlos O. Grushka. 2003. "From Reform to Crisis: Argentina's Pension System." *International Social Security Review* 56(2): 103–14.

Bhagwati, Jagdish. 1998. "The Capital Myth: The Difference between Trade in Widgets and Dollars." *Foreign Affairs* 77(3): 7–13.

———. 2002. *The Winds of the Hundred Days: How Washington Mismanaged Globalization.* Cambridge, Mass.: MIT Press.

———. 2004. *In Defense of Globalization.* New York: Oxford University Press.

Bird, Graham, and Paul Mosley. 2004. "The Role of the IMF in Developing Countries." In David Vines and Christopher L. Gilbert, eds., *The IMF and Its Critics: Reform of Global Financial Architecture.* Cambridge, Cambridge University Press, 288–315.

Blejer, Mario. 2005. "Managing Argentina's 2002 Financial Crisis." In Timothy Besley and Roberto Zahga, eds., *Development Challenges in the 1990s: Leading Policymakers Speak from Experience.* Washington, D.C.: World Bank and Oxford University Press, 167–77.

Bloomberg News. 2005. "Beijing's Fight to Cool Economy Gets Harder." May 20.

Bluestein, Paul. 2001. *The Chastening.* New York: Public Affairs.

Boorman, Jack, Timothy Lane, Marianne Schulze-Ghattas, Ales Bulir, Attish Gosh, Javier Hamann, Alex Mourmouras, and Stephen Phillips. 2000. "Managing Financial Crises: The Experience in East Asia." *Carnegie-Rochester Conference Series on Public Policy* 53(1): 1–67.

Bordo, Michael D., and Barry Eichengreen. 2002. "Crises Now and Then: What Lessons from the Last Era of Globalization?" NBER Working Paper 8716 (January).

Bordo, Michael D., and Harold James. 2000. "The International Monetary Fund: Its Present Role in Historical Perspective." NBER Working Paper 7724 (June).

Bordo, Michael D., and Christopher M. Meissner. 2005. "The Role of Foreign Currency Debt in Financial Crises: 1880–1913 vs. 1972–1997." NBER Working Paper 11897 (December).

Bordo, Michael D., Barry Eichengreen, Daniela Klingebiel, and Maria Soledad Martinez-Peria. 2001. "Financial Crises: Lessons from the Last 120 Years." *Economic Policy* 16(32): 53–82.

Boughton, J. 2000. "From Suez to Tequila: The IMF as Crisis Manager." *Economic Journal* 110(460): 273–91.

Bourguignon, François, and Christian Morrison. 2002. "Inequality among World Citizens." *American Economic Review* 92(4): 727–44.

Bourguignon, François, Anne-Sophie Robilliard, and Sherman Robinson. 2001. "Crisis and Income Distribution: A Micro-Macro Model for Indonesia." World Bank mimeo (June).

Bourguignon, François, Diana Coyle, Raquel Fernandez, Francesco Giavazzi, Dalia Marin, Kevin O'Rourke, Richard Portes, Paul Seabright, Anthony Venables, Thierry Verdier, and L. Alan Walters. 2002. *Making Sense of Globalization: A Guide to the Economic Issues.* CEPR Policy Paper 8 (July).

Boyd, John H., and Mark Gertler. 1993. "U.S. Commercial Banking: Trends, Cycles and Policy." In Olivier Blanchard and Stanley Fischer, eds., *NBER Macroeconomics Annual.* Cambridge, Mass.: MIT Press, 319–68.

Boyd, John H., Ross Levine, and Bruce D. Smith. 2001. "The Impact of Inflation on Financial Sector Performance." *Journal of Monetary Economics* 47(2): 221–48.

Boyreau-Debray, Genevieve, and Shang-Jin Wei. 2004. "Pitfalls of a State-Dominated Financial System: The Case of China." CEPR Discussion Paper 4471 (July).

Bradford, Scott C., Paul L. E. Grieco, and Gary Clyde Hufbauer. 2005. "The Payoff to America from Global Intergration." In C. Fred Bergsten, ed., *The United States and the World Economy: Foreign Economic Policy for the Next Decade.* Washington, D.C.: Institute for International Economics, 65–109.

Braudel, Fernand. 1984. *Civilisation and Capitalism, 15th–18th Century: The Perspective of the World,* vol. 3. New York: Harper and Row.

Broda, Christian, and Eduardo Levy-Yeyati. 2003. "Endogenous Deposit Dollarization." Federal Reserve Bank of New York Staff Reports 160 (February).

Broda, Christian, and Cedric Tille. 2003. "Coping with Terms-of-Trade Shocks in Developing Countries." *Federal Reserve Bank of New York Current Issues in Economics and Finance* 9(1): 1–7.

Brown, Stephen J., William N. Goetzman, and James Park. 1998. "Hedge Funds and the Asian Currency Crisis of 1997." NBER Working Paper 6427 (February).

Buira, Ariel. 2005. "Does the IMF Need More Financial Resources?" Paper presented at the Institute for International Economics Conference on IMF Reform, September 23, Washington, D.C. www.iie.com/prog_imf_reform.cfm.

Burnside, Craig, and David Dollar. 2000. "Aid, Policies and Growth." *American Economic Review* 90(4): 847–68.

Burnside, Craig, Martin Eichenbaum, and Sergio Rebelo. 2001. "On the Fiscal Implications of Twin Crises." NBER Working Paper 8277 (May).

———. 2001. "Prospective Deficits and the Asian Currency Crisis." *Journal of Political Economy* 109: 1155–97.

Caballero, Ricardo, and Arvind Krishnamurthy. 2003. "Excessive Dollar Debt: Financial Development and Underinsurance." *Journal of Finance* 58(2): 867–93.

Calomiris, Charles W. 1998. "Evaluation of Argentina's Banking Sector, 1991–1998." Columbia University mimeo.

———. 2002. *A Globalist Manifesto for Public Policy.* London: Institute of Economic Affairs.

Calomiris, Charles W., and R. Glenn Hubbard. 1989. "Price Flexibility, Credit Availability and Economic Fluctuations: Evidence from the United States, 1894–1909." *Quarterly Journal of Economics* 104(3): 429–52.

———. 1990. "Firm Heterogeneity, Internal Finance, and 'Credit Rationing.' " *Economic Journal* 100(399): 90–104.

Calomiris, Charles W., and Andrew Powell. 2001. "Can Emerging Market Bank Regulators Establish Credible Discipline? The Case of Argentina, 1992–99." In Frederic S. Mishkin, ed., *Prudential Supervision: What Works and What Doesn't*. Chicago: University of Chicago Press, 147–97.

Calomiris, Charles W., Daniela Klingebiel, and Luc Laeven. 2005. "A Taxonomy of Financial Crisis Restructuring Mechanisms: Cross-Country Experience and Policy Implications." In Luc Laeven, ed., *Systemic Financial Distress*. New York: Cambridge University Press, 25–76.

Calvo, Guillermo A., and Frederic S. Mishkin. 2003. "The Mirage of Exchange Rate Regimes for Emerging Market Countries." *Journal of Economic Perspectives* 17(4): 99–118.

Calvo, Guillermo A., and Carmen M. Reinhart. 2000. "When Capital Inflows Come to a Sudden Stop: Consequences and Policy Options." In Peter Kenen and Alexander Swoboda, eds., *Reforming the International Monetary System*. Washington, D.C.: International Monetary Fund, 175–201.

———. 2002. "Fixing for Your Life." NBER Working Paper 8006 (November).

Calvo, Guillermo A., and Ernesto Talvi. 2005. "Sudden Stop, Financial Factors and Economic Collapse in Latin America: Learning from Argentina and Chile." NBER Working Paper 11153 (February).

Calvo, Guillermo A., Leonardo Leiderman, and Carmen M. Reinhart. 1994. "The Capital Inflows Problem: Concepts and Issues." *Contemporary Economic Policy* 12(3): 54–66.

Calvo, Guillermo A., Alejandro Izquierdo, and Ernesto Talvi. 2003. "Sudden Stops, the Real Exchange Rate, and Fiscal Sustainability: Argentina's Lessons." NBER Working Paper 9828 (July).

Calvo, Guillermo A., Alejandro Izquierdo, and Luis-Fernando Mejia. 2004. "On the Empirics of Sudden Stops: The Relevance of Balance-Sheet Effects." NBER Working Paper 10520 (May).

Camdessus, Michelle. 1995. "Drawing Lessons from the Mexican Crisis: Preventing and Resolving Financial Crises—The Role of the IMF." Address at the 25th Washington Conference of the Council of the Americas on "Staying the Course: Forging a Free Trade Area in the Americas," May 22, Washington D.C.

Caprio, Gerard, Jr. 1998. "Banking on Crises: Expensive Lessons from Recent Financial Crises." World Bank Working Paper 1979 (September).

Caprio, Gerard, Jr., and Patrick Honohan. 1999. "Restoring Banking Stability: Beyond Supervised Capital Requirements." *Journal of Economic Perspectives* 13(4): 43–64.

———. 2000. "Finance in a World of Volatility." World Bank mimeo.

Caprio, Gerard, Jr., and Maria Soledad Martinez-Peria. 2000. "Avoiding Disaster: Policies to Reduce the Risk of Banking Crises." World Bank mimeo and Egyptian Center for Economic Studies Working Paper 47.

Caprio, Gerard, Jr., Daniela Klingebiel, Luc Laewen, and Guillermo Noguera. 2003. *Banking Crises Data Base* (October). http://www1.worldbank.org/finance/html/database_sfd.html.

Chang, Ha-Sung. 2002. "Korea Discount and Corporate Governance." *Corporate Governance Studies* 1: 56–71.

Chen, Shaohua, and Martin Ravallion. 2001. "How Did the World's Poorest Fare in the 1990s?" *Review of Income and Wealth* 47(3): 283–300.

Chinn, Menzie D. 2004. "The Compatibility of Capital Controls and Financial Development: A Selective Survey and Empirical Evidence." In Gordon DeBrouwer and Yunjong Wang, eds., *Financial Governance in East Asia: Policy Dialogue, Surveillance, and Cooperation.* London: Routledge, 216–38.

Chinn, Menzie D., and Hiro Ito. 2002. "Capital Account Liberalization, Institutions and Financial Development: Cross Country Evidence." NBER Working Paper 8967 (June).

Cho, Hyuk, Bong-Chan Ko, and Rene Stulz. 1998. "Do Foreign Investors Destabilize Stock Markets? The Korean Experience in 1997." NBER Working Paper 6661 (July).

Cho, Yoon-Je. 1989. "Finance and Development: The Korean Approach." *Oxford Review of Economic Policy* 5(4): 88–102.

Cho, Yoon-Je, and Joon-Hyung Kim. 1997. *Credit Policies and the Industrialization of Korea.* Seoul: Korea Development Institute Press.

Chumacero, Romulo, Rodrigo Fuentes, Rolf Luders, and Joaquin Vial. 2004. "Understanding Chilean Reforms." Banco Central de Chile mimeo (September).

Claessens, Stijn, and Marion Jansen, eds. 2000. *The Internationalization of Financial Services: Issues and Lessons for Developing Countries.* Boston: Kluwer Academic.

Claessens, Stijn, and Leora Klapper. 2005. "Bankruptcy around the World: Explanations of Its Relative Use." *American Law and Economic Review* 7(1): 253–83.

Claessens, Stijn, Asli Demiriguc-Kunt, and Harry Huizinga. 2000. "The Role of Foreign Banks in Domestic Banking Systems." In Stijn Claessens and Marion Jansen, eds., *The Internationalization of Financial Services: Issues and Lessons for Developing Countries.* Boston: Kluwer Academic.

———. 2001. "How Does Foreign Bank Entry Affect Domestic Banking Markets?" *Journal of Banking and Finance* 25(5): 891–911.

Claessens, Stijn, Rudiger Dornbusch, and Yung Chul Park. 2001. "Contagion, Why Crises Spread and How This Can Be Stopped." In Stijn Claessens and Kristin J. Forbes, eds., *International Financial Contagion.* Boston: Kluwer Academic, 9–41.

Clarke, George R., Robert Cull, Laura D'Amato, and Andrea Molinari. 2000. "On the Kindness of Strangers? The Impact of Foreign Entry on Domestic Banks in Argentina." In Stijn Claessens and Marion Jansen, eds., *The Internationalization of Financial Services: Issues and Lessons for Developing Countries.* The Hague: Kluwer Law International, 331–35.

Clarke, George R., Robert Cull, and Maria Soledad Martinez Peria. 2001. "Does Foreign Bank Penetration Reduce Access to Credit in Developing Countries? Evidence from Asking Borrowers." World Bank Policy Research Working Paper 2716 (November).

Cline, William. 1997. *Trade and Wage Inequality.* Washington, D.C.: Institute for International Economics.

Cole, Harold L., Lee E. Ohanian, Alvara Riascos, and James A. Schmitz, Jr. 2004. "Latin America in the Rearview Mirror." NBER Working Paper 11008 (December).

Collier, Paul, and David Dollar. 2002. *Globalization, Growth and Poverty: Building an Inclusive World Economy.* New York: Oxford University Press.

Council on Foreign Relations. 1999. *Safeguarding Prosperity in a Global Financial System: The Future International Financial Architecture.* Report of an Independent Task Force sponsored by the Council on Foreign Relations. Washington, D.C.: Institute for International Economics.

Cowan, Kevin, H. Kamil, and A. Izquierdo. 2004. "Macroeconomic Determinants of Dollarization: A New Look at the Evidence." Inter-American Development Bank mimeo.

Cowan, Kevin, and Jose De Gregorio. 2005. "International Borrowing, Capital Controls and the Exchange Rate: Lessons from Chile." NBER Working Paper 11382 (May).

Crockett, Andrew, Trevor Harris, Frederic S. Mishkin, and Eugene N. White. 2003. *Conflicts of Interest in the Financial Services Industry: What Should We Do About Them?* Geneva Reports on the World Economy 4. Geneva and London: International Center for Monetary and Banking Studies and Centre for Economic Policy Research.

Crystal, Jennifer S., Gerard Dages, and Linda Goldberg. 2001. "Does Foreign Ownership Contribute to Sounder Banks in Emerging Markets? The Latin American Experience." In Robert Litan, Paul Masson, and Michael Pomerleano, eds., *Open Doors: Foreign Participation in Financial Systems in Developing Countries.* Washington, D.C.: Brookings Institution Press, 217–66.

Cull, Robert, Lemma W. Senbet, and Marco Sorge. 2001. "Deposit Insurance and Financial Development." World Bank Policy Research Working Paper 2682 (September).

De Brun, Julio, and Gerardo Licandro. 2005. "To Hell and Bank. Crisis Management in a Dollarized Economy: The Case of Uruguay." Central Reserve Bank of Peru and International Monetary Fund mimeo (April).

De Gregorio, Jose. 1998. "Financial Integration, Financial Development, and Economic Growth." University of Chile mimeo (July).

De Gregorio, Jose, Barry Eichengreen, Takatoshi Ito, and Charles Wyplosz. 1999. *An Independent and Accountable IMF.* Geneva Reports on the World Economy 4. Geneva and London: International Center for Monetary and Banking Studies and Centre for Economic Policy Research.

De Gregorio, Jose, Sebastian Edwards, and R. Valdes. 2000. "Controls on Capital Inflows: Do They Work?" *Journal of Development Economics* 61(1): 59–83.

Dehejia, Rajeev H., and Roberta Gatti. 2002. "Child Labor: The Role of Income Variability and Access to Credit in a Cross Section of Countries." World Bank Policy Research Paper 2767 (January).

De Krivoy, Ruth. 2000. "Reforming Bank Supervision in Developing Countries." In Eric S. Rosengren and John S. Jordan, eds., *Building on Infrastructure for Financial Stability.* Conference Series 44. Boston: Federal Reserve Bank of Boston, 113–33.

De la Torre, Augusto. 2000. "Resolving Bank Failures in Argentina." World Bank Policy Research Working Paper 2295 (March).

De la Torre, Augusto, and Sergio L. Schmukler. 2003. "Coping with Risk through Mismatches: Domestic and International Financial Contracts for Emerging Economies." World Bank mimeo (December).

De la Torre, Augusto, Eduardo Levy-Yeyati, and Sergio L. Schmukler. 2002. "Financial Globalization: Unequal Blessings." *International Finance* 5(3): 335–57.

————. 2003. "Living and Dying with Hard Pegs: The Rise and Fall of Argentina's Currency Board." *Economia* 3(1): 43–107.

DeLong, J. Bradford, and Barry Eichengreen. 2001. "Between Meltdown and Moral Hazard: The International Monetary and Fiscal Policies of the Clinton Administration." NBER Working Paper 8443 (August).

De Luna-Martinez, Jose. 2000. "Management and Resolution of Banking Crises: Lessons from the Republic of Korea and Mexico." World Bank Discussion Paper 413 (March).

Demirguc-Kunt, Asli, and Enrica Detragiache. 1998. "The Determinants of Banking Crises: Evidence from Developed and Developing Countries." *IMF Staff Papers* 45(1): 81–109.

————. 1998. "Financial Liberalization and Financial Fragility." IMF Working Paper 98/83 (June).

Demirguc-Kunt, Asli, and Edward J. Kane. 2002. "Deposit Insurance around the Globe: Where Does It Work?" *Journal of Economic Perspectives* 16(2): 175–95.

Demirguc-Kunt, Asli, and Vojislav Maksimovic. 1998. "Law, Finance and Firm Growth." *Journal of Finance* 53(6): 2107–37.

Demirguc-Kunt, Asli, Ross Levine, and Hong G. Min. 1998. "Opening to Foreign Banks: Issues of Efficiency, Stability, and Growth." In Seongtae Lee, ed., *The Implications of Globalization of World Financial Markets*. Seoul: Bank of Korea.

De Nicolo, G., Patrick Honohan, and Alain Ize. 2003. "Dollarization of the Banking System: Good or Bad?" IMF Working Paper 03/146 (July).

Desai, Mihir, C. Fritz Foley, and James R. Hines, Jr. 2005. "Capital Controls, Liberalizations and Foreign Direct Investment." NBER Working Paper 10337 (March).

De Soto, Hernando. 2000. *The Mystery of Capital: Why Capitalism Triumphs in the West and Fails Everywhere Else*. New York: Basic Books.

Diamond, Douglas W. 1984. "Financial Intermediation and Delegated Monitoring." *Review of Economic Studies* 51: 393–414.

Diaz-Alejandro, Carlos. 1985. "Good-Bye Financial Repression, Hello Financial Crash." *Journal of Development Economics* 19(1–2): 1–24.

Djankov, Simeon, Rafael La Porta, Florencio Lopez de Silanes, and Andrei Shleifer. 2000. "The Regulation of Entry." NBER Working Paper 7892 (September).

Dollar, David, and Paul Collier. 2001. *Globalization, Growth and Poverty: Building an Inclusive World Economy*. Washington, D.C.: World Bank.

Dollar, David, and Aart Kraay. 2002. "Growth Is Good for the Poor." *Journal of Economic Growth* 7(3): 195–225.

Dominguez, Kathryn M. E., and Linda L. Tesar. 2005. "International Borrowing and Macroeconomic Performance in Argentina." NBER Working Paper 11353 (May).

Dooley, Michael. 2000. "A Model of Crises in Emerging Markets." *Economic Journal* 110(1): 256–72.

Dornbusch, Rudiger. 2002. "Malaysia's Crisis: Was It Different?" In Sebastian Edwards and Jeffrey A. Frankel, eds., *Preventing Currency Crises in Emerging Markets*. Chicago: University of Chicago Press, 441–60.

Dornbusch, Rudiger, and Andrew Warner. 1994. "Mexico: Stabilization, Reform and No Growth." *Brookings Papers on Economic Activity* 1: 253–315.

Dornbusch, Rudiger, Ilan Goldfajn, and Rodrigo Valdes. 1995. "Currency Crises and Collapses." *Brookings Papers on Economic Activity* 2: 219–93.

Drazen, Alan. 2000. *Political Economy in Macroeconomics.* Princeton, N.J.: Princeton University Press.

Easterly, William. 2001. *The Elusive Quest for Growth: Economists' Adventures and Misadventures in the Tropics.* Cambridge, Mass.: MIT Press.

———. 2003. "Can Foreign Aid Buy Growth?" *Journal of Economic Perspectives* 17(3): 23–48.

———. 2005. "A Modest Proposal." *Washington Post,* March 13, 2005, p. BW3.

———. 2005. "Reply." *Washington Post,* March 27, 2005, p. BW12.

———. 2005. "Tone Deaf on Africa." *New York Times,* Week in Review, July 3, 2005, p. 10.

———. 2005. "What Did Structural Adjustment Adjust? The Association of Policies and Growth with Repeated IMF and World Bank Adjustment Loans." *Journal of Development Economics* 76(1): 1–22.

———. 2006. *The White Man's Burden: Why the West's Efforts to Aid the Rest Have Done So Much Ill and So Little Good.* New York: Penguin.

Easterly, William, and Ross Levine. 2001. "It's Not Factor Accumulation: Stylized Facts and Growth Models." *World Bank Economic Review* 15(2): 177–219.

———. 2003. "Tropics, Germs and Crops: How Endowments Influence Economic Development." *Journal of Monetary Economics* 50(1): 3–40.

Easterly, William, Ross Levine, and David Rodman. 2003. "New Data, New Doubts: A Comment on Burnside and Dollar's 'Aid, Policies, and Growth' (2000)." NBER Working Paper 9846 (July).

Economic Report of the President. 2005. Washington, D.C.: U.S. Government Printing Office.

Economist. "A Slightly Circuitous Route." *Economist,* May 1, 2003, p. 25.

Edison, Hali J., Michael W. Klein, Luca Antonio Ricci, and Torsten Slok. 2004. "Capital Account Liberalization and Economic Performance: Survey and Synthesis." *IMF Staff Papers* 51(2): 26–62.

Edison, Hali J., Ross Levine, Luca Ricci, and Torsten Slok. 2002. "International Financial Integration and Economic Growth." *Journal of International Money and Finance* 21: 749–76.

Edwards, Franklin, and Frederic S. Mishkin. 1995. "The Decline of Traditional Banking: Implications for Financial Stability and Regulatory Policy." *Federal Reserve Bank of New York Economic Policy Review* 1(2): 27–45.

Edwards, Sebastian. 1998. "Openness, Productivity and Growth: What Do We Really Know?" *Economic Journal* 108(447): 383–98.

———. 1999. "How Effective Are Controls on Capital Inflows? An Evaluation of Chile's Experience." University of California, Los Angeles mimeo (June).

———. 2000. "How Effective Are Capital Controls?" *Journal of Economic Perspectives* 13(4): 65–84.

———. 2001. "Capital Mobility and Economic Performance: Are Emerging Economies Different?" NBER Working Paper 8076 (January).

———. 2001. "Exchange Rate Regimes, Capital Flows and Crisis Prevention." NBER Working Paper 8529 (October).

———. 2004. "Financial Openness, Sudden Stops and Current Account Reversals." NBER Working Paper 10277 (February).

———. 2004. "Thirty Years of Current Account Imbalances, Current Account Reversals and Sudden Stops." NBER Working Paper 10276 (January).

———. 2005. "Capital Controls, Sudden Stops and Current Account Reversals." NBER Working Paper 11170 (March).

Edwards, Sebastian, and Roberto Rigobon. 2005. "Capital Controls, Exchange Rate Volatility and External Vulnerability." NBER Working Paper 11434 (June).

Eichengreen, Barry. 1996. *Globalizing Capital: A History of the International Monetary System*. Princeton, N.J.: Princeton University Press.

———. 1999. "Kicking the Habit: Moving from Pegged Exchange Rates to Greater Exchange Rate Flexibility." *Economic Journal* 109: C1–C14.

———. 1999. *Toward a New International Architecture*. Washington, D.C.: Institute for International Economics.

———. 2001. "Capital Account Liberalization: What Do Cross-Country Studies Tell Us?" *World Bank Economic Review* 15(3): 341–65.

———. 2002. *Financial Crises and What to Do about Them*. New York: Oxford University Press.

———. 2004. "Financial Instability." In Bjorn Lomborg, ed., *Global Crises, Global Solutions*. Cambridge: Cambridge University Press.

———. 2004. "Financial Stability." Paper prepared for the International Task Force on Global Public Goods (December).

Eichengreen, Barry, and Ricardo Hausmann. 1999. "Exchange Rates and Financial Fragility." In *New Challenges for Monetary Policy*. Kansas City, Mo.: Federal Reserve Bank of Kansas City, 329–68.

Eichengreen, Barry, and David Leblang. 2003. "Capital Account Liberalization and Growth: Was Mr. Mahathir Right?" *International Journal of Finance and Economics* 8: 205–24.

Eichengreen, Barry, and Paul Masson. 1998. "Exit Strategies: Policy Options for Countries Seeking Greater Exchange Rate Flexibility." IMF Occasional Paper 98/168.

Eichengreen, Barry, and Richard Portes. 1995. *Crisis? What Crisis? Orderly Workouts for Sovereign Debtors*. London: Centre for Economic and Policy Research.

Eichengreen, Barry, and Marc Uzan. 1992. "The Marshall Plan: Economic Effects and Implications for Eastern Europe and the Former USSR." *Economic Policy* 14: 13–77.

Eichengreen, Barry, Andrew Rose, and Charles Wyplosz. 1996. "Contagious Currency Crises: First Tests." *Scandanavian Journal of Economics* 98: 463–84.

Eichengreen, Barry, Ricardo Hausmann, and Ugo Panizza. Forthcoming. "The Mystery of Original Sin." In Barry Eichengreen and Ricardo Hausmann, eds., *Other People's Money: Debt Denomination and Financial Instability in Emerging-Market Economies*. Chicago: University of Chicago Press.

Engerman, Stanley L., and Kenneth L. Sokoloff. 1997. "Factor Endowments, Institutions, and Differential Paths of Growth among New World Economies: A View from Economic Historians of the United States." In Stephen Haber, ed., *How Latin America Fell Behind: Essays on the Economic Histories of Brazil and Mexico, 1800–1914*. Stanford, Calif.: Stanford University Press, 260–304.

Estevadeordal, Fanz, and Alan M. Taylor. 2003. "The Rise and Fall of World Trade 1870–1939." *Quarterly Journal of Economics* 118: 359–407.

Fazzari, Steven M., R. Glenn Hubbard, and Bruce C. Petersen. 1988. "Financial Constraints and Corporate Investment: New Evidence on Financing Constraints." *Brookings Papers on Economic Activity* 1: 141–95.

Fedorov, Boris. 1999. "Open Letter to Michel Camdessus, Managing Director of the International Monetary Fund." July 9.

Feldstein, M. 1998. "Refocusing the IMF." *Foreign Affairs* 77(2): 20–33.

Ferreira, Francisco H. G., Giovanna Prennushi, and Martin Ravallion. 1999. "Protecting the Poor from Macroeconomic Shocks: An Agenda for Action in a Crisis and Beyond." World Bank Policy Research Working Paper 2160 (August).

Fischer, Stanley. 1993. "The Role of Macroeconomic Factors in Growth." *Journal of Monetary Economics* 32(3): 485–512.

———. 1999. "On the Need for an International Lender of Last Resort." *Journal of Economic Perspectives* 13(4): 85–104.

———. 2001. "Exchange Rate Regimes: Is the Bipolar View Correct?" *Journal of Economic Perspectives* 15(2): 3–24.

———. 2001. "The International Financial System: Crises and Reform." The Robbins Lecture, October 29–31, London School of Economics, mimeo.

———. 2003. "Globalization and Its Challenges." *American Economic Review* 93(2): 1–30.

Fisher, Irving. 1933. "The Debt-Deflation Theory of Great Depressions." *Econometrica* 1(4): 337–57.

Folkerts-Landau, David, Gary J. Schinasi, M. Cassard, V. K. Ng, Carmen M. Reinhart, and M. G. Spencer. 1995. "Effect of Capital Flows on the Domestic Financial Sectors in APEC Developing Countries." In Moshin S. Khan and Carmen M. Reinhart, eds., *Capital Flows in the APEC Region.* Washington, D.C.: International Monetary Fund, 31–57.

Forbes, Kristin J. 2003. "One Cost of the Chilean Capital Controls: Increased Financial Constraints for Smaller Traded Firms." NBER Working Paper 9777 (June).

———. 2004. "Capital Controls: Mud in the Wheels of Market Discipline." In William Hunter, George Kaufman, Claudio Borio, and Kostas Tsatsaronis, eds., *Market Discipline across Countries and Institutions.* Cambridge, Mass.: MIT Press, 187–211.

———. 2005. "The Microeconomic Evidence on Capital Controls: No Free Lunch." NBER Working Paper 11372 (May).

Franceschelli, Ignacio. 2005. "Poverty and Employability Effects of Workfare Programs in Argentina." Poverty Monitoring, Measurement and Assessment Network Paper, presented at the 4th PEP Research Network General Meeting, June 13–17, Colombo, Sri Lanka.

Frankel, Jeffrey. 2005. "Contractionary Currency Crashes in Developing Countries." NBER Working Paper 11508 (July).

Frankel, Jeffrey, and Eduardo A. Cavallo. 2004. "Does Openness to Trade Make Countries More Vulnerable to Sudden Stops or Less? Using Gravity to Establish Causality." NBER Working Paper 10957 (December).

Frankel, Jeffrey, and David Romer. 1999. "Does Trade Cause Growth?" *American Economic Review* 89(3): 379–99.

Frankel, Jeffrey, and Sergio Schmukler. 1996. "Country Fund Discounts and the Mexican Crisis of 1994: Did Mexican Residents Turn Pessimistic before International Investors?" *Open Economies Review* 7 (Fall): 511–34.

Freidman, Jed, and James Levinsohn. 2002. "The Distributional Impacts of Indonesia's Crisis on Household Welfare: A 'Rapid Response' Methodology." *World Bank Economic Review* 16(3): 397–423.

Friedman, Milton, and Anna J. Schwartz. 1963. *A Monetary History of the United States 1867–1960.* Princeton, N.J.: Princeton University Press.

Furman, Jason, and Joseph E. Stiglitz. 1998. "Economic Crises: Evidence and Insights from East Asia." *Brookings Papers on Economic Activity* 2: 1–114.

Galindo, Arturo, and Leonardo Leiderman. 2003. "Living with Dollarization and the Route to Dedollarization." Paper prepared for IDB/World Bank Conference, Financial Dedollarization: Policy Options, December 1–2, Washington, D.C.

Gallego, Francisco, and Leonardo Hernandez. 2002. "Microeconomic Effects of Capital Controls: The Chilean Experience during the 1990s." Central Bank of Chile mimeo.

Galor, Oded, and J. Zeira. 1993. "Income Distribution and Macroeconomics." *Review of Economic Studies* 60(202): 35–52.

Garber, Peter M., and Subir Lall. 1996. "Derivative Products in Exchange Rate Crises." In Federal Reserve Bank of San Francisco, *Proceedings.* San Francisco: Federal Reserve Bank of San Francisco, 206–31.

———. 1996. "The Role and Operation of Derivative Markets in Foreign Exchange Market Crises." Brown University, Department of Economics mimeo.

Garten, Jeffrey. 1998. "In This Economic Chaos, a Global Central Bank Can Help." *International Herald Tribune,* September 25, p. 8.

Gavin, Michael, and Ricardo Hausman. 1996. "The Roots of Banking Crises: The Macroeconomic Context." In Ricardo Hausman and Liliana Rojas-Suarez, eds., *Banking Crises in Latin America.* Baltimore: Inter-American Development Bank, distributed by Johns Hopkins University Press, 27–63.

Gertler, Mark, and Simon Gilchrist. 1994. "Monetary Policy, Business Cycles, and the Behavior of Small Manufacturing Firms." *Quarterly Journal of Economics* 109(2): 309–40.

Glaeser, Edward, Rafael La Porta, Florencio Lopez-de-Silanes, and Andrei Shleifer. 2004. "Do Institutions Cause Growth?" NBER Working Paper 10568 (June).

Glick, Reuven, and Michael Hutchison. 1999. "Banking and Currency Crises: How Common Are Twins?" In Reuven Glick, F. Moreno, and M. Spiegel, eds., *Financial Crises in Emerging Markets.* New York: Cambridge University Press.

———. 2005. "Capital Controls and Exchange Rate Instability in Developing Countries." *Journal of International Money and Finance* 24(3): 387–412.

Glick, Reuven, Xueyahn Guo, and Michael Hutchison. 2005. "Currency Crises, Capital Account Liberalization, and Selection Bias." Federal Reserve Bank of San Francisco Working Paper 2004-15 (June).

Goldberg, Linda. 2004. "Financial Sector FDI and Host Countries: New and Old Lessons." Federal Reserve Bank of New York Staff Reports 183 (April).

Goldberg, Linda, Gerard Dages, and Daniel Kinney. 2000. "Foreign and Domestic Bank Participation in Emerging Markets: Lessons from Mexico and Argentina." Federal Reserve Bank of New York Economic Policy Review 6(3): 17–36.

Goldfajn, Ilan, and Poonam Gupta. 2003. "Does Tight Monetary Policy Stabilize the Exchange Rate?" IMF Staff Papers 50(1): 90–114.

Goldstein, Morris. 1998. The Asian Financial Crisis: Causes, Cures, and Systemic Implications. Washington, D.C.: Institute for International Economics.

———. 2002. Managed Floating Plus. Policy Analyses in International Economics 66. Washington, D.C.: Institute for International Economics.

———. 2003. "IMF Structural Programs." In Martin Feldstein, ed., Economic and Financial Crises in Emerging Market Countries. Chicago: University of Chicago Press, 363–437.

———. 2005. "Currency Manipulation and Enforcing the Rules of the International Monetary System." Paper presented at the Institute for International Economics Conference on IMF Reform, September 23, Washington, D.C.

———. 2005. "The International Financial Architecture." In C. Fred Bergston, ed., The United States and the World Economy: Foreign Economic Policy for the Next Decade. Washington, D.C.: Institute for International Economics, 373–407.

Goldstein, Morris, and Philip Turner. 1996. "Banking Crises in Emerging Economies: Origins and Policy Options." BIS Economic Paper 46 (October).

———. 2004. Controlling Currency Mismatches in Emerging Markets. Washington, D.C.: Institute for International Economics.

Gourinchas, Pierre-Olivier, and Olivier Jeanne. 2005. "Capital Mobility and Reform." University of California, Berkeley mimeo (October).

Greenspan, Alan. 2000. "Global Challenges." Remarks at the Financial Crisis Conference, Council on Foreign Relations, July 12, New York. http://www.federal reserve.gov/boarddocs/speeches/2000/20000712.htm.

Haber, Stephen. 2005. "Banking without Deposit Insurance: Mexico's Banking Experiments, 1884–2004." Stanford University mimeo (August).

———. 2005. "Mexico's Experiment with Bank Privatization and Liberalization, 1991–2002." Journal of Banking and Finance 29(8–9): 2325–53.

———. 2005. "Political Institutions and Financial Development: Evidence from the Economic Histories of Mexico and the United States." Stanford University mimeo (October).

Haber, Stephen, ed. 1997. How Latin America Fell Behind: Essays on the Economic Histories of Brazil and Mexico, 1800–1914. Stanford, Calif.: Stanford University Press.

Haber, Stephen, and Aldo Musacchio. 2005. "Foreign Banks and the Mexican Economy, 1997–2004." Stanford University mimeo (August).

Haber, Stephen, Armando Razo, and Noel Maurer. 2003. The Politics of Property Rights: Political Instability, Credible Commitments, and Economic Growth in Mexico, 1876–1929. Cambridge: Cambridge University Press.

Hackethal, Andreas, and Reinhard H. Schmidt. 2004. "Financing Patterns: Measurement Concepts and Empirical Results." Johann Wolfgang Goethe-Universität Working Paper 125 (January).

Haggard, Stephen. 2000. *The Political Economy of the Asian Financial Crisis*. Washington, D.C.: Institute for International Economics.

Hahm, Joon-Ho. 2003. "The Government, the Chaebol and Financial Institutions before the Economic Crisis." In Stephan Haggard, Wonhyuk Lim, and Euysung Kim, eds., *Economic Crisis and Corporate Restructuring in Korea*. Cambridge: Cambridge University Press, 79–101.

———. 2004. "Financial Restructuring." In Duck-Koo Chung and Barry Eichengreen, eds., *The Korean Economy Beyond the Crisis*. Cheltenham: Edward Elgar, 172–93.

Hahm, Joon-Ho, and Wonhyuk Lim. 2003. "Turning a Crisis into Opportunity: The Political Economy of Korea's Financial Sector Reform." Yonsei University mimeo (August).

Hahm, Joon-Ho, and Frederic S. Mishkin. 2000. "The Korean Financial Crisis: An Asymmetric Information Perspective." *Emerging Markets Review* 1(1): 21–52.

Halac, Marina, and Sergio L. Schmukler. 2004. "Distributional Effects of Crises." World Bank mimeo (June).

Hall, Robert, and Chad I. Jones. 1999. Why Do Some Countries Produce So Much More Output per Worker Than Others?" *Quarterly Journal of Economics* 114(1): 83–117.

Haluk, Unal, and Miguel Navarro. 1999. "The Technical Process of Bank Privatization in Mexico." *Journal of Financial Services Research* 16: 61–83.

Hanke, Steve H. 2002. "On Dollarization and Currency Boards: Error and Deception." *Policy Reform* 5(4): 203–22.

Harrison, Ann. 1996. "Openness and Growth: A Time-Series, Cross-Country Analysis for Developing Countries." *Journal of Development Economics* 48(2): 419–47.

Henry, Peter Blair. 2000. "Equity Prices, Stock Market Liberalization, and Investment." *Journal of Financial Economics* 58(1–2): 301–34.

———. 2000. "Stock Market Liberalization, Economic Reform, and Emerging Market Equity Prices." *Journal of Finance* 55(2): 529–64.

———. 2003. "Capital Account Liberalization, the Cost of Capital and Economic Growth." *American Economic Review* 93(2): 91–96.

Herrera, Luis O., and Rodrigo O. Valdes. 2003. "Dedollarization, Indexation and Nominalization: The Chilean Experience." Banco Central de Chile manuscript (November).

Heston, Alan, Robert Summers, and Bettina Aten. 2002. Penn World Table Version 6.1. Philadelphia: Center for International Comparisons, University of Pennsylvania (CICUP) (October).

Higgins, Andrew. 2006. "Liberté, Precarité: Labor Law Ignites Anxiety in France." *Wall Street Journal*, March 29, p. A8.

Honig, Adam. 2003. "Dollarization, Exchange Rate Regimes and Government Myopia." Columbia University mimeo (March).

Honohan, Patrick. 2004. "Financial Development, Growth and Poverty: How Close Are the Links?" World Bank Policy Working Paper 3203 (February).

Honohan, Patrick, and Daniela Klingebiel. 2000. "Controlling Fiscal Costs of Banking Crises." World Bank Policy Research Paper 2441 (September).

Hoshi, Takeo, and Anil Kashyap. 2005. "Solutions to Japan's Banking Problems: What Might Work and What Definitely Will Fail." In Takatoshi Ito, Hugh Patrick, and David Weinstein, eds., *Reviving Japan's Economy: Problems and Prescriptions*. Cambridge, Mass.: MIT Press, 147–95.

Hubbard, R. Glenn. 1995. "Is There a 'Credit Channel' for Monetary Policy?" *Federal Reserve Bank of St. Louis Review* 77: 63–74.

Hufbaur, Gary Clyde, and Kimberly Ann Elliott. 1994. *Measuring the Costs of Protection in the United States.* Washington, D.C.: Institute for International Economics.

Institute for International Economics. 1997. "The Effects of Corruption on Growth, Investment and Government Expenditures." In Kimberly Ann Elliott, ed., *Corruption and the Global Economy.* Washington, D.C.: Institute for International Economics, 83–107.

Institute for International Finance. 2005. "Update of Capital Flows to Emerging Market Economies." March 31. http://www.iif.com/verify/data/report_docs/cf_0305.pdf.

Inter-American Development Bank. 2004. *Unlocking Credit: The Quest for Deep and Stable Bank Lending. 2005 Report, Economic and Social Progress in Latin America.* Washington, D.C.: Inter-American Development Bank and Johns Hopkins University Press.

International Financial Institution Advisory Commission. 2000. *Report.* Washington, D.C.: International Financial Institution Advisory Commission.

International Monetary Fund. 1999. *The Poverty Reduction and Growth Facility (PRGF)— Operational Issues.* Washington, D.C.: International Monetary Fund.

———. 2000. *External Evaluation of IMF Research Activities: Report by a Group of Independent Experts.* Washington, D.C.: International Monetary Fund.

———. 2000. *World Economic Outlook.* Washington, D.C.: International Monetary Fund.

———. 2001. *World Economic Outlook.* Washington, D.C.: International Monetary Fund.

———. 2003. *Financial Sector Assessment Program—Review, Lessons, and Issues Going Forward.* Washington, D.C.: International Monetary Fund.

———. 2003. *The Fund's Transparency Policy—Issues and Next Steps.* Washington, D.C.: International Monetary Fund.

———. 2003. *International Standards—Background Paper on Strengthening Surveillance, Domestic Institutions, and International Markets.* Washington, D.C.: International Monetary Fund.

———. 2003. *Republic of Korea Financial System Stability Assessment.* Washington, D.C.: International Monetary Fund.

———. 2004. *Direction of Trade Statistics.* Washington, D.C.: International Monetary Fund.

———. 2004. *International Financial Statistics.* Washington, D.C.: International Monetary Fund.

———. 2005. *Review of the 2002 Conditionality Guidelines.* Washington, D.C.: International Monetary Fund.

International Monetary Fund Independent Evaluation Office. 2003. *Evaluation Report: The IMF and Recent Capital Account Crises: Indonesia, Korea, Brazil.* Washington, D.C.: International Monetary Fund.

———. 2005. *Evaluation of the IMF's Approach to Capital Account Liberalization.* Washington, D.C.: International Monetary Fund.

Ip, Gregg, and Neil King, Jr. "Ports Deal Shows Roadblocks for Globalization." *Wall Street Journal,* March 11, p. A1.

Irwin, Gregor, Christopher L. Gilbert, and David Vines. 2004. "How Should the IMF View Capital Controls?" In David Vines and Christopher L. Gilbert, eds., *The IMF and Its Critics: Reform of Global Financial Architecture.* Cambridge: Cambridge University Press, 181–206.

Isaacson, Walter. 2003. *Benjamin Franklin: An American Life.* New York: Simon and Schuster.

Isard, Peter. 2005. *Globalization and the International Financial System: What's Wrong and What Can Be Done.* Cambridge: Cambridge University Press.

Ize, Alain, and Eduardo Levy-Yeyati. 2003. "Financial Dollarization." *Journal of International Economics* 59(2): 323–47.

Japelli, Tullio, and Marco Pagano. 2001. "Information Sharing in Credit Markets: Theory and Evidence." In Marco Pagano, ed., *Defusing Default: Incentives and Institutions.* Washington, D.C.: Inter-American Development Bank.

———. 2003. "Public Credit Information: A European Perspective." In Margaret J. Miller, ed., *Credit Reporting Systems and the International Economy.* Cambridge, Mass.: MIT Press.

Jeanne, Olivier, and Jeronim Zettelmeyer. 2001. "International Bailouts, Moral Hazard, and Conditionality." *Economic Policy* 16(33): 409–32.

———. 2004. "The Mussa Theorem: And Other Results on IMF-Induced Moral Hazard." IMF Working Paper 04/192 (October).

Jeong, Hyeok, and Robert M. Townsend. 2005. "Sources of TFP Growth: Occupational Choice and Financial Deepening." University of Chicago mimeo (April).

Jewsiewicki, Bogumil. 1983. "Rural Society and the Belgian Colonial Economy." In David Birmingham and Phylis M. Martin, eds., *The History of Central Africa,* vol. II. New York: Longman, 95–126.

Joh, S. W. 1999. "The Korean Corporate Sector Crisis and Reform." Korea Development Institute mimeo (August).

Johnson, Simon, and Todd Milton. 2002. "Cronyism and Capital Controls: Evidence from Malaysia." *Journal of Financial Economics* 67(2): 351–82.

Jonas, Jiri. 2002. Argentina's Crisis and Its Implications for the Exchange Rate Regime Debate." IMF mimeo (June).

Jones, Benjamin F., and Benjamin A. Olken. 2005. "The Anatomy of Start-Stop Growth." NBER Working Paper 11528 (July).

Kahler, Miles. 2005. "Internal Governance and IMF Performance." Paper presented at the Institute for International Economics Conference on IMF Reform, September 23, Washington, D.C. www.iie.com/prog_imf_reform.cfm.

Kaminsky, Graciela L., and Carmen M. Reinhart. 1999. "The Twin Crises: The Causes of Banking and Balance of Payments Problems." *American Economic Review* 89(3): 473–500.

Kaminsky, Graciela L., and Sergio Schmukler. 2003. "Short-Run Pain, Long-Run Gain: The Effects of Financial Liberalizations." NBER Working Paper 9787 (June).

Kaminsky, Graciela L., S. Lizondo, and Carmen M. Reinhart. 1997. "Leading Indicators of Currency Crises." IMF Working Paper 97/79 (July).

Kaminsky, Graciela L., Carmen M. Reinhart, and Carlos A Vegh. 2003. "The Unholy Trinity of Financial Contagion." NBER WorkingPaper 10061 (October).

Kane, Edward J. 1977. "Good Intentions and Unintended Evil: The Case against Selective Credit Allocation." *Journal of Money, Credit and Banking* 9(1): 55–69.

———. 1989. *The S&L Insurance Mess: How Did It Happen?* Washington, D.C.: Urban Institute Press.

———. 1991. "Zombies on the Loose: The S&L Insurance Mess." *Financier: The Journal for Private Sector Policy* 15 (July): 9–19.

———. 2000. "How Offshore Financial Competition Disciplines Exit Resistance by Incentive-Conflicted Bank Regulators." *Journal of Financial Services Research* 17(1): 265–91.

Kane, Edward J., and Daniela Klingebiel. 2004. "Alternatives to Blanket Guarantees for Containing a Systemic Crisis." *Journal of Financial Stability* 1(1): 31–63.

Kaplan, Ethan, and Dani Rodrik. 2002. "Did the Malaysian Capital Controls Work?" In Sebastian Edwards and Jeffrey A. Frankel, eds., *Preventing Currency Crises in Emerging Markets.* Chicago: University of Chicago Press, 393–440.

Karp, Jonathan. 1997. "India's Laws a Mixed Blessing for Investors—U.S. Firms Struggle in Court but Copyright Laws Improve." *Wall Street Journal,* Eastern edition, July 11, p. A10.

Kearl, James R., Clayne L. Pope, Gordon C. Whiting, and Larry T. Dimmer. 1979. "A Confusion of Economists." *American Economic Review Papers and Proceedings* 69(2): 28–37.

Kenen, Peter. 2001. *The International Financial Architecture: What's New? What's Missing?* Washington, D.C.: Institute for International Economics.

Keynes, John Maynard. 1920. *The Economic Consequences of the Peace.* New York: Harcourt, Brace and Howe.

Khan, Aubhik. 2000. "The Finance and Growth Nexus." *Business Review of the Federal Reserve Bank of Philadelphia,* no. 1: 3–14.

Kiguel, Miguel. 2001. "Structural Reforms in Argentina: Success or Failure?" Paper prepared for the Croatian National Bank Conference on Current Issues in Emerging Market Economies, June 28–30, Dubrovnik.

Kim, E. Han, and Vijay Singal. 2000. "Stock Market Opening: Experience of Emerging Market Economies." *Journal of Business* 73(1): 25–66.

King, Mervyn. 2006. "Reform of the International Monetary Fund." Speech made at the Indian Council for Research on International Economic Relations (ICRIER), New Delhi, February 20.

King, Robert, and Ross Levine. 1993. "Finance and Growth: Schumpeter Might Be Right." *Quarterly Journal of Economics* 108(3): 717–37.

Klein, Michael. 2003. "Capital Account Openness and the Varieties of the Growth Experience." NBER Working Paper 9500 (January).

———. 2005. "Capital Account Liberalization, Institutional Quality and Economic Growth: Theory and Evidence." NBER Working Paper 11112 (February).

Klein, Michael, and Giovanni Olivei. 1999. "Capital Account Liberalization, Financial Depth and Economic Growth." NBER Working Paper 7384 (October).

Kletzer, Lori G., and Howard Rosen. 2005. "Easing the Adjustment on U.S. Workers." In C. Fred Bergsten, ed., *The United States and the World Economy: Foreign Economic Policy for the Next Decade.* Washington, D.C.: Institute for International Economics, 313–43.

Klingebiel, Daniela, and Luc Laewen. 2002. "Managing the Real and Fiscal Effects of Banking Crises." World Bank Discussion Paper 428.

Kohler, Horst. 2000. "Toward a More Focused IMF." Address given at the International Monetary Fund Conference, May 30, Washington, D.C.

Kose, M. Ayhan, Eswar Prasad, Kenneth Rogoff, and Shang-Jin Wei. 2005. "The Macro-economic Implications of Financial Globalization: A Reappraisal and Synthesis." IMF mimeo (November).

Kraay, Aart. 1998. *In Search of the Macroeconomic Effects of Capital Account Liberalization.* Washington, D.C.: World Bank, Development Research Group.

———. 2003. "Do High Interest Rates Defend Currencies during Speculative Attacks?" *Journal of International Economics* 59(2): 297–321.

Kroszner, Randall. 1998. "On the Political Economy of Banking and Financial Regulatory Reform in Emerging Markets." *Research in Financial Services* 10: 33–51.

———. 2003. "Is It Better to Forgive Than Receive: An Empirical Analysis of the Impact of Debt Repudiation." University of Chicago mimeo (December).

Krueger, Anne O. 1998. "Whither the World Bank and the IMF?" *Journal of Economic Literature* 36(4): 1983–2021.

———. 2000. "Conflicting Demands on the International Monetary Fund." *American Economic Review* 90(2): 38–42.

———. 2001. "International Financial Architecture for 2002: A New Approach to Sovereign Debt Restructuring." Address given at the National Economists Club Annual Members' Dinner, November 26, Washington, D.C.

Krueger, Anne O., and Aaron Tornell. 1999. "The Role of Bank Restructuring in Recovering from Crises: Mexico 1995–98." NBER Working Paper 7042 (March).

Krugman, Paul. 1998. "The Confidence Game." *New Republic,* October 5, pp. 23–25.

———. 1998. "Saving Asia: It's Time to Get Radical." *Fortune,* September 7, pp. 74–81.

———. 1998. "What Happened to Asia?" MIT mimeo (January).

———. 1999. "Balance Sheets, the Transfer Problem and Financial Crises." In P. Isard, A. Razin, and A. Rose, eds., *International Finance and Financial Crises.* Dordrecht: Kluwer Academic, 31–45.

———. 1999. "Depression Economics Returns." *Foreign Affairs* 78(1): 56–75.

Laban, Raul M., and Felipe B. Larrain. 1997. "Can a Liberalization of Capital Outflows Increase Net Capital Inflows?" *Journal of International Money and Finance* 16(3): 415–31.

Lachman, Desmond. 2005. "How Should IMF Resources be Expanded?" Paper presented at the Institute for International Economics Conference on IMF Reform, September 23, Washington, D.C. www.iie.com/prog_imf_reform.cfm.

Laidi, Ashraf. 2005. "China Answers Back,Yen Soars." *Forex News,* April 24.

Landerretche, Oscar, Felipe Morandé, and Klaus Schmidt-Hebbel. 1999. "Inflation

Targets and Stabilization in Chile." Central Bank of Chile Working Paper 55 (December).

Lane, Timothy. 2005. "Tension in the Role of the IMF and Directions for Reform." *World Economics* 6(2): 47–66.

La Porta, Rafael, Florencio Lopez-de-Silanes, and Andrei Shleifer. 2002. "Government Ownership of Banks." *Journal of Finance* 57(1): 265–301.

La Porta, Rafael, Florencio Lopez-de-Silanes, Andrei Shleifer, and Robert W. Vishny. 1997. "Legal Determinants of External Finance." *Journal of Finance* 52(3): 1131–50.

———. 1998. "Law and Finance." *Journal of Political Economy* 106(6): 1113–55.

La Porta, Rafael, Florencio Lopez-de-Silanes, and Guillermo Zamarippa. 2003. "Related Lending." *Quarterly Journal of Economics* 118(1): 231–68.

Lederman, Daniel, Ana Maria Menendez, Guillermo Perry, and Joseph E. Stiglitz. 2001. "Mexico: Five Years After the Crisis." In Boris Pleskovic and Nicholas Stern, eds., *Annual Bank Conference on Development Economics, 2000*. Washington, D.C.: World Bank, 263–83.

Lee, Ha Yan, Luca Antonio Ricci, and Roberto Rigobon. 2004. "Once Again, Is Openness Good for Growth?" *Journal of Development Economics* 75(2): 451–72.

Lee, Joung-Woo. 2004. "Social Impact of the Crisis." In Duck-Koo Chung and Barry Eichengreen, eds., *The Korean Economy beyond the Crisis*. Cheltenham: Edward Elgar, 137–59.

Lensink, Robert, and Howard White. 2001. "Are There Negative Returns to Aid?" *Journal of Development Studies* 37(6): 42–65.

Levine, Ross. 1996. "Foreign Banks, Financial Development and Economic Growth." In Claude E. Barfield, ed., *International Financial Markets: Harmonization versus Competition*. Washington, D.C.: American Enterprise Institute Press, 224–55.

———. 1997. "Financial Development and Economic Growth: Views and Agenda." *Journal of Economic Literature* 35(2): 688–72.

———. 2005. "Finance and Growth: Theory and Evidence." In Philippe Aghion and Steven Durlauf, eds. *Handbook of Economic Growth*, vol. 1, part A. Amsterdam: North-Holland, 865–934.

———. 2005. "Law, Endowments, and Property Rights." NBER Working Paper 11502 (August).

Levine, Ross, and Sara Zervos. 1998. "Capital Control Liberalization and Stock Market Development." *World Development* 26: 1169–84.

———. 1998. "Stock Markets, Banks, and Economic Growth." *American Economic Review* 88(3): 537–58.

Levine, Ross, Norman Loayza, and Thorsten Beck. 2000. "Financial Intermediation and Growth: Causality and Causes." *Journal of Monetary Economics* 46(1): 31–77.

Levy-Yeyati, Eduardo. 2003. "Financial Dollarization: Where Do We Stand?" Paper presented at the IDB/World Bank Conference, Financial Dedollarization: Policy Options, December 1–2, Washington, D.C.

Levy-Yeyati, Eduardo, and Federoci Sturzenegger. 2003. "To Float or to Fix: Evidence on the Impact of Exchange Rate Regimes on Growth." *American Economic Review* 93(4): 1173.

Levy-Yeyati, Eduardo, Maria Soledad Martinez Peria, and Sergio Schmukler. 2004. "Market Discipline under Systemic Risk: Evidence from Bank Runs in Emerging Economies." World Bank mimeo (April).

Li, Hongyi, Lyn Squire, and Heng-fu Zou. 2001. "Explaining International and Intertemporal Variations in Income Inequality." *Economic Journal* 108(1): 26–43.

Licandro, Gerardo, and Jose Antonio Licandro. 2003. "Building the Dollarization Agenda: Lessons from the Uruguayan Case." Central Bank of Uruguay mimeo (September).

Lim, Wonhyuk. 2000. *The Origin and Evolution of the Korean Economic System.* Seoul: Korea Development Institute Press.

Lindert, Peter, and Jeffrey Williamson. 2001. "Does Globalization Make the World More Unequal?" NBER Working Paper 8228 (April).

Lucas, Robert. 1990. "Why Doesn't Capital Flow from Rich to Poor Countries?" *American Economic Review* 80(2): 92–96.

Lukas, Richard. 1997. *The Forgotten Holocaust: The Poles under German Occupation, 1939–44.* New York: Hippocrene.

Lustig, Nora. Forthcoming. "Crises and the Poor: Socially Responsible Macroeconomics." *Economia.*

Maddison, Angus. 2001. *The World Economy: A Millennial Perspective.* Paris: Development Centre of the Organisation for Economic Co-operation and Development.

———. 2003. *The World Economy: Historical Statistics.* Paris: Organisation for Economic Co-operation and Development.

Mankiw, N. Gregory. 1986. "The Allocation of Credit and Financial Collapse." *Quarterly Journal of Economics* 101(3): 455–70.

Martinez Peria, Maria Soledad, and Sergio L. Schmukler. 2001. "Do Depositors Punish Banks for Bad Behavior? Market Discipline, Deposit Insurance and Banking Crisis." *Journal of Finance* 56(3): 1029–51.

Mathieson, Donald J., and Liliana Rojas Suarez. 1993. "Liberalization of the Capital Account: Experience and Issues." IMF Occasional Paper 103.

Mauro, Paolo. 1995. "Corruption and Economic Growth." *Quarterly Journal of Economics* 110(3): 681–712.

———. 1997. "The Effects of Corruption on Growth, Investment and Government Expenditures." In Kimberly Ann Elliott, ed., *Corruption and the Global Economy.* Washington, D.C.: Institute for International Economics, 83–107.

McArthur, John W., Guido Schmidt-Traub, Margaret Kruk, Chandrika Bahadur, Michael Faye, and Gordon McCord. 2004. "Ending Africa's Poverty Trap." *Brookings Papers on Economic Activity* 1: 117–216.

McKinnon, Ronald, and Huw Pill. 1999. "Exchange Rate Regimes for Emerging Markets: Moral Hazard and International Overborrowing." *Oxford Review of Economic Policy* 15(3): 19–38.

McKinnon, Ronald, and Gunther Schnabl. 2004. "The East Asian Dollar Standard, Fear of Floating and Original Sin." *Review of Development Economics* 8(3): 331–60.

Mishkin, Frederic S. 1991. "Asymmetric Information and Financial Crises: A Historical Perspective." In R. Glenn Hubbard, ed., *Financial Markets and Financial Crises.* Chicago: University of Chicago Press, 69–108.

———. 1992. "An Evaluation of the Treasury Plan for Banking Reform." *Journal of Economic Perspectives* 6(1): 133–53.

———. 1996. "The Channels of Monetary Transmission: Lessons for Monetary Policy." *Banque de France Bulletin Digest* 27(3): 33–44.

———. 1997. "The Causes and Propagation of Financial Instability: Lessons for Policymakers." In Federal Reserve Bank of Kansas City, *Maintaining Financial Stability in a Global Economy*. Kansas City, Mo.: Federal Reserve Bank of Kansas City, 55–96.

———. 1997. "Evaluating FDICIA." In George Kaufman, ed., *Research in Financial Services: Private and Public Policy*, vol. 9. *FDICIA: Bank Reform Five Years Later and Five Years Ahead*. Greenwich, Conn.: JAI Press, 17–33.

———. 1997. "Understanding Financial Crises: A Developing Country Perspective." In Michael Bruno and Boris Pleskovic, eds., *Annual World Bank Conference on Development Economics, 1996*. Washington, D.C.: World Bank, 29–62.

———. 1998. "Bank Consolidation: A Central Banker's Perspective." In Yakov Amihud and Geoffrey Miller, eds., *Mergers of Financial Institutions*. Boston: Kluwer Academic, 3–19.

———. 1998. "The Dangers of Exchange Rate Pegging in Emerging-Market Countries." *International Finance* 1(1): 81–101.

———. 1999. "Financial Consolidation: Dangers and Opportunities." *Journal of Banking and Finance* 23(2–4): 675–91.

———. 1999. "Global Financial Instability: Framework, Events, Issues." *Journal of Economic Perspectives* 13(4): 3–20.

———. 1999. "International Experiences with Different Monetary Policy Regimes." *Journal of Monetary Economics* 43(3): 579–606.

———. 2000. "Inflation Targeting in Emerging Market Countries." *American Economic Review* 90(2): 105–9.

———. 2000. "What Should Central Banks Do?" *Federal Reserve Bank of St. Louis Review*, 82(6): 1–13.

———. 2003. "Financial Policies and the Prevention of Financial Crises in Emerging Market Countries." In Martin Feldstein, ed., *Economic and Financial Crises in Emerging Market Countries*. Chicago: University of Chicago Press, 93–130.

———. 2005. "Getting Financial Globalization Right." Paper presented at the World Bank/Journal of Banking and Finance conference Globalization and Financial Services in Emerging Market Countries, June 20–21, Washington, D.C.

———. 2005. "How Big a Problem Is Too Big to Fail?" NBER Working Paper 11814 (December), forthcoming in the *Journal of Economic Literature*.

———. 2007. *The Economics of Money, Banking and Financial Markets*, 8th edition. Boston: Addison-Wesley.

———. Forthcoming. "Can Inflation Targeting Work in Emerging Market Countries?" In Carmen M. Reinhart, Carlos Vegh, and Andres Velasco, eds., *A Festschrift for Guillermo Calvo*.

Mishkin, Frederic S., and Jiri Jonas. 2005. "Inflation Targeting in Transition Countries: Experience and Prospects." In Michael Woodford, ed., *Inflation Targeting*. Chicago: University of Chicago Press, 353–413.

Mishkin, Frederic S., and Miguel Savastano. 2001. "Monetary Policy Strategies for Latin America." *Journal of Development Economics* 66(2): 415–44.

———. 2002. "Monetary Policy Strategies for Emerging Market Countries: Lessons from Latin America." *Comparative Economic Studies* 44(2): 45–83.

Mishkin, Frederic S., and Klaus Schmidt-Hebbel. 2002. "One Decade of Inflation Targeting in the World: What Do We Know and What Do We Need to Know?" In Norman Loayza and Raimundo Soto, eds., *Inflation Targeting: Design, Performance, Challenges*. Santiago: Central Bank of Chile, 171–219.

Moffett, Matt, and Geraldo Samor. 2005. "Opportunity Cost: In Brazil, Thicket of Red Tape Spoils Recipe for Growth." *Wall Street Journal*, May 24, pp. A1, A9.

Morck, Randall, Daniel Wolfenzon, and Bernard Yeung. 2005. "Corporate Governance, Economic Entrenchment and Growth." *Journal of Economic Literature* 43(3): 655–720.

Morganthau, Tom, Rich Thomas, and Eleanor Clift. 1989. "The S&L Scandal's Biggest Blowout." *Newsweek*, November 6, p. 35.

Mussa, Michael. 2002. *Argentina and the Fund: From Triumph to Tragedy*. Washington, D.C.: Institute for International Economics.

———. 2004. "Reflections on Moral Hazard and Private Sector Involvement in the Resolution of Emerging Market Financial Crises." In Andrew G. Haldane, ed., *Fixing Financial Crises in the Twenty-First Century*. London: Routledge, 33–56.

———. 2005. "Reflections on the Function and Facilities for IMF Lending." Paper presented at the Institute for International Economics Conference on IMF Reform, September 23, Washington, D.C. www.iie.com/prog_imf_reform.cfm.

Mussa, Michael, and Miguel Savastano. 1999. "The IMF Approach to Economic Stabilization." In Olivier Blanchard and Stanley Fischer, eds., *NBER Macro Annual, 1999*. Cambridge, Mass.: MIT Press, 79–128.

Noland, Marcus. 2005. "South Korea's Experience with International Capital Flows." Institute for International Economics Working Paper 05-4 (June).

Norberg, Johan. 2003. *In Defense of Global Capitalism*. Washington, D.C.: Cato Institute.

North, Douglass. 1990. *Institutions, Institutional Change, and Economic Development*. Cambridge: Cambridge University Press.

North, Douglass C., and Robert P. Thomas. 1973. *The Rise of the Western World: A New Economic History*. Cambridge: Cambridge University Press.

Obstfeld, Maurice, and Kenneth Rogoff. 1995. "The Mirage of Fixed Exchange Rates." *Journal of Economic Perspectives* 9(4): 73–96.

Obstfeld, Maurice, and Alan M. Taylor. 2002. "Globalization and Capital Markets." NBER Working Paper 8846 (March).

———. 2004. *Global Capital Markets: Integration, Crisis and Growth*. Cambridge: Cambridge University Press.

Oh, Junggun, Hyun-Hoon Lee, and Charles Harvie. 2001. "Financial Crisis Management in Korea: Its Processes and Consequences." In Tran Van Hoa, ed., *Economic Crisis Management: Theory Practice, Outcomes and Prospects*. Cheltenham: Edward Elgar, 112–46.

Ostry, Jonathan D., and Jeronim Zettelmeyer. 2005. "Strengthening IMF Crisis Prevention." IMF Working Paper 05/206 (November).

Oxfam. 2002. *Rigid Rules and Double Standards: Trade Globalization and the Fight Against Poverty.* Oxford: Oxfam International.

Pellegrino, Adela, and Andrea Vigorito. Undated. "Emigration and Economic Crisis: Recent Evidence from Uruguay." Universidad de la Republica, Uruguay mimeo.

Perkins, Dwight H. 1997. "Structural Transformation and the Role of the State: Korea 1945–95." In D. S. Cha, K. S. Kim, and D. H. Perkins, *The Korean Economy 1945–1995: Performance and Vision for the 21st Century.* Seoul: Korea Development Institute Press, 57–101.

Perry, Guillermo, and Luis Serven. 2002. "The Anatomy and Physiology of a Multiple Crisis: Why Was Argentina Special and What Can We Learn from It?" World Bank mimeo.

Phillips, Michael M. 2004. "More Work Is Outsourced to U.S. Than Away from It, Data Show." *Wall Street Journal,* March 15, pp. A2, A4.

Poterba, James, and Jurgen von Hagen, eds. 1999. *Fiscal Institutions and Fiscal Performance.* Chicago: University of Chicago Press.

Prasad, Eswar, Kenneth Rogoff, Shang-Jin Wei, and M. Ayhan Kose. 2003. "Effects of Financial Globalization on Developing Countries: Some Empirical Evidence." IMF mimeo (March).

———. 2004. "Financial Globalization Growth and Volatility in Developing Countries." NBER Working Paper 10942 (December).

Pritchett, Lant. 1997. "Divergence Big Time." *Journal of Economic Perspectives* 11(3): 3–17.

Qian, Yingyi. 2003. "How Reform Worked in China." In Dani Rodrik, ed., *In Search of Prosperity: Analytic Narratives of Economic Growth.* Princeton, N.J.: Princeton University Press.

Quinn, Dennis P. 1997. "The Correlates of Change in International Financial Regulation." *American Political Science Review* 91(3): 531–51.

Radelet, Steven, and Jeffrey D. Sachs. 1998. "The East Asian Financial Crisis: Diagnosis, Remedies and Prospects." *Brookings Papers on Economic Activity* 1: 1–74.

Rajan, Raghuram, and Arvind Subramanian. 2005. "Aid and Growth: What Does the Cross-Country Evidence Really Show?" NBER Working Paper 11513 (July).

Rajan, Raghuram, and Luigi Zingales. 1998. "Financial Dependence and Growth." *American Economic Review* 88(3): 559–86.

———. 2003. "The Great Reversals: The Politics of Financial Development in the 20th Century." *Journal of Financial Economics* 69(1): 5–50.

———. 2003. *Saving Capitalism from the Capitalists: Unleashing the Power of Financial Markets to Create Wealth and Spread Opportunity.* New York: Crown Business.

Ranciere, Roman, Aaron Tornell, and Frank Westermann. 2005. "Systemic Crises and Growth." NBER Working Paper 11076 (January).

Reinhart, Carmen M., and Kenneth Rogoff. 2003. "Debt Intolerance." NBER Working Paper 9908 (August).

Rodriguez, Francisco, and Dani Rodrik. 2000. "Trade Policy and Economic Growth: A Skeptic's Guide to the Evidence." In Ben Bernanke and Kenneth Rogoff, eds., *NBER Macro Annual 2000.* Cambridge, Mass.: MIT Press, 261–325.

Rodrik, Dani. 1997. *Has Globalization Gone Too Far?* Washington, D.C.: Institute for International Economics.

———. 1998. "Who Needs Capital-Account Convertibility?" In Stanley Fischer et al., *Should the IMF Pursue Capital-Account Convertibility?* Essays in International Finance 207. Princeton, N.J.: Department of Economics, Princeton University.

———. 2001. *The Global Governance of Trade: As If Development Really Mattered.* New York: United Nations Development Programme (October).

———. 2003. "Growth Strategies." NBER Working Paper 10050 (October).

Rodrik, Dani, Arvind Subramanian, and Francesco Trebbi. 2002. "Institutions Rule: The Primacy of Institutions over Geography and Integration in Economic Development." NBER Working Paper 9305 (November).

Rojas-Suarez, Liliana, and Steven R. Weisbrod. 1994. "Financial Market Fragilities in Latin America: From Banking Crisis Resolution to Current Policy Challenges." IMF Working Paper 94/117 (October).

Roubini, Nouriel, and Brad Setser. 2004. *Bailouts or Bail-Ins? Responding to Financial Crises in Emerging Economies.* Washington, D.C.: Institute for International Economics.

Rubin, Robert, and Jacob Weisberg. 2003. *In an Uncertain World.* New York: Random House.

Sachs, Jeffrey D. 1994. "Do We Need an International Lender of Last Resort?" Presented as the Frank D. Graham Lecture, Princeton University, Princeton, N.J., April 20.

———. 1997. "IMF Is a Power unto Itself." *Financial Times,* December 11, 1997, p. 21.

———. 1997. "The Wrong Medicine for Asia." *New York Times,* November 3, p. 23.

———. 2005. "Can Extreme Poverty Be Eliminated?" *Scientific American,* September, pp. 55–66.

———. 2005. *The End of Poverty: Economic Possibilities of Our Time.* New York: Penguin Press.

———. 2005. "Four Easy Pieces." *New York Times,* June 25, 2005, p. 15.

———. 2005. "Up from Poverty." *Washington Post,* March 27, p. BW12.

Sachs, Jeffrey D., and Andrew Warner. 1995. "Economic Reform and the Process of Global Integration." *Brookings Papers on Economic Activity* 1: 1–118.

Sala-i-Martin, Xavier. 2002. "The Disturbing 'Rise' of Income Inequality." NBER Working Paper 8904 (April).

Sala-i-Martin, Xavier, and Elsa V. Artadi. 2004. "The Economic Tragedy of the XXth Century: Growth in Africa." In Ernesto Hernandes-Cata, ed., *The African Competitiveness Report, World Economic Forum, Geneva,* 1–19 (March).

Schmukler, Sergio L. 2004. "Financial Globalization: Gain and Pain for Developing Countries." *Federal Reserve Bank of Atlanta Review* 89(2): 39–66.

Schwartz, Anna J. 1998. "Time to Terminate the ESF and IMF." Cato Foreign Policy Briefing 48.

———. 1999. "Is There a Need for an International Lender of Last Resort?" Shadow Open Market Committee Report, March 7–8, Bradley Policy Research Center, Rochester University, http://www.somc.rochester.edu/archive1999.htm.

Serletis, Apostolos, and Karl Pinno. 2004. "Corporate Financing in Canada." University of Calgary mimeo (February).

Sewell, John W., Nancy Birdsall, and Kevin Morrison. 2000. "The Right Role for the IMF in Development." ODC Policy Brief (May).

Shadow Open Market Committee. 1998. "Policy Statements and Position Papers, March 15–16, 1998." Bradley Policy Research Center Working Paper PPS 98-01 (March).

Shiller, Robert J. 1997. "Public Resistance to Indexation: A Puzzle." *Brookings Papers on Economic Activity* 1: 156–229.

Shleifer, Andrei. 2003. "Will the Sovereign Debt Market Survive?" *American Economic Review* 93(2): 85–90.

Shleifer, Andrei, and Robert W. Vishny. 1998. *The Grabbing Hand: Government Pathologies and Their Cures.* Cambridge, Mass.: Harvard University Press.

Simone, Francisco Nadal de, and Piritta Sorsa. 1999. "A Review of Capital Account Restrictions in Chile in the 1990s." IMF Working Paper 99/52 (April).

Sobel, Robert. 1968. *Panic on Wall Street: A History of America's Financial Disasters.* London: Macmillan.

Soros, George. 2002. *On Globalization.* New York: Public Affairs Books.

Stern, Gary H., and Ron J. Feldman. 2004. *Too Big to Fail: The Hazards of Bank Bailouts.* Washington, D.C.: Brookings Institution Press.

Stiglitz, Joseph E. 2002. *Globalization and Its Discontents.* New York: W. W. Norton.

Stiglitz, Joseph E., and Andrew Weiss. 1981. "Credit Rationing in Markets with Imperfect Information." *American Economic Review* 71(3): 393–410.

———. 1983. "Incentive Effects of Terminations: Applications to Credit and Labor Markets." *American Economic Review* 73(5): 912–27.

Strahan, Phillip E., and James Weston. 1996. "Small Business Lending and Bank Consolidation: Is There Cause for Concern?" *Federal Reserve Bank of New York Current Issues in Economic and Finance* (March): 1–6.

Sturzenegger, F., and M. Tommasi. 1998. *The Political Economy of Reform.* Cambridge, Mass.: MIT Press.

Su Bei. 2005. "Investment Growth Splits Opinion." *China Daily*, May 20.

Summers, Lawrence. 1999. "The Right Kind of IMF for a Stable Global Financial System." Speech delivered at the London School of Business, December 14, London.

Suryahadi, A., S. Sumarto, and L. Pritchett. 2000. "The Evolution of Poverty in Indonesia, 1996–99." World Bank mimeo (September).

Svalaeryd, H., and J. Vlachos. 2002. "Market for Risk and Openness to Trade: How Are They Related?" *Journal of International Economics* 57(2): 364–95.

Svensson, Jakob. 2003. "Why Conditional Aid Does Not Work and What Can Be Done about It?" *Journal of Development Economics* 70(2): 381–402.

Tarullo, Daniel K. 2005. "The Role of the IMF in Sovereign Debt Restructuring." *Chicago Journal of International Law* 6(1): 289–311.

Taylor, Alan M. 1992. "External Dependence, Demographic Burdens and Argentine Economic Decline after the *Belle Epoque.*" *Journal of Economic History* 52: 907–36.

———. 2002. "Globalization, Trade and Development: Some Lessons from History." NBER Working Paper 9326 (November).

Temple, Jonathan. 1999. "The New Growth Evidence." *Journal of Economic Literature* 37(1): 112–56.

Tommasi, Mariano, Sebastian Saiegh, and Pablo Sanguinetti. 2001. "Fiscal Federalism in Argentina: Policies, Politics, and Institutional Reform." *Economia* 1(2): 147–201.

Tornell, Aaron, Frank Westermann, and Lorenza Martinez. 2004. "Nafta and Mexico's Less-than-Stellar Performance." NBER Working Paper 10289 (February).

———. 2004. "The Positive Link between Financial Liberalization, Growth and Crises." NBER Working Paper 10293 (February).

Truman, Edwin M. 2003. *Inflation Targeting in the World Economy.* Washington, D.C.: Institute for International Economics.

Truman, Edwin M., ed. 2006. *Reforming the IMF for the Twenty-First Century.* Washington, D.C.: Institute for International Economics.

Unite, Angelo, and Michael Sullivan. 2003. "The Effect of Foreign Entry and Ownership Structure on the Philippine Domestic Banking Market." *Journal of Banking and Finance* 27(12): 2323–45.

United Nations. 2004. *Common Database.* New York: United Nations Statistics Division.

———. 2005. *Trade Statistics.* New York: United Nations Statistics Division.

Vasquez, I. 1999. "The International Monetary Fund: Challenges and Contradictions." Paper presented to the International Financial Advisory Commission, September 28, Washington, D.C.

Velasco, Andres, and Emre Deliveli. 2003. "The International Monetary Fund: Origins, Objectives, Controversies and Challenges." Paper presented at the Plenary Meeting of the Club de Madrid, November 1–2, Madrid.

Volcker, Paul. 1998. "Can We Bounce Back?" Remarks at the Institute of International Finance, Washington, D.C., October 10.

Von Hagen, Jurgen, and Ian J. Harden. 1994. "National Budget Processes and Fiscal Performance." *European Economy Reports and Studies* 3: 311–408.

Wall Street Journal. 1987. "Terrible Tuesday: How the Stock Market Almost Disintegrated a Day after the Crash." *Wall Street Journal,* November 20, p. 1.

———. 2001. "Economic Front: How Policy Makers Regrouped to Defend the Financial System." *Wall Street Journal,* September 18, p. A1.

Wei, Shang-Jin. 1997. "How Taxing Is Corruption on International Investors?" NBER Working Paper 6030 (May).

Wei, Shang-Jin, and Yi Wu. 2002. "The Life-and-Death Implications of Globalization." Paper presented at the NBER Inter-American Seminar on Economics, November 15–16, Monterey, Mexico.

Weil, David N. 2005. "Accounting for the Effect of Health on Economic Growth." NBER Working Paper 11455 (July).

———. 2005. *Economic Growth.* Boston: Addison-Wesley.

Weitzman, Martin. 1970. "Soviet Postwar Economic Growth and Capital Labor Substitution." *American Economic Review* 60(4): 676–92.

Williamson, John, and M. Mahar. 1998. *A Survey of Financial Liberalization.* Princeton Essays in International Finance 211. Princeton, N.J.: Princeton University.

Winters, Alan, Neil McCulloch, and Andrew McKay. 2004. "Trade Liberalization and Poverty: The Evidence So Far." *Journal of Economic Literature* 42(1): 72–115.

Wolf, Martin. 2002. "Exchange Rates in a World of Capital Mobility." *Annals of the American Academy of Political and Social Science* 579(1): 38–52.

———. 2004. *Why Globalization Works.* New Haven, Conn.: Yale University Press.

Woods, Ngaire. 1998. "International Financial Institutions and the Mexican Crisis." In Carol Wise, ed., *The Post-NAFTA Political Economy.* University Park: Pennsylvania State University Press.

———. 2004. "Accountability, Governance and the Reform of the IMF." In David Vines and Christopher L. Gilbert, eds., *The IMF and Its Critics: Reform of Global Financial Architecture.* Cambridge: Cambridge University Press, 396–416.

World Bank. 1998. *Argentina: Financial Sector Review.* Report 17864-AR. Washington, D.C.: World Bank.

———. 2001. *Finance for Growth: Policy Choices in a Volatile World.* Oxford: World Bank and Oxford University Press.

———. 2002. *Argentina: Insolvency and Creditor Rights Systems.* Report on the Observance of Standards and Codes (ROSC). Washington, D.C.: World Bank.

———. 2003. *Global Development Finance.* Washington, D.C.: World Bank.

———. 2005. *Doing Business in 2005: Removing Obstacles to Growth.* Washington, D.C.: World Bank, International Finance Corporation, and Oxford University Press.

———. 2005. *World Development Indicators Online.* Washington, D.C.: World Bank.

Yao, Kevin, and Tamora Vidaillet. 2005. "Fast China Investment Shows Tough Rebalancing Task." Reuters, May 19.

Zhou, Xiaochuan. 2004. "Improve Legal System and Financial Ecology." Speech at the Forum of 50 Chinese Economists, December 2, Beijing.

Acknowledgments

I have been blessed with two extraordinary editors on this project: Peter Dougherty, my acquisitions editor and now the director of Princeton University Press, and Jane Tufts, my developmental editor. Both care deeply about making a difference in the world, not by being in the spotlight but by helping authors like me to hone their ideas. Peter has been my brilliant strategist: he encouraged me to write a more ambitious book than I had originally planned. Jane has been my brilliant tactician: she has helped me write far more clearly and engagingly than I ever could have on my own. I have worked with Jane for over twenty years, and there is no one better in the business. I thank both Peter and Jane deeply.

I have also had the help of numerous readers, whose comments have made this a far better book. Bill Easterly, Ross Levine, and Sergio Schmukler have done the yeoman duty of reading two full drafts of the book. Their extensive comments have been invaluable to me. I have also had excellent comments from David Archer, Mario Blejer, Christian Broda, Charlie Calomiris, Jerry Caprio, Luis Cespedes, Jose De Gregorio, Barry Eichengreen, Bob Flood, Rodrigo Fuentes, Reuven Glick, Morris Goldstein, Steve Haber, Joon-Ho Hahm, Taka Ito, Jiri Jonas, Peter Kenen, Michael Klein, Arnold Leitner, Geraldo Licondro, Carlos Lozada, Paul Masson, Maury Obstfeld, Junggun Oh, Raghu Rajan, Dani Rodrik, Guido Sandleris, Klaus Schmidt-Hebbel, and Ted Truman. I have benefited from comments from participants in seminars at Columbia University, Cornell University, the University of Delaware, the Federal Deposit Insurance

Corporation, the Federal Reserve Bank of New York, the New School University, Penn State University, Purdue University, Williams College, and the World Bank.

Emilia Simeonova has provided me with excellent research assistance.

I also thank the Chazen Institute at the Graduate School of Business of Columbia University for providing me with research support.

Last, but not least, I thank my wonderful family for being my wonderful family: Sally, my wife of nearly thirty years, who always keeps me on my toes, and my children, Matt and Laura, who bring me joy because they make me laugh.

Index

Italicized page numbers indicate the locations of definitions of key terms.